P9-DEY-342

Sea

Cape Wilberforce
Gove Peninsula · *Cape Arnhem*
Groote Eylandt

DRIVE 16
pp178–189

Gulf of Carpentaria

nathan ver

Vanderlin Island
Manangoora
Mornington Island
Wellesley Islands
Bentinck Island

Bamaga · *Horn Island* · *Cape York*
Heathlands
Cape Grenville
Duyfken Point
Worbody Point · Moreton Telegraph Station
Princess Charlotte Bay
Coen

Coral Sea

Lizard Island
Cape Flattery

SOUTH PACIFIC OCEAN

Burketown · Normanton
Gregory Downs
Mugana
Georgetown
Esmeralda
Lyndhurst

Laura · Cooktown

DRIVE 1
pp30–39
Cairns
Innisfail
Dunk Island
Hinchinbrook Island

Townsville
Mt Elliot 1234m

Mount Isa · Cloncurry · Julia Creek · Hughenden
Mt Stewart 997m
Charters Towers · Bowen
Whitsunday Islands

Mt Dalrymple 1259m · Mackay

Carandotta · Chatsworth
Nortbumberland Isles
Long Island
Reef Point

DRIVE 17
pp190–201

Boulia · Winton · Muttaburra

QUEENSLAND

Barcaldine

Emerald
Rockhampton
Gladstone
Bunker Group

Cluny · Tonkoro
Simpson Desert
Birdsville · Windorah
Mt Drummond 859m
Mt Hutton 940m
Bundaberg
Fraser Island
Maryborough

Clifton Hills
Arrabury
Charleville
Roma
Noosa
Caloundra

Mungerannie Roadhouse
Thargomindah
Cunnamulla
St George
Chinchilla
DRIVE 2
pp40–45
Brisbane

DRIVE 3
pp46–55

dwards Creek
Bollards Lagoon
Tibooburra
Mt Fitton

DRIVE 14
pp156–165

Lismore
Glen Innes
Coffs Harbour

Port Augusta
Mt Booroondarra 441m
Bourke
Narrabri

DRIVE 5
pp70–79

Whyalla
Port Pirie
Broken Hill
Cobar
Tamworth
Port Macquarie

Renmark · Mildura
NEW SOUTH WALES
Dubbo
Taree
Parkes
Maitland
Newcastle

Adelaide
Griffith
Orange
Bathurst
Penrith
DRIVE 6
pp80–91

DRIVE 4
pp56–69

Kangaroo Island
Kingston SE
Wagga Wagga
Temora
Goulburn
Sydney

VICTORIA
Albury
Shepparton
Wangaratta
A.C.T.
Canberra
Nowra-Bomaderry

Mount Gambier
DRIVE 10
pp120–129
Bendigo
Cooma
Batemans Bay

DRIVE 13
pp148–155

Portland
Geelong
Melbourne
DRIVE 8
pp102–107
Bega
Green Cape
Cape Howe

DRIVE 9
pp108–119

DRIVE 7
pp92–101

King Island
Bass Strait
Kent Group

TASMANIA
Flinders Island
Hunter Island
Burnie
Devonport
Launceston

DRIVE 12
pp138–147
Hobart
DRIVE 11
pp130–137

EYEWITNESS TRAVEL

BACK ROADS
AUSTRALIA

EYEWITNESS TRAVEL

BACK ROADS
AUSTRALIA

CONTRIBUTORS

Jarrod Bates, Lara Dunston, Andrew Harris,

Elizabeth Re, Jessica Syme, Steve Womersley

DK

LONDON, NEW YORK,
MELBOURNE, MUNICH AND DELHI
www.dk.com

PUBLISHER Douglas Amrine

LIST MANAGER Vivien Antwi

EDITORIAL Michelle Crane, Georgina
Palffy, Hugh Thompson, Fay Franklin,
Vicki Allen

DESIGN Shahid Mahmood, Steve Bere

PRODUCTION CONTROLLER
Linda Dare

PICTURE RESEARCH Ellen Root,
Marta Bescos

DTP Jason Little, Jamie McNeill

CARTOGRAPHY MANAGER
Uma Bhattacharya

SENIOR CARTOGRAPHIC EDITOR
Casper Morris

CARTOGRAPHY
Stuart James, Jasneet Arora

ILLUSTRATIONS
Arun Pottirayil

Colour reproduction by Media
Development Printing Ltd, UK

Printed and bound in China by
South China Printing Co Ltd

First published in the United States in 2011 by
Dorling Kindersley Publishing, Inc., 345 Hudson
Street, New York 10014

First American Edition 2011

13 14 15 16 10 9 8 7 6 5 4 3 2

Reprinted with revisions 2014

**Copyright 2010, 2014 © Dorling
Kindersley Limited, London**

A Penguin Company

Front cover The Olgas, Uluru Kata-Tjuta National Park

CONTENTS

Above Golden sandy beach, near Darwin,
Northern Territory

Below The impressive Devils Marbles, near
Tennant Creek, Northern Territory

Below The Yarra River, in the heart
of Melbourne, Victoria

Above Spectacular Triplet Falls, Great Otway National Park, Victoria

Above The majestic Twelve Apostles, Port Campbell National Park, Victoria

Above Pleasure boats in the marina in Manly Harbour, Queensland

Title page: Road winding around Cape Byron, New South Wales **Half-title page:** Scenic route through Walpole-Nornalup National Park, Western Australia

Below Simpsons Gap waterhole in the West MacDonnell Ranges, Northern Territory

Below Traditional 19th century building, near Castlemaine, Victoria

Below Wild flowers near the coast in Cape Le Grande National Park, Western Australia

About this Book

The 22 driving tours in this guide reflect the fantastic diversity of Australia. The sixth-largest country in the world, yet relatively sparsely populated, Australia has great expanses of road – from multi-lane freeways to bumpy dirt tracks. The majority of its towns and cities are strung out around the country's coastal circumference. While distances are daunting, flying means missing the gradually changing scenery – a quintessential aspect of the Australian experience. And while you might spot a wedge-tailed eagle or a kangaroo from a bus or a train, it will be a fleeting moment. In your own vehicle, you can stop and take it all in at a pace that suits you. Whether it is a drive through the vineyards of the Hunter Valley from Sydney or the Great Ocean Road from Melbourne, tackling the red-dirt tracks of the Outback in a 4WD, exploring remote beaches, or sleeping in a national park under the stars, Australia is made for driving tours.

Getting Started

The front section of the guide gives you all the practical information you need to plan and enjoy a driving holiday in Australia. It includes an overview of when to go and how to get there, advice on hiring a vehicle and details of any documentation required. In-depth motoring advice ranges from driving rules to road conditions, from buying fuel to breakdown or accident procedures – the kind of background knowledge that helps make a driving trip stress-free. There is information on money, opening times, communications, health and safety and other practical matters, as well as advice on accommodation and dining options, to ensure that you enjoy the authentic Australian experience.

The Drives

The main section of the guide is divided into drives, ranging from two to seven days in duration. The tours can all be driven in a standard vehicle, although there are a few excursions suitable for 4WD vehicles only.

The drives encompass every region of the country, from the glorious beaches of Queensland's Sunshine Coast to the wilderness of the Northern Territory's Top End, and from the vineyards of the Barossa Valley to the wheatbelt of Western Australia.

Each drive begins with a list of highlights and a clearly mapped itinerary. There is advice on the best time of year to undertake the drive, road conditions, market days and major festival dates. The tour pages contain descriptions of each stop on the route, linked by clear driving instructions. Side panels contain information on the most authentic places to stay and eat, as well as details of local activities, and tinted boxes relate background information.

Most drives feature a mapped town or countryside walking tour, designed to take a maximum of three hours at a gentle pace with stops along the way.

The tours are flexible: some can be linked to create a longer driving holiday; or they can be dipped into as day trips while based in a region.

Using the Sheet Map

A pull-out road map of the entire country is attached inside the back cover. This map contains all the information you need to drive around the country and to navigate between the tours. All freeways, major roads and airports – both domestic and international – plus all the ferry ports are easily identified. This makes the pull-out map an excellent addition to the drive itinerary maps within the book. The pull-out map also has a comprehensive index to help you find your destination, and is further supplemented by a clear distance chart so you can gauge the distances between the major cities in Australia.

Top far left Driving in the Flinders Ranges, South Australia **Top left** Hay bale at a Shepherds Flat farm, Central Victoria **Centre far left** Night view of Perth's waterfront centre **Centre left** Roadside letterboxes in front of Mount Roland, Tasmania **Far left** Bakery in Hobart, Tasmania **Left** Two Peoples Bay Nature Reserve, Western Australia **Right** Sculpture at Wave Rock, Western Australia

Introducing Australia

Australia is an immense country with a vast interior filled with wildlife but very few human settlements and a 19,000-km (11,800-mile) coastline of wild surf, protected harbours, world-renowned coral reefs and myriad national parks. It is a destination that demands you slow down and stop along the way to appreciate what each region has to offer. Travelling by road, you can experience the ever-changing landscape as you drive from the famous sandy beaches to the isolated interior, with fascinating Aboriginal sites, unique flora and fauna, and the colours of the countryside along the route. On top of all these natural wonders, there are many wine regions where you can savour internationally renowned New World wines, sophisticated, multi-cultural cities with excellent restaurants and lively and diverse arts scenes, and the easy-going nature of the locals at every stop of your trip.

When to Go
Each of the drives suggests the best time of year to make the trip, whether it is because the scenery is at its most spectacular or the weather is particularly pleasant. The top half of the continent is tropical and has two seasons: "the Wet" and "the Dry". The dry season (May–Sep) is the best time to visit because flooding has ceased and all roads are open. The wet season (Oct–Apr) is hot and humid, but it also offers spectacular wildlife and thundering waterfalls at places such as Kakadu National Park.

The southern half of Australia has seasons that are opposite to those of Europe and the US. The Outback is best explored in winter (Jun–Aug), as summer (Dec–Feb) brings flash floods and high temperatures. Autumn is temperate and spring brings on stunning wild flowers, especially in South Australia and Western Australia.

Summer means time at the beach in Australia and it appears that every Australian takes the latter half of December and all of January off to watch cricket and work on their tans.

Winter in New South Wales and Victoria sees snow in the mountains and wet weather almost everywhere else, although in some areas April brings the most rain, while in Brisbane, the capital of Queensland, the most rain falls in January – often with amazing thunderstorms – the result of the sub-tropical conditions there.

Times to Avoid
Summer may be the best time to enjoy many of the coastal drives, but accommodation will be booked up well in advance. Unlike in most of Europe, though, you can still find empty stretches of beach. Easter signals the end of the beach season and all of Australia heads to the surf for one last plunge. In the wet season, many roads are closed by flooding and landslides in the tropical north.

Festivals
The Melbourne Cup, the famous horse race, does not quite bring the nation to a halt in early November as it used to, but it is still a big affair. All over the country, a plethora of spring flower festivals, sporting events and arts fairs take place and every region has its own annual agricultural show. Details of main festivals, where they are held and when, are given in each drive.

Public Holidays
New Year's Day (1 Jan)
Australia Day (26 Jan NSW, 1st Mon after 26 Jan in other states)
ANZAC Day (25 Apr)
Adelaide Cup Day (2nd Mon in Mar, South Australia)
Good Friday (variable)
Easter Monday (variable)
Labour Day (1st Mon in Mar, WA; 2nd Mon in Mar, Victoria; 1st Mon in May, NT; 1st Mon in Oct, NSW, QLD, ACT & SA)
Foundation Day (1st Mon in Jun, WA)
Queen's Birthday (2nd Mon in Jun, most states; last Mon in Sep, WA)
Melbourne Cup Day (1st Tue Nov, Victoria)
Christmas Day (25 Dec)
Boxing Day (26 Dec)

Left Idyllic Two Peoples Bay Nature Reserve, Western Australia **Right** Craft market, St Kilda Esplanade, Melbourne, Victoria

Getting to Australia

The vast majority of visitors to Australia arrive by air, although cruise ships do visit from as far away as Europe and North America. If you are flying from Europe or the Americas, be prepared to have a stopover or endure jet lag for the first couple of days in Australia. Once you have arrived, domestic travel between state capitals is easily done by air, with flights usually not longer than a couple of hours. The exception being from the east coast to Perth, of course, which is around 6 hours from Sydney or Melbourne. However, it is also possible to reach the other major cities in Australia by following the drives in this guide.

Above Road sign indicating routes to Coffs Harbour and airport

Arriving by Air

Flights to Australia can be very expensive, especially in December, the peak season. Off-peak or "shoulder" season fares are much more reasonable. If you can fly at short notice, check with discount travel agencies and online as the major airlines often release unsold tickets at the last minute.

Australia is well served by dozens of international airlines, as well as Australia's own **Qantas**, which has a strong worldwide network. Along with its low-cost offshoot, **Jetstar**, it operates the most flights in and out of Australia every week. Jetstar operates increasingly widely throughout Asia as well.

Key operators to and from the United Kingdom are Qantas, which stops over at Singapore, and **British Airways**, which stops over in Bangkok in Thailand as well as Singapore. **Emirates** and **Etihad Airways** (based in Dubai and Abu Dhabi respectively) have flights from London through Dubai to Asia and Australia. **Virgin Atlantic** stops in Hong Kong on the way to Australia, as does Hong Kong's

own airline, **Cathay Pacific**, while **Malaysia Airlines** stops in Kuala Lumpur from London. Most of the big airlines fly to Australia from major continental cities such as Paris, Berlin and Rome. These include Qantas, British Airways and **KLM**, along with the respective national airlines **Air France**, **Lufthansa** and **Alitalia**. Several airlines "codeshare", so if you book yourself on a **Singapore Airlines** flight you may actually find yourself flying on a Qantas jet, or vice versa. If travelling from Ireland, most flights will stop at London Heathrow before continuing on to Australia.

Most flights from North America to Australia are offered by **United Airlines**, Qantas, **Air New Zealand** and **V Australia**, while flights from Canada with **Air Canada** stop at Los Angeles – virtually every airline's last US stop before heading to Australia, although you can stop over in Hawai'i. From South Africa with **South African Airways**, Johannesburg is the main point of departure and Perth the most likely destination. One of the largest airline operators in Asia, **Japan Airlines**, also flies to Australia.

Before arrival in Australia, you will be given customs documents to fill in. Foodstuffs and untreated wood are items that interest customs people, as they constitute a biological hazard. Officials will not hesitate to confiscate any food or banned items and issue you with a fine. Australia is a country with a large agriculture industry and it takes great care on this issue, routinely using sniffer dogs around the baggage halls. Always fill out the customs form correctly and declare anything you are uncertain about rather than risk a fine, and discard uneaten travel snacks before landing.

Australian Airports

The main airports for international travellers are **Sydney Airport** (often called **Kingsford Smith Airport**), which is always busy, and **Melbourne** (also called **Tullamarine Airport**), which is much less frenetic than Sydney. Most overseas flights land at these two airports.

Brisbane Airport and **Darwin Airport** increasingly receive Asian airline traffic, while **Perth Airport** handles flights from the UK, Asia and

South Africa. **Adelaide Airport** has direct flights from Asia but for flights from Europe and North America you will be stopping in Melbourne or Sydney first. Hobart in Tasmania only handles domestic flights.

Domestic flights are very frequent in Australia and it is easy to add a domestic connection to your flight plans. It only takes an hour to fly between Sydney and Melbourne and Sydney and Brisbane, for instance. However, the costs are pretty high compared to travelling by road.

Before booking check what the luggage allowance is, as this can be lower on domestic flights and excess baggage costs are expensive. Always take into account the distance between domestic and international terminals if you are taking a domestic flight to your final departure point from Australia and make sure you leave enough time. Check-in queues, particularly in Sydney and Melbourne, can be a problem.

International Flight Times

Flights between Australia and Europe can take at least 24 hours with a minimum of one stop. A stopover is an excellent idea, however, especially for those travelling with children. Asia is the most common stop, which leaves a much shorter flight of around 8 hours to Australia and ensures you arrive reasonably fresh. It is also possible to stop over in Dubai, the most popular hub in the Middle East, then fly direct to Australia. Two or three nights is usually enough time to refresh and explore a little.

From North America, most direct flights from Los Angeles last around 14 hours. With Hawai'i only around 5 hours from Los Angeles, a stopover there is more of a luxury than a necessity, but can be worthwhile in one direction on your trip.

Also, you might consider arranging flights so that they account for international time differences. Arriving at your destination in the afternoon, spending the rest of the day awake and then going to sleep at night will help to counteract jet lag by getting your bodyclock in sync with local time.

Arriving by Sea

Obviously, being an island, Australia can be reached by sea. However, most of the ships arriving are on around-the-world cruises or cruises taking in Australia and New Zealand. Companies such as **Princess Cruises**, **Holland America** and others do complete South Pacific cruises. While the cruises are limited and quite expensive, there are few more glamorous ways to arrive in Sydney than cruising into one of the most beautiful harbours in the world.

If you wish to take in Tasmania, Australia's island state, on your trip you can take a ferry, the *Spirit of Tasmania*. This journey south takes 14 hours to sail across the choppy Bass Strait from Melbourne. The ship has plenty of different classes to suit all kinds of travellers. There is also a frequent **Sealink** ferry to Kangaroo Island in South Australia.

Below far left Aeroplane landing at Sydney Airport **Below centre** Airline signs at Sydney Airport **Below left** Sydney Opera House in its spectacular harbour location **Below right** Cruise ship docked in Hobart's harbour

DIRECTORY

ARRIVING BY AIR

Air Canada
www.aircanada.com

Air France
www.airfrance.com

Air New Zealand
www.airnewzealand.com.au

Alitalia
www.alitalia.com

British Airways
www.ba.com

Cathay Pacific
www.cathaypacific.com

Emirates
www.emirates.com

Etihad Airways
www.etihadairways.com

Japan Airlines
www.jal.com

Jetstar
www.jetstar.com

KLM
www.klm.com

Lufthansa
www.lufthansa.com

Malaysia Airlines
www.malaysiaairlines.com

Qantas
www.qantas.com.au

Singapore Airlines
www.singaporeair.com

South African Airways
www.flysaa.com

United Airlines
www.united.com

V Australia
www.vaustralia.com.au

Virgin Atlantic
www.virgin-atlantic.com

AUSTRALIAN AIRPORTS

Adelaide Airport
www.aal.com.au

Brisbane Airport
www.bne.com.au

Darwin Airport
www.darwinairport.com.au

Melbourne Tullamarine Airport
www.melbourneairport.com.au

Perth Airport
www.perthairport.net.au

Sydney Kingsford Smith Airport
www.sydneyairport.com.au

ARRIVING BY SEA

Holland America
www.hollandamerica.com

Princess Cruises
www.princess.com

Spirit of Tasmania
www.spiritoftasmania.com.au

Sealink
www.sealink.com.au

Practical Information

Australia is a major tourist destination and has all the facilities you would expect to cater for international travellers. It is a relatively safe, friendly and relaxed destination, and visitors should encounter few problems once past the customs counter at the airport. The standard of accommodation is relatively high, the quality of the cuisine is fine, and the major roads and public transport are able to cope with the number of visitors. The only caveat is that Australia's Outback and coastal waters are wild and sometimes inhospitable places where those unused to the conditions can get into trouble if they do not stay alert and use sound judgement.

Above Australian banknotes, all made of strong, light and durable polymer plastic

Passports and Visas

Visitors to Australia must have a passport valid for longer than the intended duration of their visit. All visitors, other than New Zealand passport holders, need a pre-arranged visa to enter the country. For visitors from most countries, this will be in the form of an **Electronic Travel Authority** (ETA), which can be obtained through a travel agent, airline or applied for online. This electronically stored authority is for short-term visits to Australia of up to three months. Another electronic visa that can be issued over the Internet is **eVisitor**, available to European Union and a number of other European countries. No paperwork or special passport stamps are required for entry – the visa is stored electronically.

Travel Insurance

Most travel insurance policies will cover you for loss or theft of luggage and other property as well as personal accident and repatriation in case of a serious medical condition. Delayed or cancelled flights are generally covered, as are the expenses incurred because

of this. Policies also cover lost luggage, allowing you to replace missing items (such as clothes and toiletries) immediately. Note that if you do wish to undertake activities and sports considered dangerous by the insurer, this will generally require a different insurance policy or an extra premium to the normal policy. Read the terms and conditions carefully because coverage, excess amounts, exclusions and deductibles vary widely. Also check to see what kind of cover, if any, is offered under your home insurance policy. Some credit card companies also offer limited travel insurance benefits if you use your card to book your trip or to hire a rental car.

Health

Australia's medical services are generally world-class. Under reciprocal arrangements, visitors from the UK, New Zealand, Malta, Italy, Finland, Sweden and the Netherlands are entitled to free hospital and medical treatment, provided by Australia's National Insurance scheme, **Medicare**. Note that dental emergencies are not covered under this arrangement, nor

with standard travel insurance, so make sure your insurance policy covers this. Visitors not covered by these arrangements can face hefty bills for medical treatment, so ensure that you have adequate travel insurance.

Dial "000" nation-wide for ambulance assistance. Most public hospitals have a casualty ward for accidents and emergencies, but note that if your case is not urgent, waiting times can be very long. There are 24-hour medical centres in the larger cities that have shorter waiting times for non-urgent care and most smaller country towns always have a doctor on call. The state capitals also have emergency dental centres.

Pharmacies are known as chemist shops in Australia and they are generously scattered throughout the cities, suburbs and small towns – often with competing "discount" chemist shops on opposite sides of the road. There is a good range of over-the-counter medicines, although the brand names of items you are familiar with may be different. A pharmacist will always be on duty and can offer assistance with

Above left NSW fire engine **Above centre** An Australian park ranger **Above right** Transferring a patient from the air ambulance

minor ailments. Foreign prescriptions will not be filled unless endorsed by a local General Practitioner (GP). Hotel staff, hospital and medical practitioners' staff will direct you to after-hours pharmacies as required. If you have medicines that you need to take regularly, always take the prescription with you.

Personal Security

Few areas within Australia are "no-go" for visitors. While a big city's red-light district can be seedy, the constant police presence makes it safer than poorly lit suburban streets. Things can get quite lively late at night at the weekend. As with any country, take the usual precautions, however, and avoid poorly lit areas and parks late at night. Public transport is relatively safe, but hitchhiking, particularly for women or even couples, is not recommended. Taxis are generally a safe means of travel.

Also, note that country areas are "early to bed and early to rise" – restaurants can have their last sittings at 8pm – so it is advisable to always have a hotel or caravan park booking at your destination and arrive before dark to avoid wandering around in poorly lit places. In rural areas, note that if you need police assistance at

night, most police stations will be closed, but dial "000" and an officer will handle any important problems.

Disabled Travellers

Disabled travellers are very well catered for in Australia and the facilities are usually excellent. Hotels, restaurants, most tourist sights, cinemas, theatres, airports and shopping centres all have wheelchair access and most nature park trails have wheelchair routes. While public transport can occasionally be a problem, there are radio taxis that have wheelchair-accessible vehicles in a surprising number of places, even smaller rural centres.

Tourist information centres, or visitor centres as they are sometimes called, are a great source of information regarding wheelchair access and facilities. The **National Information Communication Awareness Network** has comprehensive information for travellers, including a database of accommodation and services that have disabled facilities.

Below left Controlled swimming area at Burleigh Heads beach, Queensland **Below centre** Road sign warning drivers of road trains in the Outback **Below right** Driving on a dusty dirt track through the deserted Outback

DIRECTORY

EMBASSIES AND CONSULATES

British High Commission
Commonwealth Avenue,
Yarralumla, ACT, 2600;
(02) 6270 6666; ukinaustralia.fco.gov.uk

Canadian High Commission
Commonwealth Avenue,
Canberra, ACT, 2600;
(02) 6270 4000; www.australia.gc.ca

Embassy of Ireland
20 Arkana Street,
Yarralumla, ACT, 2600;
(02) 6214 0000;
www.embassyofireland.au.com

New Zealand High Commission
140 Commonwealth Avenue,
Canberra, ACT, 2600;
(02) 6270 4211; www.nzembassy.com

**Embassy of the
United States of America**
Moonah Place,
Yarralumla, ACT, 2600;
(02) 6214 5600; canberra.usembassy.gov

VISAS

**Electronic Travel Authority
and eVisitor**
www.immi.gov.au

HEALTH

Medicare
www.medicareaustralia.gov.au

Police, Fire and Ambulance
Dial 000

DISABLED TRAVELLERS

**National Information
Communication Awareness
Network (NICAN)**
www.nican.com.au

Telephone

Payphones still operate in Australia and, depending on the type, may accept phonecards or credit cards instead of coins. Prepaid phonecards are available at newsagents and can save time and money. For international calls, rates vary depending on the time, and the day of the week. Long-distance calls within Australia use Subscriber Trunk Dialling (STD). All numbers have an area code before the actual number.

Mobile (cellular) phones are ubiquitous in Australia and numbers always begin with 04. Australia uses a GSM standard network, compatible with all European phones, but only some US phones. Most Australians use phones with complex contracts rather than a pre-paid system. Travellers wishing to use an Australian Subscriber Identity Module (SIM) card during their stay can buy prepaid SIM cards, but they are not as common a purchase as you would expect. The three main companies are **Telstra**, **Vodafone** and **Optus**, although others are also available. If you are travelling to remote areas, Telstra, the ex-government telephone company, has the best and widest coverage with a 4G (4th Generation) network. Many rural areas of Australia only have mobile coverage within town limits, quickly dropping away as you leave town. Keep this in mind if you are on the road and need to call ahead to the next stop to get directions or make accommodation bookings.

If remaining in contact is crucial to you, consider hiring or buying a satellite telephone. Some companies hire all over the country, so you can rent in one city and drop the phone off at another. Car hire companies may also offer these for rent. These phones can be expensive to hire and calls are not cheap. Companies to consider include **Satellite Phone Hire** and **Realtime Platform**.

Internet service in Australia is not as fast as in the US or Europe, nor as widespread in hotels. Although Internet access (either by broadband cable or Wi-Fi) is becoming more widespread in hotels in the state capital cities, it is less so in old motel-style accommodation or caravan parks. Internet cafés and cafés providing Wi-Fi are quite common in popular tourist areas. If you need broadband access at all times for a wireless device such as a Blackberry, iPhone or other smart phone, Telstra's Next G service is probably your best solution. If you require constant Internet access for your laptop computer, you can buy a USB broadband dongle/modem from the same telecommunications companies. Note that these also only work where you have mobile phone coverage – which excludes many rural and Outback areas.

Banks and Money

The currency in Australia is the Australian dollar (AU$), which breaks down into 100 cents (¢). One and two cent pieces are no longer in circulation – the smallest coin is a 5 cent piece. It can be difficult to change large denomination notes, especially in rural areas, so change AU$50 and AU$100 notes whenever you can. Taxi drivers like to know in advance if you want to pay with a large denomination note to make sure they have change.

Automatic Teller Machines (ATMs) are found at virtually every bank,

Above Signs at the tourist destination of Hepburn Springs, Victoria

shopping mall and tourist centre. It is a good idea to tell your bank that you are going to Australia, as they may restrict the use of your credit or debit cards for security reasons. Remember that if you use a credit card to withdraw cash you may incur bank charges, so ask your bank about this before travelling. Australians use debit and savings cards to cut down on credit card charges. Using EFTPOS (Electronic Funds Transfer at Point of Sale), purchases are debited directly from your account and often you will be asked by cashiers if you wish to take out extra cash at the point of purchase. This can be handy in rural and Outback areas where there are no ATMs. Visa and MasterCard credit cards are accepted almost everywhere, while American Express is not as commonly accepted in rural areas. Bureaux de change are usually found in areas popular with tourists.

Tourist Information

The **Tourism Australia** is the national tourism body, but each state and territory also has its own tourism authority. The state capital city branches have plenty of brochures

Above left Open-topped bus, Perth – a good way to quickly see the city's main sights **Above right** City centre information kiosk

and information on events state-wide, while the smaller tourist offices focus on regional activities. The offices located in small towns – often staffed by volunteers – are a wealth of local information, including road and weather conditions. Before heading off on remote roads, especially 4WD-only tracks, always consult with the local tourism office about the conditions and potential problems such as swollen rivers or roadworks.

Opening Times

Most Australian sights are open daily and are busiest at the weekend. Standard shopping hours are 9am–5 or 5:30pm Mon–Sat. Late-night shopping (until 9pm) is generally Thursday night, sometimes Friday night. On Saturdays and Sundays, hours vary widely, but generally shops are open until at least 1pm on Saturdays in the country, while supermarkets and shopping centres in cities open right across the weekend. Banks are generally open 9:30am–4pm weekdays and to 5pm on Fridays, but hours vary from bank to bank. Restaurants usually open from noon to 3pm, with dinner served from 6:30pm. In rural areas, last orders may be as early as 8pm, but most city restaurants will serve food until around 10:30pm.

Time

Australia is divided into three time zones: Western Standard Time, Central Standard Time and Eastern Standard Time. Western Australia is usually 8 hours ahead of GMT and Eastern Australia is usually a further 2 hours ahead. Central Australia is 1.5 hours ahead. Daylight saving is observed in New South Wales, the ACT, Victoria, South Australia and Tasmania from October to April, which adds an hour to the time differences.

Electricity

Australia's electrical system is 240–250 volts AC. Electrical plugs have either two or three pins and are virtually unique to Australia. As soon as you arrive, buy a flat, two- or three-pin adaptor from an electronics store.

Smoking

Australia has banned smoking inside restaurants, cafés and bars. Smoking is permitted at outside tables, although exactly what constitutes "outside" varies slightly from state to state.

Below far left Darwin City Information Centre kiosk **Below centre** Sign outside a post office **Below left** Sign for a local visitor information centre, Castlemaine, Victoria **Below right** Old-fashioned red post box, Castlemaine

DIRECTORY

TELEPHONE COMPANIES

Optus www.optus.com.au

Telstra www.telstra.com.au

Vodafone www.vodafone.com.au

CALLING AUSTRALIA

From the UK
Dial 0061, the area code, then the local number

From the USA or Canada
Dial 01161, the area code, then the local number

CALLING WITHIN AUSTRALIA

For long-distance calls outside your local area but within Australia, dial the appropriate area code, then the number.

CALLING FROM AUSTRALIA

For international calls from Australia, dial 0011, then the country code (USA and Canada: 1; UK: 44; New Zealand: 64), then the city or area code – omitting the initial 0 – then the local number.

SATELLITE PHONE HIRE

Realtime Platform
www.realtimeplatform.com
0409 372 379

Satellite Hire
www.satellitehire.com.au
1800 426 552

TOURIST INFORMATION

Tourism Australia
www.tourism.australia.com

Australian Capital Territory
www.canberratourism.com.au

New South Wales
www.tourism.nsw.gov.au

Northern Territory
www.nttc.com.au

Queensland
www.tq.com.au

South Australia
www.southaustralia.com

Western Australia
www.westernaustralia.net

Victoria
www.visitmelbourne.com

Tasmania
www.discovertasmania.com

Driving in Australia

Driving in Australia is a great way to see the country. With a relatively small population concentrated at the edge of its vast coastal circumference, Australia offers the opportunity for some extraordinary drives, from gorgeous coastal roads through quaint seaside towns to near-deserted trails across the rugged Outback. Driving in Australian cities is easy, with well maintained and well signposted roads, although finding a parking space can be a problem. If you hire a 2WD car, you will be able to visit most parts of Australia, but a 4WD vehicle will offer more options for exploring the wilderness *(see p22)*.

Above Rural petrol pump or 'bowser', as it is sometimes called in Australia

Car Rental

Most of the big international vehicle hire companies have branches at airports, in the large cities and at popular tourist destinations. These companies, such as **Avis**, **Budget**, **Hertz** and **Thrifty**, offer a wide range of vehicles, with standard 2WD cars most commonly on offer in the more urban areas and along the east coast, and 4WD vehicles being more standard in the remoter regions. Talk to the hire company about your trip and pick the vehicle most suitable for your journey – 4WDs use more fuel, so do not hire one if you do not need it. But, on the other hand, do not limit your route by hiring a 2WD if you may want to venture off the main road onto dirt tracks through national parks. As well as the big car hire firms, there are local companies, which may offer cheaper deals but can be less convenient in terms of picking up and dropping off vehicles at different locations, or provision of substitute vehicles in case of breakdown. **Britz** and **Maui** are two firms that specialize in 4WD and campervan hire *(see p20)* and also rent vehicles nationwide.

Insurance

In Australia, third party insurance is included in car hire. While insurance against damage to the hire vehicle (comprehensive insurance) is also included with the rental, the excess payment on a standard contract can be up to AU$2,000. This can generally be reduced to about AU$100 by negotiation, and paying more for the rental. With 4WD vehicles, the excess can be much higher; however, this too can be reduced to an acceptable amount by hiring from companies that specialize in renting off-road vehicles, such as Britz and Maui. Higher rates of insurance apply to drivers under the age of 25 and many companies will not rent to drivers under 21. A credit card is almost mandatory for rentals in Australia, especially for 4WD vehicles. It is a good idea to have everyone in the vehicle with a valid licence on the list of drivers – driver fatigue is a common cause of accidents in Australia due to the long distances often covered, especially in areas such as the Nullarbor Plain, the Top End and the Red Centre. The vehicle

hire company will have an arrangement with a breakdown service and will supply a toll-free number to ring for assistance.

What to Take

A valid national driving licence is generally all you need to hire a car in Australia. However, if you have a driving licence from a country that has a licence in a language other than English, it is best to check. In this case, it might be prudent to get an International Driving Licence. It is a legal requirement that you have your licence with you at all times while driving. Equipment recommended for tough cross-country trips, such as shovels, GPS units, ropes, vehicle recovery equipment and satellite phones, can usually be hired with the vehicle. A tyre pressure gauge and foot pump are also useful tools to take or hire, as driving on sand often requires reducing tyre pressure. If travelling a long way, especially in the Outback, take spare fuel and oil, plenty of water to drink and a good supply of emergency snacks *(see p22–3* for tips on driving in the Outback).

Above left Treelined road in Fryerstown, Victoria **Above centre** Road sign warning of kangaroos **Above right** Post office clock tower, Castlemaine, Victoria

Road Systems

Australia has a comprehensive and well maintained road network. The more popular routes are the best served, with multi-lane highways, while other routes generally consist of good two-lane roads. There are plenty of unsealed country roads but these are usually well-graded and can be driven easily. The exceptions are the iconic 4WD-only routes such as the Mereenie Loop to Kings Canyon from Alice Springs *(see p200)*. Note that rental companies will generally not insure a 2WD vehicle for unsealed roads. Toll-ways are the preserve of the major capitals such as Sydney – highways between states do not attract tolls outside the built-up areas.

Speed Limits and Fines

In built-up areas, the default speed limit is 50 km/h (31 mph), although it can be 60 km/h (37 mph) when signposted. Keep a look out for school zones where it generally drops to 40 km/h (25 mph). The speed limit on highways is generally 100 km/h (62 mph), sometimes 110 km/h (68 mph) and in the Northern Territory, it is 130 km/h (69 mph) where signposted. Fines and penalties for speeding and other offences vary from state to state.

Drink-driving laws are strictly enforced in Australia and the maximum legal blood-alcohol level is 0.05 per cent. Should you be involved in an accident while over the drink-driving limit, your vehicle insurance will be invalidated.

Rules of the Road

Australians drive on the left-hand side of the road and give way to the right in all circumstances unless otherwise indicated, including on roundabouts, where the flow of traffic is clockwise. One exception is in Melbourne, where, because of trams, motorists intending to turn right must pull over to the left and give way to all traffic (known as a "hook turn"). Drivers must always give way to emergency vehicles. The wearing of seatbelts is compulsory for driver and passengers. Australians are generally easy-going drivers, especially in rural areas where it is common to wave to other drivers on the road – on some trips you will only see a few vehicles a day. However, make an error in the city and you may be greeted with a different kind of hand signal.

Below far left Signage at South Walkerville and Cape Liptrap, Victoria **Below centre** Parking outside theatre, Castlemaine, Victoria **Below left** Road leading to Mount Warning, Murwillumbah, NSW **Below right** Dirt road warning sign

(see p200)

DIRECTORY

GENERAL DRIVING INFORMATION

Australian Automobile Association
02 6247 7311; www.aaa.asn.au

Four Wheel Drive Australia
www.anfwdc.asn.au

Foreign and Commonwealth Office
www.fco.gov.uk/en/
travel-and-living-abroad

EMERGENCIES

Police, Fire and Ambulance
Dial 000

CAR HIRE COMPANIES

Avis
136 333; www.avis.com.au

Budget
132 727; www.budget.com.au

Hertz
133 039; www.hertz.com.au

Thrifty
1300 367 227; www.thrifty.com.au

Road Conditions

Road conditions in urban areas of Australia are similar to those in any big city. Although well signposted, the inner cities of Sydney and Melbourne are not for the indecisive or unprepared driver. If you get lost, pull over safely to the side of the road and look at the map or ask for directions. Australia's other capital cities are slightly less hectic to navigate and drivers a little more forgiving. Try to time your arrival in a large metropolis to avoid the peak "rush hour" traffic times of 7:30–9:30am and 4:30–7pm. Traffic reports are broadcast on city radio stations. If you are just driving through a city, make sure your map has well-marked highway numbers on it so that you are not distracted by multiple signposts and destinations – it is best to look at the highway or route number to keep your bearings. On the approach to smaller towns, keep a look out for the changes in speed limits and school zones.

On straight stretches of road in the country, make sure you are happy with the distance you have to overtake and the acceleration of your vehicle – larger four-wheel drives laden with luggage and camping gear need plenty of distance to overtake other vehicles safely. On small winding highways through hilly country, overtaking lanes generally occur every 5 km (3 miles) or so. This extra lane allows slower vehicles (such as trucks and vehicles towing boats and caravans) to pull over to the left lane and allow faster vehicles to overtake. (For further tips on Outback driving, *see pp22–3*.) Another point to take into account when planning a driving trip in Australia is how many kilometres/miles you are willing to drive a day. While Australians are used to driving long distances, especially in the Outback where it is not uncommon to drive up to 700 km (450 miles) a day, this might not leave you enough time to explore – or enjoy yourself. Always take into consideration that driving before sunrise and after sunset is not advisable in the Outback and rural areas – kangaroos, wombats and much of Australia's other wildlife often move around more and can be road hazards. If you are doing serious four-wheel driving, take into account that sandy tracks or tracks with loose dust will see you not travelling much faster than 60 km/h (38 mph) safely.

Buying Fuel

Petrol is considered expensive by Australians, but is relatively inexpensive compared to Europe. In remote areas, however, the price can shoot up, sometimes being up to 50¢ a litre more expensive than in urban areas. There are two grades of unleaded fuel as well as diesel and bio-diesel, which is becoming more popular – ask your vehicle hire company if you can use this. Note that diesel is generally slightly less expensive than unleaded fuel and if you hire a heavy-duty 4WD it will probably be a diesel model. Most service stations are self-service and you pay after you have filled up, quoting the number of the pump (also called a bowser). Because of the large distances involved in driving in Australia, it is advisable to carry a spare plastic tank of fuel.

Taking a Break

Australian road authorities are aware that the long distances that people drive in Australia can cause accidents through fatigue and advise taking a break every two hours, sometimes providing free coffee stops for this purpose. There are plenty of well-signposted roadside stops, ranging from merely a place to pull over and nap, to picturesque picnic spots and overnight camping areas. Note that service stations in Australia are key break points – quite often the only stop with food and refreshments you might see for hundreds of kilometres. They sometimes have amusements such as small wildlife parks and offbeat museums. It is advantageous to fill up your fuel tank, buy water and top up snack supplies at these stops before continuing your journey.

Breakdown and Accident Procedures

Any accident involving injury in Australia must be reported to the police within 24 hours. For insurance purposes, you should report every accident with vehicle damage to the police and to your vehicle hire company. Always get insurance details and never admit fault – that is for the police to decide.

Above left Kangaroos on the Bamurru Plains   **Above centre** Helpful signage along a route   **Above right** Coastal road on Wilsons Promontory, Victoria

If you break down, try to head to the hard shoulder or side of the road, put your hazard lights on, and phone your vehicle hire company. If you are in the Outback, always stay with your vehicle when you break down. Deaths in remote areas are most often caused when people leave their vehicle and cannot be located. Your vehicle offers the best protection from the elements.

Parking

As with most cities, the bigger and busier the city, the harder it is to find a car park in the city centre. Parking restrictions are well signposted in Australia and street parking is usually limited to one or two hours during business hours with metered parking. There is often a parking ticket machine within 50 m (50 yds) of your parking spot – it is a good idea to have plenty of loose change as the machines generally only take coins. Display the ticket on the dashboard of your vehicle – and note that it is not unusual to find a parking inspector hovering as your time counts down. If you wish to park for longer periods of time, there are usually multi-storey car parks (above and below ground) in close proximity – look for blue "P" signs. Something to look out for is that many cities have "clearaway" zones, where parking is only permitted outside peak traffic hours. These actually become road lanes during peak times and your vehicle will be towed away if it is parked in this zone during these times. You will need to contact the local traffic authority or the police to find out where the vehicle pound is and retrieve your car – but only after paying the fine.

Maps

If you are on a long Australian road trip, one map will not suffice. While **Hema Maps** have quality maps, including ones tailored for 4WD tours, your best bet for a long trip is to purchase a road atlas. Keep in mind that all major vehicle hire companies now also rent Global Positioning Systems (GPS) with their vehicles, which take away a lot of the stress from driving and navigating in unknown areas. The motoring organizations opposite all have searchable driving directions and maps online. **Where is** is a useful online source for maps and directions.

Below far left Corrugated iron shed next to the road   **Below centre** Cow sculpture outside petrol station, Timboon   **Below left** Koala hazard sign   **Below right** Road through the Cape Schanck Lighthouse Reserve, Victoria

DIRECTORY

MOTORING ORGANIZATIONS

Automobile Association of Northern Territory (AANT)
08 8925 5901; www.aant.com.au

New South Wales and ACT National Roads and Motorists' Association (NRMA)
131 122; www.mynrma.com.au

Royal Automobile Club (RAC)
131 111

Royal Automobile Club of Queensland (RACQ)
131 905; www.racq.com.au

Royal Automobile Association of South Australia (RAA)
08 8202 4600; www.raa.com.au

Royal Automobile Club of Tasmania (RACT)
132 722; www.ract.com.au

Royal Automobile Club of Victoria (RACV)
137 228; www.racv.com.au

Royal Automobile Club of Western Australia (RACWA)
131 703; www.rac.com.au

MAPS

Hema Maps
www.hemamaps.com.au

Where is
www.whereis.com

Caravans, Campervans and Mobile Homes

There is a great tradition among Australians of exploring their country with a caravan in tow. For most Australians today, this simply means towing it to a favourite beachside caravan park, unhitching it and going fishing or surfing for the duration. One of the reasons for this, is that most caravans are unsuited to sandy or rough road driving, so Australians tend to use the caravan as a base and explore the surrounding area using 4WD vehicles, returning to base every night or occasionally camping out.

However, hiring a 4WD vehicle and a caravan will seem too complicated and expensive to most visitors to Australia. It makes more sense to hire a campervan. The two main rental companies that specialize in hiring out campervans and motorhomes are **Britz** and **Maui** (although you can compare deals on sites like **Fetch**). There are even 4WD campervans, which sacrifice a little comfort for the ability to get to the more remote (and sometimes most beautiful) places.

Large mobile homes can be rented, but these are even less suited to going anywhere off the main highways. Only those who prefer comfort (including a real toilet, shower and kitchen) above all else should consider this option.

The most important decision is to choose which sights you wish to see, plan your route and then assess what kind of vehicle can make the journey. Then decide on whether you prefer comfort versus convenience.

Generally, the more you want to get off the main road and explore the wilderness, the more comforts you will likely have to forego.

Motorbikes

Australia is an excellent destination for motorbike touring. You can rent any kind of motorcycle, from small 250 cc cycles to larger tourers, such as the BMW 1200 GS. Bikes that can handle some dirt riding (such as the BMW) are more useful than Harley Davidsons if you are heading off down unpaved roads. A good book to use on your motorbike trip is the *Australia Motorcycle Atlas* from Hema Maps.

Driving with Children

The law in Australia requires securely attached baby and toddler seats for children under four years old and approved booster seats for children aged four to seven. The major vehicle hire companies all carry an extensive range of infant and baby seats, so if you need one ensure you request these at the time of booking. It is now a fineable offence everywhere except the Australian Capital Territory (ACT) and the Northern Territory (NT) to smoke with minors (those under 18) in the car.

Australia has beautiful sandy beaches, fascinating wildlife and plenty of open spaces to keep children entertained. However, the main challenge that you will face travelling with children is keeping them entertained on the long-distance drives that exploring Australia entails. Obviously, games, MP3 and DVD players, and the like, are useful devices for killing the long hours when the scenery and wildlife are not at their most interesting. Use your stops wisely, choosing to stop and refuel at places that offer something entertaining for children, such as a playground or mini-zoo.

Above Campervan on the road in Victoria

Campervans that can cater for a full family of five or six (complete with fridge, stove, microwave, shower and toilet) are available and make a good option, particularly if you are not looking for major driving challenges.

Disabled Drivers

There is no Disabled Driving Association in Australia as such, but national organizations such as **NICAN** and **NDS** provide information on access and facilities for the disabled.

Vehicles are available with hand controls from most vehicle hire companies, but it is necessary to book these well in advance.

Most public car parks and parking areas have dedicated parking bays for disabled drivers, clearly identified by the international disabled sign. The bays are often close to ramps and lifts and are generally wider than the regular parking spaces. The use of disabled parking bays is closely monitored and heavy fines apply to unauthorised users. In order to use disabled parking, you must obtain a temporary disabled parking permit.

Bring your overseas permit with you as these may be used in Queensland, ACT (Canberra), Tasmania, South Australia, Western Australia and the NT. In New South

Above left Clear and comprehensive signage, Round Mountain, New South Wales **Above right** Lookout car park at Cradle Mountain, Tasmania

Wales (NSW), application may be made for a temporary permit at any **NSW Roads and Traffic Authority** office. In Victoria, a temporary permit for a holder of an overseas parking permit may be arranged before arrival through **VicRoads**. Apply at least one month before arrival by fax or by post, enclosing a copy of your overseas permit together with the dates you will be in Australia and your address on arrival. A temporary permit issued in NSW or Victoria will be recognized throughout Australia.

Driving in Rain and Heat

It is best to avoid driving during heavy rain in the tropical north, if possible. During the wet season in the NT (Nov–Apr), many roads are closed due to flooding and possible land slips. The **Road Report website** gives up-to-date information about which roads are impassable or closed in the NT at any time, as well as more general information on likely closures and when routes are expected to reopen after the rains. It can take a while for damaged roads to be repaired at the start of the dry season. The website has recommendations for restrictions by weight and type of vehicle too, although these mainly apply to road haulage and heavy freight transport.

If planning to drive in extreme heat on a desert drive in summer (Dec–Mar), carry spare water, food and fuel, and make sure you travel in an air-conditioned vehicle. It is worth taking some kind of shade covering in case of vehicle breakdown. The **Bureau of Meteorology** website is useful for weather forecasts, including bushfire weather warnings and has a helpful UV index, which advises when to project skin from harmful UV rays.

Driving in Winter

Australia's winter is quite short and snow generally only falls on the higher slopes in NSW, Victoria and Tasmania. The most dangerous aspect of this is black ice, which can affect the lower slopes of the mountain ranges. If you are heading to the ski areas of Victoria and NSW, snow chains must be carried during the declared ski season – snow or no snow. These can be hired from local service stations before heading up the mountain and if you do not know how to put them on, have a trial run *before* attempting it in a blizzard.

Below far left The single-track Vaughan-Tarilta Bridge, Victoria **Below centre** Quaint bakery in Hobart **Below left** Vintage Aussie truck in Tyabb, Victoria **Below right** Compact motorhome on a camp site at Hellyer Gorge, Tasmania

DIRECTORY

CAMPERVAN HIRE COMPANIES
Britz
www.britz.com.au

Fetch
www.fetchcampervanhire.com.au

Maui
www.maui-rentals.com

DISABLED DRIVING
NDS
www.nds.org.au

NICAN
www.nican.com.au

NSW Roads and Traffic Authority
www.rta.nsw.gov.au

VicRoads
www.vicroads.vic.gov.au

DRIVING IN RAIN AND HEAT
Bureau of Meteorology
www.bom.gov.au

Road Report website
www.ntlis.nt.gov.au/roadreport

Driving in the Outback

For many visitors, driving in the Outback is the highlight of the trip. It gives them the opportunity to really explore the wilderness and get close to nature. However, time should be spent preparing for Outback travel. Check your route, looking ahead on the map. Although some Outback areas now have roads of a good enough standard to carry conventional (2WD) cars, a 4WD is essential if you want to travel to some of Australia's best wild and remote regions. Remember that conventional vehicles in Australia are not insured for travel on dirt roads.

Safety

There are a number of basic points of safety that should be observed on any trip of this kind. Plan your route carefully and carry up-to-date maps. If you are travelling off-road on 4WD tracks between remote destinations, travel with another vehicle, if possible, and inform the authorities (either the local police, national park office, or visitor centre) of your departure and expected arrival times. Ask them about the road conditions, too.

Make sure you have plenty of food, water and fuel for the trip. Calculate your fuel economy and then plan where to get more fuel and supplies.

If you do break down, run out of fuel or become stuck, stay with the vehicle unless it is unsafe to do so. Your vehicle will provide good protection from the elements and is a much bigger target for a search party to spot from the road or air. If you fail to arrive at your destination at the expected time and have informed the authorities of your plans, a search party will be sent out to look for you.

While some travellers try to tackle 4WD trails and tracks in a 2WD vehicle, this is a very dangerous thing to do. If it rains in Outback areas, it quite often floods suddenly and a 2WD vehicle will have much difficulty negotiating creek crossings and muddy tracks. Conventional vehicles are not made for the constant bumps and juddering that occur on Australia's Outback tracks, making the reliability of even recent model vehicles suspect in these conditions. Taking on these tracks and becoming stuck will waste the resources of locals and rescue personnel who should be available to tackle legitimate emergencies rather than those who have taken unnecessary risks. Finally, your insurance will not cover you when driving a 2WD on these roads.

Another factor to take into account with Outback driving is that nobody drives at night except truck drivers hauling large road trains – up to four lorry trailers linked together. (Be warned that these huge vehicles can produce large amounts of dust, so slow down if one is approaching and pull over a little to your side of the road.) This is because animals such as kangaroos, small marsupials, emus, and farm stock will often be active at night. Plan to arrive at your final destination of the day at least an hour before sunset – this is a safety margin in case you are delayed en route – plus it gives you time for a refreshing sundowner when you arrive. Early mornings on the road can be dangerous as well, but the danger decreases as the day goes on.

Above Fording a shallow river after rain in a 4WD

4WD Driving Tips

If you do hire a 4WD, you will have access to some of Australia's most jaw-dropping scenery, but with this comes the responsibility of driving on some of the country's most remote roads in extremely rugged country where the results of poor judgement can be catastrophic – and, in very rare circumstances, even fatal.

First, get to know the vehicle before you leave the rental agency. Their staff will take you through the basics – on engaging 4WD and how to check the oil levels and water. Ask as many questions as you like as they prefer this to answering an emergency via satellite phone. Make sure you learn to use the Emergency Position Indicating Radio Beacon (EPIRB), which you should get as part of an Outback driving kit when you hire the car. (If it is not included see if you can hire one.) This is to be used only as a last resort. A satellite phone is a good idea if you are travelling with just one vehicle in remote areas and can usually be hired from the rental agency or independently (see p14). Keep in mind that even with a 4WD some roads are considered too dangerous to be covered by insurance. Make sure you are aware of any restrictions when booking your vehicle.

Above left Cars parked in the shade in the Outback **Above right** Iconic road sign warning about the dangers of wildlife on the open road

Most 4WDs are taller and narrower than conventional vehicles; keep this in mind when you are heading to a shopping centre underground car park or even hotel driveways with low awnings. These vehicles are also heavy and generally lack the acceleration of a standard 2WD vehicle, so bear this in mind when you first try overtaking on the highways. Learn the characteristics of the vehicle before heading off to remote areas. For your first time on dirt roads, do not try to drive like the locals do. They have often been driving these roads every day for years and have a highly tuned (if sometimes incorrect) idea of how fast they can go safely. Do not schedule a heavy day's driving for your first day off-road. If you feel that you do need some assistance to become a more confident off-road driver you can take a **Britz 4WD Tag-a-long Tour** or a **4WD Training Course** to hone your extreme driving skills first.

Roof Racks and Transporting Bicycles

If you are hiring a vehicle and want to carry extra gear and bicycles, it is best to rent a dedicated 4WD with racks or a campervan with a bicycle rack.

Protecting the Land

It is extremely important that you do not damage the environment you are enjoying. Do not cut down trees or disturb vegetation in any way. It may not seem so romantic, but cook using your stove rather than lighting a fire wherever possible – and remember that bush fires devastate large areas of the country every year. Do not use soap in rivers and creeks as the detergent can damage the fragile ecosystem. Some Aboriginal areas require a permit just to drive through, so make sure you have the correct permit. Camp at least 100 m (110 yds) from water and use existing tracks and camp sites – do not create new ones. Take plenty of rubbish bags and carry your rubbish out of untouched areas – do not bury food waste. If you need to make a bush toilet, dig it at least 30 cm (1 ft) deep and at least 100 m (110 yds) from any creeks and rivers. Never feed the wildlife – no matter how cute – and do not touch any Aboriginal rock art: the oil from your skin can permanently damage it.

Below far left 4WD hire car on a red dirt road **Below centre** Unforgettable scenery from a well-sealed, well-marked road **Below left** Old petrol pumps **Below right** Road train approaching in a cloud of dust

DIRECTORY

4WD DRIVING TIPS

Britz 4WD Tag-a-long Tour and 4WD Training Course
www.britz.com.au/4WD-adventures-australia

USEFUL INFORMATION

Northern Territory Road Conditions
www.ntlis.nt.gov.au/roadreport

Kakadu National Park Road Conditions
www.environment.gov.au/parks/kakadu/explore/safety

Weather Reports and Warnings
www.bom.gov.au/weather

Where to Stay

Australia has a wide variety of accommodation. The standard is generally good, with a growing number of stylish boutique hotels, charming guesthouses and eco-lodges, but there are also plenty of basic rooms. In line with Australia's egalitarian nature, places such as Uluru's Ayers Rock Resort offer a range of accommodation from camp sites to a superb luxury hotel. Sometimes, in the more remote areas, you will find motel-style rooms and caravan parks that are only meant for overnight stays for those on long driving trips.

Above Luxury safari-style room at the Ayers Rock Resort, Uluru, NT *(see p200)*

Facilities and Prices

Australia has no national grading system for accommodation. However, some state tourism organizations have their own rating systems. These are a handy indicator of standards and facilities. As always, however, they tend to focus on amenities and fail to take into account charm and service.

In hotels and motels, air conditioning is the norm and often there are tea- and coffee-making facilities, a small refrigerator, TV, and occasionally a microwave or electric stovetop. En suite bathrooms are standard, but often only with a shower, not a bath-tub. These rooms will also usually contain one double bed and one single bed.

The big city and boutique hotels are in line with international standards and are often good value for money. The average country motel rooms and caravan park cabins are fairly utilitarian and often quite expensive – but in these destinations, supply and demand dictate the prices.

Hotels, Motels and Resorts

The capital cities are well supplied with luxury hotels including the international brands such as the **Hyatt**, **Hilton**, **Sheraton**, **InterContinental** and **Westin**. There

are also boutique offerings, and these tend to be individually owned and operated and can provide a more interesting experience than many of the luxury brands and chain hotels. Of note in Australia are eco-friendly and/or safari-style luxury resorts such as **Longitude 131°** at Uluru and **Southern Ocean Lodge** on Kangaroo Island.

The chains hotels – often calling themselves "motels" – that populate the main stops on the driving trips are **Choice Hotels**, **Best Western** and **Travelodge**. They are reliable and clean choices – if offering uninspired and dated decor. Many of these have restaurants serving familiar Australian menu standards, but they do tend to close early, so phone ahead to check the closing times if you are on the road.

The term "hotel" can also simply denote a pub with a couple of basic rooms out the back, meant for the occasional pub-goer to sleep off the effects of a big night. That said, some of these characterful Aussie pubs make great places to overnight.

In the more remote areas, these convenient but no-frill rooms are often used to house government workers on short-term contracts in

the area and can – somewhat surprisingly – be in short supply, as they are booked well in advance.

Bed and Breakfast Accommodation

Bed and breakfast (B&B) accommodation is popular in Australia, particularly in areas where there were early settlers, as the accommodation tends to be in charming, heritage-listed, colonial houses or mansions. Quite often these B&Bs have only two or three rooms and no en suite bathrooms. Some host dinners featuring top-quality, locally sourced produce.

An interesting option is a farmstay, where you can get a taste of the life of the cattle drover, without having to endure the discomfort.

Camping and Caravan Parks

Caravan parks with pitches for both tents and caravans are found all over Australia, along the vast coastline, in the isolated interior, and at popular locations in national parks. These often offer much better access to the natural sights and wilderness than the nearest hotel-style accommodation. In national parks, some camping areas are free to use and offer very

Above left Jacobs Creek Retreat, Barossa Valley, SA *(see p160)* **Above centre** Chic interior of a Margaret River hotel, WA **Above right** Charming hotel in Pemberton, WA

little in the way of facilities – so you will need to be well prepared.

As well as room for caravans and campers, caravan parks often have on-site static caravans and, increasingly, cabins, units and chalets with air conditioning and small kitchens for self-caterers. Caravan parks in Australia are generally well equipped, with plenty of shower and bathroom facilities as well as a laundry, kitchen, and a very welcome outdoor swimming pool.

Self-catering
There is an increasing trend for self-catering apartments in Australia, which can be rented for anything from one night to one month or more. These generally come with kitchen and laundry facilities, satellite television and Internet, and are found in cities, large towns and popular tourist destinations throughout the country. These self-catering apartments are great for holiday-makers who like to cook, families with children, and travellers who want to stay in one place for a couple of days, do some washing and regroup on a long trip. Prices for apartments can be on a par with motels, making them great value, as cooking your own meals can

be a lot cheaper than dining out every night.

Booking
Outside the main hotel groups and chains, which have the usual sophisticated online systems, bookings can be made by telephone, often without the need to provide a credit card number. There are many websites, such as **Discover Australia**, that can help if you want to plan it all in advance. On the other hand, last-minute websites such as **Wotif** and **Last Minute** offer great rates if you are flexible about travelling – this can be a good way to travel outside school holidays, Easter and the height of the summer. If you are travelling during busy periods you will need to book months in advance. Keep in mind that if you are driving through rural areas, mobile phone reception can be a problem if you are trying to book from the road rather than in a town. **Stayz** is a useful online booking service for holiday apartments, and state and local tourist offices can also help with finding accommodation.

Below left Gracemere Grange B&B, Dorrigo, NSW **Below centre** Hotel on Burleigh Heads beach *(see p50)*, Queensland **Below right** Luxury cabins and pool at Ayers Rock Resort, Uluru, NT *(see p200)*

DIRECTORY

PRICE BANDS USED IN THIS GUIDE
The following price bands are based on a room for two people for one night.
Inexpensive: under AU$150
Moderate: AU$150–AU$250
Expensive: over AU$250

HOTELS, MOTELS AND RESORTS
Best Western
131 779; www.bestwestern.com.au

Choice
1300 668 128; www.choicehotels.com.au

Hilton
1300 445 866; www.hilton.com

Hyatt
13 12 34; www.hyatt.com

InterContinental
1800 669 562; www.ichotelsgroup.com

Longitude 131°
02 8296 8010 (select option 3); www.longitude131.com.au

Sheraton
1800 073 535; www.starwoodhotels.com

Southern Ocean Lodge
02 9918 4355 (select option 3); www.southernoceanlodge.com.au

Travelodge
1300 886 886; www.travelodge.com.au

Westin
1800 656 535; www.westin.com.au

BOOKING
Discover Australia
www.discoveraustralia.com.au

Last Minute
www.lastminute.com.au

Stayz
www.stayz.com.au

Wotif
www.wotif.com.au

Where to Eat

By absorbing the culinary traditions of Asian and Mediterranean immigrants, Australia's cuisine has improved immensely over the past 20 years and reflects the multi-cultural makeup of the country. Australians are equally at home with a curry laksa, seafood spaghetti or kangaroo steak. There is also a better appreciation of the country's natural bounty – superb fruit, vegetables, seafood and meats – and a meal is not complete without an excellent local beer or an award-winning, home-grown bottle of wine.

Above Excellent espresso from a café at Battery Point, Hobart, Tasmania

Practical Information

Most restaurants serve lunch between noon and 3pm, with dinner served from 6:30 to 10:30 pm. However, once away from the major cities and towns, you will need to be seated by 6:30–7pm to get an evening meal – many Outback and rural kitchens close by 8pm. Cafés in tourist destinations will often open right through from breakfast to late at night and generally seven days a week. While it is fine to just drop in to casual eateries for a meal, it is always advisable to make a booking for peak times at popular restaurants in holiday destinations. Some of the most celebrated restaurants can be booked up many weeks in advance. Major credit cards are accepted in the majority of Australian restaurants.

In casual cafés, the tip is generally your coin change. In more formal restaurants, it is good to leave a more substantial tip, but it is not mandatory. A tip of 10% would be seen as a generous reward for good service.

With proactive legislation in place, wheelchair access and bathroom facilities for disabled visitors in Australian restaurants and cafés are generally very good, but it is often advisable to phone ahead to discuss your needs to avoid disappointment.

Restaurants

Restaurants in Australia range from fine-dining establishments regarded as some of the best in the world, to simple, local BYO (Bring Your Own beer/wine) eateries specializing in ethnic cuisine. Restaurants that can legally sell alcohol are called "licensed restaurants". While the large cities have every type of cuisine you could imagine, rural and Outback towns will mainly have a pub offering "counter meals" (order from a blackboard menu, pay at the counter and collect your meal from the counter when your number is called) and a couple of unpretentious restaurants generally featuring Asian (usually generic Chinese) or Italian fare.

Every state capital city has a chef or two who is well regarded in Australia, and sometimes on the world stage, and meals at these restaurants can be extraordinarily good value by world standards. In Europe, the term "fusion food" – a combination of cuisines and flavours from different countries – has become a somewhat maligned style of cuisine. However, in Australia, the fresh local produce, plus expert use of the techniques and ingredients of European and Asian cooking, can result in some splendid

cuisine. As a result, the term "fusion" has been supplanted by "Mod Oz".

Another interesting element of Australian cuisine is "bush tucker". This makes use of the vegetables, animals, reptiles and insects that are native to the country and have been eaten for thousands of years by the indigenous peoples. Top restaurants often use wattle seeds, lemon myrtle and yabbies (crayfish); while bush tucker tours in the Northern Territories *(see p175)* will usually give visitors the chance to learn about and taste food such as goanna (lizard), kangaroo, and wichetty grubs (moth larvae).

While the dedicated Italian and Asian (Thai, Vietnamese, Chinese) restaurants are reasonably authentic, many restaurants and bistros found in tourist destinations serve ubiquitous dishes such as Caesar salad, salt and pepper squid, "surf and turf" (seafood and beef), lamb shanks and lasagne.

Cafés and Bars

Most cafés in Australia offer good breakfasts, salads and sandwiches, as well as fresh juices, smoothies and coffee. Aside from Melbourne and Sydney, which have large Italian-Australian populations, the country has not had a tradition of bars that

Above left Vineyard in the Margaret River region, WA **Above centre** Quirky Outback pub in Daly Waters, NT **Above right** Harbourside dining in Darwin, NT

also serve good coffee – mainly because of the prohibitive licensing laws. There are good independent cafés serving home-made cakes and excellent coffee, sometimes even made from locally grown beans. Bar food can vary from "counter meals" to sophisticated waiter-service, restaurant-style dining, akin to "gastro pubs" in the UK.

Picnics and BBQs

As a result of immigration in the mid-20th century, Australia is home to a wide range of nationalities who now run some amazing delicatessens. Salamis, cured meats and cheeses, marinated vegetables and olives, dips, and other goodies are all on offer at the local deli and make perfect picnic fare – and the weather is usually sunny, too. Load up with a picnic hamper and a chilled bottle of Australian white wine for a memorable picnic. Even more of an Australian tradition is the barbecue (BBQ). While you are on the road you will see BBQs – free or coin-operated – everywhere, from public parks to camping grounds. Australians do not need much encouragement to throw some prawns or steaks on the BBQ, and on weekends the parks are full of groups chatting around a hot barbie.

Gourmet Shopping

An obvious thing to shop for is Australian wine. With over 200 years of experience, "New World" wine is a bit of a misnomer. From the Hunter Valley (NSW) (see p90), to the Mornington Peninsula (VA) to the Barossa Valley around Adelaide (see p152) and all the way west near Perth to the Margaret River (see p230), you will find superb, fruity white wines and big juicy reds. Most wineries also have excellent restaurants so be sure to book a tour that includes dining. The wine regions also have farmshops selling local cheeses, chutneys and other produce.

While excellent seafood is caught all along the coast, the irony is that it is not available locally as it is whisked off to the big east coast cities. You will often have to buy fish from the supermarket. However, there is plenty of excellent produce on offer. Best of all are the farmers' markets. These are a showcase for regional producers and you should be able to stock up on home-made breads, cheeses, honey, and fruit. Each tour notes the location and day of the week for these markets.

Below far left Pavement café in Fremantle, WA **Below centre** Outside dining in Uluru, NT **Below left** Boathouse Café, Daylesford Lake, Victoria **Below right** Animal jerky (dried meat)

THE DRIVES

Reef and Rainforest

Mission Beach to The Daintree

Highlights

- **The Great Barrier Reef**
  Admire the myriad colourful creatures living in the world's largest coral system – one of the natural wonders of the world

- **Tropical rainforest**
  Explore some of the world's oldest forests in North Queensland, home to an amazing number of insects, plants, reptiles, birds and mammals

- **Secluded beaches**
  Relax on the area's many quiet, sandy beaches, fringed by swaying palm trees and washed by gentle waves

- **Cairns Esplanade**
  Stroll along the seafront at Cairns, swim in the Lagoon, or simply enjoy a coffee while overlooking the marina

Tropical rainforest vegetation in Mossman Gorge, Daintree National Park

Reef and Rainforest

North Queensland beaches feature pristine white sands and tantalizing aquamarine waters. Protected from big waves by the Great Barrier Reef, they provide a playground for watersports and seaside relaxation. The Cassowary Coast road, heading north out of Mission Beach, is unsurpassed in its display of natural beauty, with palm-lined sands and secluded coves. The Tablelands that overlook the coastal strip are home to ancient rainforests with skyscraping trees, spectacular waterfalls and quiet lakes. On this drive, enjoy the lazy tropical sun and the surprise afternoon rain showers. Take a cruise on a crater lake, or travel on the scenic Skyrail over the rainforest canopy. Snorkel in clear, green-blue waters and walk among rare, primitive plants. After all this, enjoy the excellent local produce in the cafés, restaurants and markets.

Above View from the Atherton Tablelands down to the coast through Barron Gorge, *see p37*

ACTIVITIES

Snorkel in the Great Barrier Reef, alternately admire the corals from a sailing boat or a high-speed catamaran from Mission Beach or Cairns

Fish for supper at Garners Beach or Flying Fish Point

Take a rainforest and wildlife cruise on Lake Barrine near Malanda

Fly high over the plateau of the Atherton Tablelands in a hot-air balloon

Glide over the dense treetop canopy on the Skyrail at Kuranda

Swim in the saltwater of Cairns Lagoon

Below Rainforest-backed sandy beach on the coast between Cairns and Port Douglas, *see p39*

Above Colourful Art Deco façades of Innisfail's Central Business District, *see p35*

KEY

🚗 Drive route

Trinity Bay

Double Island

Green Island

TRINITY BEACH 16
🏖️🍽️ **YORKEYS KNOB** 15

RANDA

Machans Beach

✈ Cairns Airport

Cape Grafton

CAIRNS 14
🏖️🍽️

Yarrabah

Fitzroy Island

White Rock

Edmonton

Gordonvale

Aloomba

High Island

CRATER LAKES NATIONAL PARK
Lake Barrine
ake Eacham

Normanby Island

Russell Island

Bellenden Ker

ALANDA

Babinda

Bramston Beach

Miriwinni

Ella Bay National Park

Ella Bay

Daradgee

MILLAA MILLAA

Belvedere

🏖️ **FLYING FISH POINT** 6
INNISFAIL 5
🏖️🍽️

South Johnstone

Mourilyan
Mourilyan Harbour

PARONELLA PARK 4
🏖️🍽️

Mena Creek

Double Point
Cowley Beach

Japoonvale
Japoon National Park

Silkwood

Stephens Islands

Carter Falls

El Arish

KURRIMINE BEACH 3
GARNERS BEACH 2

Koombooloomba Dam

Bingil Bay

Clump Point

🏖️ **MISSION BEACH** 1

Tully

Wongaling Beach

South Mission Beach
🍽️

Dunk Island

Lower Tully

Family Islands

Tully Heads

0 kilometres   20
0 miles   20

Great Barrier Reef

PLAN YOUR DRIVE

Start/finish: Mission Beach to The Daintree.

Number of days: 4 days.

Distance: Approx. 393 km (244 miles).

Road conditions: Check weather details as some roads may be closed during the wet season, at its worst between January and March. All main routes on this drive are sealed, apart from the 2WD-accessible track to Garners Beach.

When to go: The best time to visit tropical North Queensland is the dry season (May–Oct), when the temperature is not so hot and the beaches are swimmable. In the wet season (Nov–Apr), jellyfish can make swimming in the river mouths and ocean dangerous, and at its peak (Dec–Feb) cyclones and heavy rain can cause serious flooding.

Opening times: Most museums and shops in Australia are open 9am–5pm. It is often difficult to find restaurants open in smaller towns on Monday and Tuesday nights.

Main market days: Mission Beach: 1st Sat & 3rd Sun of month; **Malanda:** 3rd Sat of month; **Yungaburra:** 4th Sat of month; **Kuranda:** local produce and handicrafts, daily; **Cairns:** Rustys Markets, Fri–Sun (fruit and veg); Esplanade Markets, Sat (local crafts); City Place Markets, Mon–Fri (crafts); Mud Markets, Sat & Sun (arts & crafts); **Port Douglas:** Cotters Market (crafts made by stallholders), Sun am.

Shopping: Cairns Night Market is a permanent covered market selling arts, crafts and souvenirs. Look out, too, for fruit stalls along the route selling delicious locally grown produce.

Major festivals: Cairns: Cairns Festival, late Aug–early Sep annually (theatre, music, film, food and visual arts; www.festivalcairns.com.au).

Above Secluded Garners Beach, backed by dense rainforest where cassowaries roam

VISITING THE GREAT BARRIER REEF

Big Mama's Sailing: *0437 206 360; www.bigmamasailing.com*
Calypso Dive: *07 4068 8432; www.calypsoadventures.com.au*

WHERE TO STAY

MISSION BEACH

Eco Village Mission Resort *moderate*
Boutique beachfront accommodation in the rainforest, with good facilities.
Clump Point Road, Clump Point, 4852; 07 4068 7534; www.ecovillage.com.au

KURRIMINE BEACH

Kurrimine Beach Holiday Park *inexpensive*
Basic self-contained villas, with a saltwater pool and tropical gardens.
Jacobs Rd, 4871; 07 4065 6166; www.kurriminebeachholidaypark.com.au

AROUND PARONELLA PARK

Mena Creek Eco Gardens *inexpensive*
These comfortable units nestle in the foothills of the Misty Mountains and offer great views and tropical gardens.
17 Mena Creek Rd, Mena Creek, 4871; 07 4065 3421; www.menacreekgardens.com.au

INNISFAIL

Innisfail Riverside Motel *inexpensive*
This quaint motel has balconies that overlook the Johnstone River.
Cnr Fitzgerald Esplanade and Grace St, 4860; 07 4061 2444

FLYING FISH POINT

Flying Fish Point Tourist Park *inexpensive*
Large sites with a choice of cabins and camp sites, and a saltwater pool.
Flying Fish Point; 07 4061 3131; www.ffpvanpark.com.au

❶ Mission Beach
Queensland; 4852

The hamlet of Mission Beach on the Cassowary Coast is the gateway to two World Heritage-listed areas: the **Great Barrier Reef** in the waters to the east and Japoon National Park on its western flank. Daily trips from Clump Point boat ramp, at the northern end of Mission Beach, allow visitors to experience the beauty of the reef by snorkelling, scuba diving and sailing. For secluded beaches and a taste of tropical paradise, take a boat trip from Clump Point to **Dunk Island** *(half- or one-day cruises; 0437 206 360; www.bigmamasailing.com)*, or a dive tour to the outer reef *(07 4068 8432; www.calypsoadventures.com.au)*. Good fishing is also to be had at Clump Point Jetty and the rock wall at Clump Point boat ramp. For a land-based activity, try the 7-km (5-mile) **Edmund Kennedy Walking Track** (3–4hrs) at the southern end of the beach, which passes through mangroves and a rainforest.

🚗 *Leave Mission Beach north along beach on Porter Promenade. Around Clump Point on Alexander Dr, turn left into Bingal Bay Rd, then right into unsealed Garners Beach Rd to beach.*

❷ Garners Beach
Queensland; 4852

This secluded beach is home to the **Garners Beach Cassowary Rehabilitation Facility** *(www.arf.net.au/garners_beach.html)* where these large (up to 2-m/6-ft tall), flightless birds are looked after when injured. Look out for the birds in dense rainforest on

The Great Barrier Reef

The world's largest coral reef, the Great Barrier Reef Marine Park runs for 3,000 km (1,800 miles) parallel to the Queensland Coast – at times only 15 km (9 miles) offshore. With 400 types of vivid coral, more than 1,500 species of tropical fish, 4,000 varieties of mollusc and rare green sea turtles and dugong, the reef is one of the world's natural wonders.

the edges of Maria Creek National Park (but do not approach – or enter creeks, where crocodiles swim). The area is popular with locals who fish off shore for barramundi and mangrove jacks.

🚗 *Return to Bingal Bay Rd, turn right to the Bruce Hwy (A1), turn right then right again down Murdering Point Rd.*

❸ Kurrimine Beach
Queensland; 4871

On the way to the beach (on the left soon after turning onto Murdering Point Road), look out for **Murdering Point Winery** *(open daily; 07 4065 2327; www.murderingpointwinery.com.au)*. The winery offers a wide range of fruit wines made from local mango, passionfruit and mulberry. Enjoy free tastings – the flavour is Australian and the bouquet is tropical Queensland.

At the end of Murdering Point Road lies Kurrimine Beach, a quiet hamlet and a popular fishing spot, perhaps due to the protection of King Reef, just offshore. The long, sandy beaches are ideal for exploring and the waters are good for snorkelling in season (beware of stinging jellyfish). Be sure to visit **Kurrimine Beach Conservation Park** and take a walk along the path

Below Dramatic sunset over the islands of the Great Barrier Reef south of Mission Beach

through a rare mesophyll vine forest, featuring huge fan palms, giant tree ferns and strangler vines.

🚗 *Return to the Bruce Hwy, but cross straight over it onto Japoonvale Rd, the "Canecutter Way", to Paronella Park, passing Japoon National Park.*

④ Paronella Park
Queensland; 4871
In 1929, José Paronella purchased land at Mena Creek to fulfil his dream of creating an exotic pleasure garden in a natural environment. **Paronella Park** *(open daily; 07 4065 0000; www.paronellapark. com.au)* opened to the public in 1935. Its design was inspired by the Moorish architecture and gardens of its creator's homeland, Spain. This is a romantic playground, full of diverse flora and fauna. The park offers rainforest walks, guided tours and firefly-lit night tours through an atmospheric avenue of tall kauri trees.

🚗 *Carry on along Japoonvale Rd (Canecutter Way) north to Innisfail.*

Canecutter Way
Japoonvale Road, from Silkwood to Innisfail, was the Old Bruce Highway, with all its quaint twists and turns, and is also known as Canecutter Way. This 52-km (32-mile) long road derives its name from the itinerant gangs who used to travel this route cutting the sugar cane. It winds through sections of virgin rainforest, past waterfalls, and meanders alongside sugar cane fields. Look out for canecutter barracks, old-world sugar towns, a sugar mill and several characterful Queensland pubs.

---

⑤ Innisfail
Queensland; 4860
The area was originally inhabited by the Mamu people, who led migratory lifestyles, moving along the Johnstone River in bark canoes. They resisted land seizure by European settlers and gold miners in the late 19th century, but were eventually displaced.

Canecutter statue, Innisfail

Now a centre for fruit growing, Innisfail is known for its Art Deco architecture. Take time to admire the ornamented façades in the Central Business District (CBD). The large Chinese community here grew from the immigrant workers brought in to clear the scrub for growing fruit trees. They built the carved **Lit Sing Gung Chinese Temple** *(open daily)* in Owen Street in 1940. There is also a strong Italian community, so look out for delis and stock up for picnics. To learn more about the area, visit the **Innisfail Visitor Information Centre** *(Bruce Highway, Innisfail; 07 4061 2655).*

🚗 *Follow the Fitzgerald Esplanade over the Geraldton Bridge onto Flying Fish Point Rd to the point.*

⑥ Flying Fish Point
Queensland; 4860
Situated where the Johnstone River meets the Coral Sea, on the edge of the Great Barrier Reef Marine Park, Flying Fish Point is a stunning locale. It is worth the trek along the peninsula just for a look, a relaxed afternoon in the sun and a swim. It is also a top fishing spot and a 45-minute walk to Ella Bay Beach and National Park. There is a good camp site at the point.

🚗 *Return to Innisfail and take the Palmerston Hwy (25) to Millaa Millaa.*

Above left Flying Fish Point, a great place for fishing from the beach **Above centre** Avenue of impressive kauri trees in Paronella Park **Above right** Innisfail, described as Australia's Art Deco capital

NORTH QUEENSLAND FRUIT

It is impossible to be in far North Queensland and not be tempted by the delicious tropical fruit. Pull over to roadside fruit stalls and stock up on bananas, paw-paws, mangoes and other fruit in season. **Stevo's Fruit Stall** *(Japoonvale Rd, Mena Creek, 4871; 07 4065 3244)* is a great place to stop, refresh and buy produce straight from the farm.

EAT AND DRINK

AROUND MISSION BEACH

Nana Thai *inexpensive*
Nana's serves authentic Thai dishes in an attractive house with a tropical garden, and offers friendly service 5 km (3 miles) south of Mission Beach. *165 Reid Rd, Wongaling Beach, 4852; 07 4068 9101; open Tue–Sun 6–8:30pm*

AROUND PARONELLA PARK

Off the Rails *inexpensive*
This delightful café and gallery sources local produce to use throughout its menu. It is conveniently located on South Johnstone's main street which is directly on the sugar train's route. *37 Hynes St, South Johnstone, 4859; 07 4064 2596*

INNISFAIL

Jagad's Epicurean Emporium *inexpensive*
A small, award-winning café, which provides friendly service and great food featuring fresh, local produce. *49 Edith St, 4860; 07 4061 1480; jagads@bigpond.net.au; open daytime only, closed Sat pm & Sun*

Oliveri's Continental Deli *inexpensive*
A good place to stock up on meats and cheeses for the road ahead, or have an authentic Italian coffee and one of their gourmet lunch rolls. *41 Edith St, 4860; 07 4061 3354; open Mon–Fri 8:30am–5pm, Sat 8:30am–1pm*

Eat and Drink: inexpensive under AU$60; moderate AU$60–AU$100; expensive over AU$100

HOT-AIR BALLOONING

Hot-air balloon flights leave from Mareeba. Book at **Atherton Tableland Information Centre** *(cnr Main and Silo rds, Atherton, 4883; 07 4091 4222; www. athertoninformationcentre.com.au)*.

WHERE TO STAY

MILLAA MILLAA

Acton Ridge Farmstay *moderate*
Large farm offering an Australian-style country holiday, with home-cooking. *122 Nash Rd, 4886; 07 4097 2293; www.actonridgefarmstay.com*

MALANDA

Malanda Lodge Motel *inexpensive*
This comfortable lodge is centrally located and set in tropical gardens and lawns with views across lush pastures. *Cnr Merragallan and Millaa Millaa Rds, 4885; 07 4096 5555; www.malandalodgemotel.com.au*

AROUND MALANDA

Riversong Retreat *inexpensive*
This secluded retreat, with its Balinese-inspired tranquility and surrounded by rainforest, is 7 km (11 miles) beyond Millaa Millaa, along Palmerston Highway. *Mullins Rd, Millaa Millaa, QLD; 0402 208 377; www.grandviewcountry.com.au*

ATHERTON

Barking Owl Retreat *moderate*
This B&B retreat with cottages is set on a large rural plot nestled in a secluded valley minutes from Lake Tinaroo. *409 Hough Rd, 4872; 07 4095 8455; www.barkingowlretreat.com.au*

AROUND MAREEBA

Jabiru Safari Lodge *moderate*
This stay offers safari-style tents in the Mareeba Tropical Savanna and Wetland Reserve (follow signs from Biboohra). *Pickford Rd, Biboohra, 4880; 07 4093 2514; www.jabirusafarilodge.com.au*

Below left Walkway through Barron Gorge National Park **Below right** The 260-m (853-ft) cascade at Barron Falls, near Kuranda

⑦ Millaa Millaa
Queensland; 4886

The Palmerston Highway (25) from Innisfail weaves for a scenic 60 km (37 miles) up to the Atherton Tableland. Allow time to explore walks and waterfalls along the way.

Millaa Millaa is a quiet country village at the centre of the 17-km (11-mile) **Waterfall Circuit** *(get a map at www. millaamillaa.com)* that includes Millaa Millaa Falls, Zillie Falls and Ellinjaa Falls, all with swimming holes *(head east on Palmerston Hwy (25) then turn left on Theresa Creek Rd to Millaa Millaa Falls to start the circuit)*. Just west of town, on McHugh Road, is the **Millaa Millaa Lookout**, with fabulous 180-degree vistas over the Tableland peaks. For more walking opportunities, try one of the Misty Mountain Trails *(see box)*, over 130 km (80 miles) of forest tracks.

🚗 *From Palmerston Hwy (25) take Millaa Millaa–Malanda Rd to Malanda.*

⑧ Malanda
Queensland; 4885

Originally a dairy farming town, Malanda reflects the rural ambience of this region. Highlights include the **Malanda Environmental Centre** *(open daily)*. This explains the geology of the Tablelands, with interactive displays and guided tours. Just west of town, on the Malanda–Atherton Road, **Malanda Falls Conservation Park** has a walking track to Malanda Falls on the North Johnstone River, which tumble over ancient volcanic rock to a refreshing creek and swimming hole – an excellent place for a picnic. Tree kangaroos and platypuses can be spotted from the viewing platform.

🚗 *Take Malanda–Gordonvale Rd, turn right into Lakes Drive to Crater*

Misty Mountain Trails

In high-altitude rainforest, the 130-km (80-mile) Misty Mountain Trails give a rich sensory experience. The northern end of **Cannabullen Creek Track** is accessible from Millaa Millaa. Take the Palmerston Highway (25) west then Maalan Road/Sutties Gap Road to the Hinson Creek Trailhead. The trail leads to Carter Falls Lookout. Bring a hat, water and binoculars. This is a tough walk that requires a fair level of fitness as it is steep in parts and includes creek crossings. Access may be closed in the rainy season. Visit www.mistymountains. com.au for more information.

Lakes National Park. After Lake Eacham, turn right into Wrights Creek Rd and right onto Atherton–Gordonvale Rd to Lake Barrine.

⑨ Crater Lakes National Park
Queensland; 4883

This park contains two ancient volcanic crater lakes set in tranquil rainforest. Lake Eacham has an easily accessible tarmac track around it, as well as BBQ sites, picnic areas and toilet facilities.

Lake Barrine is the largest crater lake on the Tablelands. It is a two-hour walk around the lake, with the first section accessible to wheelchairs. Water birds, fish and turtles thrive in the ecologically rich habitat. Enjoy a **lake cruise** from the jetty by the teahouse, or swim in the tranquil 10,000-year-old lake.

🚗 *Return back along Gordonvale–Atherton Rd but carry on straight past Wrights Creek Rd to Yungaburra.*

⑩ Yungaburra
Queensland; 4884

Yungaburra is a quaint village with many buildings that have kept their heritage façades and old-world charm,

and some are listed by the National Trust of Queensland. Collect an Old Town Loop Heritage Walk map from the **Visitor Centre** in Cedar Street.

A major attraction is the **Curtain Fig Tree** – it is about a 20-minute walk along Fig Tree Road to this amazing tree (the boardwalk is wheelchair accessible), the aerial roots of which drop 15 m (49 ft) to the ground.

🚗 *Take Gordonvale–Atherton Rd to Atherton and Kennedy Highway (1).*

⑪ Atherton

Queensland; 4883

With wide streets, overhanging trees and old-world architecture, Atherton is the oldest town on the Tablelands. Built on an extinct volcano, it offers a scenic outlook over hills known as "The Seven Sisters". Visit **Hallorans Hill Conservation Park** (open daily; www. derm.qld.gov.au), or take a self-guided tour through the **Crystal Caves** (open daily; closed Feb; www.crystalcaves.com.au), in Main Street, for a display of gemstones and fossils. The **Hou Wang Temple** (open Wed–Sun; 07 4091 6945) is one of only two temples outside China dedicated to Hou Wang. It was built by Chinese immigrants who were early settlers here, running market gardens.

🚗 *Take Kennedy Hwy (1) to Mareeba.*

⑫ Mareeba

Queensland; 4881

This fascinating little town has a population of Aboriginals, miners, hippies and farmers. Its name is derived from an Aboriginal word meaning "meeting of the waters", and the Barron and Granite rivers form the backdrop to this friendly community. Visit the **Mareeba Heritage Museum**

(open daily; www.mareebaheritagecentre. com.au) on Byrnes Street for historic displays as well as information on hot-air ballooning (see left). Mareeba can also provide a superb bird-watching experience at the **Tropical Savanna and Wetland Reserve** (open daily; www. mareebawetlands.org).

🚗 *Take Kennedy Hwy (1) to Kuranda.*

⑬ Kuranda

Queensland; 4872

The town is close to the **Barron Gorge National Park** and has a wonderful boarded walkway through the park's rainforest down to **Barron Falls**, where a platform overlooks the spectacular crashing waters. Once a hippy hangout, Kuranda now has a well-developed infrastructure. Try the **Skyrail Rainforest Cableway** (www. skyrail.com.au), an aerial cableway over the top of the rainforest canopy, or the historic **Kuranda Scenic Railway** (www.ksr.com.au). It is possible to take the Skyrail out and then the railway back to Kuranda.

🚗 *Take Kennedy Hwy (1) then Captain Cook Hwy (44) to Cairns. Turn left at Florence St and right on Esplanade for Pier Point Rd and car park (on left).*

Above left A view of the Tablelands from the Kennedy Highway **Above right and below** Kuranda Scenic Railway, a spectacular way to travel

EAT AND DRINK

MILLAA MILLAA

Out of the Whey Teahouse *inexpensive*
This teahouse and dairy serves delicious home-made food, often using some of their own excellent produce.
251 Brooks Rd, 4886; 07 4097 2232; www.mungallicreekdairy.com.au

YUNGABURRA

Nick's Restaurant *moderate*
Serving Swiss-Italian cuisine and modern Australian dishes, this place has a great reputation with the locals.
33 Gillies Highway, 4884; 07 4095 3330; www.nicksrestaurant.com.au

MAREEBA

Tree Kangaroo Café *moderate*
Serving snacks, burgers, and local coffee close to Barron Falls, this is a friendly and convenient café.
Malanda Falls, 4885; 07 4096 6658

KURANDA

Frog's Restaurant *moderate*
This smart restaurant with a terrace overlooking the rainforest has a large menu and uses fresh, local produce – it is also popular with the locals.
11 Coondoo St, 4881; 07 4093 8952; www.frogsrestaurant.com.au

⑭ Cairns

Queensland; 4870

The state tourist capital, Cairns spreads along a coastal strip from Mirriwinni in the south to Ellis Beach in the north. A popular jumping-off place for the Great Barrier Reef and the rainforest at Daintree, Cairns is also a pleasant spot to make the most of the big-town facilities and to shop, eat and explore the harbour and Esplanade. Explore the history of old Cairns, join in the wealth of seaside activities *(see box)* or simply enjoy a coffee at one of the cafés overlooking the marina.

VISITING CAIRNS

Parking
Park at the Pier Shopping Centre car park, Pier Point Road.

Visitor Information
51 The Esplanade, 4870; 07 4051 3588; www.cairns-greatbarrierreef.org.au.

VISITING THE GREAT BARRIER REEF

Most tours leave from the **Reef Fleet Terminal** at the end of Spence St by the Pier Shopping Centre. For information, visit *www.cairnsesplanade.com* or *www.cairnsvisitorcentre.com.*

WHERE TO STAY

CAIRNS

Cairns Villa & Leisure Park *inexpensive*
This award-winning holiday park is set amid tropical gardens. Stay in a villa, a large or small cabin, or just camp.
28 Pease St, 4870; 07 4053 7133; www.cairnsvilla.com.au

YORKEYS KNOB

A Villa Gail *inexpensive*
This is a quiet spot within easy reach of all of Cairns' attractions. It offers big rooms with balconies and ocean views.
36 Janett St, Yorkeys Knob Beachside Estate, 4879; 07 4055 8178; www.avillagail.com

PORT DOUGLAS

The White House *moderate*
Peaceful apartment accommodation, just minutes' walk from Four Mile Beach.
19 Garrick St, 4877; 07 4099 5600; www.whitehouseportdouglas.com.au

A one-hour walk

Start at the car park at the **Pier Shopping Centre** ①. Walk to the tip of the point and then head right along the marina, admiring the boats. After the marina follow the walkways to the right to **Fogarty Park** ②, where "The Anchor" commemorates the site of the first European landing on the coast in 1876. Take a detour to the **Visitor Information Centre** ③ for maps, then head for the bandstand in the left-hand corner of the park and cross diagonally to the Anzac Memorial Park. Take Wharf Street left past the Reef Hotel Casino, the **Barrier Reef Hotel** ④ and the **Jack & Newell Building** ⑤, both with their original façades built in 1926. Carry on along the Esplanade past **Trinity Wharf** ⑥. Here, the international ocean liners berth at the Great Barrier Reef Cruise terminal. Turn right down Lake Street to City Place, a pedestrian square. On the square is **Cairns Museum** ⑦ *(open*

Modern art in Cairns' seafront saltwater pool

Mon–Sat; www.cairnsmuseum.org.au), where visitors can learn about the town's history. From the museum, head down Shield Street back to the waterfront. Just by the Lagoon, look out for **The Herd** ⑧, shell-like sculptures designed by Hew Chee Fong and Loretta Noonan, which appear to be heading to sea. From here, turn left to walk along the boardwalk. Follow the timber deck over the mudflats to the **Cairns War Memorial Cenotaph** ⑨, commemorating locals who died in World War I. The clock reads 4:28 am, the time of the Anzac landing at Gallipoli on 25 April 1915, when many Australian lives were lost. From the Cenotaph, continue north along the Esplanade, passing the aeroplane-topped **Catalina Memorial** ⑩ to Royal Australian Air Force pilots killed in World War II, and the skate park, as far as the shady, grassy **Lover's Bower** ⑪, a popular lunch spot for locals. Return along the Esplanade to the Pier and car park.

🚗 *Return to Captain Cook Hwy (44) and head north across Barron River Bridge and over two roundabouts. Turn right at the third roundabout to Yorkeys Knob (straight on for Skyrail and Tjapukai Aboriginal Cultural Park).*

Activities on Cairns Esplanade

Cairns Esplanade has two paths for walkers and cyclists, and passes exercise stations, beach volleyball courts, a spectacular skate park, a water park and Lagoon – a huge, safe, saltwater swimming area at the southern end of the boardwalk, patrolled by lifeguards 6am–10pm in summer and 7am–9pm in cooler months. There are also play areas for children and BBQ facilities.

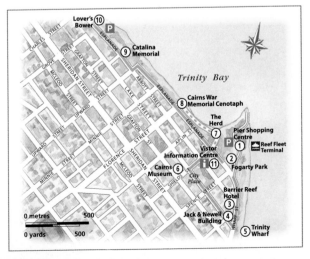

Where to Stay: inexpensive under AU$150; moderate AU$150–AU$250; expensive over AU$250

⑮ Yorkeys Knob
Queensland; 4878

On the way to Yorkeys Knob, if not visited from Kuranda (see p37), stop at the Caravonica Terminal of the **Skyrail**. Right next to it is **Tjapukai Aboriginal Cultural Park** (www.tjapukai.com.au). Here, the Tjapukai Bama, or rainforest people, of North Queensland offer a cultural experience with didgeridoo, traditional dance and spear-throwing demonstrations.

The Magic Space museum and gallery display Stone Age artifacts, and murals by Tjapukai's foremost artists, re-telling Dreamtime stories.

The beach suburb of Yorkeys Knob is quiet, laid-back and a safe haven for cruise liners, which rest offshore. There are swimming beaches and a marina. For a peaceful afternoon, enjoy lunch at Yorkeys Knob Boating Club (see right), where visitors are welcome, and relax with a beer, lulled by the warm tropical air.

🚗 *Return to Captain Cook Hwy (44), turn right and right to Trinity Beach.*

⑯ Trinity Beach
Queensland; 4879

The coastal strip between Cairns and Port Douglas hosts a string of laid-back seaside towns such as Trinity Beach. It is possible to swim here all year round as there is a large stinger-proof swimming enclosure with lifeguards on duty most days. The landscaped foreshore has paved walkways, picnic areas and a range of al fresco cafés.

🚗 *Return to Captain Cook Hwy (44), and follow it north along the coast. Turn right into Port Douglas Rd to Port Douglas.*

⑰ Port Douglas
Queensland; 4877

Port Douglas has a lively marina, a long white sandy beach and a friendly ambience. Take a stroll and breathe some exceptionally clean sea air along Four Mile Beach or walk around the headland. The town's real appeal, however, is the two great natural wonders on its doorstep – the **Great Barrier Reef** (see p34) and **Daintree Rainforest**. Do not miss the underwater world of colourful coral – seen on a dive – before heading on to the rainforest.

🚗 *Follow Hwy 44 (Captain Cook Hwy), then Mossman–Daintree Rd). Stop off at Mossman Gorge (left at Mossman). Turn right before Daintree for the Discovery Centre.*

⑱ The Daintree
Queensland; 4873

The **Daintree Discovery Centre** (Cnr Cape Tribulation Rd and Tulip Oak Rd, Cow Bay; www.daintree-rec.com.au), 59 km (37 miles) from Port Douglas on a scenic road, is the perfect introduction to the Daintree Rainforest (known as "The Daintree"). To reach the centre, take the car ferry across the Daintree River, looking out for estuarine crocodiles. The World Heritage-listed forest is the largest tropical rainforest in Australia and unrivalled for its plant diversity, supporting most of the world's primitive plant families. The award-winning centre offers guided tours of the tree canopy. Continue to **Cape Tribulation** through the Daintree National Park (www.derm.qld.gov.au) – a great place to explore the rainforest to the sound of waves crashing on the beach. The 2WD road can be bumpy.

Above left A cruise liner berthed at Trinity Wharf, Cairns **Above centre** Glorious rainforest-backed beach at Port Douglas **Above right** Boats at Port Douglas Marina

DIVING AT PORT DOUGLAS

Companies offering reef dives include **Calypso** (www.calypsoreefcruises. com), **Poseidon** (www.poseidon-cruises.com.au) and **Quicksilver** (www.quicksilver-cruises.com).

EAT AND DRINK

CAIRNS

Charlie's *inexpensive*
Charlie's at the Acacia Court Hotel has a local and international reputation for its seafood and its good-value hot buffet. *223–227 The Esplanade, 4870; 07 4051 5011; www.acaciacourthotel.com.au*

Ochre Restaurant *expensive*
This innovative restaurant's menu specializes in the use of seafood, game and native Australian foods. *43 Shields St, 4870; 07 4051 0100; www.ochrerestaurant.com.au*

YORKEYS KNOB

Yorkeys Knob Boating Club *inexpensive*
This is the place to eat fish and chips while overlooking the marina and enjoying the views across the Coral Sea, its verandah cooled by ocean breezes. *Half Moon Bay Marina, 25–29 Buckley St, 4878; 07 4055 7711; www.ykbc.com.au*

PORT DOUGLAS

Whileaway *inexpensive*
Enjoy this great little café and bookshop in the heart of town. An ideal spot for sitting in the sun and people-watching, while enjoying a coffee and browsing the books. *2/43 Macrossan St, 4877; 07 4099 4066*

Salsa Bar & Grill *moderate*
With a commitment to fresh local produce where possible and with an award-winning menu, this is one of Port Douglas' favourite dining spots. *26 Wharf St, 4877; 07 4099 4922; www.salsaportdouglas.com.au*

Eat and Drink: inexpensive under AU$60; moderate AU$60–AU$100; expensive over AU$100

Volcanic Hills
Caloundra to the Glasshouse Mountains

Highlights

- **Quiet beach town**
  Soak up the relaxed ambience of Caloundra's many cafés, galleries and safe, sandy beaches

- **Volcanic vistas**
  Witness the now extinct volcanoes of the Glasshouse Mountains rising out of an ancient plain

- **Ancient rainforest**
  Explore the rich remnant of subtropical rainforest at Mary Cairncross Scenic Reserve

- **Native Australian animals**
  Marvel at the behavior of the extraordinary range of native wildlife at Australia Zoo

View of the Blackall Range from Mapleton Falls National Park

Volcanic Hills

Starting in the laid-back beach town of Caloundra, this drive follows the coast for a short while before heading inland and climbing up into the Blackall Range. Created by volcanic activity, these hills present a spectacular backdrop for unhurried driving, while the elevated hinterland of Queensland's Sunshine Coast is dotted with galleries, wineries, dairies and cafés ideal for relaxed stop-offs. Travellers can enjoy the unique geological features of this ancient landscape, while each bend in the road brings timeless vistas.

KEY

Drive route

Above Kookaburra in the rainforest at Mary Cairncross Scenic Reserve, *see p45*

PLAN YOUR DRIVE

Start/finish: Caloundra to the Glasshouse Mountains.

Number of days: 3 days.

Distance: Approx. 188 km (117 miles).

Road conditions: All roads are paved, some are mountainous and winding. Take a map as roads are not always well signed.

When to go: This drive is delightful all year round, but most comfortable between June and August.

Opening times: Most museums and shops are open 9am–5pm. It can be hard to find restaurants open in smaller towns on Monday and Tuesday nights.

Above The long, sandy expanse of Moffat Beach at Caloundra, *see opposite*

❶ Caloundra

Queensland; 4551

Caloundra's 25-km (16-mile) shoreline is draped around the southern tip of the Sunshine Coast. The city is made up of small seaside districts with safe, sandy beaches dramatic rocky points and superb coastal views. The beaches are the great attraction and are furnished with boardwalks, picnic areas with barbecues, a tree-lined esplanade and public art. After relaxing at the beach, take advantage of the beachfront parade of cafés, restaurants and shopping spots, and allow time to wander from one beach village to the next. This walk from Moffat Beach past the SS *Dicky* to Currimundi Lake is very relaxed, just like Caloundra.

Above Art installation on the grassy promenade in front of Moffat Beach

A one-hour walking tour

Walk from the parking spot on Seaview Terrace to **Café by the Beach** ①, where locals congregate over coffee for breakfast. Continue to the corner of the main block of Seaview Terrace to the artist-run **Seaview Gallery** ② *(open daily; 07 5491 4788)*. This gallery exhibits paintings, pottery and jewellery by local artists, including the works of Redcliffe artist Barry Kidd. Continue on down Seaview Terrace to the esplanade. Walk north from Moffat Beach past the usually shallow Tooway Creek onto Dicky Beach and along the white sand to the **SS *Dicky*** ③, washed ashore during a cyclone in 1893. A century of sand has filled the old carcass, leaving its rusted ribs protruding through the beach's salty skin. It is now a playground for kids and the focal point for thousands of photos. Numerous storms and cyclones have spun past, yet still the SS *Dicky* remains in its beach grave. From the beach, head up to the esplanade and follow the walkway to the right beside an area of wallum heath, the infertile yet botanically rich scrubland that once covered much of this coast. Follow the walkway as it winds through the heath – look out for birds and wild flowers. Take the bridge over Coondibah Creek. Carry on along the walkway, past a string of houses, to the sandy point at

Currimundi Lake ④, a small wildlife reserve that is also popular with kayakers. Turn left into the car park to enjoy a drink at the popular **Coco's Resort** ⑤. Return along the beach to the parking spot on Seaview Terrace.

🚗 *Head south on Seaview Terrace and follow signs to Nicklin Way (6) north, which becomes the Sunshine Motorway (70) as it crosses the Mooloolah River. Filter left for Buderim onto the Buderim–Mooloolaba Rd (8), along the ridge up into Buderim.*

Activities in Caloundra

For windsurf, kayaking or kite-surf equipment, visit **Golden Beach Hire** *(0401 657 830; www. goldenbeachhire.com.au)*. For scuba diving, contact **Wildcat Watersports** *(72 Omrah Ave, 4551; 07 5499 6955; www.wildcatdive.com)*. For guided kayak tours, try **Blue Water Kayak Tours** *(07 5494 7789; www.bluewaterkayaktours.com)*.

VISITING CALOUNDRA

Parking
Park at the end of Seaview Terrace at the seafront.

WHERE TO STAY IN CALOUNDRA

Camping at Dicky Beach *inexpensive*
This offers tent and caravan sites, cabins, walking paths, a playground, tennis courts and a swimming pool.
Beerburrum St, Dicky Beach, 4551; 07 5491 3342; www.sunshinecoast holidaypark.com.au

Norfolks on Moffat Beach *moderate*
Ocean-front, five-storey resort with large, heated swimming pool, offering 2- and 3-bed self-catering apartments.
32 Queen of the Colonies Parade, Moffat Beach, 4551; 07 5492 6666; www.norfolksonmoffat.com.au

Estoril on Moffat *moderate*
Ideally located on Moffat Headland with comfy 2-bed apartments, Estoril has ocean views and all mod-cons.
38 McIlwraith St, Moffat Beach, 4551; 07 5491 5988; www.estoril.com.au

Pumicestone Blue Resort *moderate*
This resort offers views overlooking the Bribie Islands and Pumicestone Passage.
105–111 Bulcock Street, Caloundra, 4551; 07 5492 8989

EAT AND DRINK IN CALOUNDRA

Café by the Beach *inexpensive*
With ocean views, this café is popular with locals – try the Moreton Bay bugs.
12 Seaview Terrace, Moffat Beach, 4551; 07 5491 9505; www.cafebythebeach. com.au

Coco's Resort *inexpensive*
Friendly Currimundi café serving good value brunches in a lakeside setting.
Cnr Westaway Parade & Watson St, Currimundi, 4551; 07 5493 4173

Sandbar Cafe and Kiosk *inexpensive*
Serves fresh seafood and has great views of Bribie Island.
26 The Esplanade, Caloundra, 4551; 07 5491 0800

WHERE TO STAY

BUDERIM

Buderim Cottages *moderate*
Comfortable, air-conditioned, self-contained cottages, close to the centre of Buderim village.
62 Lindsay Rd, 4556; 07 5445 1645; www.buderimcottages.com.au

MAPLETON

Mapleton Falls Accommodation *moderate*
These units are set in bushland on the edge of Mapleton Falls National Park and feature walking paths and views over the Obi Obi Valley and Mapleton Falls.
52 Mapleton Falls Rd, 4560; 0418 976 054; www.mapletonfalls.com.au

MONTVILLE

Montville Country Cabins *moderate*
This unusual stay comprises 10 cabins by a lake, surrounded by a national park.
396 Western Avenue, 4560; 07 5442 9484; www.montvillecabins.com.au

MALENY

Maleny Hideaway *inexpensive*
A country retreat with seven guest rooms, a pool and big breakfasts.
32 Sidney Lane, 4552 (off Maleny–Kenilworth Rd); 07 5499 9520; www.malenyhideaway.com

THE GLASSHOUSE MOUNTAINS

Glasshouse Mountains EcoLodge *moderate*
A church and two train carriages have been recycled for this eco-lodge – it is also good for walks and bike hire.
198 Barrs Rd, 4518; 07 5493 0008; www.glasshouseecolodge.com

Glass on Glasshouse *expensive*
Just before the Lookout, three smart cottages with floor-to-ceiling glass on two sides offer intimate mountain views.
Glasshouse–Woodford Rd, 4518; 07 5496 9608; www.glassonglasshouse.com.au

Above right Cut-out of Steve Irwin handling a crocodile welcomes visitors to Australia Zoo
Below Mapleton Tavern in Mapleton

② Buderim
Queensland; 4556
With 360-degree vistas over the Blackall Range, Buderim is known as "The Grandstand of the Sunshine Coast" and has excellent parks, such as **Buderim Forest Park**. *(Harry's Lane, Lindsay Rd; www.buderim.com/forest.htm)*, where visitors can walk through lush, sub-tropical rainforest to see waterfalls and swim in rock pools. The town's timber-producing past is celebrated by the **Pioneer Cottage** *(open daily; 5 Ballinger Crescent; www.buderim.com/pioneer)*. Built by John Kerle Bennett in 1876, this heritage museum also has displays of period clothes and photographs. The **Buderim to Palmwoods Heritage Tramway** *(www.buderim.com.au/tramway_walk.htm)* can be followed through a rainforest featuring 120 species of native plants. For more information, visit the **Old Post Office Community Information Centre** *(open Mon–Sat; 4 Burnett St; www.bwmca.com.au/where.html)*.

🚗 Follow Mons Rd down the hill to the Bruce Hwy (1) on ramp and join the highway north. At the Bli Bli Rd exit take Bli Bli Rd (west), which becomes the Blackall–Netherton Rd and then the Nambour–Mapleton Rd. Follow it up the mountain to Mapleton, stopping off en route at the Dulong/Kureelpa Lookout car park (sharp left) for views.

③ Mapleton
Queensland; 4560
Mapleton offers exquisite views and an array of cafés, teahouses and speciality shops. However, its showpiece is the spectacular **Mapleton Falls**. These waterfalls are located on the 58-km (36-mile) **Sunshine Coast Hinterland**

Great Walk Trail *(www.derm.qld.gov.au/parks/great-walks-sunshine-coast/about.html)*, which traverses national parks and forest reserves. Follow signs out of Mapleton along Obi Obi Road to the falls, in the Mapleton Falls National Park. With little light-pollution, Mapleton is a good place to observe the star-filled skies – learn more at the **Mapleton Observatory** in the town school *(by arrangement; Flaxton Drive; 07 5445 7792; www.mapletonss.eq.edu.au/mapletonobservatory)*.

🚗 Take the Montville–Mapleton Rd through Flaxton to Montville. (The road to Kondalilla Falls is just past Flaxton.)

The Blackall Range
Created by volcanic activity millions of years ago, the Blackall Range mountains have a rich, basalt soil that supports sub-tropical rainforest. Waterfalls adorn the escarpment all year round, powerful in the summer and gentler in the winter months. To explore further, make a diversion to **Kondalilla Falls National Park** *(www.derm.qld.gov.au/parks/kondalila/about.html)*. Its name is an Aboriginal word meaning "rushing waters" and it is home to 600 protected species.

④ Montville
Queensland; 4560
With wineries, nature trails and panoramic views, Montville is a delightful town with a reputation for its arts, crafts and galleries. A traditional timber-growing and dairy-farming area, Montville, settled in 1887, has examples of Australian architecture from this era. On the drive into town look out for some of the original wooden buildings, such as "Rothley" on Main Street and visit the eclectic **Main Street**

Far left View of the Glasshouse Mountains from Mary Cairncross Reserve **Left** Bird in Kondallila Falls National Park **Below** Forest trail in Kondalilla Falls National Park

SHOPPING IN MONTVILLE

Visit **Illume Creations** (*Shop 4 Mayfield, 127–133 Main St, 4560; 07 5478 5440; www.illumecreations.com.au*) for exquisite and colourful glassware.

ACTIVITIES IN THE GLASSHOUSE MOUNTAINS

Abseiling and Climbing
For guided abseiling and climbing in the Glasshouse Mountains, visit **Pinnacle Sports** (*07 3368 3335; www.pinnaclesports.com.au*) or **Adrenalin** (*1300 791 793; www.adrenalin.com.au*).

EAT AND DRINK

BUDERIM

Harry's Restaurant on Buderim *expensive*
Modern Australian cuisine in a 120-year-old country homestead. *Harry's Lane, off Lindsay Rd, 4556; 07 5445 6661; www.harrysonbuderim.com.au; open Wed–Sun (Sun lunch only)*

MAPLETON

The Mapleton Tavern *inexpensive*
This popular stop-off offers an Australian menu and fine views to the coast. *Cnr Flaxton Dr & Obi Obi Rd, 4560; 07 5445 7499; www.mapletontavern.com.au*

The View Café *inexpensive*
Enjoy sweeping ocean views and Devonshire teas at this cosy café. *Cnr Post Office & Obei Obei Rds, 4560; 07 5445 7633*

MONTVILLE

Poet's Restaurant & Café *moderate*
In Montville's art precinct (with gallery downstairs), this café offers delicious meals, coffee and cakes. *167 Main St, 4560; 07 5478 5479*

MALENY

Maleny Cheese *moderate*
This licensed café serves regional wines, light meals, distinctive local cheese platters, coffee and dessert. *1 Clifford St, 4552; 07 5494 2207; www.malenycheese.com.au; open 9am–5pm*

AROUND AUSTRALIA ZOO

Latte Da Café and Gifts *moderate*
This delightful eatery, nestled into the mountain foothills, offers good food made from fresh, local produce. *19 Caloundra St, Landsborough, 4550; 07 5439 9555*

Gallery (*open Wed–Sun; 167 Main St; 07 5478 5050*) for displays of modern art.
🚗 *Carry along the Montville–Mapleton Rd and take signed right turn to Maleny.*

⑤ Maleny
Queensland; 4552
Maleny has a different ambience from the other towns in the area – it is not quaint and historic but hip, funky, organic and green. It is also a rich milk- and cheese-producing area. Head out from Maleny on the Landsborough–Maleny Road and to the right is **Maleny Dairies** (*Mon–Sat tours 10.30am & 2.30pm; 07 5494 2392; www.malenydairies.com*), for factory tours and tastings. Continue along the Landsborough–Maleny Road and enjoy sampling Chardonnay and Verdelho white wines and typically Australian Chambourcin red wines at **Maleny Mountain Wines** (*open daily; 07 5429 6300; www.malenymountainwines.com.au*). Head back towards Maleny but fork left down Mountain View Road to **Mary Cairncross Scenic Reserve** (*open daily; 07 5429 6122; www.mary-cairncross.com.au*). Extending across 52 hectares (128 acres) of sub-tropical rainforest, this ancient forest is home to rare species of trees and birdlife and has around 2 km (1 mile) of wheelchair-friendly tracks. Enjoy views of the Glasshouse Mountains.
🚗 *From the reserve, return to Maleny–Landsborough Rd and drive through Landsborough to Australia Zoo.*

⑥ Australia Zoo
Queensland; 4519
Whilst driving through Landsborough stop at **Landsborough Museum** (*open Wed–Sun; www.landsboroughmuseum.org.au*) in Maleny Street for displays on local history. Then head on to Steve Irwin Way, following signs to **Australia Zoo** (*open daily; 07 5436 2000; www.australiazoo.com*). This excellent zoo, made famous

by TV personality "Crocodile Hunter" Steve Irwin (1962–2006), has a good reputation for animal conservation and offers an interactive experience.
🚗 *Carry along Steve Irwin Way to the well-signed Glasshouse Mountains Visitor Centre and car park.*

⑦ The Glasshouse Mountains
Queensland; 4518
Named by Captain Cook in 1770, the mountains were formed by volcanic activity over 30 million years ago, and the area has a primordial feel. In Aboriginal legend, the mountains are a family – Mount Tibrogargan the father and Mount Beerwah the mother.
The region offers walking tracks at all levels. Visit the **Glasshouse Mountains Visitor Centre** (*www.derm.qld.gov.au/parks/glass-house-mountains/about.html*) for maps, then go to the **Glasshouse Mountain Lookout** on the Glasshouse–Woodford Road to see these impressive mountains rising from the plain and to walk along a short forest trail. New Year brings **Woodford Folk Festival** (*www.woodfordfolkfestival.com*).

Eat and Drink: inexpensive under AU$60; moderate AU$60–AU$100; expensive over AU$100

Gold Coast Back Country

Burleigh Heads to Brisbane

Highlights

- **Ancient volcanic remnant**
  Explore Springbrook Plateau with its stunning waterfalls and ancient beech forests lit at night by glow worms

- **Sub-tropical rainforest**
  Walk the trails in the vast and ancient Lamington National Park, home to a wealth of native plants and animals

- **Friendly beach hamlets and islands**
  Enjoy the calm coastal villages of the Redlands windsurf, fish or swim in the waters of Moreton Bay or explore North Stradbroke Island

- **Lively city of arts**
  Explore the vibrant communities of historic Brisbane, beside its gracious, winding river, and visit its world-class galleries and museums

Surfing the clear blue waters at Burleigh Heads on the Gold Coast

Gold Coast Back Country

This varied drive is the perfect way to appreciate the glorious attractions of South East Queensland – surf, mountains, forests, metropolitan Brisbane and its Bayside. Moving from sandy beaches to sub-tropical rainforest, the route winds its way through art-filled towns overlooking verdant mountain ranges, via the ancient flora and fauna of Lamington National Park, and then back to the ocean with its peaceful coastal villages, whale watching (Jun–late Oct) and windsurfing. Invigorating and bursting with things to see and do, the drive finishes in Brisbane with a city-and-river walk through the gallery-filled South Bank and over the snaking Brisbane River.

Above Sandy beach at Burleigh Heads, *see p50*

ACTIVITIES

Hike through Burleigh Heads National Park

Learn how to grow medicinal plants at a herb farm in Mudgeeraba

Head into the rainforest at night to see Springbrook's glow worms

Spot the indigenous wildlife in beautiful Lamington National Park

Explore the treetop canopy on the Mount Tamborine Rainforest Skywalk

Take a ferry trip to "Straddie" from Cleveland for a whale-watching adventure

Eat Moreton Bay bugs looking out over the bay itself at Manly

Below The protected harbour at Manly Marina, *see p54*

PLAN YOUR DRIVE

Start/finish: Burleigh Heads to Brisbane.

Number of days: 3–4 days.

Distance: Approx. 287 km (178 miles).

Road conditions: All roads are paved some are steep and winding. Take a map but be ready to ask for directions as roads are not always well signed.

When to go: Although the beaches are most fun in summer (Dec–Feb), check the forecast for heavy rain in rainforest areas and cyclonic weather on the Queensland coast, which can bring torrential rain and wind to the southeast corner. The most comfortable time to visit is in late winter/spring (late Aug–Nov) and autumn/early winter (Mar–early Jun).

Opening times: Most museums and shops in Australia are open 9am–5pm. It is often difficult to find restaurants open in smaller towns on Monday and Tuesday nights.

Main market days: Burleigh Heads: arts and crafts market, last Sun of month; **Tamborine:** fruit and veg, cheeses, plants, herbs, and arts and crafts, 2nd Sun of month; **Brisbane:** arts and crafts market and fresh produce, every Sun.

Shopping: Many of the small coastal resorts – such as Burleigh Heads, Sanctuary Cove and Raby Bay – are home to boutiques and speciality shops. Brisbane is a large city with a central mall, arcades and many smaller shops selling fashion, books and jewellery.

Major festivals: Sanctuary Cove: International Boat Show, May (www.sanctuarycoveboatshow.com. au); Redland Bay: Strawberry Harvest Festival, Sep (www. redlandspringfestival.com.au); Brisbane: Buddha Birth Day Festival, May (www.buddhabirthdayfestival. com.au); Queensland Music Festival (classical to contemporary), Jul, biennial, odd years (qmf.org.au); Brisbane Writers' Festival, Sep (www. brisbanewritersfestival.com.au); Brisbane Festival (arts), Sep (www. brisbanefestival.com.au).

VISITING BURLEIGH HEADS

Parking
Arriving from the Gold Coast Hwy (2) north, cross into Burleigh and before the Esplanade, turn right into Goodwin Terrace for Burleigh Bluff car park.

Burleigh Heads National Park
The walk from Burleigh Bluff is a 2-km (1-mile) round trip, with a steep section near Tumgun Lookout. Keep an eye out for whales.
1711 Gold Coast Hwy, 4220; www.nprsr.qld.gov.au

WHERE TO STAY

BURLEIGH HEADS

The Village at Burleigh *moderate*
These modern apartments have large balconies, share a swimming pool and are handy for the beach.
4 Park Avenue, 4220; 07 5520 5400; www.thevillageatburleigh.com

SPRINGBROOK

Hardy House B&B *inexpensive*
Friendly and comfortable with delicious breakfasts, this B&B is close to the National Parks Information Centre.
15A Old School Rd, 4213; 07 5533 5402; www.hardyhouse.com.au

LAMINGTON NATIONAL PARK

Binna Burra Mountain Lodge & Campsite *expensive/inexpensive*
Both the comfortable lodge and the more basic camp site offer a secluded stay with magnificent views and easy access to forest activities.
Binna Burra Rd, 4211; 07 5533 3622; www.binnaburralodge.com.au

O'Reilly's Rainforest Guesthouse *moderate*
A family-run guesthouse at the Green Mountains park entrance offers stays that celebrate the area's rare birds and wildlife and a memorable tree-top walk.
Lamington National Park Rd, 4275; 07 5502 4911; www.oreillys.com.au

Below Dense forest beside a creek along Springbrook Road

1 Burleigh Heads
Queensland; 4220

Amid the tourist frenzy of the Gold Coast, Burleigh is a relaxed haven offering a protected cove, beach cafés and delicate, bird-filled casuarina trees along its esplanade. From Burleigh Bluff car park *(see left)*, walk into town, along the beach, or, for breathtaking views, around tiny **Burleigh Heads National Park**. Take this walk in the early morning to watch the surfers paddling out to catch the waves.

In town, check out the shops, cafés, restaurants and ice-cream parlours. Do not miss **East Coast Bulk Foods** *(open daily; 29 James St, 4220)* – a great place to stock up on vital picnic supplies for the road ahead. On the last Sunday of the month, there is an arts and crafts market in Justins Park on the Esplanade.

🚗 **Leave Burleigh on Reedy Creek Rd (80) to M1 north. Take Mudgeeraba exit.**

2 Mudgeeraba
Queensland; 4213

This historic village has a friendly feel and its quaint shop-front signage helps to preserve the old village atmosphere. With a local pub and home-style bakery *(see right)*, an old post office turned into a library, and a public swimming pool, this is a bit of real Australia, without the advertising or visitor-attracting thrills. Eat in town or at one of the interesting teashop-cum-galleries along Springbrook Road on the way out of Mudgeeraba *(see right)*. Also on Springbrook Road is **Mudbrick Cottage Herb Farm** *(open Fri–Mon; 07 5530 3253; www.herbcottage.com.au)*. Wander around the garden filled with culinary, medicinal and fragrant herbs or purchase local

Above The sandy expanse of Burleigh Heads beach from afar **Below** The Surf Club on Burleigh Heads Esplanade

handicrafts, soaps, books, jams and beeswax. The farm also runs herbal medicine workshops *(phone ahead for workshop bookings)*.

🚗 **From Railway St, take Gold Coast–Springbrook Rd (99) up the mountain to Springbrook.**

3 Springbrook
Queensland; 4213

The winding road up Springbrook Mountain is cooled by rainforest air from the McPherson Range. At the top is Springbrook Plateau, a remnant of a massive volcano that last erupted more than 22 million years ago. Pockets of ancient rainforest are a living reminder of the age of this land. Stop off at one of the many cafés or places to stay en route *(see left and right)*, and enjoy the natural beauty.

Springbrook National Park covers 2,954 ha (11 sq miles) including Mount Cougal to the east and Natural Bridge and Numinbah Valley to the west. There are several lookouts in the park, all worth visiting, with picnic areas. Head

Left Secluded creekside spot along Springbrook Road

EAT AND DRINK

BURLEIGH HEADS

The Bluff Café *moderate*
This café has a friendly feel and tasty food, so sit and enjoy the view.
The Old Burleigh Theatre Arcade, 66 Goodwin Terrace, 4220; 07 5576 6333

MUDGEERABA

Gumnut Café Bakery *inexpensive*
Friendly local bakery with seating.
Shop 26, Mugdeeraba Shopping Centre, 4213; 07 5530 4766

Woodchopper's Inn *moderate*
This restaurant-bar has a cozy, old-world style, good food and friendly service.
66 Railway Street, 4213; 07 5525 3500; www.woodchoppersinn.com

The Old Teahouse Gallery *moderate*
This historic Queensland house serves lunches and teas in a fine setting.
7 Johns Rd (off Springbrook Rd), 4213; 07 5525 3053; www.theoldteahousegallery.com

SPRINGBROOK

Rosellas *moderate*
In a truly magical location, this historic homestead café-restaurant is next to the Canyon Lookout (book for dinner).
8 Canyon Parade, 4213; 0427 335 384; www.springbrookrosellas.com.au; open Thu–Sun

LAMINGTON NATIONAL PARK

Laurel Cottage Garden Café and Restaurant *inexpensive*
Run by Sydney chef Michael Beer, this superb café-restaurant serves home-made pizzas, pasta, pies and desserts and features local music and art.
707 Beechmont Rd, 4211; 07 5533 1213; www.laurelcottage.com.au; closed Thu

Below Panoramic view from Lower Beechmont Lookout

south on Springbrook Road and turn left to the **Visitor Information Centre** *(open daily)* for maps. See the forest glow worms on a night tour with **Springbrook Research Centre** *(07 5533 5239)* – for the best glow-worm experience, avoid the full moon.

🚗 *Take Springbrook Rd (99) back towards Mudgeeraba, turning left on Pine Creek Rd and right on Nerang–Murwillumbah Rd (97), then left on Beechmont Rd to Beechmont.*

④ Beechmont

Queensland; 4211
The **Beechmont Plateau** is a spur off the McPherson Range, part of the Great Dividing Range that runs down the east coast of Australia. It is covered with magnificent, ancient rainforest and offers views back to the Gold Coast. **Beechmont** is set on a forested ridge overlooking the Scenic Rim, a chain of mountains stretching as far as Mount Mistake in the Northern Territory. This pleasant village is a great place to stop for a cup of tea, fill up with petrol and stock up on supplies, including water for the walking trails of Binna Burra.

🚗 *Take the signed road to Binna Burra.*

Gondwana Rainforest

The story of the Gondwana Rainforest began some 250 million years ago when the great landmass Pangea split in two, creating Gondwana and Laurasia. About 70 million years ago, Gondwana split up, creating Australia. The continent then experienced a long period of tectonic movement and volcanic activity. Volcanic flows occurred in the Lamington region about 20–23 million years ago and then, when the volcanoes became dormant, the rainforest took over.

⑤ Lamington National Park

Binna Burra, Queensland
Lamington National Park *(www.derm. qld.gov.au)* is the largest sub-tropical rainforest in Australia, on the Scenic Rim. It features more than 160 km (100 miles) of walking trails, leading to spectacular waterfalls and bubbling creeks. The ancient forest supports Antarctic beech, native wild flowers and rare animals such as the spotted-tailed quoll and Albert's lyrebird.

Access the park at **Binna Burra** for short walks – try the Rainforest Circuit to Bellbird Lookout with views of Turtle Rock, Egg Rock and Numinbah Valley, or the longer Caves Circuit. Pick up maps at **Binna Burra Information Centre** at the Mountain Lodge *(see left)*. Keen walkers may opt for the 21-km (13-mile) Border Track from Binna Burra to the Green Mountains park entrance by O'Reilly's *(see left; take Lamington National Park Road from Canungra)*.

🚗 *Return to Beechmont Rd. Turn left, left onto Beaudesert–Nerang Rd (90) to Canungra, Benobble and Mundoolun Connection Rd (90) to Beaudesert–Beenleigh Rd (92) for Tamborine.*

Eat and Drink: inexpensive under AU$60; moderate AU$60–$100; expensive over AU$100

Right Mangrove trees seen from the esplanade at Redland Bay

Below White gum trees, much loved by koalas, at Victoria Point

⑥ Tamborine
Queensland; 4272

Tamborine is set on a plateau, about 600 m (2,000 ft) above sea level, on the northern edge of the volcanic crater that rings Lamington National Park. The drive up reveals spectacular views of the Nerang-Gold Coast hinterland. The area is lush with remnants of ancient rainforest that offer waterfall walks, cafés *(see right)*, art galleries, wineries and picnic areas. About 10 km (6 miles) down Tamborine Mountain Road (95) towards Oxenford, the **Tamborine Rainforest Skywalk** *(07 5545 2222; www.rainforestskywalk. com.au)* soars above the creek, offering panoramic views across the valley for the 300-m (1,000-ft) long canopy walk. There are also rock pools and waterfalls and a butterfly lookout. The walk returns along the rainforest floor to the gallery and café.

Sign warning of koalas

🚗 *Follow 95 east, down to the Old Pacific Hwy at Oxenford. Turn left then right onto the overpass. Cross M1 onto Oxenford–Southport Rd (4) and follow signs via Hope Island to Sanctuary Cove.*

⑦ Sanctuary Cove
Queensland; 4212

This coastal village was created in 1987 with a marina, shopping centre and smart restaurants and cafés. It is a good place to stop for a coffee and browse the boutiques and galleries – find Hollywood memorabilia and other interesting stuff at **Sanctuary Cove Antique Gallery** *(Marine Village 4212; 07 5514 8070)*. Each May, the Cove hosts an international boat show, reputed to be the largest on-water exhibition in the Asia-Pacific region.

🚗 *Head down Santa Barbara Rd to Oxenford–Southenport Rd (4). Take the M1 (Pacific Hwy) north, turn right onto Beenleigh–Redland Bay Rd (47), then Longland Rd into Redland Bay.*

⑧ Redland Bay
Queensland; 4165

After the seclusion of the rainforests, the drive heads back to the Pacific Ocean. Rather than the rolling surf of the Gold Coast beaches, Redland Bay offers access to numerous islands, ferry rides, watersports and gentle esplanade walks. From Redland Bay, regular ferry services *(www.stradbrokeferries. com)* depart for the Russell, Lamb-Macleay Islands. These islands, ringed with mangroves and sandy beaches, and rich in flora and fauna, are ideal for day-trips and great for fishing. "The Redlands", as the region is called, is known for its strawberries – look out for signs to Pick Your Own. For more local produce, try a tasting tour at the **Sirromet Winery** *(850–938 Mt Cotton Rd (45), Mt Cotton, 4165; 07 3206 2999; www.sirromet.com)* with award-winning wines and a highly regarded restaurant (the winery shuttles visitors to and from the coast).

🚗 *Head north back to 47, turning right on Benfer Rd to Victoria Point.*

⑨ Victoria Point
Queensland; 4165

Still part of the Redlands and the seaside backyard of Brisbane, Victoria Point is a good place to go for a lazy weekend or to take a ferry out to **Coochiemudlo Island** for the day. "Coochie", as it is known to locals, is ringed by safe, sandy beaches and is ideal for young families. Victoria Point also has a multitude of parks, picnic areas, BBQ spots, and esplanades for cycling and walking and there are several interesting environmental reserves. **Point Halloran Conservation Reserve** *(Orana Street)* has a large concentration of gum trees, which support the densest communities of koalas in the state. It offers places to view the creatures in the wild. At the **Egret Colony Wetlands**, between Victoria Point and Point Halloran, both egrets and ibis can be seen in the trees.

🚗 *Return to Cleveland–Redland Bay Rd (47) and turn right for Cleveland. To reach the jetty, turn right on 22.*

Above Tree-lined avenue in the suburban town of Cleveland

⑩ Cleveland
Queensland; 4163
A contender for state capital in the 1840s, today Cleveland is almost a suburb of Brisbane. The town has several interesting buildings: the octagonal wooden **Cleveland Lighthouse** *(Cleveland Point Reserve)* was built in 1864 and served the area for 110 years before being replaced and rebuilt 30 m (100 ft) away; the old courthouse in Paxton Street dates back to 1853 when it was built as a dwelling for timber-cutters and the Grandview Hotel in North Street dates back to 1849. Visit **Ormiston House**

Above One of a series of small, protected beaches at Raby Bay

(277 Wellington St; open Mar–Nov, Sun pm only), built 1848–56, to see a fine example of colonial architecture. Take the ferry to **North Stradbroke Island** *(www.stradbrokeferries.com.au)* or "Straddie," one of the largest sand islands in the world. Enjoy its clean beaches and walking trails or take a fishing trip from **Point Lookout** *(www.stradbrokeholidays. com.au)*. The island is a good place to spot turtles, whales and manta rays.

🚗 *From the Ferry Point, head west on Shore St West (22) to Raby Bay Marina.*

⑪ Raby Bay
Queensland; 4163
This man-made enclave sits behind Cleveland and takes full advantage of the bay. It features expensive houses, a busy marina, galleries such as **Raby Bay Galleries** *(open daily; 1 Anchorage Dr; www.rabybaygalleries.com.au)* and smart restaurants. Drive from the Raby Bay Marina, along Masthead Drive to **Foreshore Park**. This is a popular place to stop for a picnic, or to enjoy walking, swimming or cycling in the cooling bay breezes beside the string of sandy beaches.

🚗 *From Shore St West in Raby Bay, follow 46, along Sturgeon St, past Ormiston Manor. Turn right into Main Rd and follow this to Wellington Point.*

Above Green and leafy park in the quiet settlement of Cleveland

EAT AND DRINK

TAMBORINE
Tea and Niceties *moderate*
An enchanting teahouse – all pink detail and bone china. Book ahead.
1/21 Southport Ave, 4272; 07 5545 3645; www.teaandniceties.com.au

The Heritage *expensive*
This winery and restaurant offers views over to the Gold Coast. The cellar door is open daily for wine tasting and sales.
Cnr Shelf Rd & Bartle Rd, 4272; 07 5545 3177; www.theheritage.net.au/ restaurant

AROUND SANCTUARY COVE
The Boardwalk Tavern *moderate*
This smart local pub, just off Santa Barbara Road before it joins Oxenford–Southport Rd (4), offers a good Aussie menu and live entertainment several nights a week.
Marine Village, Santa Barbara Rd, Hope Island, 4212; 07 5510 8022; www.boardwalktavern.com.au

REDLAND BAY
Redland Bay Hotel *inexpensive*
This is an authentic Aussie pub experience with great food, local music and a relaxed bay-side atmosphere.
The Esplanade, 4165; 07 3206 7231; www.redlandbayhotel.com.au

CLEVELAND
The Lighthouse Restaurant, Bar, Café & Take-Away *moderate*
With spectacular views, an à la carte seafood menu, and an ice-cream bar, this spot is a local favourite.
237 Shore St North, Cleveland Pt, 4163; 07 3286 5555

The Courthouse Restaurant *expensive*
Classic cuisine, softly tinkling piano and crackling fires in winter create a romantic atmosphere in this popular restaurant in the old courthouse.
1 Paxton St, 4163; 07 3286 1386; www.courthouserestaurant.com.au

Eat and Drink: inexpensive under AU$60; moderate AU$60–$100; expensive over AU$100

Right Boats packing the busy marina in Manly Harbour **Far right** Mosaic mural on the outside of the State Library, Brisbane

WHERE TO STAY

MANLY

Manly Marina Cove Motel *moderate*
Situated next to the Royal Queensland Yacht Squadron on the esplanade, this is a great spot to enjoy harbour activities, and a taste of the Manly nightlife.
578a Royal Esplanade, 4179; 07 3348 1000; www.manlymarinacove.com

AROUND MANLY

Birkdale B&B
A B&B offering private, comfortable lodgings with rooms looking out over large tropical gardens.
3 Whitehall Avenue, Birkdale 4159; 07 3207 4442; www.babs.com.au/birkdale

BRISBANE

Bridgewater Terrace Apartments *moderate*
This well-maintained complex in lush, tropical gardens offers self-contained units, each with a balcony or courtyard, and sharing an outdoor swimming pool.
56 Wharf St, Kangaroo Point 4169; 07 3435 5216; www.bridgewaterterraces.com

Urban Hotel *moderate*
A stylishly refurbished 200-room hotel, close to the city centre with views of the western ranges. It has well-equipped rooms, a restaurant and small pool.
345 Wickham Terrace, 4000; 07 3831 6177; www.hotelurban.com.au/brisbane

Below left The clock tower of Brisbane's City Hall in King George Square **Below right** Brisbane's elegant Roma Street Parklands

⑫ Wellington Point

Queensland; 4160
Wellington Point has long been a spot popular with locals for a picnic and a paddle in protected bay-side waters with views over **Moreton Bay**. The village is situated right at the tip of the peninsula and is a favourite spot for children, cyclists, anglers and relaxing in the shade. In recent years, it has become slightly busier, with funky café-restaurants such as **Tanjas Cafe Restaurant** *(372–4 Main Rd; 07 3207 3120)*, and windsurfing and sailing clubs. At low tide, walk along the sandy spit to the small **King Island Conservation Park**, which is visible from the mainland and has extensive mangrove vegetation. Another point of interest is the **Wellington Point Conservation Wetland**, created to protect the shore from wave action, reduce the impact of floods and provide a habitat for animals and plants. Keep an eye out for dolphins playing in the shallow water and turtles swimming among mangroves.

🚗 *Return to Main Rd, head south, turn right on the roundabout and follow 43, turning right into Manly Rd (43, then 30) and follow to Gordon Parade, Manly, for on-street parking.*

Whale watching in Moreton Bay

Moreton Bay is a great place to spot frolicking humpback whales as they migrate north in winter *(Jun–late Oct)*. **Brisbane Whale Watching** cruises depart from Redcliffe Jetty, 30 minutes' drive north of Brisbane – a shuttle picks whale watchers up from the city centre *(07 3880 0477; www.brisbanewhalewatching.com.au)*.

⑬ Manly

Queensland; 4179
A waterfront hamlet, Manly is built on a hill with quiet streets meandering down into a centre that buzzes with small shops, cafés and pubs. Walk a little further down to the esplanade and along to the marina. Yachts from all over the world berth here – the largest marina on Australia's east coast. Enjoy the fresh air off the bay, or sit in the pub at **Wilson's Boathouse** *(4 Trafalgar St; 07 3893 3586; www. wilsonsboathouse.com.au)* and tuck into a dish of the local Moreton Bay bugs (scampi) for a sunset dinner by the bay.

🚗 *Follow Manly Rd (30, then 43) into Wynnum Rd (23) and follow city centre signs, bearing left off Bradfield Hwy (15) ramp onto Ann St to the car park entrance on the corner of Roma St.*

⑭ Brisbane

Queensland; 4000

Set on a serpentine river where every bend is home to a community with its own particular flavour, Brisbane offers shops, galleries, cafés and interesting historic sights. Across the river from the centre of the city sits Brisbane's South Bank, a collection of arts buildings created for the World Expo in 1988 – its man-made beach and pool are ideal in the summer months. Other major attractions include the Queensland Maritime Museum, Brisbane City Botanic Gardens and Mount Coot-tha Gardens. The Brisbane City Cat is a fun way to explore the city from the river, and walking, cycling and public transport are the best ways to get around Brisbane and its surroundings.

A two-hour walking tour

Walk up from the King George Square Car Park to admire the exterior of City Hall, and its 70-m (250-ft) clock tower, based on St Mark's Campanile, Venice. Turn right and right again down Ann Street to the **Museum of Brisbane** ① *(open daily; www.museumofbrisbane.com. au)*, an excellent social history museum and arts gallery. Continue along Ann Street and turn right to cross Turbot Street at the lights, and enter **Roma Street Parkland** ② at the pedestrian entry in Albert Street. This is a delightful place to wander through sub-tropical gardens or relax by the lake. Pick up a map at the information booth in the centre of the park. From the Roma Street pedestrian exit, cross over, turn left into George Street and right into Tank Street to cross the pedestrian Kurilpa Bridge over Brisbane River to the South Bank *(www. visitsouthbank. com.au)*. The **Gallery of Modern Art (GoMA)** ③ *(open daily; qag.qld.gov.au)*, at Kurilpa Point, was opened in 2006. Highlights include *Adventure Series 2* by Tracey Moffatt, one of Australia's best known 21st-century artists, along with a strong indigenous collection with a contemporary focus. It is also home to one of the best modern Asian and Pacific art collections in the world. Turn left into Grey Street for the stunning new **State Library** ④ *(book tours in advance on 07 3840 7666; www.slq.qld.gov. au)*. Opened with great fanfare, it won the Royal Australian Institute of Architects' Building of the Year award in 2007. Next on Grey Street is the **Queensland Art Gallery** ⑤ *(open daily; qag.qld.gov.au)*. Established in 1895, it has been housed in the architecturally acclaimed building by Robin Gibson since 1982. Both galleries and the library have good cafés. From the

Queensland Art Gallery, take the pedestrian overpass to the **South Bank Parklands** ⑥. Follow the path under bougainvillea arches and tropical gardens, past the man-made beach and along the esplanade. Ahead is the **Queensland Maritime Museum** ⑦ *(open daily; www.maritimemuseum.com. au)* with boats, wrecks and displays on navigation and shipping. Cross the river on Goodwill Bridge, known as the people's bridge. Explore the **City Botanical Gardens** ⑧ – large, well-tended sub-tropical gardens, with a mangrove boardwalk and fine paths over bridges and ornamental ponds. Head back along George Street past King George Square and the Neo-Italianate **Old Queensland Government Treasury Building** ⑨, built 1896–1928. Turn right into Queen Street mall and left into Albert Street to return to the car park.

VISITING BRISBANE

Parking
Park underground in the King George Square Car Park, between Ann and Adelaide Sts, in central Brisbane.

Visitor Information
Brisbane Visitor Information Centre: *Queen St, 4000; 07 3006 6290; www. ourbrisbane.com.* For information and maps about City Cat and ferries etc, visit **Transport Information Centre:** *King George Square, 4000; closed Sun.* For information on **Cycling in Brisbane**, visit *www.visitbrisbane.com.au.*

SHOPPING

Markets are held every Sun at the Riverside Centre, 123 Eagle St, with stalls selling arts and crafts and fresh produce. The **Queen Street Mall** is a centre for mainstream shopping, while **Fortitude Valley** is home to alternative fashion.

EAT AND DRINK IN BRISBANE

New Farm Deli and Café *inexpensive*
This is Brisbane's oldest Italian deli and café, offering tasty gourmet delights. *900 Brunswick St, New Farm, 4005 (4 km/2 miles from City Hall); 07 3358 2634; www.newfarmdeli.com.au*

Swiss Gourmet Deli *inexpensive*
Enjoy coffee and a bagel at this popular West End deli, close to South Bank. *181 Boundary Rd, West End, 4101; 07 3844 2937; www.swissgourmet.com.au*

Belesis *moderate*
This popular Greek place is in the suburb of Coorparoo (take Southeast Freeway). *198 Old Cleveland Rd, Coorparoo, 4151; 07 3324 2446; open Tue–Sun*

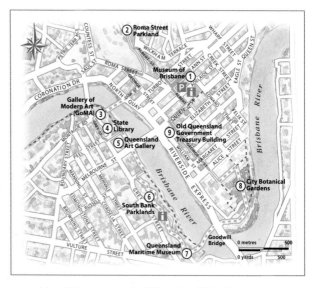

Eat and Drink: inexpensive under AU$60; moderate AU$60–$100; expensive over AU$100

Classic East Coast Drive

Noosa to Manly

Highlights

- **Spectacular beaches**
  Enjoy the beaches all along the coast: there is something for everyone, from dream surf at Nambucca Heads to safe and sandy waters at Cove Beach, Manly

- **Marine wildlife**
  Watch the seas for the unforgettable sight of humpback whales, dolphins and turtles, from lookout points at Cape Byron, Maclean, Noosa and Iluka

- **Convict heritage**
  Explore Australia's fascinating immigrant history at South West Rocks, Port Macquarie, Newcastle and Manly

- **National parks**
  Walk or canoe through wild and beautiful reserves at Noosa, Maclean, Red Rock and Lake Macquarie

Cape Byron lighthouse, a famous landmark
on Australia's most easterly point

Classic East Coast Drive

This classic coastal drive winds down the eastern edge of Queensland and New South Wales, and features appealing beach towns with arty communities and great places to stay, eat and drink, from little-known seaside hamlets to the popular havens of Noosa, Byron Bay and Manly. But it is the coastline itself, from the openness and warmth of Queensland's beaches to Sydney's capacious harbour, that is the main attraction. It offers breathtaking views from numerous headlands overlooking the Pacific Ocean, while every cove, bay and inlet comes with a pristine sandy beach, some stretching as far as the eye can see – there are countless opportunities to swim, surf and dive. When the drive meanders inland, it encounters diverse settlements, such as Eumundi in Queensland, with its lively markets, and Maclean in NSW, home to Scottish clan gatherings. After a leisurely drive along the coast, it is exhilarating to arrive on Sydney's north shore, at the charming and lively Manly, where the iconic trip on the Manly Ferry across Sydney Harbour to Sydney can be taken.

Above View of the coastline from the lighthouse at Cape Byron, *see p61*

ACTIVITIES

Watch for humpback whales at Noosa, Cape Byron or Iluka

Learn to surf at Coolangatta or Nambucca Heads

Enjoy splendid fish 'n' chips at Brunswick Heads

Walk around Cape Byron and look for dolphins, turtles and stingrays

Tuck into an authentic Punjabi curry at Woolgoolga

Explore the wetlands of the Arakoon National Park, South West Rocks

Scuba dive the reefs and wrecks at North Haven

Take a camel safari or seaplane flight at Port Macquarie

Go on a sport fishing cruise from Swansea

Kayak close to nature along the waterways of Lake Macquarie

Take a ghost tour in Manly's old Quarantine Station

Below The delightful coastal road to Point Danger, Coolangattta, see *p60*

PLAN YOUR DRIVE

Start/finish: Noosa to Manly (NSW), *see p64 for Emerald Beach to Manly map.*

Number of days: 6 days.

Distance: Approx. 1,244 km (778 miles).

Road conditions: All roads are paved, but take a map as some roads are not well signed. Always carry drinking water.

When to go: This drive is delightful all year round, but most comfortable in early winter–spring (late Aug–Nov) and autumn–early winter (Mar–early Jun). The best time to swim at the beach is Oct–Apr in NSW (all year in Queensland).

Opening times: Most museums and shops are open 9am–5pm. It is often difficult to find restaurants open in smaller towns on Mon and Tue nights.

Main market days: Eumundi: Wed & Sat; **Byron Bay:** craft market, 1st Sun of month, Butler St; **Bangalow:** craft and produce, 4th Sun of month, at Showground; **Woolgoolga:** general market, 2nd Sat of month, Beach Reserve; **Newcastle:** Olive Tree Market (arts and crafts), 1st Sat of month, Union Street, The Junction; **Manly:** arts and crafts, Sat & Sun, The Corso.

Shopping: Noosa is known for its boutique shopping. Eumundi Markets draw the crowds for arts and crafts and local produce. Newcastle has all types of shops from department stores to boutiques. Manly is great for surf gear.

Major festivals: Brunswick Heads: Fish 'n' Chips Festival, Jan; **Byron Bay:** Bluesfest Festival, Apr; Writers' Festival, Aug; **Woolgoolga:** CurryFest, Easter; **Newcastle:** Surfest, Mar.

VISITING NOOSA

Noosa Visitor Information Centre
61 Hastings St, 4567; 07 5430 5000;
www.visitnoosa.com.au; open daily

SHOPPING IN EUMUNDI

The **Eumundi Markets** *(www.eumundi markets.com.au)*, and **BerkelouW Book Barn and Cafe** offer a range of new and second-hand books in the historic Trading Post building *(87 Memorial Drive, 4562; 07 5442 8366; www. berkelouw.com.au).*

WHERE TO STAY

NOOSA

The Emerald Noosa *expensive*
Situated in Noosa's main street, this offers 45 comfortable, self-contained apartments, all with balconies.
42 Hastings St, 4567; 07 5449 6100; www.emeraldnoosa.com.au

EUMUNDI

Eumundi Hidden Valley B&B
moderate
Boutique B&B with big rooms, pool and a restored railway carriage as alternative accommodation, close to the town.
39 Caplick Way, 4562; 07 5442 8685; www.eumundibed.com

COOLANGATTA

Crystal Beach Holiday Apartments
moderate
Spacious 2- and 3-bed apartments, with swimming pool and direct beach access.
329 Golden Four Drive, Tugun, 4224; 07 5534 6633; www.crystalbeach.com.au

CAPE BYRON

Cavvanbah Beach House *expensive*
Luxury B&B with pool and spa. Very close to the beach.
28 Cavvanbah Street, Byron Bay, 2481; 02 6685 6625; www.cavvanbahbyronbay.com.au

Above The superb scenery and surf of Cabarita Beach and headland **Below** A pool of dolphins seen from the Cape Byron Lookout

❶ Noosa
Queensland; 4567
Cosmopolitan Noosa is set in the outstanding natural environment of **Noosa National Park** *(ww.derm.qld.gov. au/parks).* Follow the track along the boardwalk from Hastings Street and around the point to the Headland Section. Walk through pockets of rain-forest past sandy coves with places to swim. The park is home to koalas, wallum froglets, glossy black cockatoos and swamp orchids, and humpback whales can be seen off the coast *(Aug–Nov).* Browse Noosa's boutiques or take the **Noosa Ferry** *(daily; www.noosaferry. com)* from the Sheraton Hotel along beautiful waterways to the historic timber town of Tewantin.
🚗 *Take the Eumundi–Noosa Rd.*

❷ Eumundi
Queensland; 4562
Traditionally dairy and timber country, Eumundi's landscape is dominated by Mount Eerwah and dotted with pockets of rainforest and bush. The town is known for its markets and the usually quiet centre gets pretty busy on market days *(Wed and Sat).* Browse the arts and crafts stalls for handmade jewellery, health food and palm readers, all to the beat of live music.

🚗 *Take Eumundi Memorial Drive onto Bruce Hwy (A1) and follow the A1/M1 south (on Pacific Hwy after Brisbane) to Coolangatta (224 km/140 miles). An option is to turn off at Strathpine to Brisbane (see p55).*

❸ Coolangatta
Queensland; 4225
The drive south on the Pacific Highway into **Coolangatta** reveals the region's beauty. Follow the coast road around Greenmount to Point Danger for fabulous views on to Rainbow Bay. Drive down from the point to explore Greenmount Beach – a top surf spot: contact **Walkin' on Water** *(www.walkin onwater.com)* for lessons. Just across the NSW state border along Dixon Street lies Coolangatta's more arty sister, **Tweed Heads** (they are known as "Twin Towns"). Down Minjungbal Drive in Tweed Heads South is **Minjungbal Aboriginal and Cultural Centre** *(Kirkwood Rd; open Mon–Fri; 07 5524 2109),* with interesting exhibits on Aboriginal history and culture.
🚗 *Leave on Minjungbal Drive south, join Pacific Hwy (1), then turn left on Tweed Coast Rd to Cabarita Beach.*

❹ Cabarita Beach
New South Wales (NSW); 2488
Along the coast south of Tweed Heads, the seaside hamlet of Cabarita Beach enjoys fine views north to Coolangatta across the white sands and grassy headlands. The Cabarita beach headland is the perfect spot to enjoy a cool drink, before walking up to the top of the hill for spectacular views. Aboriginal artists sometimes sell their wares on the hillside.
🚗 *Follow the Tweed Coast Rd south. At Pottsville, turn right to Pacific Hwy (1) south. Take Brunswick Heads turn-off.*

⑤ Brunswick Heads
NSW; 2483

This relaxed riverside town offers the opportunity to have an authentic Australian fish 'n' chips experience. Follow the Old Pacific Highway (1) through town, with the river on the left, to the car park and entrance to the **Fishermen's Co-op**. With picnic tables and a small fishing boat marina, this is an idyllic place to eat and take a stroll. Every year in January, the town holds a **Fish 'n' Chips Festival** (02 6685 0186; www.brunswickvalley.com.au), with fireworks, side-shows and carnival rides. Continue from the co-op along the river through the laid-back ambience of small shops and past a splendid old, centrally located hotel.

📷 *Follow signs back to Pacific Hwy (1) south and take the Byron Bay turn-off. Park in the car park on Lighthouse Rd.*

⑥ Cape Byron
NSW; 2481

Byron Bay is the centre of the region's alternative lifestyle. Along with activities such as surfing and diving, the town offers retreats, spiritual workshops and a host of festivals. But it also boasts smart hotels and restaurants, upmarket boutiques and galleries and, of course, its famous lighthouse, with stunning ocean views. Take the path around Cape Byron to appreciate its natural grandeur.

Above Roads curving around Cape Byron

A two-hour walking tour

From the Captain Cook car park cross the road and head up Lee Lane to the start of the Cape Byron Walking Track. Follow the path through the coastal rainforest to reach the **viewing platform** ① with inspirational vistas. Hang-gliders frequently take off from here. Continue past the cottages to the gleaming white-washed **lighthouse** ②, which dates from 1901, and then walk down to the most easterly point in mainland Australia. On the way back up, instead of going back to the lighthouse, take the path around the hillside and down to the sands of **Watego's Beach** ③,

which is an excellent spot for surfing. Follow the walking trail over the next headland, to the **Pass Café** ④. There is a path from the café back to the car park in Lighthouse Road, or alternatively visitors can walk along a scenic boardwalk or Clarkes and Main beaches to Byron Bay. Between June and October, thousands converge on Cape Byron to watch the annual migration of the hump-back whales. Most of the year, dolphins, turtles and stingrays can be spotted swimming off the point.

📷 *Turn left from Jonson St into Browning St. Take the third roundabout onto Bangalow Rd into Bangalow.*

VISITING CAPE BYRON

Parking
Captain Cook Car Park, Lighthouse Rd.

Byron Visitor Centre
Stationmaster's Cottage, 80 Jonson St, 2481; 02 6680 8558; www.visitbyronbay. com; open daily

EAT AND DRINK

NOOSA

Cato's Restaurant & Bar *expensive*
Cato's, in the Sheraton Hotel, is popular for drinks, dining and music.
16 Hastings St, 4567; 07 5449 4754

EUMUNDI

Food @ Eumundi *moderate*
Locally grown food prepared by a five-star hotel trained chef.
1/104 Memorial Drive, 4567; 07 5442 7072

COOLANGATTA

café d'bar *inexpensive*
This café-gallery with great views offers alfresco dining and take-away food.
275 Boundary St, 4225; 07 5599 2031; www.cafedbar.com.au

BRUNSWICK HEADS

Fishermen's Co-op *inexpensive*
The place for fantastic, fresh, local fish 'n' chips eaten overlooking the river.
Old Pacific Hwy, Boat Harbour, 4225; 02 6685 1773

CAPE BYRON

Fishmongers *inexpensive*
Excellent gourmet fish dishes to eat in or take away – bring your own wine.
Bay Lane, 2481; 02 6680 8080

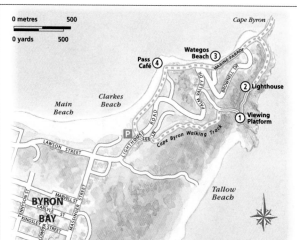

Eat and Drink: inexpensive under AU$60; moderate AU$60–AU$100; expensive over AU$100

ACTIVITIES

Richmond River Cruises
A 2-hour trip up the river from **Ballina**. *02 6687 5688; www.rrcruises.com.au; from mooring by Naval Museum; Wed & Sun 10am & 2pm; booking essential.*

Clarence Coast Visitor Information
Details of fishing, surfing and other activities around **Iluka** and **Yamba**. *Ferry Park, Pacific Hwy, Maclean, 2463; 02 6645 4121; www.clarencetourism.com.au*

National Parks Information
Details of walks in the region's parks. *Level 3, 49 Victoria St, Grafton, 2466; 02 6640 2500; www.environment.nsw. gov.au/NationalParks; open Mon–Fri.*

Boat & kayak hire
Boats can be hired from **Iluka Boatshed and Marina** *(1 Charles St, Iluka, 2466; 02 6646 6106)* or **Yamba Marina** *(3 Yamba Rd, Yamba, 2466; 02 6646 9898)*, and kayaks from **Yamba Kayaks** *(230 Gardiners Rd, Maclean, 2463; 0438 452 702).*

WHERE TO STAY

BALLINA

Ballina Manor *moderate*
This excellent boutique hotel offers rooms with wide verandas within walking distance of shops, bay and river. *25 Norton St, 2478; 02 6681 5888; www.ballinamanor.com.au*

ILUKA

Anchorage Holiday Park *inexpensive*
Set beside the river, this park offers a wide range of cabins and is ideally located for Bundjalung National Park. *Golding St, 2464; 02 6646 2930; www.yambawaters.com.au*

CORINDI BEACH

Corindi Beach Holiday Park *inexpensive–moderate*
This caravan park offers one-bedroom cabins situated on the beachfront. *93 Pacific St, 2456; 02 6649 2803; www.corindi.com.au*

Other options
Arrawarra Beach Holiday Park *(inexpensive)* offers villas, cabins and camp sites close to the water at Arrawarra *(46 Arrawarra Beach Rd, Arrawarra Beach, 2456; 02 6649 2753)*, as does **Darlington Beach Holiday Park** *(inexpensive)*, on the edge of the Wedding Bells State Forest *(104–134 Eggins Drive, Arrawarra, 2456; 02 6640 7444; www.darlingtonbeach.com.au)*. For non-campers, **Headlands Beach Guesthouse** *(moderate)* offers stylish rooms on the beach *(17 Headland Rd, Arrawarra Headland, 2456; 02 6654 0364; www.headlandsbeach.com.au)*.

Right Ballina, at the mouth of the Richmond River

⑦ Bangalow
NSW; 2479
Combining tradition with a touch of the alternative, Bangalow is a well-polished town. It features heritage architecture, several galleries and a Buddhist shop. Park down by the river and walk up to the main street to potter among the bookshops, boutiques and galleries. Stop in **The Urban** *(see right)* for something to eat, and watch the world go by.

🚗 *Take Bangalow Rd east to Pacific Hwy (1) south. At Ballina, continue straight on to the centre on Cherry St.*

⑧ Ballina
NSW; 2478
At the mouth of the Richmond River, Ballina is a great spot to take a **river cruise** *(see left)* for stunning country views. Also of interest is the **Naval and Maritime Museum** *(www.ballinamaritime museum.org.au)*, home to a collection of model ships. It houses the raft *La Balsa*, which made a trans-Pacific expedition from Ecuador in 1973, landing in Ballina. Head through town, over the creek, along Hill Road, then Pine Road, right into Sulva Street and left into Shelley Beach Road to **Shelley's on the Beach** *(see right)*, a café by the sea, to enjoy a coffee as the frill-necked lizards sunbathe on the walkways.

🚗 *Return to Pacific Hwy (1) south, after Woodburn turn left to Iluka.*

⑨ Iluka
NSW; 2466
The peaceful town of Iluka is known for its riverbank fishing and surfing beaches, and the area is a haven for wildlife such as coastal emus, sea eagles and ospreys. The town also offers easy access to **Bundjalung**

Above Bird of paradise flower, frequently seen in gardens along the NSW coast

National Park for rainforest walks. Most accessible is **Iluka Nature Reserve**, a patch of littoral rainforest that is home to over 100 species of birds including the striking black and yellow regent bowerbird. The reserve is reached along a walking track from **Iluka Bluff and Whale Watching Platform** – a superb spot for whale watching: humpback whales can be seen with their calves *(Jun–Nov)*. Before visiting, pick up a whale watching brochure from the **Visitor Information Centre** *(see left)* or pick up a map at the Makuti Café by the **Iluka Boatshed** – the departure point for the ferry to the working port of **Yamba**, where kayaks can be hired to explore the waterways, and dolphin-spotting boats taken out into the bay.

🚗 *Return to Pacific Hwy (1) south and take the Maclean turn-off (left ramp).*

⑩ Maclean
NSW; 2463
Set on the Clarence River, Maclean has an abundance of natural beauty, bounded on the north by Bundjalung National Park, on the south by the Yuraygir National Park and on the west by Banyabba Nature Reserve. Its eastern border is formed by miles of sandy beaches. Maclean is famous for

its annual **Scottish Clan Gathering** *(www.macleanhighlandgathering.com.au)* – the town's first settlers were Scots – held at Easter. Follow signs to **Maclean Lookout** for expansive views across the Clarence River and picnics. Near it is Pinnacle Rock, a fascinating rock formation with a network of caves.

🚗 *Return to Pacific Hwy (1) south past Grafton and on to Red Rock.*

⑪ Red Rock
NSW; 2456

Secluded and peaceful, the southern bank of the Red Rock River has a public park for picnics and a sandy beach. The river offers canoe access to **Yuraygir National Park** on its northern bank – wetlands teeming with important birdlife, rare reptiles and amphibians, including the bearded dragon and rocket frog. It is also the traditional home of the Yaegl and Gumbaynggirr indigenous peoples of NSW, and is a protected reserve. The park can be accessed by car at Station Creek *(turn right off Pacific Hwy (1) north of Red Rock).* The parks office at Grafton has maps.

🚗 *Take Pacific Hwy (1) to Corindi Beach.*

Above The Sikh Temple, Woolgoolga, a result of Sikh immigration in the 1940s **Right** Red Rock River, slowly flowing to the ocean

⑫ Corindi Beach
NSW; 2456

The coastline opens out as it extends south to Corindi Beach, a small town with a few facilities and several arts and crafts centres. As well as beach activities, a boardwalk leads through rainforest from the northern end of the beach. Be sure to visit **Yarrawarra Aboriginal Cultural Centre** *(170 Red Rock Rd; 02 6649 2669)* and take a bush

tucker walk to learn about indigenous food. Look out for wallabies, then head south on Pacific Hwy (1) to **Arrawarra**, another fabulous beach for surfing, swimming and fishing, with a good choice of places to stay *(see left).*

🚗 *Return to Pacific Hwy (1) south to Woolgoolga and turn left at the roundabout to the town centre.*

⑬ Woolgoolga
NSW; 2456

Known as "Whoopi" by the locals, its name comes from "Wel-gul-ga", an Aboriginal name for a local wild berry. Woolgoolga was predominantly built by Sikh immigrants from the Indian Punjab who came in the 1940s to work the banana plantations. Today, most of the town's banana industry is owned and operated by Australians of Sikh ancestry. An attractive seaside town, Woolgoolga offers a picnic area along the banks of the creek that is part of **Sherwood Reserve**, a remnant of lowland subtropical rainforest. It is ideal for bird-watching and water sports. Many restaurants in town offer Punjabi cooking and there is a Curryfest *(www.curryfest.com.au)* at Easter.

🚗 *Return to Pacific Hwy 1 south and take Fiddaman Rd left to Emerald Beach.*

Left The long expanse of Corindi Beach, stretching north to Red Rock

EAT AND DRINK

BANGALOW

Fishheads Bangalow *inexpensive*
Offering fresh seafood, Fishheads uses produce sourced from local farmers. *2 Byron St, Bangalow, 2479; 02 6687 2993; www.restaurantbyronbay.com.au; open daily for breakfast, lunch and dinner*

BALLINA

Manor Restaurant *moderate*
Enjoy modern Australian cuisine at this fine dining restaurant that has a marble fireplace, a wide verandah and a courtyard with a sandstone fountain. *25 Norton St, 2478; 02 6681 5888; www.ballinamanor.com.au; open daily for dinner*

CORINDI BEACH

Amble Inn Tavern *inexpensive*
This older-style timber pub offers counter lunches and dinners – speciality of the house is its Surf and Turf (seafood and meat). On top of the pub's chimney is a stone-carved akubra hat and outside the building are several wooden carvings, in particular one of a Killer Whale. It also has great ocean views. *1 Tasman St, 2456; 02 6649 2622; open daily for lunch and dinner*

WOOLGOOLGA

Bluebottles Brasserie *moderate*
This restaurant has a tasty, refreshing menu offering seafood, curries and lamb dishes based on fresh, local produce. *Cnr Beach & Wharf Sts, 2456; 02 6654 1962; open daily for lunch, Fri & Sat also dinner*

Eat and Drink: inexpensive under AU$60; moderate AU$60–AU$100; expensive over AU$100

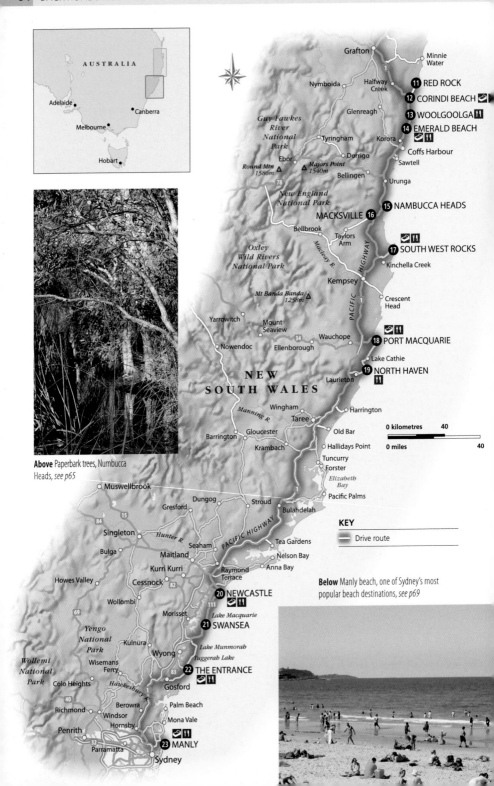

AUSTRALIA

Adelaide

Canberra

Melbourne

Hobart

Grafton

Minnie Water

Nymboida

Halfway Creek

11 RED ROCK

12 CORINDI BEACH

Glenreagh

13 WOOLGOOLGA

Guy Fawkes River National Park

Tyringham

Korora

14 EMERALD BEACH

Ebor

Dorrigo

Coffs Harbour

Round Mtn 1586m

Majors Point 1540m

Sawtell

New England National Park

Bellingen

Urunga

Oxley Wild Rivers National Park

Bellbrook

15 NAMBUCCA HEADS

MACKSVILLE **16**

Taylors Arm

17 SOUTH WEST ROCKS

Mackay R.

Kinchella Creek

Mt Banda Banda 1258m

Kempsey

Crescent Head

Yarrowitch

Mount Seaview

Lake Cathie

Nowendoc

Ellenborough

Wauchope

18 PORT MACQUARIE

NEW SOUTH WALES

Laurieton

19 NORTH HAVEN

Wingham

Manning R.

Harrington

Taree

Old Bar

Barrington

Gloucester

Hallidays Point

Krambach

Tuncurry

Forster

Elizabeth Bay

0 kilometres 40

0 miles 40

Above Paperbark trees, Numbucca Heads, see p65

Muswellbrook

Dungog

Stroud

Pacific Palms

Gresford

Bulahdelah

Singleton

Hunter R.

Seaham

Tea Gardens

Bulga

Maitland

Nelson Bay

Kurri Kurri

Anna Bay

KEY

Drive route

Howes Valley

Cessnock

Raymond Terrace

20 NEWCASTLE

Wollombi

Morisset

Lake Macquarie

21 SWANSEA

Yengo National Park

Kulnura

Wyong

Lake Munmorah Tuggerah Lake

Below Manly beach, one of Sydney's most popular beach destinations, see p69

Wollemi National Park

Wisemans Ferry

Gosford

22 THE ENTRANCE

Colo Heights

Hawkesbury R.

Berowra

Richmond

Palm Beach

Windsor

Mona Vale

Penrith

Hornsby

23 MANLY

Parramatta

Sydney

⑭ Emerald Beach

NSW; 2456

Emerald Beach is one of many beautiful expanses of sand and blue Pacific water along this stretch of coastline, perfect for a relaxed walk and a picnic *(see p74)*. There is also a children's playground and BBQ areas. Take a walk through the Moonee Beach Nature Reserve, where you are bound to see kangaroos, on your way to the Look at Me Headland. This headland is an Aboriginal site with panoramic views of the ocean and Solitary Island as well as its lighthouse. Head a short distance south, just off the Pacific Highway (1), to try your hand at a cheese-making course at **Lake Russell** *(62 Lake Russell Drive, 2456; www.thecheesemakingworkshop. com.au; book ahead)*.

📷 *Return to Pacific Hwy (1) south, past Coffs Harbour (see New England Tableland drive, pp74–5) turning left to Nambucca Heads.*

Surfing in Nambucca Valley

Nambucca Valley's coastline runs south from Nambucca Heads and includes Valla Beach, Grassy Head and Scotts Head. Popular with skilled (and not so skilled) surfers from all over the world, it is a great place to learn to surf. Try **Scotts Head Surf School** *(Shop 3, Short St, Scotts Head, 2447; 02 65 697 065; scottsheadsurfschool@hotmail.com)* or **Trent Munro Surf Academy** *(Nambucca Heads, Valla Beach, Grassy Head, Scotts Head, 2447; 02 6569 7127; www.trentmunro.com).*

⑮ Nambucca Heads

NSW; 2448

In the 1800s, Nambucca Heads was an important coastal port, but today it is a surfing mecca. Visitors can make use of the vast pristine beaches for surfing, swimming and various other watersports. Learn to surf on the beaches south of Nambucca Heads with **Scotts Head Surf School** and **Trent Munro Surf Academy** *(see box)*.

To explore the central **John Davies Rainforest Walk** *(4 Wellington Drive; 02 6568 6954)*, turn into Wellington Drive for signed entry points. Follow the trail through the eucalyptus and brush box trees. Listen for the call of the whipbird and other birdlife and enjoy the cooling shade of the figs and paperbark trees in the swampy areas of the walk. The **Headland Historical Museum** *(open 2–4pm Wed, Sat–Sun, or by appt on 02 6569 5802)* at Nambucca Heads has an eclectic collection of local memorabilia and Aboriginal artifacts.

📷 *Continue south on Pacific Hwy (1) to Macksville.*

Above left Surfing at Nambucca Heads
Above right Al fresco dining at Saltwater on the Beach

AROUND EMERALD BEACH

WHERE TO STAY

Saltwater on the Beach *expensive*
This sophisticated beachfront accommodation offers a luxurious three-bedroom apartment with excellent views of the Coffs coastline. There is also a huge balcony with outdoor seating. *104 Fiddaman Rd, 2456; 0401 681 170; www.saltwateronthebeach.com*

EAT AND DRINK

Saltwater on the Beach *inexpensive–moderate*
Enjoy a sumptuous breakfast, lunch or a delightful dinner by candlelight at this casual café, which is also an ideal spot for whale watching. Book in advance. *104 Fiddaman Rd, 2456; 02 6656 1888; www.saltwateronthebeach.com*

Below Scenic Lake Russell, surrounded by trees, near Emerald Beach

Eat and Drink: inexpensive under AU$60; moderate AU$60–AU$100; expensive over AU$100

Above One of the sandy beaches in the heart of Newcastle **Below** Lily pond in a park at the heart of Macksville

WHERE TO STAY

SOUTH WEST ROCKS

South West Rocks Tourist Park *moderate*
Located on the tidal waterway, this park offers cabins and camping with great facilities, in a scenic, central location. *Gordon Young Drive, 2431; 02 6566 6264; www.southwestrockstourist.com.au*

Stillpoint *moderate*
This self-catering apartment is in a great position, close to good beaches and on the edge of the Arakoon National Park. *78 Cardwell St, 2431; 02 6566 6679; www.stillpoint.com.au*

PORT MACQUARIE

Flynns on Surf *inexpensive*
Set in landscaped gardens, this resort offers modern, self-catering units, within a 5-minute walk from Flynns Beach. *25 Surf St, 2444; 02 6584 2244; www.flynns.com.au*

Beachport B&B *inexpensive*
This welcoming B&B is opposite Sea Acres Nature Reserve and only a short stroll along a rainforest boardwalk to the beach. *155 Pacific Drive, Port Macquarie, 2444; 02 6582 5268; www.beachportbnb.com.au*

NEWCASTLE

Crowne Plaza *expensive*
In the historic Honeysuckle Precinct, this hotel has old-world elegance and charm and ocean-side windows. *Cnr Merewether St & Wharf Rd, 2300; 02 4907 5000; www.crowneplaza.com*

Noah's On the Beach *moderate*
This hotel offers rooms overlooking the town's historic East End, the harbour and foreshore, or the Pacific Ocean. *Cnr Shortland Esplanade & Zaara St, 2300; 02 4929 5181*

---

16 Macksville
NSW; 2447

This town is situated on the Pacific Highway (1). After the bridge over the Nambucca River, look out for the **Star Hotel** on the left on the riverbank – a historic hotel with a veranda overlooking the river, ideal for sitting with a drink. Locals say dolphins have been seen from the veranda. Explore the town's history with a visit to **Mary Boulton's Pioneer Cottage** *(open Wed & Sat pm; 02 6568 6954)*, a replica of a rough-sawn timber home of the European settlers, filled with original tools and memorabilia.

Head south on Pacific Hwy (1) to the South West Rocks turn-off. Follow signs to Gregory St, to the coast.

17 South West Rocks
NSW; 2431

The small town of South West Rocks is situated at the mouth of the Macleay River, one of several rivers that flow down from the Great Dividing Range, carving wide estuaries and winding creeks through the coastal rainforest and ending at long sandy beaches. South West Rocks is a classic example of river-mouth beauty, with the aquamarine waters and coastal forest reserve of Trial Bay sheltered by the fish-hook promontory of Laggers Point and **Arakoon National Park**. Follow the foreshore boardwalk over wetlands or walk out to the point to see the ruins of **Trial Bay Gaol** *(open daily)*, established as a public works prison in the 1870s to provide men to build a breakwater in the bay. From there, wander over Monument Hill to the **Little Bay picnic area** or take a half-day walk to **Smoky**

Cape Lighthouse in Hat Head National Park. The coast here is ideal for surfing, swimming and fishing (rent a line and bait at the kiosk), and scuba diving – especially at **Fish Rock Cave**.

Return to Pacific Hwy (1) south, turning left on Hastings River Drive to Port Macquarie.

Diving Fish Rock Cave

Fish Rock Cave, 2 km (1 mile) off Smoky Cape at South West Rocks, is one of Australia's top dive sites. **South West Rocks Dive Centre** *(5/98 Gregory St, 2431; 02 6566 6474; www.southwestrocksdives.com.au)* and **Fish Rock Dive Centre** *(134 Gregory St, 2431; 02 6566 6614; fishrock.com.au)* both arrange dives.

---

18 Port Macquarie
NSW; 2444

As well as sandy beaches for picnics, walks and swimming, Port Macquarie offers more adventurous attractions – try a **camel safari** *(Sun–Fri am; Lighthouse Beach; 0437 672 080)* along the shore or take a **seaplane flight** *(Town Wharf, 2444; www.australiabyseaplane.com.au)*. There is some historical interest, as a penal settlement was established here in 1821. Remnants of early architecture include the convict-built buildings of **St Thomas' Church** and the **Historical Museum** *(open Mon–Sat; 22 Clarence St; www.pmhm.org.au)*. There are plenty of other heritage buildings to see including the National Trust-listed **Roto House**, built in 1891 and set in the **Macquarie Nature Reserve** (with Koala Hospital) *(open daily; off Lord St)*. There are several museums in town,

including the **Mid-North Coast Maritime Museum** *(02 6583 1866)*, in one of the small Pilot Station cottages on the river, built 1896–1937 on the corner of William Street and Pacific Drive. For information about other heritage sites, visit the **Visitor Information Centre** *(Cnr Gordon & Gore Sts)*. For a change of pace, head to the **Cassegrain Winery Cellar Door** *(open daily)*, just off the Pacific Highway (1).

🚗 *Return towards Pacific Hwy (1) and at the junction of Oxley Hwy (34) and Hastings River Drive, turn left down Hindman St to Ocean Drive. Follow signs to Laurieton along the coast, through Lake Cathie to North Haven.*

Scuba Diving at North Haven

To dive the reefs, wrecks and rich waters of Port Macquarie and North Haven, contact **Scuba Haven** *(5/559 Ocean Drive, Laurieton, North Haven, 2443; 02 6559 5530; www.scubahaven.com.au)*. They provide lessons, too, for all levels of experience, including beginners.

🔟 North Haven

NSW; 2443

North Haven sits below North Brother Mountain and beside the Camden Haven River. It offers an array of sandy surf beaches, reefs for scuba diving, and river inlets and lakes for fishing, sailing and windsurfing. The best way to appreciate the beauty of the area is to drive to the top of North Brother Mountain in **Dooragan National Park** *(cross the bridge to Laurieton and follow Ocean Drive to West Haven, then turn left up Captain Cook Bicentenary Drive)*. There are several tracks from here.

🚗 *Follow Ocean Drive through Laurieton, turn left onto Pacific Hwy (1, becoming 111) to central Newcastle.*

🔟 Newcastle

NSW; 2300

This once grimy coal port – Australia's sixth largest city – has had a clean-up. Head to the rejuvenated waterfront **Honeysuckle Precinct** for Newcastle's café scene, before driving around the headland for expansive views. Stop at the open-air **Newcastle and Merewether Ocean Baths** *(closed Thu for cleaning)* and swim in the man-made seawater pools. Alternatively take the **Newcastle East Heritage Walk** past the Customs House, the Convict Lumber Yard and Fort Scratchley. Pick up maps from the **Visitor Information Centre**.

Newcastles beaches include family-oriented Bars Beach in the harbour and Nobbys Reef and Caves Beach in the south, great for swimming and surfing.

The **Christ Church Cathedral** contains many fine fittings including stained glass by Pre-Raphaelite artist Edward Burne-Jones, nave windows by prolific Victorian stained-glass artist C E Kempe and the bishop's throne by English architect W D Caröe.

Take a tour of the nearby **Hunter Valley Wineries** *(see box and pp90–91)*.

🚗 *Take King St to Pacific Hwy (111), then Lake Rd into Swansea's centre.*

Lower Hunter Valley Wineries

Australia's oldest wine region, the fertile Hunter Valley harbours many superb wineries creating world-class Semillon and Shiraz wines, among others, alongside quality food producers and restaurants. With over 120 cellar doors there is plenty of scope for tasting tours. For more information go to *www.winecountry. com.au*. **Rover Coaches** *(02 4990 1699; www.hunterwinetours.com.au)* arranges coach tours and will pick up passengers from Newcastle.

VISITING NEWCASTLE

Parking
Park on King Street or Wharf Road.

Visitor Information Centre
3 Honeysuckle Drive, 2300; 1800 654 558; www.visitnewcastle.com.au

EAT AND DRINK

SOUTH WEST ROCKS

Barnetts Rainbow Reach Oyster Barn *moderate*
Follow Rainbow Beach Road to one of the best oyster farms on the coast.
Rainbow Reach Rd, 2431; 02 6565 0050

PORT MACQUARIE

The Restaurant at Cassegrain *expensive*
This delightful restaurant at the Cassegrain Winery serves French-inspired food in a verdant setting.
764 Fernbank Creek Rd, 2431; 02 6582 8320; www.cassegrainwines.com.au; open daily, dinner Fri only; book ahead

NORTH HAVEN

The Addictive Pie Shop *inexpensive*
The pie is a great Australian staple and few places make better pies than this shop – all made and baked on site.
559 Ocean Drive, 2443; 02 6559 9522

The Sandbar Café *inexpensive*
Café on the river serving excellent food made with fresh, local ingredients.
621 Ocean Drive, 2443; 02 6559 6945

NEWCASTLE

Jonah's On the Beach *moderate.*
This restaurant offers quality dining, ocean views and live music Thu–Sat.
Cnr Shortland Esplanade & Zaara St, 2300; 02 4929 5181

Chinois Chinese Restaurant *moderate*
A friendly fusion restaurant with a great reputation, offering a range of Western and Asian dishes.
326 King St, 2300; 02 4926 2333

Eat and Drink: inexpensive under AU$60; moderate AU$60–$100; expensive over AU$100

WHERE TO STAY

THE ENTRANCE

Lakeview Tourist Park *inexpensive*
This handy tourist park has tent sites, cabins and caravans for visitors and also offers a wide range of activities.
491 The Entrance Road, Long Jetty, 2261; 02 4332 1515; www.lakeviewtouristpark.com.au

Annabell's B&B *moderate*
Four 1930s-style rooms close to the waterfront and near al fresco cafés and restaurants.
5 Bent St, 2261; 02 4333 5669

MANLY

Q-Station *moderate*
Located on Sydney's North Head, the historic Quarantine Station has been turned into a resort offering individual rooms, some with ensuites. The on-site restaurant, The Boiler House, offers fine dining. This is more than somewhere to stay, it is an insight into Sydney's past.
1 North Head Scenic Drive, 2095; 02 9466 1500; www.qstation.com.au

Below The Corso, Manly's palm-tree-lined main street **Below right** The still waters of Lake Macquarie at sunset **Below left** Jetskis churn up saltwater Lake Macquarie, the largest of its kind in Australia

Lake Macquarie Activities

For information on watersports, biking and other activities, visit **Lake Macquarie Visitor Information Centre** *(228–34 Pacific Hwy, Swansea, 2281; 02 4921 0740; www.visitlakemac.com.au)*. To hire kayaks or bikes, contact **Lake Macquarie Kayaks** *(0437 772 939; www.lakemacquariekayaks.com.au)* and for scenic lake cruises try **Lake Macquarie Cruises** *(02 4973 2513; www.lakemacquariecruises.com.au)*. For fishing trips contact **B & L Fishing and Cruises** *(0427 713 323; www.blfishingcruises.com)*.

㉑ Swansea
NSW; 2281

Swansea is located on the eastern shores of **Lake Macquarie**, the largest coastal saltwater lake in Australia. The town developed by the deep channel leading from the ocean to a sheltered harbour, used to export coal from inland mines. The lake is perfect for watersports – swimming, surfing, boating, water-skiing and fishing – and its banks for hiking and horseriding. The less sporty may prefer to visit the **Lake Macquarie State Conservation Area** to enjoy the natural beauty of the region. Established in 1996, this spectacular bushland region encompasses 16 km (10 miles) of

foreshore in six different sections around Lake Macquarie. An important habitat for wallabies, kangaroos and squirrel gliders, it also provides excellent opportunities for wildlife photography. A good way to see the lake in all its glory and to get close to the wildlife is from a kayak *(see box)*.

🚗 *Take Pacific Hwy (111) south to Lake Munmorah. Turn left on Elizabeth Bay Drive (Coastal Rd) to The Entrance.*

㉒ The Entrance
NSW; 2261

Getting its name from its position at the entrance of the Tuggerah Lakes to the Tasman Sea, The Entrance is a popular Australian coastal holiday resort and offers an array of water-based activities. Its serene and picturesque landscapes are captivating for photographers, but there is plenty of opportunity for watersports such as boating and sailing – ask at **Long Jetty Catamaran and Boat Hire** *(Foreshore, cnr Tuggerah Pde & Pacific St; 0408 506 661; www.longjettyboathire.com)*. Watch the daily **pelican feeding** *(3.30pm, The Esplanade, Memorial Park)* and walk or cycle the track that runs along the lake's foreshore to Chittaway Bay. On the foreshore next to Memorial Park, **Vera's Water Garden** *(open daily)* is popular

with youngsters, who enjoy splashing about in its pools and fountains.

🔁 *Return to Pacific Hwy (83) south, then Pacific Hwy (1). Turn left on the multi-lane freeway, following signs to Manly. Turn off on Military Rd (10), then right on Sydney Rd (22) to the Esplanade. Turn left for the Peninsula car park.*

The Manly Corso

In 1853, Henry Gilbert Smith, a wealthy speculator, began buying up tracts of land on the Manly Peninsula. His vision was to establish a seaside resort, offering fresh air and sea baths in the English style. In 1855, he built a boardwalk from Manly Cove to the sea along a well-trodden Aboriginal track. This he named **The Corso** after the famous route in Rome. Smith was also instrumental in establishing the famous Manly Ferry; a regular service that began in June 1859.

23 Manly
NSW; 2095

The historic Sydney suburb of Manly is a lively centre on the north shore, linked to central Sydney by the **Manly Ferry** *(Cnr West Esplanade & Corso; 131 500; www.sydneyferries.info)*, which carves its way across the harbour waters every 30 minutes from Circular Quay. Driving towards Manly's famous **Corso**, it is easy to see why a town was established here, with the Pacific Ocean on one side and the harbour on the other. At the tip of the peninsula, sandstone cliffs jut into the ocean, forming **North Head** at the mouth of Sydney Harbour. This area is part of **Sydney Harbour National Park** *(www.environment.nsw. gov.au/NationalParks)* and houses the

historic buildings of the old Quarantine Station, where immigrants suspected of carrying disease were kept in isolation for 40 days to avoid contagion. The **Q-Station** *(see left)* also runs **Ghost Tours** *(02 9466 1500; www.qstation.com.au).* To see more of Manly's history, try the **Heart of Manly Heritage Walk**, which starts from the **Visitor Centre** *(Forecourt, Manly Wharf, 2095; 02 9976 1430).* Children will enjoy **Oceanworld Manly** *(open daily; 02 8251 7877; www.oceanworld.com.au)* on Cove Beach as they can see Australia's dangerous marine animals close up. From the headland, watch the constant flow of ships, yachts, ferries and small boats shuttling to and from the harbour. Manly's spectacular position, bounded by ocean and harbour, does not distract from its other attractions – shops, cafés and restaurants – at locations such as **Manly Wharf Shopping Fair**. After exhausting the shops, enjoy a harbour crossing on the famous Manly Ferry.

EAT AND DRINK

THE ENTRANCE

Ocean Restaurant *moderate*
A seaside restaurant with ocean views, serving fresh local seafood accompanied by a good wine list.
102 Ocean Parade, 2262; 02 4334 4600; open lunch daily, dinner Mon–Sat

MANLY

The Boilerhouse Restaurant *expensive*
Fresh modern cuisine, prepared with care and attention to the smallest detail. Worth the effort and the price.
1 North Head Scenic Drive, 2095; 02 9466 1511; www.qstation.com.au

Hugo's Manly *moderate*
The spectacular location of this restaurant allows you to watch the ferries go by while enjoying a cocktail and pizza.
Manly Wharf, East Esplanade, 2095; 02 8116 8555; www.hugos.com.au

Above left View from the Q-Station, set in the verdant Sydney Harbour National Park
Above right Manly façade **Below** Manly Ferry and Sydney Harbour Bridge

Eat and Drink: inexpensive under AU$60; moderate AU$60–AU$100; expensive over AU$100

New England Tableland

Coffs Harbour to Tweed Heads

Highlights

- **Glorious Coffs Coast**
  Enjoy the many attractions of Coffs Harbour and the coast's sandy beaches

- **Galleries galore**
  Browse the excellent art collections of Armidale and Murwillumbah

- **Australia's historic heritage**
  Admire the area's mix of Art Deco, Federation and Colonial architecture

- **Wonderful waterfalls**
  Picnic by cool cascades flowing from waterfalls that feed the Tableland

- **Extraordinary geology**
  Clamber over the massive boulders of Cathedral Rock and Bald Rock national parks and enjoy the wilderness

The marina at Coffs Harbour

New England Tableland

This drive covers a wide range of Australian countryside, winding through some magnificent scenery and stopping at local cultural sights. Starting on the white sandy beaches of Coffs Coast, the route heads up on to the Dorrigo Plateau, where it zig-zags into the ancient rainforest and past the pretty waterfalls of ten national parks. The drive then moves across the New England Tableland, through the farming communities and early Australian settlements of the region. As it heads down again from the heights of the Great Dividing Range, the route takes in the characterful villages of Nimbin and Tumbulgum, the cultural centres of Armidale and Murwillumbah and a host of colourful hippy markets in the hinterland, before finishing up at Tweed Heads on the Gold Coast.

Above Paperbark trees in Knox Park, Murwillumbah, *see p78*

ACTIVITIES

Get close to seals and dolphins at Coffs Harbour

View the Federation architecture in Bellingen, Dorrigo and Murwillumbah

Explore the dense rainforest canopy of Dorrigo National Park

Enjoy a picnic by the cascading waters of pretty Dangar Falls

Learn about Aboriginal culture in Armidale

Clamber over the extraordinary Bald Rock in the national park near Tenterfield

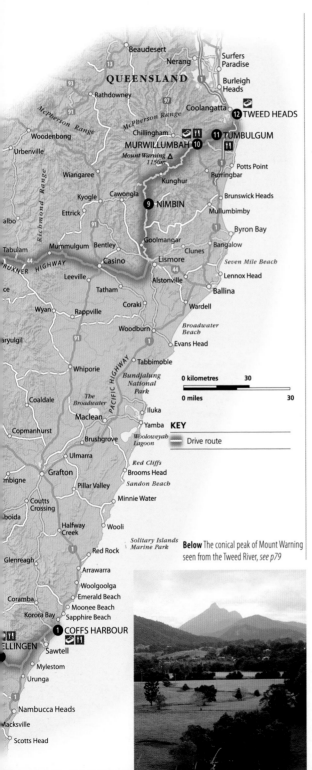

QUEENSLAND

Beaudesert

Nerang

Surfers Paradise

Burleigh Heads

Rathdowney

Coolangatta

TWEED HEADS ⑫

McPherson Range

McPherson Range

Woodenbong

Chillingham ⑩ **MURWILLUMBAH**

TUMBULGUM ⑪

Urbenville

Mount Warning △ 1156m

Potts Point

Wiangaree

Kunghur

Burringbar

Richmond Range

Kyogle

Cawongla

Brunswick Heads

Ettrick

NIMBIN ⑨

Mullumbimby

albo

Byron Bay

Tabulam

Mummulgum

Bentley

Goolmangar

Clunes

Bangalow

RUXNER HIGHWAY

Casino

Lismore

Seven Mile Beach

Leeville

Alstonville

Lennox Head

ce

Tatham

Ballina

Coraki

Wardell

Wyan

Rappville

Woodburn

Broadwater Beach

aryulgil

Evans Head

Whiporie

Tabbimoble

Bundjalung National Park

0 kilometres   30

0 miles   30

Coaldale

The Broadwater

Iluka

Copmanhurst

Maclean

Yamba **KEY**

Brushgrove

Woolooweyah Lagoon

Ulmarra

Drive route

Grafton

Red Cliffs

mbigne

Pillar Valley

Brooms Head

Sandon Beach

Coutts Crossing

Minnie Water

boida

Halfway Creek

Wooli

Glenreagh

Solitary Islands Marine Park

Red Rock

Arrawarra

Woolgoolga

Coramba

Emerald Beach

Moonee Beach

Korora Bay

Sapphire Beach

COFFS HARBOUR ①

ELLINGEN

Sawtell

Mylestom

Urunga

Nambucca Heads

Macksville

Scotts Head

Below The conical peak of Mount Warning seen from the Tweed River, see p79

PLAN YOUR DRIVE

Start/Finish: Coffs Harbour to Tweed Heads.

Number of days: 6 days.

Distance: Approx. 679 km (424 miles).

Road conditions: All roads are paved, though some are mountainous and winding. Take a map and be sure to check current road conditions before setting out for the Tableland.

When to go: This drive is delightful all year round, but most comfortable in late winter–spring (late Aug–Nov) and autumn–late winter (Mar–early Jun).

Opening times: Most museums and shops are open 9am–5pm. It is often difficult to find restaurants open in smaller towns on Monday and Tuesday nights.

Main market days: Coffs Harbour: Growers' Market, Thu; Bellingen: Community Markets (arts, crafts and local produce), 3rd Sat of month (www.bellingenmarkets.com.au); Organic Market, 2nd and 4th Sats of month; Dorrigo: 1st Sat of month; Armidale: farmers' market and car boot sale, 1st and 3rd Sat of month; Murwillumbah: cottage markets at Knox Park, 3rd Sat of month; markets on showgrounds, 4th Sat of month.

Shopping: Coffs Harbour has a good range of independent boutiques in the village centre and speciality shops in its Plaza. Nimbin has an array of hippy-style shops selling alternative-lifestyle paraphernalia and New Age items. Tumbulgum is a good place to pick up craft gifts.

Major festivals: Coffs Harbour: Coffs Harbour Show, late Apr; Buskers and Comedy Festival, late-Oct; Bellingen: Jazz and Blues Festival, mid-Aug; Global Carnival, early Oct; Dorrigo: Folk and Bluegrass Festival, last weekend Oct; Glen Innes: Glen Innes Show, Feb; Australian Celtic Festival, first weekend May (www.australiancelticfestival.com); Gourment in the Glen, Oct; Land of the Beardies Festival, early Nov; Murwillumbah: Tweed Valley Banana Festival, Aug; Speed on Tweed festival, Sep.

VISITING COFFS HARBOUR

Visitor Information Centre
*Cnr Pacific Hwy & McLean St, 2450;
02 6648 4990; www.coffscoast.com.au*

WHERE TO STAY

AROUND COFFS HARBOUR

Opal Cove Resort *inexpensive*
Situated 7 km (4 miles) north of Coffs
Harbour, just off the Pacific Hwy (1), this
beachfront resort offers modern rooms,
villas and apartments with good facilities.
*Pacific Hwy, Coffs Harbour 2450; 1 800
008 198; www.opalcove.com.au*

The Big Windmill Motor Lodge
inexpensive
This motor lodge has a restaurant set
in a large windmill and is situated
2 km (1 mile) south of Coffs Harbour.
*168 Pacific Hwy, Coffs Harbour 2450; 02
6652 2933; www.bigwindmill.com.au*

BELLINGEN

Finders Keepers Cottage *inexpensive*
A comfortable country cottage-style
B&B with fragrant gardens and a spa,
within easy reach of the centre.
*8 Coronation St, 2454; 02 6655 0603;
finderskeeperscottage.com.au*

AROUND DORRIGO
NATIONAL PARK

Gracemere Grange *moderate*
This B&B is owned by author Helen
Proud, who knows the rainforest well.
The peaceful country-style home is only
3 km (2 miles) from the park entrance.
*325 Dome Rd, 2453; 02 6657 2630;
www.gracemeregrange.com.au*

Above Waves crashing against rocks at Coffs
Harbour **Below left** Federation-style
shopfronts in the heart of Bellingen **Below
right** Wallaby on the route to Dorrigo

① Coffs Harbour
New South Wales (NSW); 2450
The town of Coffs Harbour sits at the
heart of a region of great natural
beauty and abundant wildlife, where
the Great Dividing Range descends
from the tableland to the coast. Its
string of golden beaches stretches
90 km (55 miles) from Red Rock in the
north to Scotts Head in the south. In
the migratory season (May–Nov), this
whole stretch of coast is ideal for
humpback whale-watching.

In Coffs Harbour itself, walk along
the Jetty, overlooking Jetty Beach and
the marina. Visit **Dolphin Marine
Magic**, aka the Pet Porpoise Pool *(open
daily; www.dolphinmarinemagic.com.au)*
by the rivermouth, which offers close-
up encounters with dolphins and
seals. It works with the national parks
and wildlife service to provide
sanctuary for endangered marine life.

The southern end of the **Solitary
Islands Marine Park**, which stretches
the length of northern Coffs Coast, lies
off Coffs Harbour. It provides refuge for
hundreds of species of fish and corals,
and is an important habitat for
endangered grey nurse sharks. Despite
strict regulations for access to the park,
there are plenty of opportunities for
watersports. For diving and whale
watching, contact **Jetty Dive Centre**

*(398 Harbour Drive, The Jetty Strip; 02 6651
1611; www.jettydive.com.au)*. For
information about walking, bird-
watching and fishing, visit **Coffs Coast
Visitor Information Centre** *(see left)*.
🚗 *From Park Beach Rd, turn left on to
Pacific Hwy (1) south and take the
Bellingen/Armidale exit on the left.*

Coffs Coast Beaches
Along the northern Coffs Coast,
Sapphire, Moonee and **Emerald
beaches** *(all signed off Pacific Hwy (1)
north)* are worth exploring for their
white sandy beaches, headlands,
inlets, coves and creeks – perfect
for swimming and picnics. To the
south are the sheltered waters of
Urunga, where the Bellingen and
Kalang rivers reach the ocean, and
the surf beaches around **Mylestom**
(both signed off Pacific Hwy (1)).

② Bellingen
NSW; 2453
This picturesque village marks the turn
from the coast towards the mountains
and the tableland beyond. Surrounded
by rich farmland and nestled on the
banks of the Bellingen River, Bellingen
tempts visitors to stay overnight and
explore its Federation architecture,
galleries and cafés. The three-storey
weatherboard and brick building of
Lodge 241 on the main street was built

Where to Stay: inexpensive under AU$150; moderate AU$150–AU$250; expensive over AU$250

as a Masonic temple in Federation style in 1912. It is now a gallery and café *(see right)*. Visit **The Old Butter Factory** *(1 Doepel St (off Waterfall Way); www. bellingen.com/butterfactory)*, a labyrinth of arts and crafts galleries, antiques shops, fashion boutiques and a café. On the third Saturday of the month, **Bellingen Park** holds one of the liveliest markets in NSW *(see p73)*.

🚗 *Take Waterfall Way (78) past tumbling cascades up to Dorrigo National Park, turning right, about 3 km (2 miles) before the town of Dorrigo. Park at the Dorrigo Rainforest Centre and Skywalk.*

Waterfall Way
A narrow winding road up the escarpment to the Dorrigo Plateau, Waterfall Way is an extremely scenic drive (take care as there are sharp turns and steep inclines). On the way, expect to see wide panoramic mountain vistas and cascading waterfalls. The first is **Newell Falls**, which has spectacular views (and a lookout with a car park) that reveal the extent of the wilderness beyond. Other pretty waterfalls along the road include **Sherrard Falls** and **Crystal Shower Falls**.

③ Dorrigo National Park
NSW; 2453
A section of the ancient Gondwana Rainforest *(see p51)*, the **Dorrigo National Park** was World Heritage-listed in 1986. The **Dorrigo Rainforest Centre and Skywalk** *(Dome Rd, Dorrigo 2453; open daily; 02 6657 2309; www.*

environment.nsw.gov.au/nationalparks/) offers a starting point for exploring the region. It has interactive displays, information and walk maps as well as a shop and café. At the rear of the centre is a viewing platform that stretches out over the edge of the escarpment with astonishing views of the rainforest. Look down on the tree canopy from the stunning Skywalk, 70 m (230 ft) in the air, or walk along the forest floor between the huge tree trunks, while keeping an eye out for bright-coloured butterflies and native birds, such as bower birds, fruit doves cockatoos and parrots. Marsupials in the forest include wallabies, possums, koalas and bandicoots. On the walks, look out for Aboriginal sites and inspirational views of McGrath's Hump and the Great Escarpment.

There are forest walks that range from easy 15-minute strolls to serious 4½-hour hikes, including ranger-guided **Discovery Tours** *(book at the Rainforest Centre)*. Wheelchairs can access the boardwalks and child carry-packs are available. It is also possible to drive 10 km (6 miles) along Dome Road to the Never Never picnic area and set off on walks from there.

🚗 *Continue up Waterfall Way (78). Follow the signs into Dorrigo.*

Below left Dorrigo National Park seen from the Rainforest Centre **Below** The Dorrigo Rainforest Visitor Centre with café and shop **Below right** Fertile, green farmland around the town of Dorrigo

EAT AND DRINK

COFFS HARBOUR
Wild Harvest Seafood Restaurant *moderate*
Wild Harvest is a co-op owned by 45 local fishermen. Not surprisingly, it specializes in fresh seafood meals, served in a relaxed, licensed restaurant overlooking the harbour. The co-op also offers fresh and cooked seafood to take away from retail outlets along the wharf.
69 Marina Drive, Coffs Harbour 2450; 02 6652 2811; www.coffsfishcoop.com.au

Tahruah Thai Restaurant *moderate*
This traditional Thai restaurant has a good reputation with the locals. Its open kitchen provides diners with a chance to witness their meals being prepared, amid the tantalizing aroma of fragrant spices.
366 Harbour Drive, Coffs Harbour 2450; 02 6651 5992

BELLINGEN
Lodge 241 Gallery Café *moderate*
This building, at the mountain end of town, is one of Bellingen's finest examples of Federation architecture. It serves excellent food and is a great place by the river to stop for a coffee.
117–212 Hyde Street, 2454; 02 6655 2470; www.bellingen.com/thelodge; open Wed–Sun

Above left Brightly painted shop façade in Nimbin **Above right** Dangar Falls as they begin their 30-m (100-ft) plunge

VISITING ARMIDALE

Armidale Visitor Information Centre
The centre can provide information on and bookings for all Armidale's cultural events and other activities in the area.
82 Marsh St, 2350 (behind the Mobil service station); 02 6770 3888; www. armidaletourism.com.au; open daily

WHERE TO STAY

AROUND DORRIGO

Matt & Dina's Ridgetop Hideaway *inexpensive*
This self-contained stone house with kitchen facilities has three bedrooms, a wood fire and large spa bath. The ingredients for a delicious breakfast are supplied. The house is located 5 km (3 miles) north of Dorrigo and also offers stunning views.
44 Parberys Lane, 2453; 02 6657 2243; www.ridgetophideaway.com.au

EBOR

Ebor Falls Hotel Motel *moderate*
A clean and comfortable hotel, with a decent restaurant. It is a useful place for local information and a half-hour return walk to the falls.
Waterfall Way, Ebor 2453; 02 6775 9155; www.eborfallshotelmotel.com.au

ARMIDALE

Cotswold Gardens *moderate*
This heritage building has 24 guest rooms in a country cottage-style with an old-world charm. Close to town, it also has its own restaurant, a boutique atmosphere and offers plenty of personal attention.
34 Marsh St, 2350; 02 6772 8222; www. cotswoldgardensarmidale.com.au

Petersons Guesthouse *expensive*
Located within the grounds of Petersons Armidale Winery and Vineyard, this guest house offers a luxury stay in a restored historic 1912 homestead.
Dangarsleigh Rd, 2350; 02 6772 0422; www.petersonsguesthouse.com.au

➍ Dorrigo
NSW; 2453
On Waterfall Way, Dorrigo is the hub of this region, with a strong community spirit that keeps the public spaces well-maintained. **Heritage Hotel Motel Dorrigo** on the main street is a classic example of Federation architecture and a good place to eat *(see right)*. Take the short drive to **Dangar Falls** *(turn right to the falls at the monument in town, along Falls Rd)*, which plunge 30 m (100 ft) over a basalt rock face. There is a viewing platform by the car park with a stunning top-down view. It is also a lovely place for a picnic.

Trompe l'oeil shopfront, Nimbin

🚗 *From Dorrigo, continue on Waterfall Way (78) to Ebor.*

Federation Architecture
Federation architecture refers to a style prevalent in the period c1890–1920. The term refers to Australia's Federation, when its six colonies became the Commonwealth of Australia on 1 January 1901. There are many examples of the style in NSW, including several in Bellingen, such as **The Old Bellingen Chambers** *(1 Oak St)* and in Dorrigo, such as the **Heritage Hotel Motel Dorrigo** *(www. hotelmoteldorrigo.com.au)*.

➎ Ebor
NSW; 2453
This tiny town (roughly 100 residents) is next to the gorgeous two-tier **Ebor Falls** just to the south and has a general store and a roadhouse (selling petrol and food). Ebor is also known for its trout fishing, attracting anglers from around the world. The Ebor Falls Hotel Motel *(see left)* can provide information on fishing. Anglers may wish to visit

the **L P Dutton Trout Hatchery** *(open daily; 02 6775 9139)*, off Waterfall Way south, where two million trout are bred each year for release into the rivers.

Off Waterfall Way to Armidale, a right turn *(signed)* leads to **Cathedral Rock National Park** *(02 6657 2309; www. environment.nsw.gov.au)*, famous for its boulders, granite tors and wedge-tailed eagles. Access to the park is by unpaved roads, so ask about road conditions at the roadhouse in Ebor – and carry plenty of water and a full tank of petrol.

🚗 *From Ebor, continue along Waterfall Way (78) to Armidale.*

➏ Armidale
NSW; 2350
With churches, a university, several museums, cinema and theatres, as well as regular musicals and classical and choral performances, Armidale is the major cultural centre on the New England Tableland. It is also the highest, sitting at 1,000 m (3,300 ft) above sea level. The **New England Regional Art Museum** *(closed Mon; www.neram. com.au)*, regarded as the best of its kind in NSW, has valuable collections. Next door, the extensive **Aboriginal Cultural Centre and Keeping Place** *(open daily)* includes a film-viewing area and a bush tucker walk. **Armidale Playhouse Theatre** *(309 Beardy St; www. armidaleplayhouse.org.au)* puts on a season of amateur shows in March. A **heritage walk map** can be obtained from the Visitor Information Centre.

🚗 *From Erskine St take Glen Innes Rd to the New England Hwy (15) north to Glen Innes. This road is known as "The New England Country Way" and connects Sydney and Brisbane.*

Where to Stay: inexpensive under AU$150; moderate AU$150–AU$250; expensive over AU$250

❼ Glen Innes
NSW; 2370

This town is known as "Celtic Country" due to the large number of Scottish settlers. The heritage is valued by the residents, who have their own **Standing Stones** – a sort of mini-Stonehenge – to celebrate the community's Celtic roots. An annual spring food festival called **Gourmet in the Glen** is held in King Edward Park and the agricultural **Glen Innes Show** is held in February. Check the **Visitor Information Centre** *(02 6730 2400)*, a Tudor-style building on New England Highway, for details.

🚗 *Follow the New England Hwy (15) to Tenterfield.*

❽ Tenterfield
NSW; 2372

A symbolic town, Tenterfield is known to Australians as "The Birthplace of Our Nation" – Sir Henry Parkes delivered his Federation Speech here on 24 October 1889. It has historic buildings aplenty, such as the **Tenterfied Saddlery** *(123 High St; www.tenterfieldsaddler.com; open daily)*, built in 1860 of quarried blue granite. This National Trust-listed building was immortalized in the

song "Tenterfield Saddler" (1972), written by "The Boy from Oz" – Australian singer-songwriter Peter Allen – as a tribute to his grandfather, who was the town saddle maker for over 50 years. For more information on the town's history and buildings, stop at the **Tenterfield Visitor Centre** *(Rouse St; 02 6736 1082)*. Also ask about access to nearby **Bald Rock National Park** to see the famous exposed 200-m (650-ft) high granite-type rock that gives the park its name.

🚗 *Take Bruxner Hwy (44) to South Lismore. To bypass Lismore, take Union St exit, turn left on Bridge St, then left on Terania St, which becomes Nimbin Rd, and follow it to Nimbin.*

❾ Nimbin
NSW; 2480

In the heart of so-called "Rainbow Country", Nimbin's shops, cafés and public spaces are all brightly painted. A dairy-farming and banana-growing area, Nimbin became a major centre of the alternative counter-culture movement in the 1960s and 70s. Communities grew up in the hills and self-subsistence and art collectives were the order of the day. Today, Nimbin is still an alternative hang-out, but it is also a thriving business centre, skilfully balancing community interests with tourism aspirations. The colourful stalls and shops make the town an interesting place to wander through – visit the **Nimbin Museum** *(62 Cullen St, 2480)* for local art and artifacts.

🚗 *Head north on Cullen St to Blue Knob Rd, then right on Kyogle Rd, which becomes Riverview St and bends right into Wollumbin St in Murwillumbah. Park in Knox Park car park on right.*

Above Classic Australian-style architecture in the centre of Nimbin **Centre left** Colourful, hippy-heritage Cullen Street, Nimbin

EAT AND DRINK

DORRIGO

Heritage Hotel Motel Dorrigo *moderate*
This hotel's family bistro offers fresh local produce, such as honey-smoked trout, on a menu that changes regularly.
Cnr Hickory & Cudgery St, 2453; 02 6657 2016; www.hotelmoteldorrigo.com.au

ARMIDALE

The Wicklow *moderate*
Serving an extensive menu cooked with fresh, local produce, this hotel restaurant is child-friendly and has a relaxed atmosphere and a courtyard.
Cnr Dumaresq & Marsh St, 2350; 02 6772 2421; www.wicklow.com.au

Manor at Cotswold Gardens *expensive*
A classy yet relaxed restaurant, the Manor offers fresh local ingredients cooked in an international style.
34 Marsh St, 2350; 02 6772 8222; www.cotswoldgardensarmidale.com.au

GLEN INNES

The Crystal Room Glen Innes & District Services Club *moderate*
This small, classy and modern club offers a great Australian menu with seafood, steak, lamb and pasta dishes. It serves a roast of the day and a pie of the day.
Cnr Grey St, 2370; 02 6732 1355; www.giservices.com.au

Below The rolling green farmland of the New England Tableland

VISITING MURWILLUMBAH

Parking
There is on-street parking along **Main Street** and surrounding streets and all-day parking at **Knox Park** (right down Wollumbin St on the way into town).

Visitor Centre & World Heritage Rainforest Centre
Alma St & Tweed Valley Way, 2484; 02 6672 1340; open daily.

WHERE TO STAY

MURWILLUMBAH

Town Palms Motel *inexpensive*
Centrally located and family friendly, the Town Palms Motel offers decent rooms in the heart of the CBD.
3 Wharf St, 2484; 02 6672 8600

AROUND MURWILLUMBAH

Hillcrest Mountain View Retreat *moderate*
Offering a luxury B&B or self-contained cottage, the accommodation here is relaxed and friendly with spa baths and a solar-heated pool. This retreat does not cater for children. Leave Murwillumbah north on Queensland Rd, then left on Numinbah Rd, and right at Crystal Creek.
Upper Crystal Creek Rd, 2484; 02 6679 1023; www.hillcrestbb.com

TWEED HEADS

Berger Houseboats *moderate*
A houseboat on the Tweed River makes an interesting weekend stop – cruise where the spirit leads (lessons are provided). It is also an excellent way to get close to the wildlife.
Cnr Dry Dock Rd & Minjungbul Drive, 2486; 07 5524 3222; www.bergerhouseboats.com.au

❿ Murwillumbah
NSW; 2484

Murwillumbah's name comes from the Aboriginal for "place of many possums", although the town is better known today for its stunning river location, eco-tourism retreats, museums and art galleries. Relax with a coffee or a cool drink overlooking the surrounding landscape before setting off on a tour of the town's Federation architecture and art galleries.

A one-hour walking tour

From Know Park walk up Wollumbin Street and turn right up Nullum Street to the **Uniting Church** ① on Main Street. From here, there are views across farm-quilted countryside and the river. Walk down Main Steet, passing **St Stephen's Cathedral** ②, and turn into Queensland Road and walk up to the **Tweed River Regional Museum** ③ *(2 Queensland Rd; open 11am–3.30pm Wed & Fri and the 4th Sun of each month)*. The museum's collection includes a rare 1896 steam engine, a specialist radio collection and countless historical photographs. Return to Main Street and head towards the river, turn right to walk down to Wharf Street, taking note of the eclectic mix of architecture, including examples of Colonial, Federation and Art Deco styles. The antique shop and Town Palms Motel *(see left)* at the end of the street are two Art Deco classics. Turn left into Tumbulgum Road and follow it to the **Tweed**

War Memorial, Murwillumbah

Shire Civic and Cultural Centre ④. There is a Remembrance Wall and War Memorial in the park outside the centre. Cross Tumbulgum Road and follow it back over Wharf Street, continuing along Commercial Road, past the bridge and the intersection at Wollumbin Street, where visitors can take a look at the **Treasures of the Tweed Mural** ⑤. This art project features rare and endangered flora and fauna of the Tweed Valley region, painted by local artists. Walk back along Commercial Road to the bridge. Cross the river to the **Visitor Centre and World Heritage Rainforest Centre** ⑥ to pick up maps for Mount Warning and other walks, as well as information about local architecture, festivals and events. Retrace the route over the bridge and along Wharf Street, then Main Street, to the car park.

Murwillumbah's best art gallery is outside town, a short drive away. Drive back along Main Street, Wharf Street and over the bridge, then turn right

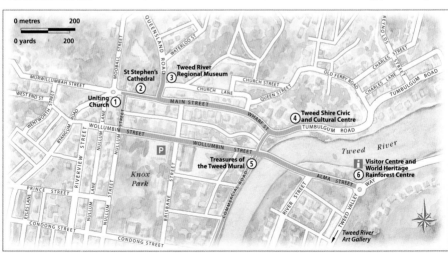

Above The tranquil Tweed River flowing through a pastoral landscape at Muriwillumbah, with Mount Warning in the background **Above right** Cyclist on a quiet road leading to Murwillumbah

along Tweed Valley Way for the **Tweed River Art Gallery** *(Cnr Mistral Rd & Tweed Valley Way; closed Mon & Tue)*. The gallery houses Australian and international art and also has great views of Mount Warning and the Tweed Valley.

Murwillumbah holds two major annual festivals. First held in 1955, the Tweed Valley Banana Festival is a lively event with a street parade, and the Speed on Tweed festival sees hundreds of classic racing cars from Australia and around the world gathered for sprint-racing through the town's streets.

🚗 *Take Tweed Valley Way. Turn left into Riverside Drive and then into Tumbulgum – the turn-off is on the left, past the Condong sugar mill.*

Mount Warning

Mount Warning, a sacred place of the Bundjalung people, is the first place in mainland Australia to see the sun rise. To visit Mount Warning in Wollumbin National Park, take Kyogle Road west from Murwillumbah, turn right on to Mount Warning Road up to Breakfast Creek picnic area at the park's entrance. Allow four hours for the 9-km (5-mile) walk; a reasonable level of fitness is required, as are good walking shoes *(www.mtwarning.com)*.

11 Tumbulgum
NSW; 2490
It is hard to conceive of a more picturesque village than Tumbulgum (pronounced tum-BUL-gim). The

quaint one-street village sits on the banks of the wide, slow-moving Tweed River, overlooked by Mount Warning, and is an ideal spot for a riverside picnic or a cream tea in one of its cafés. Visit **Tumbulgum Art Gallery** *(110 Riverside Drive; closed Mon)* for a range of candles, soaps and jewellery, alternatively take a walk along the river bank.

🚗 *Take Tweed Valley Way to the Pacific Hwy (1) into Tweed Heads.*

12 Tweed Heads
NSW; 2485
Tweed Heads *(see p60)* is a lively town with access to some great beaches. Along with its "twin town", Coolangatta across the border in Queensland, it is known as the gateway to Queensland's Gold Coast. Drop in to the **Visitor Information Centre** *(see right)* for information about activities up and down the coast or, for an account of local history, visit the **Tweed River Regional Museum** *(Pioneer Pk, 230 Kennedy Dr; www.tweed.nsw.gov.au)*.

Below Water-skiing on the Tweed River between Murwillumbah and Tweed Heads

VISITING TWEED HEADS

Visitor Information Centre
Corner of Bay & Wharf Street, 2485; 07 5536 6737; www.tweedtourism.com.au; open daily

EAT AND DRINK

MURWILLUMBAH

The White Olive *inexpensive*
This family-run modern Italian restaurant is a favourite with locals.
7 Nullum St, 2484; 02 6672 3000; www.thewhiteolive.com.au

TUMBULGUM

Bird Wing Café and Curios *inexpensive*
This cafe overlooks the Tweed River, and as well as great food it also sells art, books, second-hand stuff – and the best pizza in town.
116 Riverside Drive, 2490; 02 6676 6048; www.tweedcoolangatta.com.au

Eat and Drink: inexpensive under AU$60; moderate AU$60–AU$100; expensive over AU$100

Mountains, Valleys and Vines

Sydney to Brooklyn

Highlights

- **Incomparable harbour**
  See Sydney's scenic heart by taking a ferry across its iconic harbour

- **Blue Mountains**
  Look out across an ocean of trees from a scary height aboard the Scenic Skyway cable car at Katoomba

- **Valley vines**
  Drink some of the finest Australian wines – especially the sparkling Shiraz – in the renowned Hunter Valley

- **Gourmet river**
  Cruise down the tranquil waterways of the Hawkesbury River, tasting the delightful produce of the oyster farms

The unmistakable Sydney Opera House and harbour

Mountains, Valleys and Vines

From the heart of cosmopolitan Sydney, west to the dramatic escarpments, gullies, cliffs and flat peaks of the Blue Mountains, this drive goes north on the Bells Line of Road, across to the Hawkesbury River and along the length of the Hunter Valley. Finally, it heads south towards Sydney, to the mouth of the Hawkesbury River, at the scenic fishing village of Brooklyn. The trip takes in the sights of Sydney's city centre and its world-famous harbour, before taking more of a natural focus, offering a taste of Royal National Park and the Blue Mountains National Park, and descending to cross Yengo National Park, along one of the most scenic stretches of the drive. Expect wine, cheese, olives and Art Deco architecture along the way, as well as some of the most stunning vistas in the state.

Above Beautiful fertile landscapes in the Lower Hunter Valley, *see p89*

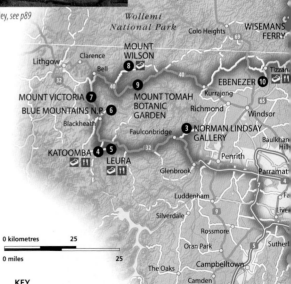

ACTIVITIES

Go camping on an island in Sydney Harbour

Make a splash canyoning in the Blue Mountains

Hang out in the open air on the Scenic Skyway cable car in Katoomba

Take a trip down memory lane at the Leuralla Toy and Railway Museum near Leura

Smell the flowers in the colourful gardens of Mount Wilson

Take a fully guided tasting tour of the Hunter Valley's vineyards

Enjoy the scenic Hawkesbury River with a Brooklyn Water Taxi Tour

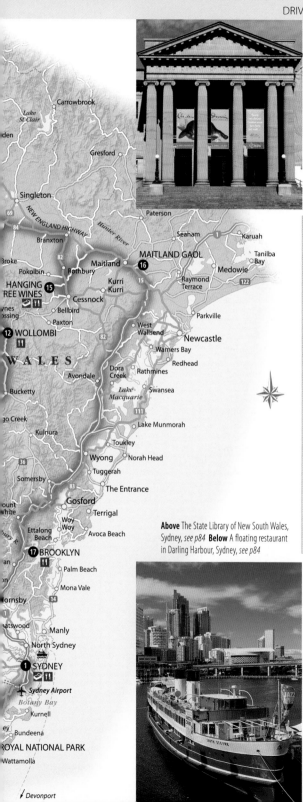

Above The State Library of New South Wales, Sydney, *see p84* **Below** A floating restaurant in Darling Harbour, Sydney, *see p84*

PLAN YOUR DRIVE

Start/finish: Sydney to Brooklyn.

Number of days: 4–5 days, allowing half a day for the Sydney city walk and at least half a day to drive from Ebenezer to Denman.

Distance: Approx. 766 km (476 miles).

Road conditions: Mostly sealed and signposted, with some very narrow, winding roads used by trucks. The roads through the Blue Mountains are sometimes snowbound in winter and the roads from Wisemans Ferry to Wollombi are unsealed dirt roads, but quite driveable in good conditions.

When to go: Highly changeable weather in the Blue Mountains most of the year, with a severe bushfire risk in summer. April to May is the most scenic time to go, with a fabulous display of autumn leaves.

Opening times: Most museums and shops are open 9am–5pm. It is often difficult to find restaurants open in smaller towns on Mon & Tue nights.

Main market days: Sydney: Balmain, Sat; Glebe, Sat; Paddington, Sat; The Rocks, Sat & Sun; **Blue Mountains National Park:** Springwood, 2nd Sat of the month; **Leura:** 1st Sun of the month; **Maitland:** 1st Sun of the month, Apr–Dec.

Shopping: In Sydney, the Queen Victoria Building *(www.qvb.com.au)* has some brilliant designer boutiques, and Oxford Street is a top spot for shopping. There is also the gigantic Japanese bookshop Kinokuniya *(Level 2, The Galeries Victoria, 550 George St; 02 9262 7996; www.kinokuniya.com)*. In the Blue Mountains, Leura's tree-lined mall and arcades are filled with speciality shops selling candles and sweets. Elsewhere on the drive, the shopping is limited, but Hunter Valley is good for buying wines, olive oil and cheeses.

Major festivals: Sydney: Sydney Festival, Feb; **Katoomba:** Yulefest, Jun–Aug; **Wollombi:** Wollombi Valley Scarecrow Festival, Apr–May; **Hunter Valley** Hunter Valley Wine and Food Month, Jun.

① Sydney
New South Wales (NSW); 2000

A vast urban sprawl snaking around huge national parks, and the stunning Botany Bay and Sydney Harbour, Australia's biggest city is more a collection of villages than a unified metropolis. From the well-forested North Shore to the built-up city centre, and from the exclusive Eastern Suburbs and the southern reaches fringing Royal National Park to the well-known beaches of Bondi and Manly, Sydney has something for everyone. This walk goes through the 19th-century heart of Sydney en route to the iconic Sydney Opera House, before returning by ferry across the harbour.

A three-hour walking tour

From the Secure Parking car park on Harris Street, turn right into Allen Street, cross Pyrmont Street, continue along Murray Street and turn right to reach Pyrmont Bridge. Cross the **Pyrmont Bridge** ① to Cockle Bay Wharf. The central portion of the 1902 bridge swivels out to allow tall ships to sail underneath, and was one of the first of its type to be powered by electricity. Go straight ahead and up the stairs to road level, along Market Street and into the beautiful **Queen Victoria Building** ② *(open daily; www.qvb.com.au)* on the right. The Neo-Romanesque QVB, as it is known, was built in 1898 on the site of the old Sydney markets. Exit the far end of the QVB to Druitt Street and turn left to Park Street and on to Hyde Park. Turn left up Elizabeth Street to the Neo-Gothic 1878 **Great Synagogue** ③ *(tours Tue & Thu at noon; 02 9267 2477; www. greatsynagogue.org.au)*, one of the oldest and most aesthetically impressive synagogues in Australia. Cross back into Hyde Park, heading left to the ornate 1934 Archibald Fountain. Exit the park north, up Macquarie Street, and walk past a string of impressive 19th-century buildings: the **Hyde Park Barracks** ④ (1817) *(open daily; 02 8239 2311; www.hht. net.au)*, now a museum of convict history; **The Mint** ⑤ (1811) *(open daily; 02 8239 2288; www.hht.net.au)*, originally part of the hospital and site of Australia's first coin factory; the **Sydney Hospital** ⑥ (1811), the oldest hospital building in Australia, with the shiny-snouted Il Porcellino outside (see box, p88); the understated **Parliament House** ⑦ (1829); and

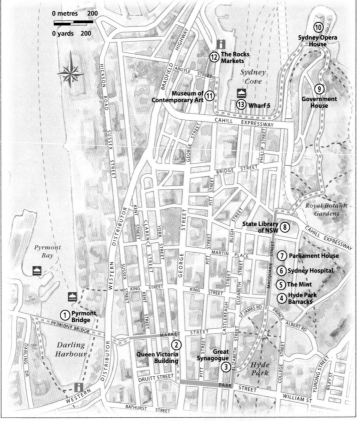

the **State Library of NSW** ⑧ (1869) *(open daily; 02 9273 1414; www.sl.nsw. gov.au)*. Head diagonally right across the road to the Mershead Fountain, and into the Royal Botanic Gardens. Walk towards the crenellated Sydney Conservatorium of Music and, keeping it on the left, head straight past on to **Government House** ⑨ *(open daily; 02 9931 5222; www.hht.net.au)*, and all the way to the harbour wall. Head round to the left, towards the fabulous **Sydney Opera House** ⑩ *(open daily; 02 9250 7250; www. sydneyoperahouse.com)* and further around to Sydney Cove and Circular Quay. Walk around the quay, past the bustling ferry terminals, in front of the **Museum of Contemporary Art** ⑪ *(open daily; 02 9245 2400; www.mca.com. au)*, for a better view of the Opera House. Turn left into Argyle Street and right into George Street, which on weekends thrums with **The Rocks Markets** ⑫ *(open Sat & Sun; 02 9240 8500; www.therocks.com)*. Finally, to return, board the ferry *(www. sydneyferries.info)* from **Wharf 5** ⑬ to Pyrmont Bay and the car park.

🚗 *From the car park, turn onto Darling Drive south and follow green sign up ramp to Airport/Wollongong. Keep following green signs to Wollongong, turn left onto Acacia Rd and left onto Farnell Drive for Royal National Park.*

❷ Royal National Park
Sydney, NSW; 2232
Before leaving Sydney, sample some of the fabulous greenery of the world's oldest national park. Established in 1879, the 60-sq km (23-sq mile) Royal National Park is a medley of waterways, beaches and coastal and inland walking trails. It is as peaceful as if it were a million miles from the city, especially during the week. Stop at the visitors' centre at **Audley** *(open daily; 02 9542 0648; www.environment. nsw.gov.au/nationalparks/)* for maps and directions, then drive up Highway 68 to the waterfalls, rockpools and beach at **Wattamolla**. Finally, follow Bundeena Drive back down to **Bundeena** for a coffee on the wharf overlooking the bay – perhaps even enjoying a refreshing swim.

🚗 *Return to Princes Hwy (1) and turn left. Exit right onto Heathcote Rd (6) and head north, merging left off Heathcote Rd onto the South Western Hwy (5) west, then take Westlink (M7) north. Exit on Western Mwy (4) west, then Gt Western Hwy (32). At Faulconbridge, brown signs lead to Norman Lindsay Gallery.*

❸ Norman Lindsay Gallery
14 Norman Lindsay Crescent, Faulconbridge, NSW; 2776
Creator of the children's classic *The Magic Pudding*, artist, illustrator, sculptor and model ship builder, the irreverent Norman Lindsay (1879–1969) left behind a beautiful house, Springwood, which is now the Norman Lindsay Gallery *(open daily; 02 4751 1067; www.normanlindsay.com.au)*. After acquiring the property in 1912, Lindsay landscaped the garden, adding pergolas, pools and retaining walls. Take a guided tour of the grounds, studded with provocative statues of nymphs and nudes, learn about the goings on in the studio, and get an insight into a remarkable man.

🚗 *Continue along Norman Lindsay Parade then right onto Chapman Parade. Turn left onto Grose Rd and right onto the Gt Western Hwy (32). Turn left at Parke St, left at Gang Gang St and right at Katoomba St.*

Right Waterfall at Wattamolla, in the Royal National Park

Above left Archibald Fountain, Hyde Park, Sydney **Above centre** Sydney Opera House **Above right** Bondi Beach, Sydney

---

VISITING SYDNEY

Parking
Park at the **Secure Parking** car park. *320 Harris St (enter via Allen St), Darling Harbour, 2000; 1300 727 483.*

Visitor Information
A visitor centre is located near the start of the walk, in **Darling Harbour**. *Palm Grove, between Cockle Bay Wharf and Harbourside, 2000; 02 9240 8500; www.sydneyvisitorcentre.com.au*

EAT AND DRINK IN SYDNEY

David Jones Foodhall *inexpensive*
With hot meals to go, 250 sorts of bread and a deli, this store has all the ingredients for an urban picnic. *65–77 Market St, 2000; 02 9266 5544 www.davidjones.com.au*

Swagman's Post Cafe *moderate*
A tranquil, courtyard garden in The Rocks, with friendly service and good food that does not cost the earth. *35 George St, 2000; 02 9241 5557*

Botanic Restaurant *expensive*
Stylish dining in the surrounds of the lovely Botanic Gardens, this is a smart but laid-back lunch option. *Mrs Macquaries Rd, 2000; 02 9241 2419; www.trippaswhite.com.au*

Above Road sign on the drive route to the Blue Mountains National Park

VISITING THE BLUE MOUNTAINS

Visitor Centre
Echo Point, Katoomba, 2780; 1 300 653 408; www.visitbluemountains.com.au

WHERE TO STAY

KATOOMBA

The Carrington *moderate*
This Art Deco architectural gem has been in Katoomba for over a century. Rooms are spacious, and many have views over the town towards the Three Sisters. The antique elevator and large lounge area complete the package.
15–47 Katoomba St, 2780; 02 4782 1111; www.thecarrington.com.au

Waratah Cottages *moderate*
Fully self-contained, boutique accommodation in a cottage close to the main drag. It comes with breakfast provisions, top-notch appliances and two smart double bedrooms.
30 Waratah Ave, 2780; 02 4782 6740; www.waratahcottage.com.au

LEURA

The Old Leura Dairy *moderate*
A collection of quirky buildings have been turned into chic accommodation in this eco-retreat. It offers excellent breakfasts and dining, as well as landscaped gardens.
61 Kings Rd, 2780; 02 4782 0700; www.oldleuradairy.com.au

AROUND MOUNT WILSON

Chimney Cottage *expensive*
These three delightful themed stays – Alpine, English country or Heritage – lie 8 km (5 miles) off the Bells Line of Road between Bell and Mount Tomah. Charming and self-contained, the cottages also have breakfast provisions.
Waterfall Rd, 2786; 02 4756 2022; www.chimneycottage.com.au

④ Katoomba
NSW; 2780
Part tourist town, part alternative enclave and part outdoor gallery of Art Deco architecture, Katoomba is the commercial heart of the Blue Mountains and a good base to explore the nearby forest. Often cloaked in mist, its steep main street has a collection of fine second-hand book and antique shops and stylish cafés.

As soon as the mist clears over Katoomba, head over to **Echo Point** *(Echo Point Rd, 2780)* at the southern edge of town to see the **Three Sisters** rock formation and the huge gulf of forest. Paths lead down to the cliff itself, and around its rim to the left to a walkway between two of the Three Sisters, or they lead right, to **Scenic World** *(open daily; 02 4780 0200; www.scenicworld.com.au)*. The main attraction here is the spectacular Scenic Skyway – the best way to get an idea of the majesty and scale of the landscape – which glides a stomach-churning 270 m (885 ft) above the valley floor.
🚗 *Follow Cliff Drive east and green Sydney sign (left) to park in Leura Mall.*

Mountain Adventures

A rugged landscape often requires an intrepid approach to fully appreciate it. The **Blue Mountains Adventure Company** *(84a Bathurst Road, Katoomba, 2780; 02 4782 1271; www.bmac.com.au)* are experts at climbing and abseiling, and they also arrange guided mountain-biking, bushwalk and canyoning excursions into the mountains from Katoomba.

---

⑤ Leura
NSW; 2780
Like Katoomba's sophisticated aunt, nearby Leura is a pocket of upmarket restaurants and boutiques along a pretty main street, Leura Mall, which is lined with flowering cherry trees. Here, the houses are more like estates, and the gardens are wonderful, especially in autumn. From Leura Mall, turn right into Craigend Street and right into Everglades Avenue to the heritage-listed **Everglades Gardens** *(open daily; 02 4784 1938; www.everglades.org.au)*. These are a wonderful celebration of the high society that has long made Leura home. With an Art Deco mansion at its centre, the 5 hectares (12 acres) of European-style manicured gardens, designed in the 1930s by Danish architect Paul Sorenson, mesh seamlessly with patches of bushland, and are the perfect place for a picnic.
🚗 *Return to Craigend St, and left to Leura Mall, right to Gt Western Hwy (32) and left to Blackheath. Take Govetts Leap Rd on the right to the car park.*

⑥ Blue Mountains National Park
Great Western Hwy, NSW; 2780
Given the moody weather in the Blue Mountains, there is no guarantee of seeing the coloured haze that gives them their name. Some say that it is a blanket of eucalyptus oil vapour created by the forest. Others that it is light reflecting off the leaves, or the way certain particles interact with electromagnetic radiation. Whatever the case, on a fine day, it is an amazing

Below The spectacular rock towers of the Three Sisters, Echo Point

sight – a rugged landscape of rolling forest, giant boulders and plunging cliffs, featuring rainforest, woodlands and swamps. Home to kangaroos, wombats and many other creatures, the park is also a good place to spot colourful lyre birds.

For spectacular views of Govetts and Grose gorges, drive to **Govett's Leap** *(Govetts Leap Rd, 2785)*. This is a 180-m (590-ft) cascade, smashing itself on rocks below the cliff and the highest single-drop waterfall in the Blue Mountains. Known by the name of a surveyor, William Govett (1831), rather than its former moniker of Bridal Veil Falls, this is the most accessible waterfall in the area.

🚗 *Return to the Gt Western Hwy (32), turn right and drive to Mt Victoria, turning right into Station St for parking.*

Leuralla Toy & Railway Museum
One of the oldest heritage-listed houses in the Blue Mountains, **Leuralla** *(36 Olympian Parade, Leura, 2780; 02 4784 1169; www.toyand railwaymuseum.com.au; 10am–5pm daily)* is home to the largest toy, doll and model train collection. Adults and kids alike will enjoy browsing the antique tin toys from Victorian times and marvelling at the huge teddy bear collection. The wonderful garden features a model of a working railway.

⑦ Mount Victoria
NSW; 2786
Spilling down from the 1876 Post Office, the village of Mount Victoria is blessed with a number of historic buildings, including the Imperial Hotel and the **Mount Victoria & District Historical Society Museum** *(open Sat & Sun pm; 02 4787 1210)*. Housed in the heritage-listed Mount Victoria Railway Station, it offers a nostalgic insight into the lives of the early European settlers.

🚗 *Head north up Darling Causeway, turn right onto Bells Line of Road (40) and left onto Mt Wilson Rd to Mt Wilson.*

⑧ Mount Wilson
NSW; 2786
At its best in autumn, with golden leaves from its avenues of trees dusting the roads, the tiny township of **Mount Wilson** is one big garden display. Three gardens are open most of the year, others seasonally: **Windyridge** *(Queens Ave, 2786; 02 4756 2019; www.windyridge. com.au)* dates from 1877 and features delightful maples, dogwoods and nyssas; **Merry Garth** *(Davies Lane, 2786; 02 4756 2121)* has fine native sassafrass and coachwood, and a rare New Zealand Rimu Pine; and gently sloping **Sefton Cottage** *(Church Lane, 2786; 02 4756 2034)*.

🚗 *Drive back down Mt Wilson Rd, and left onto the Bells Line of Road (40). Mt Tomah Botanic Garden is on the right.*

Above left The beautiful 1930s Everglades Garden, Leura **Above right** The 1878 heritage Imperial Hotel, Mount Victoria

EAT AND DRINK

KATOOMBA
Common Ground Cafe *inexpensive*
This place serves good food – especially bakery fare – in a hand-made wooden interior that looks like an enchanted forest. Try the South American Yerba Matte tea.
45 Waratah St, cnr 214 Katoomba St, 2780; 02 4782 9744; closed Fri pm & Sat

Café Zuppa *inexpensive*
A funky student hangout serving hearty, great-value meals with a healthy twist and a cool aesthetic, right at the top end of town.
36 Katoomba St, 2780; 02 4782 9247

LEURA
Red Door Cafe *moderate*
Resisting having three courses at this chic café is futile. Three tiers of delectable soups, tarts, tortes and more, make this a rewarding meal.
134 The Mall, 2780; 02 4784 1328

Left Beautiful golden autumn foliage in Mount Wilson

Above Buildings of the Tizzana Winery, Ebenezer

WHERE TO STAY

EBENEZER

Tizzana Winery B&B *expensive*
A marvellous old stone building overlooking a vineyard, lovingly restored by Peter and Carolyn Auld, with two suites, a large common lounge and tea and coffee facilities. This functions more like a five-star boutique hotel than a B&B, with a five-course dinner, à la carte breakfast, pillow menu and spa treatments.
518 Tizzana Rd, 2756; 02 4579 1150; www.tizzana.com.au

Below Misty autumn morning at Mount Tomah Botanic Garden

⑨ Mount Tomah Botanic Garden

Bells Line of Road, NSW; 2758
At 1,000 m (3,280 ft) above sea level, **Mount Tomah Botanic Garden** *(open daily; www.mounttomahbotanicgarden. com.au)* is the cool-climate extension of The Royal Botanic Gardens in Sydney *(see p85)*. It is a stunning place, even in the frequent wet fog, with tiny waterfalls flowing down the side of Mount Tomah to giant koi-stocked pools. The gardens afford easy access to the rainforest running along the ridge, as well as offering a close-up look at a hillside wetland known as a "hanging swamp", with plenty of short trails and boardwalks throughout its specialized sections. The well-regarded restaurant, has glorious views from its terrace.

🚗 *Turn right onto Bells Line of Road and continue through Kurrajong, turning right to rejoin Bells Line of Road (40), left on Comleroy Rd, and right onto Blaxlands Ridge Rd. Turn right onto Singleton/Putty Rd, sharp left onto Bull Ridge Rd, right onto West Portland Rd and right onto Sackville Rd. Turn left onto Tizzana Rd and fork right onto Coromandel Rd.*

⑩ Ebenezer

NSW; 2756
This historic village is spread along the roads and lacks an obvious focal point. However, it is most famous as the home of Australia's oldest church. Since 1809, **Ebenezer Church** *(open 10am–3pm; 02 4579 9350; www.ebenezerchurch.org.au)* has been serving the spiritual needs of the local

Bottle of Tizzana's Aleatica rosé wine

Presbyterian community. This unassuming sandstone structure, with its well-tended little cemetery, was built by Scottish migrants. The 15 pioneer families involved in the early history of the church went on to play an important role in the development of the colony of New South Wales, and today visitors can enjoy cream tea in the 1817 **Schoolmasters House**, and take a self-guided tour of the church and grounds.

Ebenezer's other main draw is the **Tizzana Winery** *(518 Tizzana Rd, 2756; www. winery.tizzana.com.au)*. Follow the brown tourist signs 5 km (3 miles) up Tizzana Road – the winery is on the right. Established by Florentine physician Dr Thomas Fiaschi (1853–1927) in 1882 *(see box)*, it is one of the few wineries in Australia to grow the rare Aleatica grape variety, and the resulting sweet rosé is a marvellous wine with hints of Turkish delight. The present owners rescued the property over 40 years ago after a catastrophic fire.

🚗 *Continue on Tizzana Rd to Sackville Ferry Rd and turn right. Cross the river on the ferry and follow the road to Wisemans Ferry Rd (65), then left on Old Northern Rd (36) to Wisemans Ferry.*

Above Weatherboard café in the relaxed, rural village of Wollombi

⑪ Wisemans Ferry

NSW; 2775

The rustic village of Wisemans Ferry is a popular rural retreat for Sydneysiders. From here, take the ferry over the river and drive along the dirt road to the tiny old cemetery of St Albans and Wollombi; it is like traversing a lost wilderness. The drive winds through the **Yengo National Park**, a wild area of deep gorges and sandstone ridges, part of the Greater Blue Mountains World Heritage Area. Along the way, the road dips under rock overhangs amid dense birdsong.

🚗 *Turn left onto Settlers Rd, and take the left fork. Follow the unsealed road*

beside the river to St Albans, and then Wollombi Rd, which becomes Mogo Creek Rd (good-quality dirt road). Turn right to sealed Gt North Rd, with sweeping views, and left to Wollombi.

⑫ Wollombi

NSW; 2325

A manicured village of hippy drop-outs and yuppie drop-ins, Wollombi is the centre of activity in a valley of the same name. It is the best stop en route to the Hunter Valley. Try the infamous Dr Jurd's Jungle Juice (originally made from leftover drinks from the night before) at the **Wollombi Tavern** *(Old North Rd, 2325; 02 4998 3261; www.wollombitavern.com.au).*

🚗 *Follow Paynes Crossing Rd, which becomes Wollombi Rd then Wollombi St at Cessnock turn. Go through Broke, and along Broke Rd. Turn left onto Golden Hwy (84), through Denman, and right onto narrow Reedy Creek Rd. Turn right onto Wybong Rd, left onto Yarraman Rd, and the winery is on the left.*

Above left Sculpture made of scrap metal on the route to Wollombi **Above right** Native trees and scrubland on the road to Wollombi

EAT AND DRINK

EBENEZER

Tizzana Winery B&B *expensive*
Gourmand hosts Peter and Carolyn Auld serve five-course dinners in the lovingly restored old stone building overlooking a vineyard.
518 Tizzana Rd, 2756; 02 4579 1150; www.tizzana.com.au

AROUND WISEMANS FERRY

Fickle Wombat *inexpensive*
This family-friendly café is in St Albans, on the road from Wisemans Ferry to Wollombi. It serves superior burgers, delicious topped *focaccia* and huge seafood platters. Fickle is a good name for it – the café only opens at weekends.
29 Bulga Rd, St Albans 2775; 02 4568 2078

WOLLOMBI

Wollombi Tavern *inexpensive*
Built on the site of an 1840s pub, the tavern sells Australian ales and local wines along with large plates of satisfying, if unsophisticated, food.
Old North Rd, 2325; 02 4998 3261; www.wollombitavern.com.au

Café Wollombi *moderate*
Inner-city foodie sensibilities combine with a relaxed country vibe to make this chilled-out cafe the perfect place to unwind with a soup, gourmet toasted sandwich or something more substantial. Perch on the hillside deck and watch the town pass by.
Opposite the General Store, 2325; 02 4998 3220

Left Wisemans Ferry across the placid Hawkesbury River

Eat and Drink: inexpensive under AU$60; moderate AU$60–AU$100; expensive over AU$100

WHERE TO STAY

AROUND PUKARA ESTATE

Grapevine Motel *moderate*
In the town of Denman, just southeast of the olive estate, this modern motel offers 17 comfortable, well-appointed rooms, with a light breakfast included in the rate. Rooms are also available in the Denman Hotel, which houses the fine Cepes Restaurant *(see right)*.
1 Ogilvie St, Denman, 2328; 02 6547 2303; www.grapevinemoteldenman.com.au

AROUND HANGING TREE WINES

Hermitage Lodge *expensive*
Each named after a local winery, these exceptional, gleaming suites boast lovely decks that overlook the property's own vines. Lots of space, great beds and full breakfast provisions are supplied for an in-room feast.
609 McDonalds Rd, Pokolbin, 2320; 02 4998 7639; www.hermitagelodge.com.au

Below Rolling green landscape at Hanging Tree Wines, Pokolbin **Below right** Main winery building, Hanging Tree Wines **Below left** Boats on the Hawkesbury River, Brooklyn

13 Yarraman Estate
700 Yarraman Rd, Wybong; 2333
Upper Hunter Valley wineries are known for a different take on the craft from their Lower Hunter Valley compatriots. **Yarraman Estate** *(open daily; 02 6547 8118; www.yarramanestate.com)* produces a range of wines for export, as well as an exclusive boutique range only available locally. Many varieties are heavily awarded, but the deep-red Chambourcin is a standout.
🚗 *Continue along Yarraman Rd, right into Ridgelands Rd, left into Wybong Rd, right into Roxburgh Rd then Mongoola Rd, left onto the Golden Hwy, through Denman, and left into Denman Rd.*

14 Pukara Estate
1440 Denman Rd, Muswellbrook; 2333
It is a good thing that olive oil is so healthy – there are over 25,000 olive trees at **Pukara Estate** *(open daily; 02 6547 1055; www.pukaraestate.com.au)*. The olives from these are used to create a lovely fruity olive oil, fully endorsed by some of the country's finest chefs. Stop by for an "oil and condiment" tasting, and enjoy a delicious platter for lunch with local cheese, olives, golden oil, caramelized balsamic vinegar and tapenade, mopped up with crackers and bread.

🚗 *Drive back down Denman Rd, and turn left onto Golden Hwy (84), right onto New England Hwy (still 84), and right onto Hwy 82, which leads to Wine Country Drive. Turn right onto O'Connors Rd for the winery.*

A Taste Apart
The winemakers of the Upper Hunter are a boutique clique, and distinguish themselves from their kin in the Lower Hunter under the umbrella of the **Winemakers of the Upper Hunter** *(www.upperhunterwine.com.au)*. For a guided tasting tour, contact **Upper Hunter Tours** *(02 6547 1030; www.upperhuntertours.com.au)* or for a gourmet experience take a tour with **Hunter Tours** *(02 4933 2537; www.huntertours.com.au)* and sample artisan cheeses, fine olive oils and breads, and hand-made chocolates, all washed down with big-tasting reds and sparkling whites.

15 Hanging Tree Wines
294 O'Connors Rd, Pokolbin; 2320
This winery features picturesque cottages and outbuildings, studded down a fertile hill into a valley. **Hanging Tree Wines** *(open Fri–Sun; 02 4998 6601; www.hangingtreewines.com.au)* has an aspect that is every bit as good as its red and white wines. However, it is the

creamy sparkling red Shiraz that really is the star – it was top rated at the main Hunter Valley Wine Show in 2005.

🚗 *Continue along O'Connors Rd, right into O'Connors Lane, and left onto Pinchen St, right onto Fletcher St and left onto Wine Country Drive. Turn right onto Lovedale Rd and right onto the New England Hwy (84). Take the Melbourne St turn off, left to East Maitland, and turn right onto John St.*

16 Maitland Gaol

6–18 John St, East Maitland; 2323
Australia's longest continuously operating prison (1844–1996) also had a reputation for being one of its hardest. Backpacker Murderer Ivan Milat was held here in the 1990s, as were a who's who of serious criminals. **Maitland Gaol** *(open daily; 02 4936 6482; www.maitlandgaol.com.au)* also happens to be a stunning sandstone creation, and a chilling, blackly humorous insight is offered into the history of the place through a self-guided audio tour. Tours by former inmates and ghost and history tours are available at weekends and some evenings.

Hawkesbury River Tours
Join a Brooklyn local aboard a water taxi for an informative and enjoyable tour of one of Sydney's most important food basins, the Hawkesbury River, where many residents continue to benefit from oyster farming and prawn fishing. The trips range from two hours to a full day, for up to 20 people *(0410 554 777; www.brooklynwatertaxis.com).*

🚗 *Drive back along John St, left onto Melbourne St, and left onto New England Hwy. Turn off right to Sydney–Newcastle Fwy (1) to Brooklyn.*

17 Brooklyn

NSW; 2083
At Sydney's northern fringes, the mouth of the Hawkesbury River is awash with oyster farms *(see right)*, fishermen and the sleek craft of wealthy Sydneysiders. The town of Brooklyn is built on cliffs behind the river banks, across a causeway from the thickly forested **Long Island Nature Reserve**. There are plenty of watersports available, such as boating, fishing and water-skiing, or explore the river islands by water taxi. Try **Hawkesbury Cruises** *(02 9985 9900; www.hawkesburycruises.com.au)*, which runs trips to historic **Dangar Island**, which Captain Arthur Phillip, founder of Sydney, discovered in 1788.

EAT AND DRINK

AROUND PUKARA ESTATE

Cepes Restaurant *moderate*
In the Denman Hotel, Denman's prime dinner spot takes steaks and fish fillets to new heights, serving modern Australian cuisine with country gusto. *3 Ogilvie St, Denman, 2328; 02 6547 2207; www.denmanhotel.com.au*

Noah's in the Valley *moderate*
A la carte dining in Muswellbrook, along Denman Rd from Pukara Estate. The modern exterior does not do justice to the food. A Comfort Inn, it has rooms. *91 Bridge St, Muswellbrook, 2333; 02 6543 2833; www. noahsinthevalley.com.au*

AROUND HANGING TREE WINES

Il Cacciatore *expensive*
This fine-dining destination is by far the best restaurant in the area. North Italian cuisine with the freshest ingredients – try the melt-in-your-mouth *gnocchi.* *609 McDonalds Rd, Pokolbin, 2320; 02 4994 7639; www.hermitagelodge.com.au*

BROOKLYN

Life Boat Seafood *moderate*
Indulge in fresh seafood in a pleasant outdoor garden setting from the retail arm of the Hawkesbury River Fishermen's Co-op. *www.brooklynwatertaxis.com*

Other options
Hire a BBQ motorboat from Brooklyn Marina and enjoy preparing your own lunch while cruising around the waters of the Hawkesbury River, or stop at one of the many oyster farms along the banks for some freshly shucked oysters *(02 9985 7722; www.brooklynmarina. com.au).*

Above Sun-parched Yarraman Estate vineyards **Below** Maitland Gaol, Australia's longest-serving prison

Glorious Gippsland

Wonthaggi to Harrietville

Highlights

- **Wilderness and wildlife**
  Explore the rugged beauty of Wilsons Promontory National Park and look for wombats and wallabies

- **Extraordinary beaches**
  Walk barefoot along secluded Squeaky Beach and enjoy the open seascapes and soft sand of Ninety Mile Beach

- **Scenic waterways**
  Cruise the calm Lake Tyers and catch a fish supper or just relax on the boat and try a glass of Gippsland wine

- **Sea of green**
  Enjoy the rolling, fertile pastureland of South and East Gippsland

- **Mountain meander**
  Drive along the winding Great Alpine Road through the stark High Country

Sheep grazing on the fertile South Gippsland pastureland

Glorious Gippsland

Gippsland covers roughly half of Victoria's eastern flank, running from the base of the Victorian Alps through to the Southern Ocean. This is a tour through three of its distinct regions – the low-lying, coal-rich west, where it is possible to go underground at Wonthaggi and see lime kilns at Walkerville South; the picturesque coastline and serene grazing land of Wilsons Promontory National Park and Ninety Mile Beach in the south; and the boating paradise and fishing heaven around Paynesville, Lakes Entrance and Lake Tyers Beach in the east – with a journey over the top of Victoria through the dramatic High Country to cap it all off.

Above Coastal road winding through Wilsons Promontory National Park, *see p97*

Right Lichen-covered boulders in the breakers at Squeaky Beach, *see p98*

PLAN YOUR DRIVE

Start/finish: Wonthaggi to Harrietville.

Number of days: Around 4–5 days, allowing half a day to explore Wilsons Promontory National Park and half a day to drive from Buchan Caves Reserve to Harrietville.

Distance: Approx. 888 km (555 miles).

Road conditions: Most roads are sealed and signposted, but some are winding, with slippery surfaces. The Great Alpine Road is snowbound in winter (Jun–Aug), when a 4WD is needed. There are also several dirt roads, especially along the coast.

When to go: The weather can be unpredictable, especially on the Great Alpine Road and at Wilsons Promontory, but Feb–Mar is generally hot and dry, while July is cold, windy and rainy, often with snow in the mountains.

Opening times: Most museums and shops are open 9am–5pm. It is often difficult to find restaurants open in smaller towns Mon–Tue nights.

Main market days: Bairnsdale: 4th Sun of every month; **Great Alpine Road:** Omeo, 2nd Sat of the month.

Shopping: Pick up an unusual timepiece at Bairnsdale Clocks in Bairnsdale, or striking jewellery at Oneofftwo Studio between Raymond Island and Lakes Entrance.

Major festivals: Wonthaggi: Bass Coast Summer Agricultural Show, Jan; **Paynesville:** Jazz Festival, Feb; **Lakes Entrance:** Lakes Skyshow, Dec.

Below Koala in a gum tree on Raymond Island, just across the water from Paynesville, *see p99*

KEY

Drive route

0 kilometres   25

0 miles   25

ACTIVITIES

Go underground at the Wonthaggi State Coal Mine

Cycle along the old railway tracks from Bairnsdale to Orbost

Kayak through the Gippsland waterways at Paynesville

Cruise through the lakes to wineries at Lakes Entrance

Catch fish from Lake Tyers Beach

Belly-crawl through Spring Creek Cave at Buchan Caves Reserve

Swim in the Tronoh Dredge Holes by the Ovens River

Right Mining huts at the Wonthaggi State Coal Mine **Far right** Granite boulders in Tidal River, Wilsons Promontory National Park

VISITING WILSONS PROMONTORY NATIONAL PARK

Parking
Park in the car park by the Visitor Centre.

Visitor Centre
Wilsons Promontory Park Office, Tidal River, 3960; 03 8627 4700; www.parkweb.vic.gov.au; open daily

WHERE TO STAY

CAPE LIPTRAP LIGHTHOUSE
Bear Gully Cottages *expensive*
Surrounded by rolling green hills and with expansive sea views, these four well-spaced villas benefit from gas-fires in winter, air-conditioning in summer, and a lovely deck for a drink any time. Enjoy the contemporary luxury just a short walk from the water.
Between Cape Liptrap Lighthouse and Walkerville South, 3956; 03 5663 2364; www.beargullycottages.com.au

WILSONS PROMONTORY NATIONAL PARK
Wilderness Retreat *expensive*
These luxury tents are the most desirable place to stay in the most popular national park in Victoria. Enjoy proper beds and linen and plenty of living space at these sheltered sites. There are also cheaper **camp and caravan sites** available by ballot only at peak periods.
Tidal River, 3960; 13 19 63; www.parkweb.vic.gov.au

Below left The inviting sea at the quiet Walkerville South Beach **Below** Walking trail through the Prom **Below right** Wonderfully isolated Cape Liptrap Lighthouse

① Wonthaggi
Victoria; 3995
The discovery of gold in the 1850s turned Victoria into the richest colony in Australia *(see pp120–29)*. When the gold ran out 30 years later, the state's lifeblood became coal. One of the first mines was the **State Coal Mine** *(site open daily; book ahead for underground tours; 13 19 63; www.parkweb.vic.gov.au)*, which opened in 1909. The small theatre near the entrance shows fascinating footage of the hard labour and grimy conditions once endured by the miners and their pit ponies. Retired miners and park volunteers take tours into the first level underground.

🚗 *Take the B460 for Inverloch, forking right onto the C442 at Inverloch. At the roundabout on entry to Tarwin Lower, take Walkerville Rd left. Turn right into Walkerville South Rd at sign for "Lime Kilns and Historic Lighthouse" and continue to beach on the unsealed road.*

② Walkerville South Beach
Victoria; 3956
The conical ruins on Walkerville South Beach could be misconstrued as some architecturally advanced civilization lost to misadventure. In fact, they are kilns, the remains of a limestone-quarrying settlement. The quiet beach is sheltered from the weather, and is a popular fishing spot. A walking track behind the beach leads up the hill towards an old cemetery and then down the hill towards Walkerville North – perfect for building up an appetite for a picnic at its beach.

🚗 *Return along Walkerville South Rd, and left into unsealed Cape Liptrap Rd and follow it to the lighthouse.*

③ Cape Liptrap Lighthouse
Victoria; 3956
Standing on a windswept outcrop, Cape Liptrap Lighthouse is a concrete, automatic beacon with priceless views over Bass Strait, and fearsome seas breaking on the rocks below. A viewing platform juts over the cliff, with views back to the lighthouse.

🚗 *Drive back along Cape Liptrap Rd, turn left onto Walkerville South Rd, right onto Walkerville Rd, and left on Acacia Rd, following the "Wilsons Prom" sign. Continue onto the C445 and then right onto the C444, all the way to Tidal River for Wilsons Promontory National Park.*

❹ Wilsons Promontory National Park

Victoria; 3960

The summertime darling of Victoria's national parks, the "Prom" offers granite mountains, sheltered beaches and rainforest gullies ideal for walking, surfing, fishing and diving – for more information, ask at the Visitor Centre. In 2009, around 50 per cent of the park was burned in a bushfire – the worst in Australia's history. However, it has regenerated itself in a remarkable display of resilience.

A 90-minute walking tour

The only permanent settlement on the Prom, Tidal River is the national park's centre of operations. In addition to accommodation and food, there is also a **Parks Victoria Visitor Centre** ①, which has displays on local fauna and flora, as well as expert guides.

From the back of the Tidal River car park, directly opposite the Visitor Centre, the Loo-Errn track leads through the vegetation to the riverbank. Follow the river west towards the ocean. The river is tidal and the gravelly path is so close to the waterline in places that at high tide the hollows can fill with water – waterproof shoes are advisable. Look out for wombats along this stretch. The gravel path soon becomes a raised **boardwalk** ② that protects the fragile wetland ecosystem from walking boots. Take the **bridge** ③ on the right over Tidal River, and stop on the other side to take in the view of Mount Oberon, above the Tidal River settlement, with rust-coloured

boulders in the foreground. Turn left at the trail junction to begin the Tidal Overlook Circuit. As the trail ascends, views of bright-blue Norman Bay and Beach open up on the left. Around the hill's eastern face, there is the option of a diversion to Pillar Point, a granite outcrop overlooking Norman and Squeaky beaches and the Prom's islands. Follow the path up to the top of the hill – there may be wallabies here – and take in the views from the **Tidal Overlook Quiet Place** ④, a memorial to park rangers worldwide who have lost their lives in the line of duty. From here, Norman Bay, Leonard Bay and Norman Island are clearly visible.

Continue up the track, following the northern face of the hill. Turn right at the **Lilly Pilly Link junction** ⑤ to return to the bridge, and walk back down the Loo-Errn track to return to the Tidal River car park.

🚗 *From Tidal River, drive back along the C444 and turn left at the sign for Squeaky Beach.*

EAT AND DRINK

AROUND WONTHAGGI

Koonwarra Store *expensive*
Slow food, seasonal produce and locally made conserves and wines come together here for memorable meals.
Cnr South Gippsland Hwy & Koala Drive, Koonwarra, 3960 (take Bass Hwy from Inverloch, forking right for Koonwarra); 03 5664 2285

WILSONS PROMONTORY NATIONAL PARK

Tidal River Store & Takeaway *inexpensive*
This small store at the very end of the C444, in the heart of the park, is the only option for decent coffee and takeaway meals in Tidal River. It is the ideal place to stock-up before hikes.
Tidal River, 3960; 03 5680 8520

AROUND WILSONS PROMONTORY NATIONAL PARK

Flying Cow Café *moderate*
At the junction of the C444 and the C445, just outside the park, this place offers bovine adornments and hearty meals, alongside huge ANZAC biscuits. The coffee is good, and the atmosphere is urbane.
9 Falls Rd, Fish Creek, 3960; 03 5683 2338

Rhythm Café *inexpensive*
Positioned where the C445 meets the A440, the Rhythm Café is a great place to stop for a coffee and a slice of homemade flan or pie.
3 Bridge St, Foster, 3960; 03 5682 1612

Above left The boulder-studded shoreline of Squeaky Beach. **Above right** Signpost at the entrance to Ninety Mile Beach

WHERE TO STAY IN BAIRNSDALE

Bairnsdale Holiday Park *inexpensive*
Caravanners, motorhomers and budget travellers are well served here with good facilities, a swimming pool and tennis court and animal feeding for the little ones.
139 Princes Hwy, 3875; 03 5152 4066; www.bairnsdaleholidaypark.com

Tara House *moderate*
Capture some period charm at this tastefully appointed slice of old-fashioned hospitality, set in manicured gardens in a quiet part of town, minutes from the centre. Expect ensuite rooms, daily papers and an early evening cheese-and-wine snack, with a terrific deck to relax on.
37 Day St, 3875; 03 5153 2253; www.tarahouse.com.au

⑤ Squeaky Beach
Wilsons Promontory National Park, Victoria; 3960
On all but the very coldest of days, there are travellers walking barefoot on Squeaky Beach – the ultra-fine sand chirps and sings against bare skin. To the right of the beach, along the access path, naturally "rusting" boulders – actually covered in a type of lichen – make an exciting, if slippery, natural playground.

The Clock Museum, Bainsdale

🚗 *Turn left onto the C444 to Fish Creek, fork right onto the C446 and veer right onto the C445 to Foster. Turn right onto the South Gippsland Hwy (A440) towards Yarram. Turn right at sign for Seaspray and follow it to the town and Ninety Mile Beach.*

⑥ Ninety Mile Beach
Seaspray, Victoria; 3851
Yes, it really is 90 miles (145 km) long. Stretching almost to the horizon in both directions, even at high tide there is enough soft white sand for everybody. Head south from Seaspray along the coast, or drive north up Shoreline Drive to find a quiet stretch of beach to relax on; but obey the warnings against swimming at certain points – the sea can be hazardous.

🚗 *Take the C496 back to the A440 and fork right, through Sale onto Princes Hwy (A1) to Bairnsdale. Park in centre.*

Koala-spotting tips
If on foot, keep quiet. If you are in the car, drive slowly and turn off any music. Look for forks in tree trunks where koalas can sleep safely, and keep an eye on fresh, young foliage, where they could be eating.

⑦ Bairnsdale
Victoria; 3875
The grand old dame of East Gippsland, Bairnsdale is an important commercial centre for the surrounding district. At its heart is an attractive collection of pleasant old buildings – well-kept Victorian cottages – as well as all the modern retailing a sizeable rural community requires. A little over an hour from winter snowfields, and only a short drive from the beach, Bairnsdale is ideal as a base for exploring eastern Victoria.

On the highway to the left on the way in to Bairnsdale, time ticks away more frantically than usual at the **Clock Museum** *(open daily; 03 5152 6962; www.bairnsdaleclocks.com.au)*. As well as selling Art Deco jewellery, Bakelite radios and many interesting timepieces, there are 800 clocks on display out the back. The showpiece is the Monks' Clock, a mechanical dolls' house in which monks operate a guest house, with diners who say "cheers" in a multitude of languages, including an Aboriginal dialect.

On the main street stands the impressive red-brick **St Mary's Catholic Church**. Begun in 1913, this distinctive structure's crowning glory is actually on the inside. During the Great Depression in the 1930s, itinerant Italian painter Francesco Floriani was commissioned to paint the frescoes in the interior. The intricate, passionate result depicts the stations of the cross, heaven and hell.

🚗 *Continue along Main St and the A1 and turn off left onto the C604, which leads all the way to Paynesville.*

⑧ Paynesville
Victoria; 3880

Before heading across the water to Raymond Island, take a wander along the main strip of Paynesville, which lays claim to the title of "Boating Capital of Victoria". Bobbing watercraft line the exclusive marina, while the pub, cafés and fuel station lie across the road. Paynesville is the ideal place to hire a boat or kayak to explore the Gippsland lakes and waterways – try **Bulls Cruisers** *(54 Slip Rd, 3880; 03 5156 1200; www. bullscruisers.com.au).* Or, if pushed for time, simply walk along the esplanade and admire the views of the waterways and foreshore. The town church, **St Peter-by-the-Lake** (1961), is filled with interesting nautical motifs – the pulpit looks like the prow of a boat and the font is shaped like a ship's bollard.

🚗 *Follow Main Rd to the waterfront and continue to the left for the ferry to Raymond Island (every half hour).*

Rail Trail Cycle Ride
Converting abandoned railways into cycling trails is a popular way of re-using the tracks in Victoria, and the 100-km (60-mile) trail from Bairnsdale to Orbost, in Snowy River country, is the longest continuous stretch in the state. The 10-km (6-mile) section from **Bairnsdale** to **Nicholson** rewards cyclists with a trip over the lovely wooden bridge crossing the Mitchell River. Hire bikes from **Riviera Cycles** *(193 Main St, Bairnsdale, 3875; 03 5152 1886; eastgippslandrailtrail.com).*

---

⑨ Raymond Island
Victoria; 3880

Isolated from Paynesville and the mainland by a short stretch of salty water, bridged by a ferry, Raymond Island maintains a dense population of koalas, those must-see, bear-like Australian icons. If there is time, explore the island on foot and do not forget to look up at the trees *(see box).* Otherwise, take the dirt roads around the coast to **Gravelly Point Beach** – the roads are fine with a 2WD car. Tracks through the centre of the island can be overgrown and require a 4WD.

🚗 *From Paynesville, take the C604 back to Bairnsdale, cross Princes Hwy (A1) and turn left on it, right to stay on it, right onto Nungurner Rd, left onto Nungurner Jetty Rd and first left onto Kleinitz Rd, then Loop Rd, to Oneofftwo Studio.*

Above left Koala in the fork of a gum tree, Raymond Island **Top right** Dirt road to Gravelly Point Beach, Raymond Island **Above right** Jetty and boats at Raymond Island

---

EAT AND DRINK

NINETY MILE BEACH

Ronnie's Tea Rooms *inexpensive*
Among the holiday shacks of Ninety Mile Beach, Ronnie's serves a divine Devonshire Cream Tea.
13 Trood Street, Seaspray, 3851; 03 5146 4420

BAIRNSDALE

Lake Whadie Cafe *inexpensive*
There are fabulous lake views from the outdoor deck at this café, which offers all-day breakfasts and gourmet pies.
1 Princes Hwy, 3875; 03 5152 6060

Riversleigh *expensive*
The restaurant at this surprisingly quiet, chic Comfort Inn, located in three renovated 1886 Victorian terraces by the Mitchell River, serves decent Australian fare in its conservatory bistro and dining room.
1 Nicholson Street, 3875; 03 5152 6966; www.riversleigh.info

PAYNESVILLE

Fisherman's Wharf Pavillion *moderate*
Uses fresh local produce and serves up modern Australian cuisine, including a first-class seafood chowder, by the water.
70 The Esplanade, 3880; 03 5156 0366

Above The ornately decorated interior of St Mary's Catholic Church, Bairnsdale

---

Eat and Drink: inexpensive under AU$60; moderate AU$60–$100; expensive over AU$100

LAKES ENTRANCE CRUISES

Book a lunch or dinner cruise to **Wyanga Park Winery** (*222 Baades Road, 3909; 03 5155 1508; www.wyangapark.com.au*) or a dolphin cruise on the **Lonsdale** (*03 9013 8363; www.lakesentrance.com/cruises/lonsdale-cruises.html*) from the Post Office Jetty at Lakes Entrance.

WHERE TO STAY

LAKES ENTRANCE

Goldsmiths in the Forest *moderate*
Enjoy a truly special night's stay here, where cute marsupial sugar gliders (like skydiving "squirrels") "fly" among the treetops, parrots crack seeds on the balcony, and forest-grown spices find their way into the house-cooked, three-course meal. For a treat, enjoy a twilight soak in a clawfooted bath at the front, or try the covered spa out in the forest. *Harrisons Track, 3909; 03 5155 2518; www.goldsmithsintheforest.com.au*

Other options
Caravanners can stop just out of town at the **Swan Reach Gardens Tourist & Holiday Park** (*2143 Princes Hwy (A1), 3909; 03 5156 4366; www.swanreachgardens.com.au*).

BUCHAN CAVES RESERVE

Wilderness Retreat *moderate*
Replete with communal kitchen and shared amenities, these high-end tents are great value, and make a fine base from which to explore the Buchan Caves Reserve. There are also some prime caravan sites and camp sites at the reserve, all with access to modern, clean facilities (inexpensive). *Buchan Caves Reserve, 3885; 13 19 63; www.parkweb.vic.gov.au*

HARRIETVILLE

Shady Brook Cottages *moderate*
Set in landscaped gardens away from the Great Alpine Road and bordered by forested hills, these self-contained, spacious villas are great for families, while the cozy bed and breakfast in the main house is a more personal option. Encounters with local wildlife are common. *Great Alpine Rd, Harrietville, 3741; 03 5759 2741; www.shadybrook.com.au*

10 Oneofftwo Studio
96 Kleinitz Rd, Nungurner, Victoria; 3909
Without so much as grid electricity, Dore Stockhausen and Marcus Foley are an inspired goldsmithing couple who fashion striking jewellery in gold, silver and palladium, as well as acrylic, enamel and glass, from their hilltop **studio** (*open Mon–Fri; 03 5156 3270*) in the East Gippsland hinterland. Join them in their light-filled workshop and showroom to see how it is done, and pick out something special. Call ahead, as opening hours vary.

🚗 *Take Kleinitz Rd and Loop Rd back to Nungurner Jetty Rd. Turn right onto Nungurner Rd and right onto the Princes Hwy (A1) to Lakes Entrance. Park along the Esplanade.*

11 Lakes Entrance
Victoria; 3909
Known locally as "Lakes", the town fills up with holiday-makers over summer. Along the Esplanade, cafés, pubs and fish-and-chip joints face the moored boats at the marina, the centrepiece of which is the Post Office Jetty, where lake cruises depart (*www.lakesentrance.com*). From the hill on the drive into town, turn off to a lookout where, on a clear day, oil platforms can be seen in Bass Strait.

🚗 *Continue through Lakes Entrance along the Princes Hwy (A1). Turn right for Lake Tyers Beach on Lake Tyers Rd, which becomes Lake Tyers Beach Rd.*

12 Lake Tyers Beach
Victoria; 3909
When the weather is right, this sheltered, sandy beach is nothing short of picturesque. Anglers might wish to try their luck, as it is a popular

Winery Cruise
Wine and boats go well together, especially when navigating the waterways of the lake system to Wyanga Park Winery, where tastings begin on board, with an expert commentary, and a three-course meal awaits ashore. The 4-hour excursion leaves from the Lakes Entrance Post Office Jetty at 11am (*03 5155 1508; www.wyangapark.com.au*).

Above Angler at the popular fishing spot, Lake Tyers Beach

fishing spot. Take a trip on the **Tambo Queen** (*No. 2 Boat Ramp, 83 Lakeside Drive; 0428 565 003*) with food, bait and equipment provided. Whatever gets thrown back is usually snapped up by the resident flock of pelicans. Nearby **Red Bluff** is one of the area's top surf spots – but it is only for fairly experienced surfers.

🚗 *Drive back to the Princes Hwy (A1), and turn right. Turn left onto the A620 at Nowa Nowa and right on the C608 to Buchan. The Buchan Caves Reserve turn-off is on the left in town.*

Right Cruise boats at the holiday spot, Lakes Entrance

⓭ Buchan Caves Reserve

Buchan, Victoria; 3885

The land on which **Buchan Caves Reserve** (13 19 63; www.parkweb.vic.gov. au) sits is a honeycomb of limestone caverns ripe for exploration. The best caves are explored by guided tours – times depend on the time of year. See the delicate stalactites and stalagmites of the Fairy Cave and the calcite-rimmed pools of the Royal Cave, among others. The reserve also has a camp site (see left), walking tracks and a picnic area. In summer, the wet **Spring Creek Cave** is open for 90-minute sessions of crawling and squeezing through tiny gaps – it is definitely not for the claustrophobic. Overalls, lights and helmets are provided; all visitors need to bring are some sturdy shoes and a reasonable degree of fitness.

🚗 *Drive back out of Buchan along the C608, turn right onto the C620, and then right onto the B500, the Great Alpine Road.*

⓮ Great Alpine Road (B500)

Victoria

Starting in Bairnsdale, in the fertile pastures of East Gippsland, and ending across the Victorian Alps in the population centre of the High Country, Wangaratta, the Great Alpine Road is 310 km (190 miles) of blissful automotive touring, and includes the highest year-round accessible stretch of sealed road in the country.

Join the Great Alpine Road at **Bruthen** (3885) and drive down onto the Tambo Valley floor, parallel to the cool Tambo River, at times closed in by rock faces on one side and forest on the other. Then start climbing again before dropping into the pretty mountain town of **Omeo** (3898), where the heritage-fronted

Post and Telegraph Office faces the old Bank across the steep main street.

Once out of Omeo, the previously thick forests give way to open, foliage-free expanses. If the weather is clear, there will be spectacular, uninterrupted views of some of the country's highest mountains, including a peek of the very highest, **Mount Kosciusko** 2,228 m (7,310 ft). On the way into **Dinner Plain** (3898), the route traverses a ridge lined with a striking line of ghost gums, a rather aptly named eucalyptus tree.

Hotham Heights (3741), known as the powder capital of Australia, is the main ski village on Mount Hotham and located at the top of a saddle-like dip on the summit. Whether it is snow, sun, winter or summer, there is plenty to do at Hotham Heights, from skiing and snowboarding to snowshoeing and dog-sledding, and in summer, alpine mountain-biking and hiking (1800 468 426; www.hotham.com.au).

🚗 *On leaving Hotham Heights, the road begins the steepest, most winding section of the drive, so keep the car in low gear and carry on along Great Alpine Rd down to Harrietville.*

⓯ Harrietville

Victoria; 3741

A sleepy little town, **Harrietville** is another good base for snowsports on Mount Hotham. It is a shadow of its former 19th-century gold-rush size (although gold is still mined in these parts) and is a fine place to wind down in its own right. In summer, have a swim in the eerily opaque-green waters of the **Tronoh Dredge Holes**, two 30-m (100-ft) pits dug to extract gold from the Ovens River. The holes, filled with water and stocked with fish, are reached from a track off the main street.

Above left The clear waters of Ovens River, running through Harrietville **Above centre** The narrow, winding and thrilling Great Alpine Road **Above right** Limestone formations at Buchan Caves Reserve

EAT AND DRINK

LAKE TYERS BEACH

Waterwheel Beach Tavern *moderate*
This pub-restaurant offers excellent fish and chips washed down with ice-cold beer as well as foreshore views and a lovely outdoor dining area beside its stilled waterwheel.
Lake Tyers Beach Rd, 3909; 03 5156 5855

BUCHAN CAVES RESERVE

Caves Hotel *inexpensive*
This traditional country hotel serves pub favourites that never disappoint, such as the popular chicken parmigiana.
49 Main St, 3885; 03 5155 9253

Other options
Buchan Valley Roadhouse (inexpensive; Main Rd, 3885; 03 5155 9484) is a fuel-stop and newsagent that sells excellent home-made brownies as well as burgers and chips, while **Buchan Caves Hotel** (moderate; Main St, 3885; 03 5155 9203) serves good pub grub.

HARRIETVILLE

Morries Ice Creamery & Café *inexpensive*
Run by two expat-Zimbabweans, the creamy delights here, at the base of Mount Hotham, are among the best in Victoria. Gourmet meals featuring local produce are available, as is good coffee and breakfasts for skiers – ring ahead.
Great Alpine Rd, 3741; 03 5759 2612

Other options
Filling pizzas and pastas and the odd Malaysian fish curry are to be found at Harrietville Hotel's **Redgum Bar** (moderate;169 Great Alpine Rd, 3741; 03 5759 2525; www.harrietvillehotelmotel. com.au), and up the road, **Snowline Hotel** (moderate; 237 Great Alpine Rd, 3741; 03 5759 2524; lunch Thu–Sun & dinner daily) offers great local wine, pub grub and house specialities.

Eat and Drink: inexpensive under AU$60; moderate AU$60–AU$100; expensive over AU$100

Peninsula Tour

Mornington to Coolart Wetlands and Homestead

Highlights

- **Espionage outpost**
  Explore secret tunnels, observation posts and interesting military fortifications at Fort Nepean

- **Vertiginous views**
  Wind down Cape Schanck's cliff boardwalk to wild rocky shores

- **Flinders fishermen**
  Wander down to Western Port Bay to see what is biting

- **Gourmet touring**
  Taste microbrewed beer, artisan wines and olive oil, all served with top-quality food in Red Hill

Rows of vines at the Montalto Winery, Red Hill

Peninsula Tour

The Mornington Peninsula is where Melbourne comes to unwind. Rolling hills, fertile valleys, tree-lined roads and dramatic ocean coastline all come together with a mixture of world-class golf, wine and gourmet produce, less than an hour from the big smoke. This tour starts in the Peninsula's café-culture heartland of Mornington, heads inland for fabulous views, dips into virgin forest and then returns to the coast to Point Nepean National Park. It then runs oceanside to the fishing town of Flinders, before trying some of the tasty attractions of Red Hill and capping it all off with a visit to the Coolart Wetlands and Homestead reserve.

KEY

Drive route

PLAN YOUR DRIVE

Start/finish: Mornington to Coolart Wetlands and Homestead.

Number of days: 1–2 days, allowing half a day to explore Point Nepean.

Distance: Approx. 156 km (98 miles).

Road conditions: Roads are mainly sealed and signposted, with some steep gradients and winding sections around Arthurs Seat.

When to go: January is generally warm and dry, while June and July are cold and wet; the landscape is spectacular in autumn (Apr–May), with green fields and fallen leaves.

Main market days: Mornington: Wed; Red Hill: 1st Sat of the month (Sep–May).

Major festivals: Mornington: October Pinot Week, Oct.

Shopping: In Red Hill, look for fine wine, olive oil, preserves and cheeses. Take a short detour from Coolart to Tyabb for collectibles and antiques.

Above The eroded limestone arch known as London Bridge, Ocean Beach, see p105

① Mornington
Victoria; 3931

Where Melbourne's peninsula playground begins, Mornington is a bayside town that is almost a suburb of the city, but runs at about half its pace, to the rhythm of the tides. Fashion and homeware boutiques line Main Street, which leads from the highway to the bay.

For an on-high look at Mornington and its surroundings, wander up the clifftop walk at **Schnapper Point**. Here, check out the plaque to 18th-century navigator and cartographer of Australia, Matthew Flinders *(see p233)*, take in the views of safe Mothers Beach and the town's famous coloured bathing boxes, and admire the sleek yachts and watercraft in the marina.

🚗 *From Schnapper Point, follow the Esplanade as it becomes Marine Drive, turn right (towards Rosebud) as it hits the Nepean Highway. Follow signs for the C789 and pass under the freeway on to Arthurs Seat Rd to Arthurs Seat.*

② Arthurs Seat
Arthurs Seat Rd, Victoria; 3936

At not much over 300 m (1,000 ft) above sea level, Arthurs Seat commands a surprisingly impressive view over the Mornington Peninsula, Port Phillip Bay and Melbourne. The steep and winding road to the top is a favourite with masochistic cyclists. On a clear day, do not forget to look through the built-in binoculars at the lookout for the stunning views.

🚗 *Carry along C789, right into Main Creek Rd, left onto Purves Rd, right onto Browns Rd, left onto C777 and left onto Limestone Rd to the park entrance gate.*

③ Greens Bush
Mornington Peninsula National Park, Victoria; 3939

The largest remnant of the tangled coastal bushland that once blanketed Mornington Peninsula, Greens Bush offers a serene escape from any big-city buzz. The forest contains gum trees, peppermint trees, eucalypts and spectacular grass trees. Walking tracks crisscross the park frequented by honeyeaters, parrots and even wedge-tailed eagles or black-shouldered kites. At dusk, look out for kangaroos, ringtail possums or flying, squirrel-like sugar gliders.

🚗 *Return to Limestone Rd across Boneo Rd and right onto Truemans Rd and left onto Browns Rd. Turn right onto Dundas St, left onto B110 through Sorrento and right to Portsea.*

④ Sorrento
Victoria; 3943/3944

Melbourne's fabulously wealthy have always built their holiday mansions in Sorrento and Portsea. The vibe along Sorrento's main street, in its boutiques, cafés and restaurants, is unsurprisingly upmarket, and it is a charming stop-off. Keep an eye out for bottlenose dolphins playing in the bay waters. Further along the B110, **Portsea** is little more than a few restaurants, a hotel and the beach – the locals and blow-ins live down impossibly long drives in private palaces on the beachfront.

🚗 *Turn left into Back Beach Rd, right onto London Bridge Rd to Ocean Beach car park and viewpoint.*

⑤ London Bridge
Portsea Back Beach, Victoria; 3944

Unlike its better-known twin on the Great Ocean Road *(see p117)*, this sandstone rock formation known as **London Bridge** has not fallen down. Better still, it is much closer to shore, and is accessible at low tide, as well as creating a stunning view from the car park lookout. Swimming on Ocean Beach is inadvisable, although it is lovely for a walk or a picnic.

🚗 *Return along London Bridge Rd, and left on Back Beach Rd, then left on Point Nepean Rd to Point Nepean.*

Above Yachts at the marina near Schnapper Point, Mornington

WHERE TO STAY IN SORRENTO

Hotel Sorrento *moderate*
On a rise overlooking the marina, this 1871 hotel is a stylish overnighter with balcony and spa-suite options.
5–15 Hotham Rd, 3943; 03 5984 8000; www.hotelsorrento.com.au

Carmel of Sorrento *moderate*
Three suites in this 1905 limestone home come with large beds and a central location, overlaid with small-town hospitality.
142 Ocean Beach Rd, 3943; 03 5984 3512; www.carmelofsorrento.com.au

EAT AND DRINK

MORNINGTON

The Boyz 4 Breakie *moderate*
With enormous servings, a bustling, camp ambience and a location close to the beach, this Mornington institution is the place to breakfast with the locals.
1a Main St, 3931; 03 5977 2888; www.theboyz4breakie.com.au

Other options
Caffeine-addicts will appreciate the wide range of coffees and treats at **Coffee Traders** *(3 Blake St, 3931; 03 5977 1177)*, while bread aficionados will enjoy the European baking at **Franks Classique Bakery** *(29a Main St, 3931; 03 5975 0205)*, and Italophiles will love the slice of the Isle of Capri that is **Via Boffe** *(74 Main St, 3931; 03 5975 7499)*.

SORRENTO

Three Palms *inexpensive*
For great tapas with a South American twist, this restaurant and bar is an essential visit. The prices are reasonable, the ambience is great, and the prawns are an absolute must.
154 Ocean Beach Rd, 3943; 03 5984 1057

Above Typical forest trees at Greens Bush, Mornington Peninsula National Park

Eat and Drink: inexpensive under AU$60; moderate AU$60–AU$100; expensive over AU$100

VISITING POINT NEPEAN

Parking and Visitor Centre
Park at Gunners Car Park by the **Point Nepean Visitor Centre**, Portsea *(03 5984 4276; www.parkweb.vic.gov.au)* and catch the tractor-powered transporter *(admission fees payable at Visitor Centre)* to Fort Nepean.

ACTIVITIES

The Mornington Peninsula has superb golf courses. Rated as the best public-access course in Australia, the **Dunes Golf Links Championship Course** at 335 Browns Rd on the route to Greens Bush *(03 5985 1334; www.thedunes. com.au)* is a picturesque place to start. See wild dolphins and seals from the family-run **Moonraker Dolphin Swims** *(03 5984 4211; www. moonrakercharters.com.au)*. Cruises leave from Sorrento Oct–Apr and take three hours, with participants actually swimming with the dolphins.

WHERE TO STAY IN RED HILL

Stony Creek Cottages *moderate*
These self-contained cottages are conveniently located – close to the attractions and yet secluded enough. They come complete with fantastic amenities, including a fireplace and spa. *1193 Morning-Flinders Rd, 3937; 03 5989 2748*

Lindenderry at Red Hill *expensive*
Garden views and fresh air abound at this vineyard, winery, restaurant and hotel, where European fabrics and down-tempo Australian style combine for a sophisticated boutique hotel stay. *142 Arthurs Seat Rd, 3916; 03 5989 2933; www.lindenderry.com.au*

Below The narrow strip of scrubland that forms Point Nepean

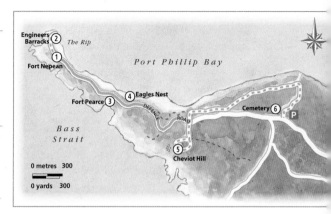

⑥ Point Nepean
Victoria; 3944

Probably the only national park in Australia with signs warning of the danger of unexploded bombs for those foolhardy enough to stray from the path or scale barbed-wire fences, Point Nepean offers a fascinating insight into the nation's military history. It is formed of a spectacular, narrow strip of bushland with incredible views of calm Port Phillip Bay to one side and the furious Bass Strait to the other. Gather a map and parking token at the Visitor Centre at the park entrance to access Gunners Car Park. Point Nepean National Park is crisscrossed with all sorts of short, loop walks, and there are myriad ways to accomplish roughly the same exploration.

A three-hour walking tour

Park the car and take the transporter to **Fort Nepean** ①. From here, take the path down the hill to the left – this will lead around the cliff along Bass Strait to the Rip, the hazardous entrance to Port Phillip Bay. Walk around to the **Engineers Barracks** ② (the only toilets are signed near here), enter and climb up through to the Engine House and a series of gun emplacements, and dip below ground through the magazine tunnels. Here, explore the main tunnel network, where echoes of the past are recreated with carefully placed sound recordings. Follow the signs to the heavily fortified Bomb Proof Room, and head up to the Battery Observation Post. Exit the tunnels to the Upper Barracks Site and walk along the Narrows towards **Fort Pearce** ③. Divert to the right for the Cheviot West lookout and then walk through the gutted fort. Follow the path, then take a diversion left towards another Battery Observation Post and head to **Eagles Nest** ④, once the site of Australia's largest "disappearing" gun: a cannon that could be lowered into its emplacement and so disappear from view. Walk back to the main path, turn left and take a right up the steep path to **Cheviot Hill** ⑤, the highest point in the area. Take the right fork past scenic lookouts, a WWII gun emplacement and a Battery Observation Post, with glorious views. Keep on the path as it loops to the left, and rejoins the main track. Cross Defence Road, take the first right and fork left to take Coles Track back to the **cemetery** ⑥ and car park.

🚗 *Travel back to Point Nepean Rd, turn right on Back Beach Rd, left on Hotham Rd then right on Melbourne Rd. Then turn right on Canterbury Jetty Rd, into Tasman Drive and then Browns Rd. Turn right at Dundas St into Sandy Rd, turn right onto Truemans Rd and follow it all the way to Gunnamatta Ocean Beach.*

Danger UXB!
Remain on the path at all times, as Point Nepean was a military installation for over a hundred years and unexploded ordnance litters the fenced-off range on a western swathe of the park.

⑦ Gunnamatta Ocean Beach
Truemans Rd, Victoria; 3939
Experienced surfers flock to wild spots like Gunnamatta Ocean Beach to pitch their skills against the best nature has to offer. Visit to see how the locals are carving up the waves. But do not be tempted to swim here – it is one of Victoria's most dangerous beaches.
🚗 *Drive back along Truemans Rd, turn right onto Limestone Rd, right onto C777 and right onto Cape Schanck Rd to Cape Schanck. The boardwalk is accessible from the car park.*

⑧ Cape Schanck
Cape Schanck Rd, Victoria; 3939
The cliffside pathway at Cape Schanck runs out to Pulpit Rock, where the foamy surf surges in from the ocean. It is a popular rock-fishing spot, but a dangerous one. Some superb rockpools are accessible via the boardwalk. The only way to see the **Cape Schanck Lighthouse** *(open daily)* is on a tour, for an interesting insight into the past – much of the original technology is still in place.
🚗 *Drive back out along Cape Schanck Rd to C777 and turn right. Continue into Flinders to Cook St. Take the Esplanade right to the foreshore and park there.*

⑨ Flinders
Victoria; 3929
Named after Matthew Flinders, a British explorer who circumnavigated Australia in 1802, this quaint fishing village on Western Port Bay, with views to Phillip Island, is a good place to ask what is biting, and then get a rod. Buy a fishing licence online *(www.new.dpi.vic.gov.au)* or book a trip with **Peninsula Fishing Charters** *(03*

9769 5544; www.peninsulafishingcharters. com) in Western Port Bay.
🚗 *Drive back along the Esplanade, turn left onto Cook St and right at the roundabout onto the C777. Turn left onto Shoreham Road towards Red Hill.*

⑩ Red Hill
Victoria; 3916/3937
More of a locality than a town, Red Hill has become the centre of a gourmet movement on the peninsula.
Look out on the right for **Ashcombe Maze and Lavender Farm** *(open daily; 03 5989 8387; www.ashcombemaze.com.au).* The lavender's in bloom year-round. Gardeners will love the themed gardens, along with the largest hedge maze in the Southern Hemisphere and the world's oldest circular rose maze.
Carry on along Shoreham Road to **Montalto Winery** *(open 11am–5pm; 03 5989 8412; www.montalto.com.au)* to enjoy award-winning wines and olive oils from a lovely verandah restaurant.
A little further on is **Red Hill Brewery** *(open Thu–Sun; 03 5989 2959; www. redhillbrewery.com.au)*, one of the only microbreweries in Australia that grow their own hops. The rich, red Scotch ale is a standout, especially with some Welsh rarebit (essentially a beer-enriched cheese-on-toast).
Just off Shoreham Road, along Arthur's Seat Road, **Red Hill Market** sells the finest condiments, crafts, cheeses, oils and spices. And do not miss nearby **Red Hill Cheese** *(open 11am–5pm Sat, Sun & public hols; 03 5989 2035; www.redhillcheese.com.au).*
🚗 *Carry on along Shoreham Rd, right onto Stanleys Rd into Sandy Point Rd, and then right onto Lord Somers Rd.*

⑪ Coolart Wetlands and Homestead
Lord Somers Rd, Victoria; 3927
This stately late-Victorian mansion, built at the turn of the 19th century as a country retreat and adorned with lush wetlands and bright-green lawns, is begging for a picnic basket. **Coolart** *(open daily; 13 19 63; www.parkweb.vic. gov.au)* boasts great biodiversity: nine species of frog, 13 species of mammal and 11 species of reptile are to be found in the reserve, not to mention more than 110 bird species. Wander down to the observatory to survey the birds before picnicking.

Above The rolling surf of sandy Gunnamatta Ocean Beach **Centre left** Fishing boats bobbing in the bay at Flinders

SHOPPING ON MORNINGTON PENINSULA

Trash and treasure
Australian antiques are not as impressive as European ones, but collectors will enjoy the town of Tyabb (15 km/9 miles along the Frankston–Flinders Road from Coolart), with main street antiques stores such as the **Tyabb Antique Centre** *(1527 Frankston–Flinders Rd; 0414 523 461; www.tyabbantiquecentre.com.au)*, and the gargantuan **Tyabb Packing House** *(14 Mornington-Tyabb Rd; 03 5977 4414, www.tyabbpackinghouseantiques.com. au)* next to the train station.

EAT AND DRINK IN RED HILL

Vines of Red Hill *expensive*
Fine dining with all the benefits of eating in a food-obsessed hamlet. Snapper and lamb loin are specialities, with plenty of vegetarian options and delightful desserts.
150 Red Hill Rd, 3937; 03 5989 2977; www.vinesofredhill.com.au

Below Part of the hedge maze at Ashcombe Maze and Lavender Farm, Red Hill

Great Ocean Road

Melbourne to Ballarat

Highlights

- **Architectural compendium**
  Wander the streets of arty Melbourne, amid a majestic array of historic and contemporary buildings

- **Surfing mecca**
  Pay homage at Bells Beach, the spiritual home of Australian surfing

- **Rainforest canopy**
  Walk through the forest treetops on the suspended Otway Fly Treetop Walk

- **Striking shoreline**
  See the extraordinary coastal rock formations of the Twelve Apostles and London Bridge

- **Gold-Rush glitz**
  Witness some of western Victoria's golden past in 19th-century Ballarat

The Twelve Apostles in the surf at Port Campbell National Park

Great Ocean Road

The Great Ocean Road is 243 km (150 miles) of largely clifftop driving along the south-western edge of the state of Victoria, starting in the surfing town of Torquay and ending in Warrnambool. Studded with breathtaking seascapes, this tour starts at the state capital of Melbourne before joining the ocean road, continues to the petrified forest of Discovery Bay, then diverts inland past hinterland rainforest, dipping into the region's wool-producing and gold-mining heritage.

Left Painted bollards on the Geelong Foreshore, *see p114*

Above The Triplet Falls in the Great Otway National Park, *see p115*

ACTIVITIES

Take a tour of the state parliament in Melbourne's city centre

Don a wetsuit and learn to surf with seasoned instructors at Torquay

Hit the mountain bike trails on a guided ride in the Otway rainforest

Attempt to keep up with the fur seals in a kayak at Marengo Reefs Marine Sanctuary

Take a helicopter over the Twelve Apostles for an aerial view

Charter a boat to whale feeding grounds near Portland

Get soaked in the spray from blowholes at Discovery Bay Coastal Park

0 kilometres 25

0 miles 25

Above Melbourne's Royal Exhibition Building, *see p112*

PLAN YOUR DRIVE

Start/finish: Melbourne to Ballarat.

Number of days: 6–7, allowing half a day to explore Melbourne and half a day to drive from Portland to Ballarat.

Distance: Approx. 944 km (590 miles).

Road conditions: Most roads are sealed and signposted but there are some unsealed dirt roads on this route; any 4WD-only roads are optional to the drive. Some roads are winding and can be slippery. Roads in the Otways may be snowbound in winter (Jun–Aug).

When to go: Weather is changeable, but February to March are generally hot and dry, while July is cold, wet and windy.

Opening times: Most museums and shops in Australia are open 9am–5pm. It is often difficult to find restaurants open in smaller towns Mon–Tue nights.

Main market days: Geelong: 2nd Sat of month; Ballarat: 2nd & last Sun of month.

Shopping: Melbourne is a shopper's paradise: hunt for bargains in Prahran's retro Chapel Street Bazaar *(www.chapelstreet.com.au)*, visit Klein's Perfumery *(www.kleinsperfumery.co.au)* on Brunswick Street in Fitzroy and Harrolds *(www.harrolds.com.au)* or Henry Bucks clothes *(www.henrybucks.com.au)* on central Collins Street.

Major festivals: Melbourne: Melbourne Food & Wine Festival, Mar; **Geelong Foreshore:** Pako Festa (multicultural celebration), last Sat in Feb; Highland Gathering, 1st Sun in Mar; **Around Bells Beach:** Lorne Falls Festival, New Year's Eve; Heywood, Wood, Wine and Roses Festival, last Sat of Feb; Apollo Bay Music Festival, last weekend in Apr.

KEY

Drive route

Right The beach and limestone formation of Loch Ard Gorge, *see p117*

VISITING MELBOURNE

Parking
Park at the **Central Smartpark** (224 Latrobe St, cnr Elizabeth St, 3000).

Visitor Information
Federation Square, 3000; www. thatsmelbourne.com.au; open daily

WHERE TO STAY

MELBOURNE

The Adelphi *expensive*
With a glass-bottom pool, the Adelphi is Melbourne's top style hotel and home to the excellent Ezard restaurant.
187 Flinders Lane, 3000; 03 8080 8888; www.adelphi.com.au

Other options
For a Victorian terraced boutique hotel, try the **Hatton Hotel** (65 Park St, South Yarra 3000; 03 9868 4800; www.hatton. com.au), or for beachside rooms, head to the **Cosmopolitan Hotel** (2–8 Carlisle St, St Kilda, 3000; 03 9534 0781; www. 8hotels.com/melbourne-hotels/cosmopolitan-hotel).

GEELONG

The Haymarket Hotel *expensive*
A six-room boutique hotel, built in 1855.
244 Moorabool St, 3220; 03 5221 1174; www.haymarkethotel.com.au

❶ Melbourne

Victoria; 3000

Victoria's sprawling state capital curls around Port Philip Bay and inland to the Dandenong Ranges. Its commercial core is filled with significant old buildings and cultural institutions alongside striking contemporary architecture. Split by the Yarra River, Melbourne is a fashion-conscious metropolis that thrives on its arty reputation, café culture and top cuisine, with global influences. This walk is a tour of its architectural gems.

A three-hour walking tour

From the car park, head east along Latrobe Street to the 1856 **State Library** ❶ *(open daily)*, on the corner of Swanston and Latrobe streets, to marvel at its glass-domed reading room. Cross Latrobe Street to see the ultra-modern (1994) façade of the **Royal Melbourne Institute of Technology** ❷ on Swanston Street, before continuing east along Latrobe Street, and left into Russell Street to the bluestone **Old Melbourne Gaol** ❸ *(open daily)* on the left, built in the 1840s, where the infamous bushranger Ned Kelly was hanged in 1880. Opposite stands the Art Deco former **Russell Street Police Headquarters** ❹.

Turn right into McKenzie Street, cross Victoria Street and continue to Carlton Gardens to the grand 1880 **Royal Exhibition Building** ❺ *(tours 2pm; 13 11 02)*, behind which is the **Melbourne Museum** ❻ *(open daily)*, built in the 1990s. Its most popular exhibit is the stuffed hide of legendary Depression-era racehorse Phar Lap. Go back to Victoria Street, turn left then right into Nicholson Street and left into Albert Street. On the left stands the 1958 glass-and-steel **ICI Building** ❼ – once Australia's tallest; next to it is the Romanesque 1901 **Salvation Army Printing Works** and then the 1877 East Melbourne **Hebrew Congregation** *(services Thu, Fri pm & Sat am)*. Cross over into **Parliament Gardens** ❽ taking the diagonal path to Spring Street and the elegant 1854 **Princess Theatre** ❾, beside the 1883 **Windsor Hotel** ❿. Opposite the hotel is the grand 1856 **Parliament House** ⑪ *(hourly tours 9:30am–2:30pm, until 3:45pm when parliament is not in session)*, and the Renaissance revivalist 1862 Treasury Building, now the **City Museum** ⑫ *(open daily)*. Return along Spring Street and turn left into Bourke Street, stopping at Melbourne's first espresso

Below Neo-Classical Flinders Street Station in Melbourne's busy Central Business District

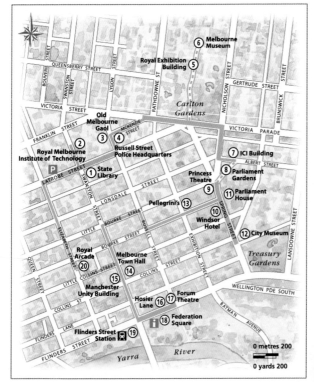

bar, **Pellegrini's** ⑬ *(open daily)*. Carry on to Russell Street, turn right and then left into Little Bourke Street, to walk through Chinatown to Swanston Walk and turn left. A few blocks along stands the **Melbourne Town Hall** ⑭ (1867), and then City Square with the Art Deco 1932 **Manchester Unity Building** ⑮. Turn left into Flinders Street and look at the graffiti up **Hosier Lane** ⑯ on the left. Back on Flinders Street carry on to the corner of Russell Street to the Moorish 1929 **Forum Theatre** ⑰. Across the road is the pink stone, glass-and-steel 2002 **Federation Square** ⑱ (and Visitor Information Centre) and the **Ian Potter Centre** art gallery *(closed Mon)*, on the Yarra River, and opposite the stately **Flinders Street Station** ⑲. Walk back up Swanston Street to Little Collins Street and turn right into the 1869 **Royal Arcade** ⑳, turning left into Elizabeth Street then right all the way up to Latrobe Street and right to the car park.

🚗 *Turn right out of car park, left at King St/Kings Wy. Cross the river and take a U-turn under the freeway to enter it from the left. Follow the signs to the West Gate Bridge/Geelong. Take the A10 exit to Geelong. Park at the National Wool Museum.*

Ned Kelly
A folk hero to many Australians for his defiance of colonial authority, bush-ranger Ned Kelly became an outlaw in 1878 after murdering three police-men. In his final showdown with the law two years later, he famously wore home-made armour. His exploits have been immortalized in the ballad of Stringybark Creek and Peter Carey's Booker prize-winning *Life and Times of the Kelly Gang*, among others.

Above Federation Square in the centre of Melbourne **Above right** Melbourne's iconic expresso bar, Pellegrini's

❷ Geelong
Victoria; 3220
Wool production was crucial to Australia's economy until the mid-20th century – it used to be said that the country "rode on the sheep's back". Geelong was Melbourne's industrial satellite until the raw materials went overseas for processing and the wool-stores closed down, but since then the bayside has been rejuvenated.

At the **National Wool Museum** *(26 Moorabool St; open daily; 03 5227 4701; www.geelongaustralia.com.au/nwm)*, learn about the industry, with tactile interactive displays and working machinery.

Just outside Geelong, on the B100, is **Narana Centre** *(410 Torquay Rd, 3216; 03 5241 5700; www.narana.com.au)*, a non-profit art and culture centre run by the indigenous community. Art, homewares, hand-crafted tools and instruments such as boomerangs and didgeridoos are available here.

🚗 *Turn right onto Moorabool St and continue to Eastern Beach and Geelong Foreshore.*

EAT AND DRINK

MELBOURNE
MoVida Bar De Tapas y Vino *moderate*
Finding a table can be tough here, but persevere to sample top Spanish nibbles. *1 Hosier Lane, 3000; 03 9663 3038; www.movida.com.au*

Other options
Try the cigar bar **Siglo** for great views, then choose between **The European** or **Melbourne Supper Club** *(all at 161 Spring St, 3000; 03 9654 0811; www. theeuropean.com.au)*. Or try the **Italian Waiters Club** *(20 Meyers Place, 3000; 03 9650 1508)*, then coffee at **Pellegrini's** *(66 Bourke St, 3000; 03 9662 1885)*.

GEELONG
Winters Café *inexpensive*
An award-winning eatery, which offers great food and excellent service at a reasonable price. *33 Pakington St, 3220; 03 5221 8832*

Other options
For fine bay dining, try the **Beach House** *(Eastern Beach Reserve, 3220; 03 5221 8322; www.easternbeachhouse.com.au)* or head to **Sabeeka Kohinoor Indian Restaurant** *(211 Moorabool St, 3220; 03 5222 7076)* for a great curry.

Left Stylish graffiti on the walls in Hosier Lane, central Melbourne **Below** Façade of the National Wool Museum, Geelong

Eat and Drink: inexpensive under AU$60; moderate AU$60–AU$100; expensive over AU$100

Above Bollards painted as local personalities lined up along the Geelong Foreshore

ACTIVITIES AROUND OTWAY FLY TREETOP WALK

Otway Eco Tours
Willing adventurers are met at the town of Forrest, 36 km (22 miles) north of Apollo Bay along the B100 and C119, for tours along purpose-built mountain bike trails through Great Otway National Park. Self-guided trips, with packed lunches, are also available. The same company runs **Paddle with Platypus Tours**, with a discount if none are seen, and **Great Ocean Walks**. *0419 670 985; www.platypustours.net.au*

WHERE TO STAY

AROUND OTWAY FLY TREETOP WALKWAY

Chris's Villas *moderate*
On winding Skenes Creek Rd on the drive to Otway Fly Treetop Walk, down a steep paddock from the forest, are Chris's self-contained villas, suitable for families. *280 Skenes Creek Rd, Apollo Bay, 3233; 03 5237 6411; www.chriss.com.au*

AROUND TRIPLET FALLS

Otway Estate
Get away from it all in these two secluded villas on the C155 north – enjoy great food, luxury accommodation and a romantic setting, but note – children only by prior arrangement. Tours and activities can be arranged for residents. *10–30 Hoveys Rd, Barongarook, 3429; 03 5233 8400; www.otwayestate.com.au*

❸ Geelong Foreshore
Victoria; 3220
The Geelong Foreshore and Eastern Beach are the seaside destinations of choice for many Melburnians. Follow artist Jan Mitchell's trail of 111 person-sized bollards, painted in the guise of local personalities; take a seaplane flight from **Bay City Seaplanes** *(Steam Packet Quay; 0438 840 205; www.baycityseaplanes.com.au)*; or simply relax by the water. Kids can try their luck at the modern skate park, on the hill overlooking the boardwalk.
🚗 *Take the A10 out of Geelong and turn off on the B100 to Torquay. For Surfworld turn right down Beach Rd.*

❹ Surfworld
Beach Rd, Torquay, Victoria; 3228
A shrine to all things surfing, **Surfworld** *(open daily; www.surfworld.org.au)* is a fine introduction to the beach culture of the area. Displays reveal major themes from the world of surfing, and outline the origins of the sport in Australia, with one of the first boards in the country on display. A board shaper -- fashioning boards out of fibreglass – operates in the museum most of the time and can be viewed working behind a glass partition.
🚗 *Rejoin the B100 and continue past Jan Juc, then left on C132 then left onto Bones Rd, which becomes Bells Beach Rd to the beach on the left.*

Retro graphics advertising Surfworld

Learn to Surf
Take to the breakers with **Go Ride a Wave** *(03 5263 2169; www.gorideawave.com.au)* at Torquay, Anglesea or Lorne. With over 20 years' experience instructing first-timers, Go Ride a Wave, which supplies soft beginner boards, leg ropes and wetsuits, could have beginners carving a path down the face of a wave after a lesson or two. Boards and kayaks are also available for hire without lessons.

❺ Bells Beach
Victoria; 3228
At any time of year and at almost any time of the day, there are experienced surfers taking on the intimidating swells at Bells Beach. The location for the world's longest-running surfing competition, the Rip Curl Pro, Bells Beach was first recognized as a top surfing spot more than 60 years ago, and remains one of the best surfing destinations in Victoria.
🚗 *Carry on along Bells Beach Rd, which becomes Jarosite Rd. Turn left at B100, which becomes Great Ocean Rd, past Anglesea, Fairhaven and Lorne all the way to Skenes Creek. Turn right down the C119, and left at Turtons Track. Head along Beech Forest–Lavers Hill Rd towards Weeaproinah and turn left to Otway Fly Treetop Walk. Park in car park.*

Below A seaplane docked at the jetty on the Geelong Foreshore

⑥ Otway Fly Treetop Walk
Weeaproinah, Victoria; 3237

It is one thing to walk in the shade of the trees, it is another to walk through the canopy itself, 25 m (80 ft) above ground. The **Otway Fly Treetop Walk** (open daily; www.otwayfly.com) is 600 m (1,970 ft) of walkway that swings and sways in a subtle (and safe) manner in the breeze – especially the cantilever section. Look out for the bright flash of the crimson rosella flying among the foliage and, on the ground, keep an eye out for platypuses and spiny echidnas, as well as any of the approximately 50 other mammal species. In addition to the many birds and creepy crawlies, there are also model dinosaurs along the way for a "Jurassic Park" experience. Pick up a map at the visitor centre, where there is also a decent café, and allow an hour and a half to explore the bright green ferns and damp, towering mountain ash, myrtle beech and blackwood trees.

🚗 *Turn right out of Otway Fly car park, turn right into Phillips Track and then on to the Great Otway National Park.*

⑦ Triplet Falls
Great Otway National Park, Victoria; 3232

Drop down to earth in Great Otway National Park, into a moist fern gully at **Triplet Falls** (www.parkweb.vic.gov.au), which flow through dense fernery, over moss-covered boulders. After a AU$2 million-dollar improvement – the walking track, on metal-grid walkways that offer grip in the wet forest – is more accessible than ever, and dips into once dense territory. The walking loop takes around one hour (1.8 km/1 mile) and passes Otways Timber Mill, with rusty old machinery scattered in the undergrowth. The ancient forest is also home to koalas, wallabies and grey kangaroos. Viewing platforms allow visitors to peer into the lower and upper reaches of the falls, while tables are perfect for picnics.

🚗 *Retrace route to Otway Fly Treetop walk and continue to C159, turning right onto it, then right onto C119 as far as Skenes Creek on the Great Ocean Rd (B100). Turn right to Marengo and park at caravan park.*

Above left Walkway through the forest at the Otway Fly Treetop Walk **Above right** View of the rainforest floor, Otway Fly Treetop Walk

EAT AND DRINK

AROUND OTWAY FLY TREETOP WALKWAY

Chris's *expensive*
This restaurant serves modern Greek fare and seafood specialities followed by baklava served with crystallized rose petals. There are sweeping sea and forest views, along with a top wine list.
280 Skenes Creek Rd, Apollo Bay, 3233; 03 5237 6411; www.chriss.com.au

Other options
Apollo Bay, between Skenes Creek and Marengo, offers reasonable **fish and chips** options along the main street, as well as **La Bimba** *(125–7 Great Ocean Rd, Apollo Bay, 3233; 03 5237 7411)*. Enjoy decent tapas and hearty pasta dishes, along with good coffee and wireless internet.

AROUND TRIPLET FALLS

Blackwood Gully *moderate*
In Lavers Hill, near the Otway Fly and Triplet Falls, this restaurant, gift shop and bird-watching centre serves delicious home-made cakes and teas.
Great Ocean Rd, Lavers Hill, 3238; 03 5237 3290; www.blackwoodgully.com

Otway Estate
A little way north along Beech Forest Road, this winery, brewery, and local arts-and-crafts gallery offers plenty of fine food, too, making it a one-stop afternoon entertainment spot. Sip Prickly Moses Organic Lager alongside one of three ever-changing mains and then taste your way through the rest of the alcoholic range at the cellar door.
10–30 Hoveys Rd, Barongarook, 3429; 03 5233 8400; www.otwayestate.com.au

Left Lush fern gully at the spectacular cascades of Triplet Falls

Above Two of the spectacular eight remaining apostles, Port Campbell National Park

VISITING MARENGO REEFS MARINE SANCTUARY

For information on diving and snorkelling at Marengo Reefs Marine Sanctuary, contact the **Parks Victoria Information Centre** *(13 1963; www.parkweb.vic.gov.au)* or **Visit Warrnambool** *(http://visitwarrnambool.com.au/)*.

WHERE TO STAY

AROUND MARENGO REEFS MARINE SANCTUARY

Room with a View *moderate*
Enjoy split-level living with sweeping views though floor-to-ceiling glass from a hilltop above the Great Ocean Rd, not far from Apollo Bay. Breakfast is included and there are koalas outside. *280 Sunnyside Rd, Wongarra 3233; 03 5237 0218; www.roomwithaview.com.au*

Johanna River Farm and Cottages *moderate*
Little extras like fresh flowers, local organic produce and hand-made soap and candles add to the comfort of this peaceful property. Greet the farm animals and enjoy views of the ocean from well-equipped cottages. *420 Blue Johanna Rd, 3238; 03 5237 4219; www.johanna.com.au*

AROUND PORT CAMPBELL NATIONAL PARK

Anchors Port Campbell *moderate*
Just outside the town centre, in a bright green field, sit two fully self-contained villas. Enjoy contemporary design and an open-plan layout with wine cooler and coffee machine. There is a spa with a view, as well as a huge kitchen. *2549 Cobden–Port Campbell Rd, 3233; 0417 434 400; www.anchorsportcampbell.com.au*

Seal Kayaking at Marengo Reefs Marine Sanctuary

See the seals up-close by paddling out in a sit-on-top kayak, either by yourself or with a guide. **Apollo Bay Surf Kayak** *(0405 495 909; www.apollobaysurfkayak.com.au)* offer instruction, as well as a figure-flattering wetsuit and a sense of humour. Catch a wave back to shore for an exhilarating finale.

⑧ Marengo Reefs Marine Sanctuary
Marengo, Victoria; 3233

The two reefs of the sanctuary, 80 m (260 ft) from shore – Henty and Little Henty – and a diverse marine habitat make for a fascinating snorkel or swim off the shore at Marengo *(see left)*. From August to February, see male six-spined leather-jacket fish go lip to lip for territory, dorsal spines erect, ready to attack each other with their tails. The beach at Marengo is less crowded and no less lovely than that at Apollo Bay, and the rocky outcrop 200 m (650 ft) or so out to sea hosts an extra attraction – a transient group of Australian fur seals that use it as a haul-out point *(see box)*.

🚗 *Rejoin B100 and turn left back towards Lavers Hill. Turn off left onto Otway Lighthouse Tourist Rd all the way to Cape Otway. Park in the main car park, and walk from site to site.*

⑨ Cape Otway Lightstation
Victoria; 3233

Cape Otway is a wild place offering dramatic clifftop walks. However, its main attraction is the lightstation complex *(open daily; www.lightstation.com)*, which includes the old light-

house and a World War II radar station. Run initially on whale oil, then kerosene and finally electricity, the 18-m (60-ft) high old lighthouse was built in 1848 after several shipwrecks at King Island, off Cape Otway in the Bass Strait. In 1994, the lighthouse was replaced by a solar-powered beacon with an inferior range, as advances in navigation technology had reduced its importance. It is possible to climb the lighthouse to take in the view.

In November 1940, the US steamship *City of Rayville* was sunk by a German mine off Cape Otway, claiming the first US casualty of the war. The bunker, built near the lighthouse two years later, though largely a shell today, is one of four once-secret **World War II radar stations** built along this coast.

🚗 *Rejoin B100, turning left – there is a possible diversion to the Gables at Moonlight Head Rd for views of some of the highest cliffs in Australia on an unsealed road, but passable by 2WD. Rejoin B100, heading east, all the way to Twelve Apostles visitor centre car park, Port Campbell National Park.*

⑩ Port Campbell National Park
Victoria; 3269

Possessing some of the most iconic rock formations and landscapes in Australia, Port Campbell National Park has also seen several tragic shipwrecks.

The iconic **Twelve Apostles** – in fact only eight remain – are eroded sandstone stacks, standing in the sea,

Above The old lighthouse at Cape Otway Lightstation

Above Loch Ard Gorge, site of a terrible tragedy, Port Campbell National Park

Apostles from Above

It might take several days to visit all the fabulous beaches, bays and rock formations from the Twelve Apostles to the Bay of Islands by road, but they can all be seen in under an hour with **12 Apostles Helicopters** *(03 5598 8283; www.12apostleshelicopters.com.au).* The choppers leave from behind the Twelve Apostles visitor centre, and take passengers on a 180-km (110-mile) round-trip with commentary.

a popular dive site. It takes a few hours on foot to fully explore the gorge, beach and tiny cemetery, where some victims of the wreck are buried. Visitors will appreciate the beautiful setting and lingering sense of tragedy. After the wreck, 11 bodies were found in the blowhole, near Loch Ard Gorge. For nights afterwards, the blowhole glowed eerily purple – supposedly caused by phosphorus matches from the ship.

A little further along the coast stands **London Bridge**. What is now a single-span, bridge-like limestone rock formation was once a twin-span structure with a passing resemblance to the English bridge that was regularly traversed by foot. Two visitors were caught out on 15 January 1990, when the span closest to shore collapsed and they had to be lifted to safety by helicopter.

🚗 *Rejoin the B100 and turn left at the sign to the Bay of Islands.*

stark against the high cliffs. Originally called the "Sow and Piglets" (the sow was Muttonbird Island at Loch Ard Gorge), they were renamed the Twelve Apostles to encourage visitors. No matter the spin, they are a fabulous sight to behold. Viewing platforms are accessed via a highway underpass leading to the visitor centre and car park.

A little further along the Great Ocean Road is the **Loch Ard Gorge**. When the *Loch Ard* ran aground near Muttonbird Island (an important nesting site for muttonbirds or shearwaters) on 1 June 1878, 52 passengers and crew were lost, with only two survivors. The wreck remains

Signs for kangaroos and echidnas, Loch Ard

Below Twelve Apostles visitor centre, Port Campbell National Park

Above The cemetery where some victims of the *Loch Ard* tragedy are buried

VISITING PORT CAMPBELL NATIONAL PARK

For information about visiting Port Campbell National Park and activities in the park, contact **Parks Victoria** *(13 1963; www.parkweb.vic.gov.au)* or drop in to the information centre at **Port Campbell** *(26 Morris St, 3269; 03 5598 6089)*, the information kiosk at the **Twelve Apostles** or the visitor centre at **Warrnambool** *(89 Merri St, 3280; 1800 637 725)*. **Daktari Sport and Dive** at Warrnambool *(453 Raglan Parade, 3280; 03 5562 4006)* organize dives.

EAT AND DRINK

AROUND PORT CAMPBELL NATIONAL PARK

Waves *expensive*
It is all about seafood at Port Campbell's fine-dining destination. Local wines and beers complement modern, Australian-style dishes. *29 Lord St, Port Campbell, 3233; 03 5598 6111; www.wavesportcampbell. com.au*

Other options
Opposite Waves, **KooAAH** *(26 Lord St, 3233; 03 5598 6408)* is a nice little outlet, which offers fast and fantastic takeaway food.

WHERE TO STAY

PORTLAND

Seascape *moderate*
Just across the road from the beach and equipped with a telescope to spy on visiting blue whales (Nov–May), this offers en suite rooms, free Internet and a communal living/kitchen area. Drink the complimentary port to the sounds of soft jazz and the crashing waves.
271 Hanlon Parade, 3305; 03 5523 3960; www.seascapeaccomm.com.au

BALLARAT

Craig's Royal Hotel *expensive*
After a long and careful refurbishment, this historic boutique hotel recaptures the glimmering heyday of Ballarat with the finest fittings available, wireless internet, cable TV and enormous suites.
10 Lydiard St South, 3350; 03 5331 1377; www.craigsroyal.com.au

Other options
Art Deco outside and contemporary design inside, **Oscar's Hotel** is a fine option *(18 Doveton St, 3350; 03 5331 1451; www.oscarshotel.com.au)*, or for character on a budget try **Sovereign Hill Lodge** *(Sovereign Hill, 3350; 03 5337 1159; www.sovereignhill.com.au)* in the recreated eponymous 19th-century gold-rush theme park.

Below The 1910 shed housing the Timboon Railway Shed Distillery **Below right** The cluster of limestone outcrops at the Bay of Islands **Below left** Copper still at the Timboon Railway Shed Distillery

⓫ Bay of Islands
Victoria; 3280
It is a 15-minute drive without stops from the Twelve Apostles and equally attractive, but the Bay of Islands is much less celebrated. A cluster of dark brown outcrops scattered throughout a small bay with a typically wild beach, fringed by cliffs, the Bay of Islands harbours a dark history. At nearby Massacre Point, local oral history tells that a group of Aborigines were driven off a cliff by European settlers. The point's alternate name, Halladale Point, refers to a 1908 shipwreck.

🚗 *Rejoin B100, turn left, and turn off right to C163 into central Timboon.*

⓬ Timboon Railway Shed Distillery
Timboon, Victoria; 3268
Who would have thought ice cream and vodka would go so well together? This historic distillery and restaurant also produces a huge range of innovative velvety ice creams. Savour the menu, learn about the history of the distillery and then walk the 3 km (2 miles) to Curdie's River Trestle Bridge along the well-signed **Timboon to Camperdown Rail Trail** (the whole trail is 34 km/21 miles long). After the walk, fill up at the gourmet café – finishing, of course, with some

delicious ice cream *(open daily; 03 5598 3555; www.timboondistillery.com).*

🚗 *Take C163 back to B100, turn right then take A1 (Princes Hwy - motorway as far as Warrnambool) left, to Portland.*

⓭ Portland
Victoria; 3305
The first European settlement in Victoria, dating from 1834, before settlement of the state was legalized by the colonial authorities, Portland possesses the only deep-water port between Melbourne and Adelaide. Today, it is supported by aluminium smelting, but its historic centre retains many attractive buildings.

It is possible to take a self-guided walk to 48 of the more than 200 noted historic buildings in Portland – a map and guide are available from the

Whale Migration
Brave the waters off the western reaches of the Great Ocean Rd in May–Sep – the coldest, wettest time of year – and be rewarded with the spectacle of whales at play. Visit the specially built whale viewing platform at **Logans Beach** and watch for southern right whales near Warrnambool. The even larger blue whales can be seen around Portland between Nov and May.

Beach Trail Horse Riding

Ride on the deserted beaches between Warrnambool and Port Ferry with **Rundell's Mahogany Trail Rides** *(Millers Lane, 3280; 0408 589 546; www.rundellshorseriding.com.au).* Rides range from one to three and a half hours. There are also rides catered for complete beginners.

Portland Maritime Discovery and Visitor Information Centre *(Lee Breakwater Rd, 3315; 1800 035 567).* Many of these are built from bluestone, a type of basalt often used in older buildings in Melbourne and elsewhere.

🚗 *Take C193 out of Portland to Cape Bridgewater, follow signs to Blow Holes.*

⑭ Discovery Bay Coastal Park

Victoria; 3350

Under the whir of electricity-generating turbines', Discovery Bay Coastal Park, a 50-km (30-mile) stretch of beaches, dunes and coastal lakes, contains some extraordinary tube-like mineral deposits of limestone that have the texture and form of fossilized tree trunks. This petrified forest overlooks a stark, rocky plain bordered by black (basalt) and brown (scoria) cliffs. As the scoria erodes faster than the basalt, the rough swells have bored tunnels, caves and blowholes into the cliffs. The waves crash into these with huge booms, sending up clouds of spray. The dramatic scenery is best at sunset.

🚗 *Drive back along C193 to Portland, take A200 to Hamilton, becoming the B160 for the long drive to Ballarat.*

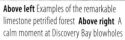

Timboon Railway Shed Distillery

⑮ Ballarat

Victoria; 3350

Central to Victoria's 19th-century Gold Rush, Ballarat is Victoria's largest inland city and retains a lot of impressive architecture from its heyday *(see p126).* Gold was discovered in 1851 and fuelled the city's growth for 50 years. Its golden heritage is evident in the legacy of fine dining and entertainment, such as **Her Majesty's Theatre** *(7 Lydiard St South; 03 5333 5888; www.hermaj.com).* Opened in 1875, this is Australia's best-preserved theatre. For further insight into the area's heritage and the inspiration artists continue to draw from its landscape and lifestyle, stop by the **Art Gallery of Ballarat** *(40 Lydiard St North; open daily; guided tours 2pm Wed–Sun; 03 5320 5858; www.balgal.com),* which exhibits everything from century-old realist depictions of sights along the Great Ocean Road and scenes from the Otway Rainforest, to cutting-edge multimedia pieces.

Above left Examples of the remarkable limestone petrified forest **Above right** A calm moment at Discovery Bay blowholes

EAT AND DRINK

PORTLAND

Bridgewater Bay Café *inexpensive*
Located around ten minutes west of Portland, this pretty beachfront café offers spectacular ocean views and delicious food. Live music on Sunday afternoons.
1661 Bridgewater Rd, 3305; 03 5526 7155

BALLARAT

Europa Café *expensive*
Seasonal lunch and dinner menu ranging from Italian to Middle Eastern to Asian cuisine, with a wide-reaching wine list and a good breakfast menu, too.
411 Sturt St, 3350; 03 5338 7672; www.europacafe.com.au

Other options
L'Espresso *(417 Sturt St, 3350; 03 5333 1789),* near the Europa Café, has a deliciously Italian flavour and excellent coffee, while **Chat for Tea** *(25 Armstrong St, 3350; 03 5331 3898)* is a relaxed vegetarian Buddhist tea house.

Left The Art Gallery of Ballarat, Lydiard Street

Eat and Drink: inexpensive under AU$60; moderate AU$60–AU$100; expensive over AU$100

Goldfields and Spa Country

Melbourne to Castlemaine

Highlights

- **Grand private gardens**
  Delight in the autumnal colours of Mount Macedon's historic private gardens

- **Fine regional wines**
  Sample Central Victoria's excellent dry-climate wines at the vineyards around Mount Macedon, Woodend and Daylesford

- **Mineral springs and day spas**
  Pamper yourself with a soak in the warm waters of the mineral spas at Daylesford or Hepburn Springs

- **Gold Rush architecture**
  Dine or sleep in elegant Gold Rush hotels or quaint miners' cottages

Rural scene at Shepherds Flat

Goldfields and Spa Country

In the 1850s and 1860s the Goldfields of Central Victoria were a magnet to hundreds of thousands of fortune seekers from across the globe. For many, the Gold Rush was to be a time of back-breaking heartache but for others – the lucky few – it was their passport to previously unimaginable wealth. This route traces the footsteps of the "diggers" north from the port of Melbourne, via the temperate slopes of Mount Macedon and the mineral springs and spas of Daylesford and Hepburn Springs, to the Goldfields. Many grand hotels and civic buildings remain, as do humble miners' cottages, old gold-diggings and memorials to the turbulent times that led to the birth of Australian democracy.

Above The old Mining Exchange in Ballarat, *see p126*

Below Field of sunflowers at Clunes, *see p126*

ACTIVITIES

Climb Hanging Rock, the setting for Joan Lindsay's evocative novel *Picnic at Hanging Rock*

Take the steam train from Castlemaine to Maldon or spa country railway from Daylesford to Bullarto

Pan for gold at Ballarat's Sovereign Hill, a re-created gold-mining town

Take to the skies in a hot-air balloon over Bendigo and the local vineyards

Cool off with a swim in the Expedition Pass Reservoir outside Chewton

Mountain bike the many trails through the Castlemaine Diggings National Heritage Park

Above Farmland at Shepherds Flat, *see p125*

KEY

Drive route

VICTORIA

Goomong
shot
Barnadown
kedale
Knowsley
Lake Eppalock
Mía Mla
Redesdale
Barfold
Langley
nsbury
Baynton
Nullavale
Kyneton
Lancefield
on
ylden
HANGING ROCK ③
Romsey
DODEND ④
② MOUNT MACEDON
Darraweit Guim
Macedon
New Gisborne
Monegeetta
kwood
Riddells Creek
Gisborne
Beveridge
llengarook
Couangalt
Kalkallo
Sunbury
Mickleham
Wollert
Toolern Vale
Diggers Rest
Greenvale
Craigieburn
Mernda
acchus Marsh
Bulla
Melbourne Airport
Epping
Melton
Taylors Lakes
Greensborough
Parwan
Exford
Preston
Yarra River
Brunswick
Doncaster
Truganina
Footscray
① MELBOURNE
Balliang East
Derrimut
Altona
St Kilda
Hoppers Crossing
Werribee
Brighton
Werribee South
Port Phillip Bay
Moorabbin

0 kilometres 15

0 miles 15

PLAN YOUR DRIVE

Start/finish: Melbourne to Castlemaine.

Number of days: 4–5, allowing a day to explore Sovereign Hill in Ballarat.

Distance: 255 km (158 miles).

Road conditions: Roads are paved and signposted. Mount Macedon can have snow in winter (Jun–Aug), when roads around Mount Macedon, Trentham, Daylesford and Ballarat are prone to black ice. Drive slowly from dusk to dawn to avoid accidents with kangaroos and wallabies (which can be seen everywhere) and wombats (between Trentham and Daylesford).

When to go: April and May are the best months in which to enjoy Mount Macedon's autumnal foliage. Spring (Sep–Nov) is the prime season for wildflowers in the box-ironbark forests. Summer (Dec–Mar) in Central Victoria is very hot and dry.

Opening times: Most museums and shops are open 9am–5pm. It is often difficult to find restaurants open in smaller towns on Mon & Tue nights.

Main market days: Trentham: farmers' market 3rd Sat, Trentham trash and treasure market 4th Sun of month; **Daylesford:** Sun, farmers' market every Sun; **Castlemaine:** Sat; farmers' market 1st Sun of month.

Shopping: Melbourne has all the big-city shopping you would expect, while Daylesford and Castlemaine both have a range of chic one-off boutiques and shops, and numerous arts and crafts galleries. Many regional vineyards offer tastings and opportunities to buy their wines.

Major festivals: Ballarat: Begonia Festival, Mar; Organs of the Ballarat Goldfields, Jan; **Newstead:** Newstead Live Folk Festival, Jan; **Maldon:** Folk Festival, Nov; Historic Hill Climb, Oct; **Fryerstown:** Antiques Fair, Jan; **Guildford:** Banjo Jamboree, Sep; **Castlemaine:** Castlemaine State Festival (odd years), Mar-Apr.

Above Tree-lined road up Mount Macedon

VISITING MOUNT MACEDON

Parking
Mt Macedon Rd winds its way up past the village to the summit of Mount Macedon, where there is a car park.

Macedon Ranges Visitor Information Centre
Garden maps and guides.
High St, Woodend, 3442; 03 5427 2033; www.visitmacedonranges.com

WHERE TO STAY

MOUNT MACEDON

Braeside Café and B&B *moderate*
This café also has a quaint cottage and a small cabin set in the gardens. Both have wood-burning heaters.
47 Taylors Rd, 3441; 03 5426 1762; www.braesidemtmacedon.com.au

WOODEND

Campaspe House *expensive*
An award-winning country retreat with rooms in the manor house and a cottage in the historic Edna Walling-designed gardens.
Goldies Lane, 3442; 03 5427 2273; www.campaspehouse.com.au

DAYLESFORD

Hotel Frangos & Frangos *moderate*
Luxurious apartment rooms hidden away on Daylesford's main street.
82 Vincent St, 3460; 03 5348 2363; www.frangosandfrangos.com

HEPBURN SPRINGS

Continental House *inexpensive*
A friendly vegan guesthouse retreat offering single, double and family rooms, a garden cottage, a tree-house cottage and a tipi (teepee).
9 Lone Pine Ave, 3461; 03 5348 2005; www.continentalhouse.com.au

① Melbourne
Victoria; 3000
When the news that gold had been discovered in Victoria spread around the globe in 1851, hopefuls from Europe, America and China set sail for Port Phillip Bay and fanned north in search of wealth. The Gold Rush spawned "Marvellous Melbourne", for a time one of the wealthiest cities in the world. It retains many fine Neo-Gothic and Neo-Classical buildings from the period and much of its Victorian charm. It is justly proud of its public gardens, elegant arcades, tree-lined boulevards, fine dining and vibrant nightlife *(see also pp112–113).*

🚗 *Follow blue and yellow Citylink signs for M2 towards Bendigo, branch left for M79 Calder Hwy. After Diggers Rest and Gisborne take C322 exit to Mount Macedon.*

② Mount Macedon
Victoria; 3441
This wealthy enclave was devastated by the 1983 Ash Wednesday bushfires, but the historic gardens scattered over its slopes have recovered and are a delight in spring and autumn, when many are open to the public. Pick up a map and guide from the visitor centre. The 21-m (69-ft) Memorial Cross at the summit, with views south, honours the fallen of World War I. Nearby Camels Hump offers views to the north.

🚗 *Rejoin C322 and follow the signs down the mountain to Hanging Rock.*

Warning of wombats near Trentham

③ Hanging Rock
Victoria; 3442
This 6-million-year-old lava outcrop was the location for Joan Lindsay's haunting novel *Picnic at Hanging Rock* and the 1975 Peter Weir film of the same name. On New Year's Day and Australia Day (26 January) the Picnic Horse Races are run here, and in February and March it hosts wine and harvest picnics. **The Reserve** *(open daily)* has a Discovery Centre with exhibitions, nature trails, guided night walks, picnic areas and a café.

🚗 *Turn right onto C322 and follow signs to Woodend. Turn left at C792. With the Macedon Ranges Visitor Centre on the right, cross Five Mile Creek into Woodend.*

④ Woodend
Victoria; 3442
This small town on the edge of the Black Forest was once a popular resting spot for diggers travelling to the Goldfields. With numerous B&Bs and holiday cottages, it makes a good base from which to explore Hanging Rock and the region's cafés, pubs, speciality shops, galleries and wineries. An easy walking trail beside Five Mile Creek is accessible from the Visitor Centre.

🚗 *From Woodend take the Tylden road (C317). Turn left at Chanters Lane. Fork right after Chanters Ridge Vineyard and pass the Pig & Whistle Hotel. Turn left. This road becomes Trentham's main street. Park here.*

Below Atmospheric and dramatically beautiful Hanging Rock

⑤ Trentham

Victoria; 3458

Deep verandas line the main street of Trentham, and its historic **Railway Station** doubles as the Information Centre. The town is surrounded by the temperate Wombat State Forest. The nearby **Garden of St Erth** *(open daily)* is a year-round delight with its lovely plantings and organic café. Just outside Trentham (signed down Falls Road), the Coliban River plunges 32 m (105 ft) down Trentham Falls.

🚗 *Continue along the main street to rejoin C317. Turn right to visit Trentham Falls or left for Daylesford.*

⑥ Daylesford

Victoria; 3460

This bustling town has over a dozen spas and almost 100 alternative health practitioners. There are wineries in the nearby hills, and restaurants and galleries line the main street. The **Daylesford Museum** *(Vincent St, open Sat, Sun & public hols)* has relics from the Gold Rush. A Sunday market operates beside the Historic Railway Station, from where the **Spa Country Railway** *(www.dscr.com.au)* operates a scenic route to Bullarto and back. Picturesque Lake Daylesford *(just off Vincent St)* offers boat hire, and the Botanic Gardens *(1 km/ half a mile east on Central Springs Road)* are dusted with snow in winter.

🚗 *At the roundabout of Vincent St and A300 (the Daylesford-Ballarat road), turn right and head north, downhill, to Hepburn Springs.*

⑦ Hepburn Springs

Victoria; 3461

This hilly town, which sits alongside Daylesford, has been famous for its mineral springs since the 1890s. Lavishly restored and redesigned in 2008, the **Hepburn Bathhouse & Spa** *(open daily)* in the Mineral Springs Reserve offers spa treatments, and the heritage-listed Pavilion Café next door serves delicious lunches. Short walks in the reserve lead to mineral springs where water bottles can be filled for free. **The Palais Theatre** *(open Wed–Sun, evenings only)* is an intimate live music venue and café-bar featuring a good mix of Australian and international acts.

🚗 *Turn left on Main Rd just downhill from The Palais Theatre and continue straight on to Shepherds Flat.*

⑧ Shepherds Flat

Victoria; 3461

Swiss-Italian migrants settled here in the 19th century, and their distinctive stone buildings are a local feature. Lavender farm **Lavandula** *(open daily Jan; weekends Jun–Aug; Fri–Tue Feb–May & Sep–Dec)* boasts an 1860s Italian-style homestead. Nearby, **Cricket Willow** *(open Sat, Sun & public hols)* has been making cricket bats from its own willow for over a century. Take a "bud to bat" tour.

🚗 *Return to Daylesford and turn right onto A300 at the roundabout. Continue straight ahead on C292. Turn right at Victoria St for central Ballarat or left to the Eureka Centre or Sovereign Hill.*

Below Trentham Railway Station

Above left Lavender farm at Shepherds Flat
Above centre Daylesford's convent **Above right** Long drop of Trentham Falls

EAT AND DRINK

MOUNT MACEDON

Top of the Range Tea Rooms and Gallery *inexpensive*
This welcoming café at the summit of Mount Macedon serves breakfasts on weekends and light lunches daily.
805 Cameron Drive, 3441; 03 5427 3466

WOODEND

Holgate Brewhouse *moderate*
This microbrewery in an old country pub also offers courtyard dining.
Keatings Hotel, 79 High St, 3442; 03 5427 2510; www.holgatebrewhouse.com

DAYLESFORD

Cliffy's *inexpensive*
Light and airy café near the market – ideal for breakfast on a sunny morning.
30 Raglan St, 3460; 03 5348 3279

Farmers Arms *moderate*
Relaxed dining and one of the best pub menus in Australia.
1 East St, 3460; 03 5348 2091; www.farmersarmsdaylesford.com.au

Lake House *expensive*
One of Australia's best restaurants, serving award-winning modern Australian cuisine by Lake Daylesford.
King St, 3460; 03 5348 3329; www.lakehouse.com.au

HEPBURN SPRINGS

Red Star *inexpensive*
Laid-back café serving breakfast and lunch, with comfortable old couches and a wall of books.
115 Main Rd, 3461; 03 5348 2297; www.theredstar.com.au

Lucini's Pasta Café and Bar *moderate*
This homely Italian restaurant is housed in Australia's first macaroni factory, established by the Lucini brothers in the 1850s.
64 Main Rd, 3461; 03 5348 4345; www.macaronifactory.com.au

Eat and Drink: inexpensive under AU$60; moderate AU$60–100; expensive over AU$100

WHERE TO STAY

BALLARAT

Craig's Royal Hotel *moderate*
This 1862 hotel has an Oriental suite with a 600-year-old Chinese wedding bed.
10 Lydiard St South, 3350; 03 5331 1377; www.craigsroyal.com.au

Quest Ansonia Ballarat *moderate*
Modern, pleasant rooms and an airy central atrium behind an 1860s façade.
32 Lydiard St South, 3350; 03 5332 4678; www.theansoniaonlydiard.com.au

Oscar's Hotel *moderate*
Stylish Art Deco hotel, café & bar that sits in the heart of Ballarat.
18 Devon St South, 3350; 03 5331 1451; www.oscarshotel.com.au

BENDIGO

Lynnevale Estate B&B *moderate*
Contemporary B&B nestled in a vineyard, minutes' drive from the city centre.
83 Cahills Rd, 3551; 03 5439 3635; www.lynnevale.com.au

Hotel Shamrock *moderate*
A Bendigo icon since 1854, this is a beautiful Victorian hotel.
Cnr Pall Mall & Williamson St, 3550; 03 5443 0333; www.hotelshamrock.com.au

AROUND BENDIGO
Byronsvale Vineyard *moderate*
A converted 1870s stable block on a vineyard 7 km (5 miles) from Bendigo.
51 Andrews Rd, Maiden Gully, 3551; 03 5447 2790; www.byronsvale.net.au

CHEWTON

Shack 14 *moderate*
A chic, one-room "eco shack", nestled in secluded box-ironbark forest.
Hoopers Rd, 3451; 03 5472 1677; www.shack14.com.au

⑨ Ballarat
Victoria; 3350
Ballarat's Lydiard Street is a lovingly-preserved Gold Rush streetscape. The **Museum of Australian Democracy at Eureka** *(open daily)* is on the site of the original Eureka Stockade *(see box)*, while **Sovereign Hill** *(open daily)* is a re-creation of a gold-mining town *(see also p119)*.

🚗 *Take Dovetown Street north towards Creswick/Castlemaine. Turn left at Howitt Street (the Showgrounds) to take C287 towards Maryborough for Clunes.*

Goldfields Rebellions
Tension over the mining licence and a lack of political suffrage simmered at the 1851 Monster Meeting in Chewton, and exploded in Ballarat in 1854. On 3 December, at 3am, soldiers and police attacked the ramshackle Eureka Stockade, erected by militant miners. Thirty people died and the revolt was crushed, but the government granted white-male suffrage in 1857.

⑩ Clunes
Victoria; 3370
Gold was discovered in Clunes in 1851, triggering the first Gold Rush. This tiny town, much loved as a film set, has a broad main street with old buildings and shady verandas. A walking track beside Creswick Creek leads to a lookout. The mullock (slag) heaps and remains of the former Port Phillip Mine are also worth seeing.

🚗 *Head north from Clunes following signs to Newstead.*

Hot Air Ballooning
An early morning hot air balloon ride over the vineyards around Bendigo is a great way to start the day. **Bendigo Ballooning** *(www.bendigoballooning. com.au)* operates flights, with a champagne breakfast, flight certificate and souvenir pack available on request.

⑪ Newstead
Victoria; 3462
The Loddon River runs through leafy Newstead. This quiet town comes alive over the Australia Day (26 Jan) weekend when it hosts the Newstead Live Music Festival, a folk music event with performances at several venues, including the popular Dig Cafe.

🚗 *Turn left from Newstead's main street on to C283 direct to Maldon.*

⑫ Maldon
Victoria; 3463
This historic town, nestled beneath Mount Tarrengower, is full of pretty old miners' cottages. The **Victorian Goldfields Railway** steam train runs to and from Castlemaine *(www.vgr. com.au)*. Take a candle-lit tour of **Carman's Tunnel** *(open Sat–Sun and holidays)*, an original 1880s mine.

🚗 *Leave town on Hornsby Street. Turn right at Fogarty's Gap Road and follow this to A79. Turn left into Bendigo.*

Below left Loddon River, Newstead **Below** Intact Gold Rush streetscape of Lydiard Street, Ballarat **Below right** Abandoned mining landscape with mullock heaps and miner's shanty, Clunes

⑬ Bendigo

Victoria; 3550

Bendigo's Gold Rush-era Pall Mall, in the centre of town, features the fine edifices of the Shamrock Hotel, the Law Courts and the former Post Office. In nearby View Street, the **Bendigo Art Gallery** *(open daily)* has a significant Colonial art collection. Behind the gallery is a former mine's pit head that offers great views over the town. Vintage trams run along Pall Mall from the **Central Deborah Goldmine** *(open daily)* to the 1860s **Joss House** *(open daily Aug–May; open Wed–Sat Jun & Jul)*. Tours of the former go 30 levels underground, while the latter provides an insight into the life of Bendigo's Chinese pioneers, as does the **Golden Dragon Museum** *(open daily)*.

A different way to see.Bendigo and the surrounding vineyard country is by hot-air balloon *(see box, left)*. Several companies offer early morning rides, finished off with a glass of local sparkling wine. Autumn is the best time for a flight.

🚗 **Leave Bendigo on the Calder Highway (A79), take the B180 exit and turn right onto the Pyrenees Highway to reach Chewton.**

Lion carving on a Bendigo building

Gold Fossicking

The Gold Rush may have run its course, but there is still gold out there to be found. **Bendigo Gold World** *(www.bendigogold.com.au)* runs fossicking tours and rents out gold (metal) detectors. Fossickers regularly turn up nuggets, sometimes as large as 550 g (20 oz), so, it could be worth setting aside a half day to give fossicking a try.

⑭ Chewton

Victoria; 3451

On the approach to Chewton from Golden Point Road take in the Expedition Pass Reservoir. Scottish explorer Major Thomas Mitchell came through here in 1836. Further along is the site of the 1851 Monster Meeting *(see box)*. This one-pub town once swarmed with miners. Now the surrounding hills are pocked with reminders of that era, including mine shafts, water races, machinery and stone ruins, the most impressive of which is the Garfield Waterwheel. The park next door to the tiny, over 150-year-old Town Hall features an old transportable gaol. On the way out of town is Wattle Gully Mine, a working gold mine since 1876.

🚗 **Chewton is only 6 km (4 miles) from Castlemaine, but detour left into Fryers Road and follow the brown Tourist Route 41 sign right to Fryerstown.**

Above Ruins of the immense Garfield Waterwheel, just north of Chewton

Above left Bendigo Art Gallery **Above centre** Golden Dragon Museum, Bendigo **Above right** Bendigo Law Courts

EAT AND DRINK

BALLARAT

Eclectic Tastes *inexpensive*
With its quirky decor and its varied menu, this is a great place for a meal or a good cup of coffee.
2 Burbank St, 3350; 03 5339 9252

Europa Café *moderate*
A café-restaurant with European, Middle-Eastern and Asian influences. The wine list is one of Ballarat's best.
411 Sturt St, 3350; 03 5331 2486; www. europacafe.com.au

L'espresso *moderate*
A fashionable Ballarat stalwart offering great coffee, ice cream and a modern Australian, Italian-influenced menu.
417 Sturt St, 3350; 03 5333 1789

BENDIGO

T'hooft *inexpensive*
A Belgian cafe in Bendigo may sound odd, but it is great for sandwiches, *focaccia*, waffles and Belgian beers.
322 Lyttleton Terrace, 3550; 03 5444 4448; www.thooft.com.au

Green Olive *inexpensive*
A breakfast and lunchtime favourite of Bendigo's smart set, with great coffee.
11 Bath Lane, 3550; 5442 2676

GPO *moderate*
This modern, stylish restaurant-lounge-café is popular with the young crowd and lawyers – it is across from the Court House.
60–64 Pall Mall, Bendigo, 3550; 03 5443 4343; www.gpobendigo.com.au

Whirrakee *expensive*
A classy French restaurant and wine bar, overlooking Pall Mall, Rosalind Park and Alexandra Fountain.
17 View Point, 3550; 03 5441 5557; www.whirrakeerestaurant.com.au

---

Eat and Drink: inexpensive under AU$60; moderate AU$60–AU$100; expensive over AU$100

Above left Creek at Vaughan Springs
Top right Scenery around Vaughan Springs
Above right The Guildford Hotel in the small town of Guildford

VISITING CASTLEMAINE

Parking
There is a car park behind the Visitor Information Centre; vehicle access from Pyrenees Hwy.

Visitor Information Centre
Maps, guides and information about the town and Castlemaine Diggings National Heritage Park.
44 Mostyn St, 3450; 03 5471 1795 (town), 03 5470 6200 (park); www.parkweb.vic. gov.au; open daily.

WHERE TO STAY

CASTLEMAINE

Albion Motel/Hotel *inexpensive*
Simple but stylish motel-style rooms at the rear of the 1850s Albion Hotel, overlooking the site of the Saturday Wesley Hill Market.
152 Duke St, 3450; 03 5472 1292

Empyre Boutique Hotel *expensive*
Six suites of contemporary luxury in a lovely 19th-century hotel with walled private garden, lounge and fine dining.
68 Mostyn St, 3450; 03 5472 5166; www.empyre.com.au

AROUND CASTLEMAINE

The Potager *expensive*
This 1860s sandstone cottage beside Forest Creek (left off the B180 from Castlemaine to Chewton) is set in its own shady gardens with a swimming pool.
Golden Point Rd, 3451; 03 5472 3714; www.thepotager.com.au

⑮ Fryerstown
Victoria; 3451
It is hard to believe that this sleepy hollow, with sheep grazing on the town common, was once home to 15,000 miners. Set in the middle of a box-ironbark forest, Fryerstown is now the setting for an annual antiques fair, which is held over the Australia Day (26 Jan) long weekend, when the population of 120 expands to over 30,000. On the road into Fryerstown the remains of the Duke of Cornwall Engine House are on the right, and the town's Mechanics Institute *(cnr of Camp St)* of 1863 commemorates pioneering explorers Burke and Wills.
🚗 *Follow the brown Tourist Route 41 sign around to the right at the fork just past Irishtown for Vaughan.*

Above Duke of Cornwall Engine House at Fryerstown

The Diggers
Fifty years after the Gold Rush, Australian and New Zealand troops in World War I were nicknamed "diggers". Almost every Australian town has a memorial to those who died in both world wars. Sadly, they now also carry the names of those who have died in subsequent wars – the monument in Clunes bears that of Australia's first military casualty in the 2003 Iraq War.

⑯ Vaughan
Victoria; 3451
On arrival in Vaughan, stop at the lookout on the right for views over the poplar-lined creek and back towards the old gold workings. A turn-off leads down to Mineral Springs Reserve, a peaceful, shady picnic ground with lovely walks beside the Loddon River and to a small Chinese cemetery.
🚗 *Continue on from Vaughan and follow the signs to Guildford.*

⑰ Guildford
Victoria; 3451
Guildford is a laid-back, one-pub, one-store town on the banks of the Loddon River. Gold prospectors flocked here in the 1850s and a large encampment of Chinese miners grew up at the meeting of Loddon River and Campbells Creek. The Guildford Hotel, venue for the Blues & Roots Explosion in March, dates back to the Gold Rush era.
🚗 *Leaving Guildford, turn right onto Midland Hwy (A300) to Castlemaine. Turn right into Pyrenees Hwy (B180) to access the car park.*

Where to Stay: inexpensive under AU$150; moderate AU$150–AU$250; expensive over AU$250

⑱ Castlemaine

Victoria; 3450

In the 1850s, 60,000 miners descended on what has since become an arty country town. The spring Castlemaine State Festival *(odd years)* celebrates the arts, and the Castlemaine Diggings National Heritage Park, between Castlemaine, Vaughan, Fryerstown and Chewton, protects sites significant to the Gold Rush and local Jaara Jaara people.

A two-hour walking tour

From the car park behind the 1861 **Market Building** ① on Mostyn Street, turn right and cross Hargraves Street. The 1857 **Theatre Royal** ②, Victoria's oldest continuously operating theatre, albeit with a 1930s façade, is on your right. Further along is the former Albion Hotel (now the Empyre Boutique Hotel). Across the road are the tiny weather-boarded 1860 Trades Hall and the 1864 Mount Alexander Hotel, now the **Restorers Barn** ③, packed to the rafters with curios and architectural salvage.

Cross Urquhart and Andrew Streets, and walk uphill (a steep but short climb) to the **Burke and Wills Monument** ④. This commemorates Robert O'Hara Burke and William John Wills, European explorers who crossed Australia from south to north in 1860–61. Burke was Castlemaine's Superintendent of Police (1858–60). Turn left along Wills Street, right at Lyttleton Street and head uphill to **Kalimna Park** ⑤. In the spring, this box-ironbark reserve blooms with wildflowers. Follow the Tourist Road as far as Hunter Track. Turn left and walk downhill to Hunter Street.

The elegant Gold Rush-era **Buda Historic Home and Garden** ⑥ *(open Wed–Sun)* on the corner of Urquhart Street houses a collection of home crafts. Turn left at Hargraves Street. After crossing Templeton Street and the 1855 **State Savings Bank Building** ⑦, the old police lock-up is on the right. At the next corner is a private residence that was once the Gold Warden's Office. On the opposite corner, the Supreme Court Hotel, built in 1859, is now **Heron's Art Gallery** ⑧. Turn right into Lyttleton Street, past the 1877 **Court House** ⑨, the 1887 School of Mines, the 1898 Town Hall and the 1889 Drill Hall. Turn right at the 1875

Post Office to see the 1857 Telegraph Office, the 1895 **Faulder Watson Hall** ⑩ and the 1857 Library. Return to Lyttleton Street and turn left to visit the **Castlemaine Art Gallery and Museum** ⑪ *(open daily)*, which has an excellent collection of Australian artworks. Turn left after the gallery and walk alongside the Uniting Church back to Mostyn Street. Across the road, beyond the Boer War Memorial, is **Christ Church** ⑫. It is on the site of Agitation Hill, where protesting miners gathered (1851–1854). Walk back down Mostyn Street and through **Victory Park** ⑬ to the car park. Pick up a map from the Visitor Information Centre and continue along Pyrenees Hwy (B180) for Castlemaine Diggings National Heritage Park. Forest Creek, just out of town, is a good start.

Art Gallery façade

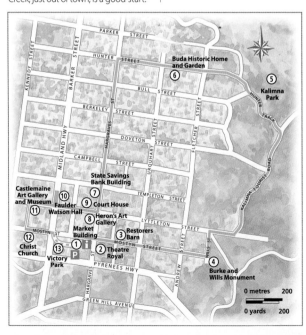

Eat and Drink: inexpensive under AU$60; moderate AU$60–AU$100; expensive over AU$100

Coastline and Convicts

Hobart to Port Arthur Historic Site

Highlights

- **Monolithic viewpoint**
  Survey all of the city, North Bruny Island and beyond from a perch atop Hobart's magnificent Mount Wellington

- **Vibrant market**
  Rummage for bargains and treasures at Salamanca Market, one of Australia's liveliest arts, crafts, produce and bric-a-brac markets

- **Cascade Brewery**
  Sample southern Tasmania's favourite brews at Australia's oldest brewery

- **Penal colony**
  Hear fascinating stories and explore remnants of Australia's convict past at the Port Arthur Historic Site

View of Hobart from Mount Wellington

Coastline and Convicts

Southeastern Tasmania is a land of islands, bays, harbours and inlets, crowned by Mount Wellington, and fringed to the west by the almost inaccessible forest of the Southwest National Park. Anchored firmly in the state capital of Hobart, this tour runs southwest into the forest's fringes, through the Huon Valley with its rich apple-growing heritage. It then returns to Hobart to travel northeast on causeways across the River Derwent and Pitt Water, before heading south to take in the rugged coastline at Eaglehawk Neck. Then it continues down onto the wave-beaten Tasman Peninsula as far as the poignant Port Arthur Historic Site for a glimpse into the nation's penal past.

KEY

Drive route

TASMANI

Levedale

Lowdina
Runnymede
Mangalore
Campania
Black Brush
Pontville
Brighton
Bridgewater
Pawlee
Hayes
Magra
Gagebrook
Richmond
Orielton
Granton
Old Beach
Grasstree Hill
Sorell
New Norfolk
Claremont
Otago
Midway Point
Brookside
Glenlusk
Lachlan
Glenorchy
Cambridge
Hobart Airport
Wellington Range
Collins Bonnet 1259m
HOBART
Rosny Park
Seven Mile Beach
White Timber Mountain 920m
MOUNT WELLINGTON
CASCADE BREWERY
Lauderdale
Mountain River
Neika
Fern Tree
Taroona
Ralphs Bay
Cremor
HUON VALLEY APPLE HERITAGE MUSEUM
Longley
Grove
Sandfly
Kingston
Opossum Bay
Clifton Beach
Judbury
Ranelagh
Barretta
Blackmans Bay
Glen Huon
Huonville
Nierinna
Howden
South Arm
Betsey Island
Snug
Dennes Point
Snug Tiers
Coningham
TAHUNE AIRWALK
Franklin
Storn Bay
Castle Forbes Bay
Glaziers Bay
Kettering
Barnes Bay
Port Huon
Cygnet
Woodbridge
Trumpeter Bay
Geeveston
North Bruny Island
Cairns Bay
Birchs Bay
Great Bay
Waterloo
Lymington
Police Point
Middleton
Cape Queen Elizabeth
Gordon
Surveyors Bay
Simpsons Bay
Adventure Bay

ACTIVITIES

Take a spectacular bike ride down from the peak of Mount Wellington into Hobart

Meet a Tasmanian Devil by spotlight on a private wildlife reserve near Eaglehawk Neck

Dive amid giant kelp forests in deep-water Eaglehawk Bay

Cruise beneath soaring sea cliffs off the Tasman Peninsula

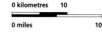

0 kilometres   10

0 miles   10

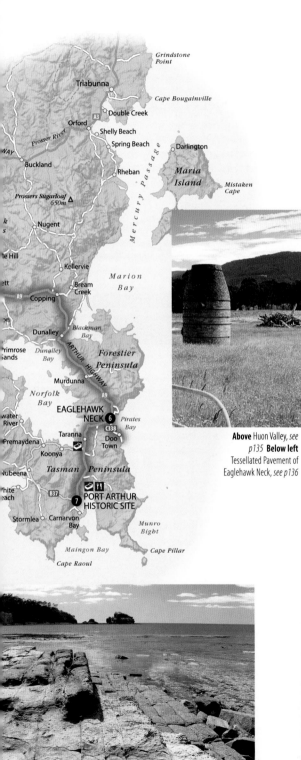

Above Huon Valley, *see p135* **Below left** Tessellated Pavement of Eaglehawk Neck, *see p136*

PLAN YOUR DRIVE

Start/finish: Hobart to Port Arthur Historic Site.

Number of days: 2–3 days, allowing half a day for Port Arthur Historic Site.

Distance: 198 km (124 miles).

Road conditions: Roads are sealed and signposted, but narrower and more winding than on the mainland. Beware of wildlife, and be prepared for snow and ice in winter (Jun–Aug) – pay attention to low-speed signs.

When to go: February is warm and dry, while June and July are cold and crisp in the day, with showers likely in the afternoon. The weather is highly changeable, though, and it can snow in the mountains at any time of year.

Opening times: Most museums and shops are open 9am–5pm. It is often difficult to find restaurants open in smaller towns on Mon and Tue nights.

Main market days: Hobart: Sat; **Glenorchy:** Sun; **New Norfolk:** Sat, Sun.

Shopping: The retail highlight is Hobart's Salamanca Market, but Huon Valley apple preserves make nice gifts.

Major festivals: Hobart: Antarctic Midwinter Festival, Jun; Festival of Voices, Jul; Seafarers' Festival, Oct; Taste Festival, Dec; Australian Wooden Boat Festival, Feb; Cygnet Folk Festival, Jan.

Below Spectacular Tahune Airwalk, *see p135*

VISITING HOBART

Parking
On-street metered parking and voucher parking in car parks in Salamanca Place and around.

Visitor Information
20 Davey Street, Hobart, 7000 (cnr Davey St and Elizabeth St); 1800 990 440; www.hobarttravelcentre.com.au

WHERE TO STAY IN HOBART

The Astor Private Hotel *inexpensive*
With its old fashioned charm, the Astor offers comfortable rooms in an ideal location. The staff is friendly and the hotel is ideal for those on a budget.
157 Macquerie St, 7000; 03 6234 6611; www.astorprivatehotel.com.au

Islington Hotel *expensive*
With a chic assemblage of antique furniture, marble bathrooms and hand-made beds, this boutique hotel welcomes you like a wealthy relative's mansion. A top-notch chef is in the kitchen, which adjoins a glass conservatory with views of Mount Wellington.
321 Davey Street, 7000; 03 6220 2123; www.islingtonhotel.com

Other options
High-end waterfront accommodation in a former Georgian warehouse and fine contemporary Australian cuisine await at the chic **Henry Jones Art Hotel** *expensive (25 Hunter Street, 7000; 03 6210 7700; www. thehenryjones.com)*, while a superbly located, if noisy, Australian pub hotel is the **Customs House Hotel** *moderate (1 Murray Street, 7000; 03 6234 6645; www.customshousehotel.com)*.

Below left Flora and fauna in the Royal Tasmanian Botanic Gardens **Below right** Cruise ship docked at Hobart's bustling port

❶ Hobart
Tasmania; 7000

Tasmania's glorious capital is like a regal outpost at the end of the world, where fine weather can easily turn to vicious winds, biting cold and a dusting of snow. Poised astride the wide River Derwent with an easy grace, it is a city where dramatic views are not only for million-dollar homes – they are commonplace. In the shadow of ever-visible Mount Wellington, Hobart's cultural heart stretches from the one-time whaling centre and now upmarket old-style neighbourhood of Battery Point to the art galleries and weekend market of Salamanca Place, and along Franklin Wharf at the border of the Central Business District to the charming row of 19th-century warehouses at Macquarie Wharf.

Immaculate Georgian buildings occupy the steep-sided hill at **Battery Point**, with brilliant water views down the main streets. There is a good handful of chic cafés and stylish restaurants here, too.

At **Salamanca Place**, no matter what the weather, every Saturday it explodes into life, with everything from South American folk music to bagpipe-playing punks and political protestors. Stalls are packed with produce, from honey, fudge and olive oil to fried doughnuts, handicrafts of all sorts, bric-a-brac, clothing and more. Arrive by 9am to beat the crowds and be gone well before 2pm, when the great pack-up begins.

Founded in 1992, the small **Lark Distillery** *(open daily)* is the first of its kind in Tasmania – surprising, given that conditions on the island are ideal for making a perfect single malt whisky. Taste the range of whiskies or take a guided tour of the distillery.

Lark Distillery sign

Walk through leafy **Queen's Domain** to the **Royal Tasmanian Botanic Gardens** *(open daily)*, the second- oldest in Australia. Here, it is possible to see the whole state's plant life at once. There is a Tasmanian fernery and a tiny but fascinating section of the gardens devoted to Macquarie Island, a sub-Antarctic island of exposed sea crust 1,500 km (930 miles) south of Hobart; its **Subantarctic Plant House** (the only one of its kind in the world) comes complete with recorded animal calls and icy gusting winds.

From the Royal Tasmanian Botanic Gardens, head east and take the ramp onto the Tasman Highway, which becomes Davey St. At the Southern Outlet turn right and follow the signs to Cascade Brewery. Park in the brewery car park on the right.

2 Cascade Brewery
140 Cascade Road, Hobart; 7004
Australia's oldest brewery was founded in 1824. The 90-minute tour *(daily 11am and 1pm; booking essential; www.cascadebrewery.com.au)* takes visitors through the moist, yeasty atmosphere of the brewing process behind southern Tasmania's favourite lager. Finish up with tastings obtained by trading bottle-cap tokens won along the way by answering beer questions.

Retrace route towards Hobart. Turn first right onto Hillborough Road then right onto Huon Road. At Fern Tree turn right at Mount Wellington sign and follow Pinnacle Road to car park at top.

3 Mount Wellington
Mount Wellington Park Reserve
On a clear day, from the top of Mount Wellington there is a fine aerial view of Hobart, North and South Bruny islands, the Southwest Wilderness, and what seems like half the state of Tasmania. It is at least 10°C (18°F) cooler up here than it is in the city, and rain, sleet or snow can roll in just as easily as howling winds, so come prepared. A few short walks lead to various magnificent vistas. The highest point, at 1,270 m (4,167 ft), is the rocky **Pinnacle**. For a descent with a difference, take a bike tour bus with **Island Cycle Tours** *(www.islandcycletours.com)* from Hobart to the top and cycle down.

Return down Pinnacle Rd and turn right onto Huon Rd. Turn left at Sandfly Rd, then right onto the Huon Hwy (A6) Continue for 12 km (8 miles) to the Apple Museum. Car park is on the right.

4 Huon Valley Apple and Heritage Museum
Huon Highway, Grove; 7109
The **Huon Valley Apple and Heritage Museum** *(open daily; www.applemuseum.huonvalley.biz)* offers, literally, a taste of an area that, in the past, farmed almost 400 varieties of apple. A terrifying historic hand-cranked corer and peeler supplies fresh fruit snacks.

Continue on Huon Hwy (A6) to Geeveston, then turn right onto C631 and follow it to Tahune.

5 Tahune Airwalk
Tahune; 7116
In a pocket of ancient stringybark gum forest by the Huon River, the 597-m (1,959-ft) suspended walkway of the **Tahune Airwalk** is thrilling – one section hovers 48 m (157 ft) above the river *(open daily; adventureforests.com.au)*.

Return on C631, turn left onto Huon Hwy (A6) into Hobart, then Macquarie St to Tasman Hwy (A3), and follow signs to Sorell. Turn right onto Arthur Hwy (A9) and follow it to Pirates Bay Drive.

Above left View over Hobart from Mount Wellington **Above right** 19th-century façade of the Cascade Brewery **Below** 19th-century warehouses at Macquarie Wharf, Hobart

EAT AND DRINK

HOBART

Fish Frenzy *inexpensive*
Fight your way in for delectable fish and chips, battered, crumbed or grilled, right by the water.
Elizabeth Street Pier, 7000; 03 6231 2134; www.fishfrenzy.com.au

Monty's on Montpelier *expensive*
Treat yourself to dinner from Monty's seasonally-changing menu. Located just minutes' walk from Salamanca Place, the restaurant is set in an 1860s building with period features such as multiple fireplaces.
37 Montpelier Retreat, 7004; 03 6223 2511; www.montys.com.au

AROUND HUON VALLEY

Ds Coffee House and Internet Lounge *inexpensive*
Good coffee, and pies so popular they are sold out by early afternoon.
34 Main Road, Huonville, 7109; 03 6264 1226

DIVING EAGLEHAWK NECK

Eaglehawk Dive Centre
*178 Pirates Bay Drive, 7179; 03 6250
3566; www.eaglehawkdive.com.au*

WHERE TO STAY

AROUND EAGLEHAWK NECK
Four Seasons Holiday Cabins
moderate
A short drive from Port Arthur, these
four cheerfully painted, self-contained
cabins look out onto Little Norfolk Bay;
ideal for sundowners on the deck or
watching storms roll past.
*5732 Arthur Hwy, Taranna, 7182;
0407 044483; www.fourseasons
holidaycottages.com.au*

PORT ARTHUR HISTORIC SITE
Sea Change Safety Cove *moderate*
Ocean and beach views abound at this
spot, with B&B or self-contained
accommodation within walking
distance of the Historic Site.
*425 Safety Cove Rd, 7182; 03 6250 2719;
www.seachangesafetycove.com.au*

Other options
The only budget option close to the
Historic Site is the **Port Arthur Caravan
and Cabin Park** *inexpensive (Garden
Point Road, 7182; 03 6250 2340)*, while
the only onsite option is the **Comfort
Inn Port Arthur** *moderate (Port
Arthur Historic Site, 7182; 03 6250
2101; www.portarthur-inn.com.au).*

Below left Tessellated Pavement, jutting out
into Pirates Bay **Below** Dramatic, but
becalmed, the Tasman Blowhole **Below right**
The Tasman Arch

Devilish Encounter
Tasmania's most famous mammal is
one of its most elusive. Tasmanian
Devils are under serious threat of
extinction due to the all-pervasive
Devil Facial Tumour Disease, spread
among them by biting, but huge
conservation efforts are underway.
The best way to see one is at night,
by spotlight, and family-run **Bangor
Farm** *(www.bangorfarm.com)*, just
north of Eaglehawk Neck, offers
Devil-watching walks as part of their
rescue and rehabilitation work.

⑥ Eaglehawk Neck
Tasmania; 7179
With the deep-water Eaglehawk Bay
to the west and the wild Tasman Sea
to the east, and a landscape of
wooded hills, mountains and sea
cliffs, pencil-thin Eaglehawk Neck is a
fascinating place to explore.

Drive around Pirates Bay, a bright
crescent of beach backed by steep
mountainsides, pausing at its lookout
for sweeping views, until reaching
the **Tessellated Pavement**. With deep
lines cross-hatched into a basalt rock-
shelf beach along fractures caused
by the movements of the earth's
crust, the Pavement almost seems
man-made, especially where huge,
angular chunks have fallen in heaps
into a tidal channel like discarded
building materials.

Continue along Pirates Bay Drive to
the A9 and turn left onto the C338 to
blink-and-you-will-miss-it **Doo Town**.
Since 1935, when Hobart architect

Eric Round called his shack here
Doo-I, it has become a tradition to
name subsequent dwellings with
similarly twee names – anything
from *Wee Doo* to *Dr Doolittle*.

Follow the C338 on the left to
the **Tasman Blowhole**. In bad
weather, powerful sea-swells rumble
through caves and gush out and up
with all the force of a depth charge.
In good weather, the beach and
wharf at nearby **Eaglehawk Bay** are
more interesting. With giant kelp
forests, underwater caves and
several ship-wrecks, including the
Andre Reboncas, the bay makes for a
great diving experience.

Drive back down the C338 and
turn left. The bushland falls away and
monolithic **Tasman Arch** rises up
from the sea floor. Nearby **Devils
Kitchen**, which can be reached on foot
by a marked track, is a geometric gorge
with pounding surf at the bottom.
🚗 *Take Blowhole Rd back to the
C338, turn left onto the A9 and follow
it to Port Arthur Historic Site car park.*

Cruising the Peninsula
The highest coastal cliffs in the southern hemisphere lie at remote Pillar
Point, which rises up 300 m (984 ft)
from the pounding waves. Visitors
can see the cliffs in all their glory, as
well as whales, dolphins, seals and
other wildlife, from the deck of a
3-hour Tasman Island Cruise *(daily;
15th Dec–15th Apr 1:30pm; 16th Apr–
14th Dec 9:30am)* from Port Arthur.

ⓞ Port Arthur Historic Site

Tasmania; 7182

Tranquil beauty belies a history of hardship at Port Arthur's former penal colony, its sandstone ruins bright against lush green lawns, and set on a picture-perfect harbour backed by coastal mountains.

Above Tranquil waterside setting of the Port Arthur Historic Site

A three-hour walking tour

From the car park by the Visitor Centre walk up to the 1857 **Penitentiary** ①. Climb the hill to its left and admire the view from the crenellated 1842 **Guard Tower** ②, the only accessible turret of three still standing. Continue left behind the 1833 **Commandant's House** ③ and turn right onto a path through the bush. On the left are four bluegum trees, planted to mark the boundaries of "civilized" land from the encroaching bush. The path zig-zags past the site of the **Nichols' Family House** ④, marked by a plaque, where three generations lived until 1985 with no amenities.

Descend alongside the rectangular depression that was the convicts' dam. Continue past the tiny **Laundry** ⑤ back up the hillside to the remains of the 1842 **Hospital** ⑥. Here, rough surgery was performed with whatever was to hand, such as a stocking needle to sew up the throat of one prisoner, and a hot frying pan to cauterize an amputation stump.

Further up the hill to the right is **Smith O'Brien's Cottage** ⑦. The Irish Protestant parliamentarian William

Gateway at Port Arthur Historic Site

Smith O'Brien, who fought for Irish independence from the British, lived here from 1849 to 1853, one of several political prisoners at Port Arthur. Back down the hill is the 1864 **Paupers' Mess** ⑧, where infirm prisoners were housed. Opposite, in the 1868 **Asylum** ⑨, is a museum and study centre. It adjoins the 1850 **Separate Prison** ⑩, built when mental punishment replaced flogging; here, men were kept apart even at church services, when they stood in cubicles with a view of the priest. Most shocking of all is the Punishment Cell where men were locked in silent darkness.

Continue down the hill to Civil Row, comprising houses for the **Magistrate and Surgeon** ⑪, the **Roman Catholic chaplain,** the **Junior Medical Officer** and the **Accountant**. The tiny chapel opposite the Parsonage is still used by the parish, however the imposing 1837 **Gothic Church** ⑫ was never consecrated. Behind the church are the ruins of the 1853 **Government Cottage** ⑬, built in order to provide comfortable lodgings for visiting dignitaries.

VISITING PORT ARTHUR HISTORIC SITE

Parking
There is a large car park by the Visitor Information Centre.

Visitor Information Centre
Port Arthur Historic Site, 7182; 03 6251 2300; www.portarthur.org.au; open daily 9am–end of evening ghost tours.

EAT AND DRINK IN PORT ARTHUR HISTORIC SITE

Port Arthur General Store
inexpensive
Do not miss trying some fish and chips fresh from the tiny fryer in the corner of the general store.
Arthur Hwy, 7182; 03 6250 2220

Other options
Eucalypt *moderate (6962 Arthur Hwy, 7182; 03 6250 2555),* delivers on its motto of "coffee art food" with innovative café fare, while **Felons Restaurant** *expensive (Port Arthur Historic Site, Arthur Hwy, 7182; 03 6251 2314)* allows guests to dine in style within the penal settlement itself.

Above The ruins of the imposing 1857 Penitentiary building

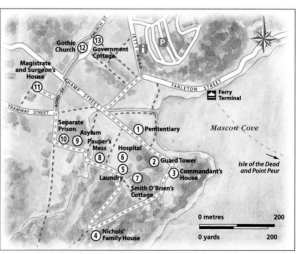

Eat and Drink: inexpensive under AU$60; moderate AU$60–100; expensive over AU$100

Wilderness and Wild Rivers

Launceston to Strahan

Highlights

- **Rocky viewpoint**
  Climb the Nut, at the centre of Stanley on Tasmania's northwest coast, for sunset views over Bass Strait

- **Pristine alpine lake**
  Walk the quiet shores of Dove Lake in the World Heritage area of Cradle Mountain–Lake St Clair National Park

- **Riveting roads**
  Drive the twisting roads between Cradle Mountain and Strahan, with stunning views around every bend

- **Serene harbour**
  Visit Strahan's Macquarie Harbour and take a boat trip into the Franklin-Gordon Wild Rivers National Park

The promontory of glacier rock in Dove Lake

Wilderness and Wild Rivers

Northern Tasmania is a jigsaw of rugged coastlines, river-hewn valleys, rolling green hills and mountains with craggy, towering peaks, fractured by the wide Tamar River. Beginning at the waterway's southern end, in the state's second city of Launceston, this tour works steadily westwards. It ducks underground at the Marakoopa Cave near Mole Creek, heads northwards to coastal cliffs at Table Cape and further west along the coast of Bass Strait to the beautiful peninsula-set town of Stanley. It then turns south to climb into Cradle Mountain–Lake St Clair National Park, negotiating some of the most winding roads in the country southwest to the forlorn mining town of Zeehan, continuing to Strahan on the expansive, peak-ringed Macquarie Harbour, the gateway to the Gordon River. From there, it traverses the copper mining-ravaged landscape around Queenstown, and the vast, untamed Franklin-Gordon Wild Rivers National Park.

ACTIVITIES

Explore the Tamar Island Wetlands with their profusion of birdlife

Descend into a glow-worm grotto at Liena's Marakoopa Cave

Watch fairy penguins returning to their burrows for the night on the aptly-named Penguin Road

Speed down Henty Dunes at Strahan on the wild west coast by sand-board or quad bike

Take a cruise into the heart of the wilderness along the Gordon River from Strahan

0 kilometres 20

0 miles 20

Above Picturesque route to Sheffield, *see p141*

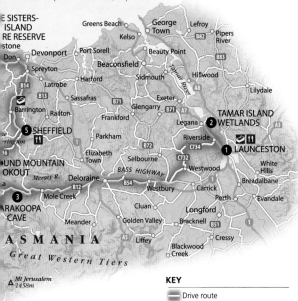

KEY

━━ Drive route

Below View of the Stanley peninsula from the Nut, *see p145*

PLAN YOUR DRIVE

Start/finish: Launceston to Strahan.

Number of days: 4–5 days, allowing half a day for the Dove Lake Walk and a day for a boat trip up the Gordon River from Strahan.

Distance: 663 km (414 miles).

Road conditions: Although mainly sealed and signposted, roads are narrower than on the mainland, and are very winding in places. Pay attention to low-speed signs. Be prepared for sudden changes in the weather, and for snow and ice in winter. Look out for wildlife, and for logging trucks.

When to go: February is generally warm and dry, while June and July are cold and crisp in the day, with showers likely in the afternoon and evening. Weather in the west, in particular, and in and around Cradle Mountain, can change rapidly, and snow is possible at any time of year.

Opening times: Most museums and shops are open 9am–5pm. It is often difficult to find restaurants open in smaller towns Mon–Tue nights.

Main market days: Port Sorell: Sat; Ulverstone: Sat; **Penguin:** Sun; **Burnie:** First and third Sat of month.

Shopping: Hand-crafted polished serpentine can be found at Zeehan.

Major festivals: Launceston: Wooden Boat Rally *(check website for dates, www. woodenboatrally.com)*; Festivale, Jan; **Deloraine:** Tasmanian Craft Fair, Nov; **Sheffield:** International Mural Festival, Apr; **Devonport:** Taste the Harvest, Mar; Devonport Cup races, Jan.

Above Peacock at Cataract Gorge gardens just outside Launceston, *see p142*

VISITING MARAKOOPA CAVE

Parking
Park by the information kiosk at Marakoopa Cave. King Solomons Cave is 15 mins away off the B12.

Visitor Information
Buy tickets for Marakoopa and King Solomons caves at the central ticket office, just before Marakookpa Cave.
330 Mayberry Road, 7304; 03 6492 1110; www.parks.tas.gov.au; tours daily

WHERE TO STAY

LAUNCESTON

Colonial on Elizabeth *moderate*
Set in a 19th-century school building, and including the excellent **Three Steps on George** restaurant, this quiet, central hotel is classy.
31 Elizabeth Street, 7250; 03 6331 6588; www.colonialinn.com.au

Other options
Find ultra-modern self-contained apartments at **twofourtwo** *moderate* *(242 Charles Street, 7250; 03 6331 9242; www.twofourtwo.com.au)*, or stay in the hidden old gem of **Airlie on the Square** *moderate (77 Cameron Street, Civic Square, 7250; 03 6334 0577; www.airlielodge.com.au)*.

AROUND SHEFFIELD

Glencoe Rural Retreat *moderate*
Comfortable rooms in a luxurious farmhouse in the midst of rolling hills, with a private library for guests. French chef Remi Bancal, formerly of the Paris Ritz, and his wife, Ginette, can serve a gourmet dinner by prior arrangement.
1468 Sheffield Road, Barrington, 7306; (8 km/5 miles from Sheffield on the B14); 03 6492 3267; www.glencoeruralretreat.com.au

Below left Fascinating Marakoopa Cave
Below right Black swans at Tamar Island Wetlands reserve

① Launceston
Tasmania; 7250

A pocket metropolis sprawling over the hills towards Lake Trevallyn at the southern end of the River Tamar, Launceston is the charming heart of northern Tasmania. Offering 19th-century architectural gems and sophisticated dining, it is also endowed with natural beauty. **Cataract Gorge** is a 15-minute walk *(signposted)* along the riverbank from the centre of town. This rock-edged stretch of the dark, deep Esk River is traversed by footbridges and the longest single-span chairlift in the world. Tracks criss-cross the area, and it is possible to catch a glimpse of pademelons – small, kangaroo-like marsupials.

🚗 *Head north from Launceston on the A7. After about 10 mins you will see Tamar Island on the right; turn into the car park.*

② Tamar Island Wetlands
Tasmania; 7250

The lagoons and mudflats of **Tamar Island Wetlands** reserve *(open daily; www.parks.tas.gov.au)* are home to native black swans, Pacific black ducks and other birds. There is an interpretation centre and a hide by the boardwalk to Tamar Island.

🚗 *Drive back along the A7 and turn right in Riverside following signs to Tasmanian Zoo onto the C734 (unsealed), then the C732. Turn right onto the B54 through Deloraine, and take left fork onto the B12 for Mole Creek Karst National Park and Marakoopa Cave (signposted on the left).*

Speed warning sign at roundabout

Giant Freshwater Crayfish
The enormous blue freshwater crayfish lives in the river systems of northwestern Tasmania. Reaching over 1 m (3 ft) long and 5 kg (11 lb) in weight, these are the largest freshwater crustaceans on earth. They take 25 years to reach maturity and, due to their delicious flesh and the resulting overfishing in the past, are now listed as a "vulnerable" species.

③ Marakoopa Cave
Liena, Tasmania; 7304

From Mole Creek to Liena, the limestone karst underfoot is riddled with caves. Of the two most accessible, **King Solomons Cave** and **Marakoopa Cave**, the latter is probably the most impressive. The only glow-worm cave in Tasmania open to the public, it boasts one of the largest pieces of flowstone (a formation composed of layers of calcite deposited down cave walls) ever found, as well as an underground river, impressively tall stalactites and stalagmites, and reflective, crystal-rimmed pools. Tours take in all these features as well as a chance to see the magical light of the glow worms. Bat-fearers can relax – the cave's only inhabitants are harmless, blind Tasmanian cave spiders, crickets and small, innocuous harvestmen spiders.

🚗 *Turn left down the B12, then the C138, and turn right at the junction with the C171. Carry on until Round Mountain Lookout, on the left.*

Above left Round Mountain lookout **Above** View from Penguin Road **Below** Sheffield mural

④ Round Mountain Lookout
Gads Hill Road, Tasmania; 7306

With all the dangerously distracting scenery flying past along the ditch-lined alpine roads, it is better to stop to enjoy the view. However, safe road shoulders are few and far between, so the small car park overlooking the unimaginatively named **Round Mountain**, with its information board detailing the geography of the landscape around, is a most welcome stop-off.

🚗 *Continue along the C138, which soon becomes the C136. Turn left onto the B14 into Sheffield.*

Tea with the Penguins

If driving along the scenic Penguin Road around dusk, pause at the Blue Wren Tea Gardens. Visitors may be rewarded with a view of fairy penguins scuttling home to their burrows. For earlier arrivals, Goat Island is only a short walk across a causeway at low tide, but take local advice on when to head back safely.

---

⑤ Sheffield
Tasmania; 7306

Take the opportunity to wander around at this unlikeliest of outdoor galleries. Mural-painting as urban renewal is nothing new, but Sheffield has taken it to extremes. In the1980s, in response to economic decline, local artists began to paint murals to attract visitors, and now scores of colourful scenes, often bucolic depictions of pioneer life in the area, adorn almost every building in town.

🚗 *Continue on the B14 to Spreyton, turn left onto the B19 to join Bass Hwy (1) at Don. Follow signs for Ulverstone. Stay on Main St, cross the river and turn right into Queen St, then Penguin Rd. The reserve lookout is on the right.*

⑥ Three Sisters-Goat Island Nature Reserve
Penguin, Tasmania; 7316

An important breeding ground for the diminutive fairy penguin, the reserve encompasses all the offshore Islands between Ulverstone and Penguin, including rocky **Goat Island** to the south and the **Three Sisters** to the north. A lookout on Penguin Road gives perspective. The Three Sisters offer good diving – the "fourth sister" is an underwater reef (www.centralcoast.tas.gov.au).

🚗 *Continue along Penguin Rd into the village of Penguin. The Big Penguin is on the right.*

EAT AND DRINK

LAUNCESTON

Burger Got Soul *inexpensive*
Gourmet burgers, vegetarian options and Coke Spiders (cola and ice cream).
243, Charles Street, 7250; 03 6334 5204

Stillwater *expensive*
This is the place for an elegant lunch, with lovely views over the Tamar River.
Ritchies Mill, 2 Bridge Road, 7250; 03 6331 4153; www.stillwater.net.au

SHEFFIELD

Skwiz Café-Gallery *inexpensive*
Great Rainforest Alliance coffee and art on the walls inside as well as out.
63 Main Street, 7306; 03 6491 1887

THREE SISTERS-GOAT ISLAND NATURE RESERVE

Blue Wren Tea Gardens *inexpensive*
Spot scuttling penguins over tea.
225 Penguin Road, 7315; 03 6425 4463; www.bluewrenteagardens.com.au

Eat and Drink: inexpensive under AU$60; moderate AU$60–$100; expensive over AU$100

WHERE TO STAY IN STANLEY

Stanley Hotel *inexpensive*
For a town-centre bargain choose one of the cheerful rooms here.
19 Church Street, 7331; 03 6458 1161; www.stanleytasmania.com.au

Abbey's Cottages *moderate*
Spend a night or two at any one of Abbey's nine accommodation options in and around Stanley, which variously suit couples, families and groups of friends, and you will feel a real part of village life. Every mod con, plenty of room, and all a short stroll from the beach or the Nut, with brightly painted, picket-fence aesthetics.
Various locations, 7331; 1800 222 397; www.abbeyscottages.com.au

@VDL *moderate*
Travellers looking for architect-designed, urbane, contemporary accommodation need look no further.
16 Wharf Road, 7331; 03 6458 2032; atvdlstanley.com.au.

Below Big Penguin at Penguin **Below right** Table Cape lighthouse **Below left** Table Cape lookout

7 Penguin
Tasmania; 7316
Apart from the iconic 3-m (10-ft) fibreglass **Big Penguin**, built in 1975 to mark the town's centenary, the town of Penguin is best known for its covered **market**, the largest in Tasmania, and purportedly one of the largest anywhere. It is only open on Sundays – on other days, see how many penguin likenesses can be spotted, and take a walk down to the lovely beach.
🚗 *Continue on Penguin Rd and turn right down Preservation Drive to Hwy 1. Turn left at Burnie towards Old Surrey Rd. Follow signs for Lactos on left.*

8 Lactos Cheese Factory
145 Old Surrey Road, Havenview; 7320
Industrial **Burnie** is not a pretty place, but it is a tasty one. **Lactos** *(open daily)* is the showroom for some of Tasmania's best cheese, made with the region's extra-creamy milk. The Tasmanian Heritage range is a highlight: try the award-winning Traditional Camembert, White Pearl or Double Brie.
🚗 *Return to Hwy 1, turning left onto it. Continue past Somerset, where it becomes the A2. Fork right onto Old Bass Hwy (C240) and right into Saunders St at Wynyard, then take Table Cape Rd to the lighthouse.*

9 Table Cape Lookout
Table Cape, Tasmania; 7325
The almost-sheer sides of flat-topped bluff **Table Cape** drop 160 m (525 ft) into the surf. Formed after a volcanic explosion in which the caldera filled with a lava lake, and then solidified, the cape is covered in rich, fertile soil, of which the tulip growers make good use. A lookout near the **lighthouse** has views as far as Low Head at the mouth of the Tamar River, and a short walking loop offers more great coastal views.
🚗 *Go back down Table Cape Rd and turn right onto Tollymore Rd. Continue to the A2 and turn right. Turn right at the B21 for Stanley.*

Far left Cheeses available to taste at Lactos
Left Chairlift up the Nut at Stanley

EAT AND DRINK IN STANLEY

Stanley Hotel *moderate*
This may well be the best pub food in Tasmania. Try the Bolduan Bay oysters, gourmet sausages and "plate-sized" smoked trout – but save room for the heavenly desserts.
19 Church Street, 7331; 1800 222 397; www.stanleytasmania.com.au

Other options
Before climbing the Nut, stop in at the **Nut Rock Café** *inexpensive (Browns Road; 1800 222 397)* and after watching the spectacular sunset, dine at the fine **Stanley's on the Bay** *moderate (15 Wharf Road, 7331; 03 6458 1404; www.stanleyvillage.com.au).*

⑩ Stanley

Tasmania; 7331

Driving the narrow strip of land off Bass Highway into Bass Strait, it is impossible not to be struck by the beauty of Stanley. Clinging to the southern base of the crag of the Nut, which rises ethereally from the water and beach, it is a sight unlike any other in Australia. Only a few hundred lucky locals call this lovely place home, flanked as it is by wide, empty, sheltered sandy beaches north and south, and graced with a decidedly laid-back and timeless air.

Its sheer sides rising around 150 m (190 ft) up from Bass Strait to a flat summit, **the Nut** is a giant rock that just begs to be climbed. Visitors can either take the steep, strenuous 20-minute paved path, or an effortless chairlift that takes 5 minutes to reach the summit.

In some parts of the world, the nightly return of penguins to their rookeries is a much-commercialized attraction. In Stanley, they do not make such a fuss. Head to the beach on the north side of town just after sunset and join a small cluster of fans quietly watching the show.

🚗 *Return to the A2 and turn left. After Wynyard, turn right onto the B26 and at Yolla right onto Murchison Hwy (A10). Hellyer Gorge is on left after bridge.*

⑪ Hellyer Gorge

Murchison Highway, Tasmania; 7325

About midway between Stanley and Cradle Mountain, **Hellyer Gorge** offers a welcome respite from the tiring, if beautiful, **Murchison Highway**. There is a picnic area and small campground set on the banks of the Hellyer River before it rushes beneath the narrow walls of the gorge itself. Visitors can pick their way across the rocks and wade in the deeper water near the bridge, but should be aware of the currents.

🚗 *Continue along the A10 (Murchison Hwy) and turn left onto the C132. Follow signs for Cradle Mountain to Dove Lake car park. If it is full, park at the visitor centre and catch a shuttle to the lake.*

Below left Tranquil Hellyer Gorge
Below right Wooden houses in Stanley

Above A signpost for walkers at Dove Lake

SHOPPING IN ZEEHAN

Zeehan Gem and Mineral Fair is held annually, the 1st weekend in Nov.

VISITING CRADLE MOUNTAIN–LAKE ST CLAIR NATIONAL PARK

Parking
Drive to Dove Lake car park if possible, or catch a shuttle bus from the Visitor Centre up to the lake (8 km/5 miles).

Cradle Mountain Visitor Centre
Sign in here for walks in the park, including the Overland Track from Cradle Mountain to Lake St Clair in the south of the park (a tough 6-day walk). *4057 Cradle Mountain Road, 7301 (at park entrance on Dove Lake approach); 03 6492 1110; www.parks.tas.gov.au*

Lake St Clair Visitor Centre
The southern access point to the park. Overland track walkers sign out here. *Derwent Bridge, 7140 (off the Lyell Hwy (A10) east from Queenstown); 03 6289 1172; www.parks.tas.gov.au*

WHERE TO STAY

CRADLE MOUNTAIN–LAKE ST CLAIR NATIONAL PARK

Cradle Mountain Lodge *expensive*
With walks from its grounds and a superb in-house restaurant, the lodge offers a cozy wilderness respite. *4038 Cradle Mountain Road, 7306; 1300 806 192; www.cradlemountainlodge.com.au*

STRAHAN

Motel Strahan *moderate*
Funky fittings, five-star bathrooms and gourmet mini-bar. *3 Andrew Street, 7468; 03 6471 7555; www.motelstrahan.com.au*

⑫ Cradle Mountain–Lake St Clair National Park

Tasmania; 7306

Cradle Mountain–Lake St Clair National Park is a vast tract of unspoiled wilderness. Dove Lake, at an altitude of 934 m (3,000 ft), is a glorious sight, backed by the craggy, twin-peaked Cradle Mountain. A 6-km (4-mile) circuit of the lake offers mountain views, shimmering waters, forest paths and sometimes a wildlife encounter or two.

A two-hour walking tour

Before starting the walk, sign in at the **Visitor Centre** ①. The walk is best done clockwise, in the afternoon, when the light is best for photos.

From the green signboard in Dove Lake car park, head for **Glacier Rock** ②. On the approach to this tiny promontory, shallow water can be glimpsed through the foliage on the right. The tea colour of the water is a result of tannins leeched by native buttongrass. Other interesting flora includes the finely fronded Alpine Coral Fern. Access Glacier Rock via rocky steps to the right. Pass the signed track that leads left to Hansons Peak, and continue on the path, which becomes a **boardwalk** ③ that crosses low forest and shrubbery. (This can ice up in winter and there are no railings, so be careful of the slippery surface.) A track to the right leads to a small **sandy beach** ④, where bands of

Above *Banksia marginata* in the national park

yellow, orange, brown and black sand lead out into the deepening water. The path leads up to a **rock face** ⑤, with views of Honeymoon Island. The route continues as a railed boardwalk. There are some amazing pandanus plants along the way.

On the western side of the lake, **Ballroom Forest** ⑥ is home to the slow-growing, iron-hard king billy pine. Found only in Tasmania, it seeds every five to seven years and lives for over a thousand. Soon after leaving the forest is a lovely **picnic spot** ⑦, after which the path becomes rocky and uneven. Pass the sign to Marions Lookout on the left to reach the **boat house** ⑧. Beside it is another beach. If the weather is good, paddle in Lake Dove's icy waters before returning to the car park.

🚗 *Drive back down Cradle Mountain Road. Turn left onto the C132, left again onto the A10 and right on the B27 for Zeehan.*

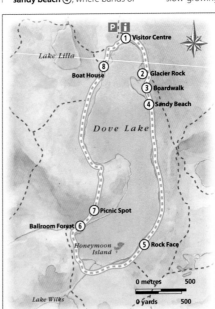

P i
① Visitor Centre
Lake Lilla
⑧
Boat House
② Glacier Rock
③ Boardwalk
④ Sandy Beach
Dove Lake
⑦ Picnic Spot
Ballroom Forest ⑥
Honeymoon Island
⑤ Rock Face
0 metres 500
0 yards 500
Lake Wilks

Far left Dove Lake, with Cradle Mountain in the background Left Dove Lake boardwalk

ACTIVITIES ON HENTY DUNES

Sand-boarding: *03 6471 7396*

GORDON RIVER TRIPS

World Heritage Cruises
5-hour cruise from Strahan into Franklin-Gordon Wild Rivers National Parks.
The Esplanade, Strahan 7468; 03 6471 7174; www.worldheritagecruises.com.au

EAT AND DRINK

CRADLE MOUNTAIN–LAKE ST CLAIR NATIONAL PARK

Lemonthyme Lodge *moderate*
Fine dining in a romantic wilderness log-cabin lodge near Dove Lake.
Dolcoath Road, Moina, 7310; 03 6492 1112; www.lemonthyme.com.au

Other options
Try the **Tavern Bar & Bistro** *(4038 Cradle Mountain Road, 7306; 03 6492 2103)* for a reasonable, hearty meal in beautiful surroundings.

STRAHAN

Schwoch Seafood Takeaway *inexpensive*
The most delectable ocean trout and chips in Tasmania can be found here.
Shop 3, 23 Esplanade, 7468; 03 6471 7500

Other options
For mind-blowing fish chowder, try **Fish Café on the Wharf** *moderate (41 The Esplanade, 7468; 03 6471 4332)*, or dine by the water's edge at **Risby Cove** *expensive (The Esplanade, 7468; 03 6471 7572; www.risbycove.com.au)*.

Centre left Elegant civic building in central Strahan Below Lush riverbank in the Franklin-Gordon Wild Rivers National Park

⑬ Zeehan
Tasmania; 7469
Zeehan is a remnant of the silver-mining boom of 1882–1914. Grand old buildings and mining relics in various stages of disrepair line the main street, one of which houses the **West Coast Pioneers Museum** *(open daily; www.westcoastheritage.com.au)*. Shop for local rose-purple crystal stichtite and green serpentine here.
🚗 *Drive back along the B27, forking right to stay on the B27 for Strahan.*

⑭ Strahan
Tasmania; 7468
On the drive down to Strahan, stop off at **Henty Dunes Lookout** to explore 35-km (22-mile) **Ocean Beach**, studded with muttonbird rookeries. The dunes are great for sand-boarding and quad-biking – but do not be tempted to swim in the treacherous waters.

Strahan itself is a charming town, with old timber buildings and a pretty port. Set on the wild-weathered, tannin-dark waters of **Macquarie Harbour** (more than twice the size of Sydney Harbour), its main business was once logging the now-protected Huon pine, but today, fishing lends it a village feel – and superb seafood.

Conservation is a contentious issue in Tasmania, especially when it comes to the exotic timbers that were once its economic mainstay. At

Morrison's Huon Pine Sawmill *(open daily; 03 6471 7235)*, the wonderful slabs of ancient, slow-growing pine come from salvaged dead trees. Adjacent **Strahan Woodworks** *(open daily; 03 6471 7244)* offers a more polished take on the timber.

To experience the enormity of Macquarie Harbour and the stunning wilderness of the **Franklin-Gordon Wild Rivers National Park**, take a 5-hour cruise from Strahan down the harbour and up the Gordon River to **Heritage Landing**. The dense, tangled national park is largely impenetrable on foot, but here a short boardwalk loops through the forest of rare Huon pine and Sassafras trees. A remnant of Gondwanaland, the growth comes from a time before avian pollination and remains eerily birdless.

Alternatively, take the B24 east from Strahan to **Queenstown** – where copper mining has ravaged the landscape, offering a stark contrast to the lush surrounds – and continue east along the Lyell Highway (A10) for another 80 km (50 miles) through the Franklin-Gordon Wild Rivers National Park to the southern entrance to Cradle Mountain–Lake St Clair National Park.

Eat and Drink: inexpensive under AU$60; moderate AU$60–AU$100; expensive over AU$100

South Australia's Coastal Gems

Adelaide to Mount Gambier

Highlights

- **Winery excellence**
  Tour one of South Australia's premier wine regions – the McLaren Vale

- **Wetland wonder**
  Discover tranquil scenery and diverse wildlife at Coorong National Park

- **Historic township**
  Wander along breathtaking beaches and enjoy fine dining in the historic fishing town of Robe

- **Volcanic lakes**
  Absorb the amazing views and colours at Mount Gambier's crater lakes

The pumping station at Blue Lake, supplying fresh water to Mount Gambier

South Australia's Coastal Gems

Golden sands, quaint seaside towns and wondrous cave formations – the southeastern coast of South Australia provides some of the country's most stunning coastline and spectacular wildlife watching experiences. Consisting of the Fleurieu Peninsula, a paradise for beach-goers, divers and surfers, and the Limestone Coast, a combination of rugged coastline, unique wetlands and labyrinthine caves and sinkholes, this former whaling region is now a thriving tourist area. After soaking up the architecture, culture and café-life in the state capital, Adelaide, the drive explores the renowned wine region of the McLaren Vale, before descending upon historic fishing towns scattered along the coast, and ending in the volcanic region of Mount Gambier.

Above Linear Park, a long green space running through the heart of Adelaide, *see p152*

| 0 kilometres | 40 |
| 0 miles | 40 |

Below Antique farm equipment at Penny's Hill Winery, Mclaren Vale, *see p153*

ACTIVITIES

Ride a Harley Davidson motorcycle around the glorious vineyards of the McLaren Vale

Cycle along the Encounter Bikeway around Horsehoe Bay, from Victor Harbor to Port Elliot

Cruise the spectacular beauty of the Coorong National Park from Goolwa

Go bird-watching in the Wetland Bird Sanctuary at Meningie

Explore the area's extinct volcanoes around Millicent

Clamber through subterranean limestone caves right under the city centre of Mount Gambier

Above Obelisk at Cape Dombey, in Robe, *see p155*

KEY

🚐 Drive route

PLAN YOUR DRIVE

Start/finish: Adelaide to Mount Gambier.

Number of days: 3 days, allowing half a day to explore the McLaren Vale and a day touring the Limestone Coast.

Distance: Approx. 557 km (346 miles).

Road conditions: Well-paved and in good condition with adequate signposting. Some roads are narrow.

When to go: Jun–Oct is whale-watching season around the Fleurieu Peninsula; Dec–Mar is the ideal time to enjoy the historic coastal towns and divine beaches in warm weather.

Opening times: Most museums and shops are open 9am–5pm. It is often difficult to find restaurants open in smaller towns on Monday and Tuesday nights.

Main market days: Adelaide: Tue–Sat; Victor Harbor: 2nd & 4th Sun of the month; Goolwa: 1st & 3rd Sun of the month; Across the region: Limestone Coast Farmers' Market – various dates and locations, www.lcfg.com.au.

Shopping: South Australia's coastal towns offer excellent opportunities to find a bargain in the many antique and craft stores run by local residents.

Major festivals: Adelaide: Adelaide Festival, Mar (even years); Fringe Festival, Feb–Mar; McLaren Vale: Sea and Vines Festival, Jun; Victor Harbor: Rotary Arts Show, Jan; Robe: Village Fair, Nov; Mount Gambier: Blue Lake Blues and Roots Festival, Jan.

Below Motorhome on the road at Meningie, on the shores of Lake Albert, *see p154*

❶ Adelaide
South Australia (SA); 5000

With wide boulevards and vibrant inner-city districts, lush gardens and grand 19th-century stone architecture, Adelaide is an entertaining place to visit. This dynamic city was named after Queen Adelaide, the consort of King William IV of England, and was founded in 1836 as the capital of the only freely settled British province in Australia. Adelaide boasts delightful cafés and shopping, and its centre is easily explored on foot.

A three-hour walking tour

Walk east along Grote Street from the car park, stopping at **Adelaide Central Market** ① *(closed Sun–Mon)*. Established in 1869, the covered market buzzes with life and colour all year. Continue along Grote Street to Victoria Square, a diamond-shaped island in the centre of the city. Admire the stately buildings, then proceed north along King William Street to North Terrace. On the way, stop to admire the beautiful architecture of the **GPO Building Clock Tower** ②, designed in the 1870s. The Town Hall opposite also boasts a fine clock tower. On the corner of King William Street and North Terrace is South Australia's **Parliament House** ③ *(open Mon–Fri)*, with its impressive façade of 10 marble

Ayres House, Adelaide

Corinthian columns. Continue east along North Terrace to uncover many wonderful attractions – all of them free. First is the **State Library** ④ *(open daily)*, home to the Sir Donald Bradman Collection of cricketing memorabilia. Alongside the library is the **South Australian Museum** ⑤ *(open daily)*, where highlights include the natural history section, the superb Australian Aboriginal Cultures Gallery, and the Mawson Gallery. The **Art Gallery of South Australia** ⑥ *(open daily)*, a major cultural focus since its creation in 1881, is just next door. Situated at the eastern end of North Terrace is the **Botanic Garden** ⑦ *(open daily; www.environment.sa.gov.au/ botanicgardens)*, a garden oasis in the heart of the city. Opened in 1857, it features a range of Australian natives and exotic plants. The restored Art Deco Palm House is a top attraction, housing a succulent garden of rare Madagascan flora. The Bicentennial Conservatory is the biggest glasshouse in the southern hemisphere. The **National Wine Centre of Australia** ⑧ *(open daily; www.wineaustralia.com.au)* is tucked away in the Botanic Garden, where visitors can taste an array of great Australian wines. Refreshed, head back along North Terrace to view **Ayres House** ⑨ *(open Tue–Sun)*, one of Australia's best examples of Colonial Regency architecture. Turn south after Ayres House down Frome Street, then first right and head west along Rundle Street to Rundle Mall, Adelaide's main shopping strip. Its star feature is the **Adelaide Arcade** ⑩, built in the 1880s and restored to its former glory. Follow Rundle Mall to King William Street, and head back to Victoria Square. Take Grote Street back to the car park.

Where to Stay: inexpensive under AU$150; moderate AU$150–AU$250; expensive over AU$250

🚗 *Head west from the centre and turn left down West Terrace (A21). Bear right onto Anzac Hwy (A5), continue to the A13 and exit on Main South Rd. Follow this to the Old Noarlunga exit.*

② Old Noarlunga
SA; 5168

This delightful town, lying within the protective curl of the Onkaparinga River, is the epitome of 19th-century charm. Feeding the ducks and picnicking under the gum trees are the order of the day at the **Market Square**. Opened in 1841, it is near the 1844 river-powered **Mill** that provided the area with flour. Up on the hill stands the 1850 church of **St Philip & St James** *(Church Hill Road)*, whose cemetery tells a tale of the early settler's hardships, such as scarlet fever. Stroll down the main street past an array of heritage-listed 19th-century colonial buildings.

🚗 *Rejoin the A13 south to the left, then left to McLaren Vale.*

③ McLaren Vale
SA; 5171

Neat green vines, excellent wines and a homely atmosphere are characteristic of the McLaren Vale. With the warmth and charm of a country town and boasting over 60 vineyards, this is South Australia's biggest wine producer, with Shiraz being the most planted variety (47.5 per cent). One of the first areas to be planted with vines in South Australia, it is now a favoured stop for wine-lovers – a vineyard tour is a must. Enjoy the open road with **McLaren Vale Harley Tours** *(0423 668 342; www.mclarenvaleharleytours.com)*, or simply concentrate on the open bottles with **McLaren Vale Tours** *(0414 784 666; www.mclarenvaletours.com.au)*.

Winery sign, McLaren Vale

🚗 *Take Main Rd back to the A13 and head south, staying on the A13 to the end. Turn right on B37 to Victor Harbor.*

④ Victor Harbor
SA; 5211

Settled in 1837 as a whaling station, Victor Harbor was a major port during the 1860s and has retained much of its early charm. The **Cockle Train** steam

Right The Granite Island Causeway, Victor Harbor

locomotive *(www.steamranger.org.au)* runs along the coast, while the **Horse Drawn Tram** *(open daily; www.horsedrawntram.com.au)*, opened in 1894, takes visitors to **Granite Island**, where fairy penguins can be seen. The **South Australian Whale Centre** *(www.sawhalecentre.com)* operates whale-watching trips (May–Oct). Visitors can also hire a bike or roller-blades from **Victor Harbor Cycle & Skate** *(73 Victoria St; 08 8552 1417)* and follow the **Encounter Bikeway** around the bay to Port Elliot and Goolwa (30 km/18 miles).

🚗 *Return on B37 into Port Elliot Rd. Turn right into the Strand to centre. Park on street.*

⑤ Port Elliot
SA; 5212

Featuring a pristine coastline, Port Elliot epitomizes the Australian seaside village lifestyle. Enjoy a walk on the golden sands or take a dip in the waters of Horseshoe Bay's **main beach** (reached from Bashman Parade). Alternatively, admire the beach views by scaling the clifftop walking path.

🚗 *Rejoin B37 to Goolwa. Turn left and right to access Hindmarsh Island Bridge.*

Above left Picturesque Granite Island, Victor Harbour **Above right** Horsedrawn tram on its way to Granite Island, Victor Harbor

EAT AND DRINK

ADELAIDE

Tincat Café *inexpensive*
Housed in a historic Victorian terrace, this café combines vibrant local culture with coffee and hospitality.
107 Rundle St, Kent Town 5067; 08 8362 4748; www.tincat.com.au

MCLAREN VALE

The Kitchen Door and Red Dot Café *moderate*
This eatery at Penny's Hill Winery delivers modern Australian cuisine, including snacks and larger meals.
281 Main Rd, 5171; 08 8556 4000; www.pennyshill.com.au

d'Arry's Verandah Restaurant *moderate*
With breathtaking views, this award-winning restaurant offers a classic winery dining experience. It offers a six-course degustation menu.
Osborn Rd, 5171; 08 8329 4848; www.darrysverandah.com.au

VICTOR HARBOR

Ocean Grill at Anchorage *moderate*
Specializing in seafood and steaks, try the delicious beef moussaka, or salt and pepper squid.
21 Flinders Pde, 5211; 08 8552 5970; www.anchorageseafronthotel.com

Above Meningie's tourist information centre and arts and crafts market **Below** Victoria Cottage, Robe, dating from 1852

VISITING ROBE

Parking
Park on James St, off Victoria St.

Visitor Information Centre
Robe Information Centre, Mundy Terrace, 5276; 08 8768 2465;
www.council.robe.sa.gov.au

VISITING MOUNT GAMBIER

Visitor Information Centre
Lady Nelson Discovery Centre, Jubilee Hwy East, 5290; 08 8724 9750, 1800 087 187 (toll free); open daily;
www.mountgambiertourism.com.au

WHERE TO STAY

ROBE

Robe House *moderate*
This charming building was the first to be built in Robe, in 1847. Constructed from locally quarried sandstone it features high vaulted ceilings and rustic floorboards.
1a Hagen St, 5276; 08 8768 2770;
www.robehouse.com.au

The Caledonian Inn *moderate*
Built in 1858 and retaining many of its original features, this charming abode offers provincial hotel rooms or seafront cottages, close to the town centre.
1 Victoria St, 5276; 08 8768 2029;
www.caledonian.net.au

MOUNT GAMBIER

Blue Lake Holiday Park *inexpensive*
Offering camp sites or roofed accommodation, this lakeside resort caters to all budgets and has breathtaking views of Blue Lake.
Bay Rd, 5290; 08 8725 9856;
www.bluelake.com.au

The Barn Accommodation *moderate*
This offers generous-sized apartments in what was once a barn used to store grain and hay in the late 1800s.
Nelson Rd, OB Flat, 5290; 08 8726 8250; www.barn.com.au

Where to Stay: inexpensive under AU$150; moderate AU$150–AU$250; expensive over AU$250

⑥ Goolwa
SA; 5214

Goolwa sits at the mouth of the Murray River, Australia's largest waterway. The nearby pristine wetlands of **Hindmarsh Island** (accessible via bridge) and the **Coorong** are ideal for viewing some of South Australia's most striking scenery. English explorer Captain Sturt used Hindmarsh Island to locate the mouth of the Murray River on his epic 1830 trip. The lakes and Coorong area are a haven for boating and fishing enthusiasts.

🚗 *Take B37 past Strathalbyn, then B45 to Wellington and across Murray River. Take Princes Hwy (B1) right to Meningie.*

⑦ Meningie
SA; 5264

On the shores of Lake Albert, Meningie was established in the 1800s as a staging post for the local cattle graziers. Serviced by paddle steamers, the town formed part of the original Melbourne to Adelaide route and is now an ideal location for messing about in boats. The Lake Albert foreshore makes for a pleasant stroll or swimming stop. A short walk to **Meningie Hill Lookout**

The Coorong

With more than 200 species of birds in its waterways, the Coorong is rich in natural beauty. The Ngarrindjeri Aboriginal people have resided here for over 6,000 years, and the area is best explored through walking trails and tours run by their descendants. Head south out of Meningie and turn right on Seven Mile Road to **Camp Coorong** (08 8575 1557), an Aboriginal cultural centre and museum. Or explore the area and its wildlife by boat on a half- or full-day boat trip with **Spirit of the Coorong Cruises** (08 8555 2203; www.coorongcruises.com.au).

provides superb views of Lake Albert and the surrounding countryside, while the **Wetland Bird Sanctuary** *(open daily)* serves as a haven for many of the birds seen in the Coorong.

🚗 *Take Princes Hwy (B1) south to Kingston SE, stopping on the outskirts of town for a photo with the Big Lobster.*

⑧ Kingston SE
SA; 5275

On pretty Lacapede Bay, Kingston, the "Gateway to the South East", offers safe, sandy shores perfect for watersports and fishing. **Cape Jaffa Lighthouse** *(Marine Parade, 5275)* was removed from Cape Jaffa and re-built on Kingston's foreshore, and is open for tours. The town is also home to a rare **analematic sundial** (a sundial that is read by standing in a specific location) as well as the 17-m (60-ft) concrete and fibreglass **Big Lobster**, built to advertize a local restaurant.

🚗 *Head south on the B101, then turn right to Robe and park on the main street or head to Mundy Terrace and the Visitor Information Centre.*

⑨ Robe
SA; 5276

Founded in 1802, Robe is a bustling tourist area and fishing port known for its maritime culture, beautiful beaches and sightseeing – it is home to over 60 buildings dating back to the mid-1800s. The main thoroughfare, Victoria Street, boasts friendly pubs, cafés, galleries, and boutiques. Head down Obelisk Road to Cape Dombey to view the **Obelisk**, built in 1853 to guide ships entering the bay, or enjoy a dip at the bay's beaches, particularly the famous 10-km (6-mile) **Long Beach** *(follow signs and park along the Esplanade)*.
🚗 *Leave via the B101 south along the coastline past Beachport to Millicent.*

⑩ Millicent
SA; 5280

Established in 1870, Millicent grew with the establishment of pine plantations in the nearby ranges in the early 20th century. Mount Muirhead, the large hill that dominates Millicent, is one of the oldest volcanoes in this region, and along with Mount Burr is a feature of the **Volcanoes Discovery Trail** – a tour of the region's volcanoes. Another tour, the **Wind Farm Tourist Drive** *(08 8733 0904)*, explores the wind farms of the Woakwine Range, where each turbine stands almost 100-m (330-ft) high. Pick up maps from

Millicent Visitor Information Centre
(1 Mt Gambier Rd; 08 8733 0904; www.wattlerange.sa.gov.au).
🚗 *Take Princes Hwy (B1) south all the way to Mount Gambier.*

⑪ Mount Gambier
SA; 5290

This city is set amid a unique and ancient landscape of breathtaking volcanic craters, lakes, caves, sinkholes, and underground waterways. The **Crater Lakes** complex is comprised of four lakes – Blue Lake (which houses the city's water supply), Valley Lake, Browne Lake and Leg of Mutton Lake. Blue Lake is famous for its striking colours, which change during the Nov–Mar period. **Engelbrecht Cave** *(open daily; park on Chute St; 08 8723 5552)* is a complex of limestone caves located beneath the city's streets. These fascinating caves feature two large chambers that expose the underground water table. Elsewhere in the city, the **Cave Gardens** *(Watson Terrace; open daily, lit up at night)* and **Umpherston Sinkhole** *(Jubilee Highway East; open day and night; 0429 349 328)*, are beautiful gardens planted in the remnants of limestone caves left exposed when the roofs collapsed. Diving and snorkelling are popular activities in the area; contact the Visitor Information Centre *(see left)*.

Top left A panoramic view from Meningie Hill Lookout **Above right** Engelbrecht Cave, an extraordinary limestone cave complex under the city of Mount Gambier **Above left** Valley Lake, one of the Crater Lakes, Mount Gambier

EAT AND DRINK

ROBE

Sails Restaurant *moderate*
Enjoy superb seasonal food and regional wines at Sails.
21 Victoria St, 5276; 08 8768 1954; www.sailsatrobe.com.au

The Caledonian Inn *moderate*
Built in 1858, the Caledonian Inn is centrally located and features a fine selection of modern Australian cuisine.
1 Victoria St, 5276; 08 8768 2029; www.caledonian.net.au

Vic Street Pizzeria *inexpensive*
An affordable array of thin-crust pizzas and pastas are on offer at this pizzeria.
6 Victoria St, 5276; 08 8768 2081

MOUNT GAMBIER

Sage and Muntries *inexpensive*
Boasting modern Australian and Mediterranean cuisine, Sage and Muntries serves delicious local seafood.
78 Commercial St West, 5290; 08 8724 8400

The Barn Steakhouse *moderate*
With beef aged on the premises, and cooked to perfection over coal from the Murray Mallee region, this steakhouse offers a quintessential Australian dining experience.
Nelson Rd, OB Flat, 5290; 08 8726 8250; www.barn.com.au

Eat and Drink: inexpensive under AU$60; moderate AU$60–AU$100; expensive over AU$100

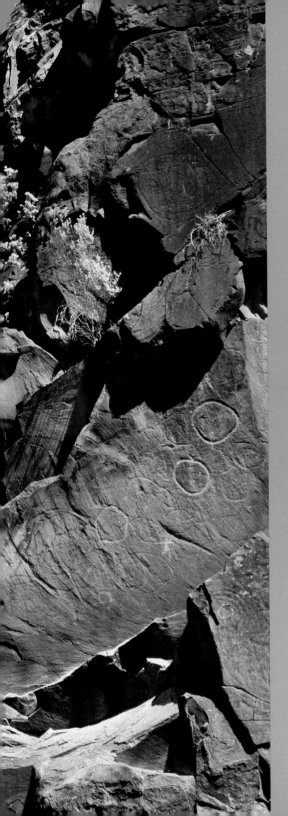

Vineyards and Rocky Ranges

Birdwood to Parachilna

Highlights

- **Delightful wines and vineyards**
  Enjoy delicious wines such as rich Barossa Valley Shiraz and zingy Clare Valley Riesling amid pretty vineyards

- **Natural wonders**
  Explore the deep red gorges and vast natural amphitheatre of the Flinders Ranges, teeming with exciting wildlife

- **Aboriginal rock art**
  Discover the ancient culture and art at the sacred sites of the indigenous people of the Adnyamathanha region

- **Old pubs and fine restaurants**
  Have a beer and a chat with the locals in 19th-century pubs and dine on the best produce in upmarket restaurants

Aboriginal rock art at Sacred Canyon in the Flinders Ranges

Vineyards and Rocky Ranges

From Adelaide, it is an easy hop east to the wineries of the Barossa Valley, known for their full-bodied Shiraz, before heading north to the Clare Valley wineries, where Riesling reigns supreme. Spend some time exploring the magnificent Mount Remarkable National Park in the Southern Flinders Ranges. Continue north to Quorn, where visitors can experience the seclusion of an old shearers' quarters at the foot of Dutchmans Stern Bluff, then take a detour to the amazing rock formations of Warren Gorge. Visit the Yourambulla Caves and their Aboriginal paintings or explore sacred rock art sites in the vast amphitheatre of Wilpena Pound. Finish the trip by staying at an Outback pub in tiny Parachilna and eating bush tucker.

Above Blinman street scene on the route to Parachilna, *see p165*

KEY

Drive route

ACTIVITIES

Blend your very own bottle of wine on the Penfolds winery tour, Nuriootpa

Glide over the stunning Barossa Valley in a hot-air balloon from Nuriootpa or Tanunda

Work up a real thirst: hire a bike and cycle the Riesling Trail between Auburn and Clare

Spend a night behind bars in Gladstone Gaol

Hike the bluff at Dutchmans Stern Conservation Park at Quorn and spot native fauna and flora along the way

Visit sacred Aboriginal sites to see the ancient rock art at Yourambulla Caves near Hawker and around Wilpena Pound

See the extraordinary rock formations of the Flinders Ranges on an aerial tour from Wilpena

Below Jacobs Creek vineyards in the Barossa Valley, *see p160*

Above Grapes ripening on the vines at Peter Lehmann vineyards, see p161

PLAN YOUR DRIVE

Start/finish: Birdwood to Parachilna.

Number of days: 5–6 days, allowing half a day to explore Tanunda and a day in Wilpena Pound.

Distance: Approx. 575 km (357 miles).

Road conditions: Sealed roads through all stops along the drive. Routes within some sights deviate onto unsealed roads. Some steep terrain through the national parks. Can be undertaken with a 2WD, but 4WD recommended.

When to go: Feb–Mar is usually very hot. Spring (Sep–Nov) is the best time to go, to appreciate the wildflowers.

Opening times: Most museums and shops in Australia are open 9am–5pm. It is often difficult to find restaurants open in smaller towns on Monday and Tuesday nights.

Main market days: Angaston: Barossa Farmers Market, Sat am.

Shopping: Tanunda has some good antiques and art shops. Throughout the Barossa and Clare valleys there will be opportunities to buy fine wine – look out too for quality local produce, such as cheeses at Birdwood Cheese and Wine Centre and in the artisan bakeries of Tanunda.

Major festivals: Tanunda: Barossa Vintage Festival, Apr; **Clare:** Clare Valley Gourmet Weekend, May.

Right The brick and bluestone winery at Chateau Tanunda

VISITING TANUNDA

Parking
Park in the car park behind the library on Murray Street.

Barossa Visitor Information Centre
Information on wine trails and tastings in the Barossa Valley wine region.
66–8 Murray St, 5352; 08 8563 0600; www.barossa.com; open daily

WHERE TO STAY

ANGASTON

Barossa Treasure *moderate*
This self-contained cottage is set on a large property with plenty of wildlife and great views over the Barossa Valley.
Lot 6, Gawler Park Rd, 5353; 1300 136 970; www.treasuredmemories.com.au

TANUNDA

The Louise *expensive*
These luxurious modern suites on a hill with views over the Barossa each feature a spa and private courtyard.
Seppeltsfield Rd, 5352; 08 8562 2722; www.thelouise.com.au

AROUND TANUNDA

Barossa Junction Motel *inexpensive*
Offering family accommodation with a pool and tennis court, the motel is only minutes from wineries and shops.
2976 Barossa Valley Hwy, 5352 (just north of Tanunda); 08 8563 3400

Jacobs Creek Retreat *expensive*
Enjoy French-inspired luxury in these restored cottages on the banks of the creek that gives its name to the winery.
Nitschke Rd, 5352 (take Barossa Valley Hwy south, turn left on Koch Rd); 08 8563 1123; www.jacobscreekretreat.com.au

Below left Vines in the Torrens Valley, near Birdwood **Below right** Jacobs Creek Retreat

① Birdwood
SA; 5234
This pretty town, with historic buildings and pleasant cafés, lies a short drive northeast of Adelaide through the winding, gum-tree-lined roads of the Adelaide Hills. Known as Blumberg until 1917, Birdwood was renamed amid anti-German feeling during World War I. Birdwood Mill is now home to the **National Motor Museum** *(open daily)*, one of the country's largest collections of vintage cars. Stop at the **Birdwood Cheese and Wine Centre** *(open Wed–Sat, & Sun pm)* to taste local wine or pick up picnic provisions.
🚗 *Take the B10 towards Angaston – for a picnic spot, turn right past Eden Valley to Eden Valley Scenic Lookout – then continue on the B10 to Angaston.*

② Angaston
SA; 5353
Named after George Fife Angas, one of South Australia's founders, Angaston – an entry point for the Barossa Valley – is a town of tree-lined streets and historic buildings. One that is worth visiting is **Collingrove Homestead** *(12–3pm Wed–Fri & 12–4pm weekends;*

entrance fees apply; 08 8564 2061), which was home to the Angas family. Explore its lush gardens or enjoy a cream tea. **Yalumba Winery** *(open daily; Eden Valley Road; 08 8561 3200; www.yalumba.com)* is worth visiting to see the landmark clock tower. Try a Yalumba red wine, such as an "Octavius".
🚗 *Follow Murray St into Nuriootpa.*

③ Nuriootpa
SA; 5355
Surrounded by vineyards, the largest town in Barossa – known to locals as "Nuri" – is laid out alongside the North Para River. The southern end of town is occupied by a number of wineries including the renowned **Penfolds** *(open daily; 30 Tanunda Rd; 08 8568 8408; www.penfolds.com)*. Enjoy the oasis of the **Barossa Bushgardens** *(open daily; Coulthard Reserve, off Penrice Rd)*, with an array of native golden wattles, eucalypts and other plants. Or, take a spectacular balloon ride over the glorious Barossa countryside with **Balloon Adventures** *(08 8389 3195; www.balloonadventures.com.au)*.
🚗 *Take B19 south to Tanunda and park behind the library, just off Murray St.*

Barossa Valley
Colonial explorer Johannes Menge described the Barossa Valley in the 1830s as "the cream, the whole cream and nothing but the cream". Soon after, passage was arranged for a community of Prussians to settle the land around present-day Angaston, Nuriootpa and Tanunda, an hour's drive from Adelaide. Barossa's early European settlers planted vines on the rolling hills and today the Barossa is famous for its manicured vineyards, fine wines and German-style breads, cheeses and cured meats produced there.

❹ Tanunda
SA; 5352

An Aboriginal word meaning "watering hole", Tanunda is the focal point of the Barossa. With its strong European heritage, distinctive church spires, wineries, German-style bakeries and cafés, there is plenty to see and do in the town. Explore the boutiques and galleries and take in the historical delights.

A two-hour walking tour
Leaving the car park, admire the fine stonework, windows, grand spire and gravestones of the **Tabor Lutheran Church** ①. Head across the road to the **Zinfandel Tea Rooms** ② *(closed Tue)* for a traditional meal in a historic building – enjoy bratwurst and sauerkraut among kitsch furnishings. A short stroll south on Murray Street is the **Barossa Museum** ③ *(open daily)*, which contains a collection of artifacts from German Lutherans, the largest group of Barossa settlers, including a wagon and butcher's cart. Cross the road to **The Old Mill Gallery Café** ④ *(open daily)*, formerly a steam-powered flour mill, dating from 1848. Today, it is home to Nosh, a trendy little café, Old Mill Past and Presence, a gorgeous gift store, and the Bull Creek book store. Walk west up Jane Place to Maria Street, where an avenue of candle pine trees line the entrance to the **Langmeil Lutheran Church and Cemetery** ⑤ *(open daily, am)*. The original church was built in 1846, but it has since been rebuilt in bluestone and its tower features stained-glass windows. The cemetery is the final resting place of Pastor Augustus Kavel, a central figure in the emigration of German-speaking Lutherans from Prussia to South Australia. Along Maria Street is **Goat Square** ⑥, the site of the *ziegenmarkt*, used by pioneers for bartering goods – admire the Germanic architecture. Continue up Maria Street, turn right into Elizabeth Street and left into Bilyara Road to find the **Tanunda Kegelbahn** ⑦ *(at the entrance to the Tanunda Oval; open from 7:30pm Wed & Fri)*. The Kegelbahn, a single-lane, nine-pin skittle alley, is the only one of its kind in the southern hemisphere. It is a longish walk north along Langmeil Road to Barossa's oldest winery, **Langmeil Winery** ⑧ *(open daily)*, so it is preferable to retrace the tour to the car park and

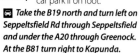

Langmeil Lutheran Church and Cemetery

drive the rest of the route. The winery is built on a vineyard dating back to the first settlement. Down Para Road is **Peter Lehmann Wines** ⑨ *(open daily)*. Art adorns the cellar walls, and the riverside lawn makes a great picnic spot. Beyond are the spires of **Richmond Grove Winery** ⑩ *(open daily)*, with early equipment. Carry on to Murray Street and turn right, then left at Basedow Road for **Chateau Tanunda** ⑪ *(open daily)*, a winery in a 19th-century building. Then continue down Murray Street to the car park if on foot.

🚌 *Take the B19 north and turn left on Seppeltsfield Rd through Seppeltsfield and under the A20 through Greenock. At the B81 turn right to Kapunda.*

EAT AND DRINK

ANGASTON
Vintners Bar and Grill *moderate*
Enjoy fine regional food with local wines in a picturesque vineyard setting. *Cnr Nuriootpa & Stockwell Rds, 5353; 08 8564 2488; www.vintners.com.au*

NURIOOTPA
Maggie Beer's Farm Shop *inexpensive*
Grab a Picnic Fare Basket and find a table by the small lake or watch a cooking demo in the kitchen where TV show *The Cook and the Chef* was filmed. *50 Pheasant Farm Rd, 5355; 08 8562 4477; www.maggiebeer.com.au*

TANUNDA
Zinfandel Tea Rooms *moderate*
Traditional German food *(see left)*. *58 Murray St, 5352; 08 8563 2822*

1918 *moderate*
This lovely wisteria-covered villa serves modern Australian cuisine. *94 Murray St, 5352; 08 8563 0405; www.1918.com.au*

Appellation *expensive*
Enjoy fine dining that showcases local products, served with great local wines (bookings essential). *Cnr Seppeltsfield & Stonewell Rds, 5352; 08 8562 4144; www.appellation.com.au*

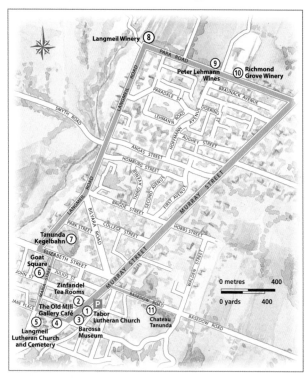

Eat and Drink: inexpensive under AU$60; moderate AU$60–AU$100; expensive over AU$100

Above Bicycling on the Riesling Trail in the Clare Valley

VISITING THE CLARE VALLEY

Visitor Information Centre
Winery maps and information.
Cnr Main North & Spring Gully rds; 1800 242 131; www.clarevalley.biz

WHERE TO STAY

CLARE

Clare Valley Motel *inexpensive*
This family-friendly hotel is set on a hill overlooking the Clare Valley and is within walking distance of several wineries.
74 Main North Rd, 5453; 08 8842 2799; www.clarevalleymotel.com.au

Riesling Trail Cottages *moderate*
These self-contained private cottages, each featuring wood fires, spa baths and BBQs, are within walking distance of Clare's centre and the Riesling Trail.
12 Stanley St, 5453; 0427 842 232; www.rtcvcottages.com.au

EAT AND DRINK

AUBURN

The Station Café *inexpensive*
Located at Mount Horrock's cellar door at the Old Auburn Railway Station, the lunches here feature mainly local produce. Delicious freshly baked cakes are available for hungry visitors.
Curling St, 5451; 08 8849 2202; www.mounthorrocks.com

CLARE

Wild Saffron *inexpensive*
Known for its fantastic coffee and an array of gourmet delights including freshly-baked bread, cheeses, olives and relishes, this café is a foodie's haven.
288 Main St, 5453; 08 8842 4255; www.wildsaffron.com.au

⑤ Kapunda
SA; 5373
This small town located just north of the Barossa Valley has a rich history, captured in the impressive **Kapunda Museum** *(open daily, pm)*. Originally a Baptist church, the Romanesque building now houses two floors of artifacts including agricultural and mining displays. Entry includes **Bagot's Fortune** *(open daily)*, an interpretive exhibition celebrating Kapunda's history as the first copper-mining town in Australia. Kapunda also lays claim to being the birthplace of "Cattle King" Sir Sidney Kidman (1857–1935), once said to be the greatest private landowner in the world, with over 100 cattle stations. The **Wheatsheaf Pub** at Allendale North, 5 km (3 miles) away, is a great example of a 19th-century pub brought back to its former glory.
🚗 *Follow signs to Marrabel on the B84 and turn left to Saddleworth.*

⑥ Saddleworth
SA; 5413
Named by early pastoralist James Masters, who grew up in Saddleworth, Yorkshire, this is a quiet country town. The old **Catholic church and cemetery** on the hill is worth visiting for its views and interesting tomb epitaphs. The **Saddleworth Historical Museum** *(open daily)* documents the history of the town as well as that of nearby Marrabel, Waterloo and Manoora.
🚗 *Take the B84 northwest to Auburn.*

⑦ Auburn
SA; 5451
Known as the gateway to the Clare Valley, Auburn is a town of preserved 19th-century bluestone buildings, fine wineries and art galleries. **St John Lutheran Church** at the end of King Street is an excellent example of original stonework, built by local stonemason, Joseph Meller, in 1878. Hire a bicycle and pedal the **Riesling Trail** *(see box)*, which follows the tracks of the old railway line between Auburn and Clare, admiring views of vineyards and bushland. The Auburn entrance to the trail is located at the Old Auburn Railway Station. Follow the brown signs off the main street.
🚗 *Take the B82 north towards Clare. Turn right at Leasingham, and follow signs along Leasingham Rd on the*

Pedal the Riesling Trail
A great way to see the sights of the Clare Valley and visit its numerous cellar doors is to cycle the **Riesling Trail**. The trail runs 25 km (16 miles) from Auburn to Clare via some of the region's finest wineries. Bike hire is available from **Cogwebs Bicycle Hire** *(30 Main North Rd, Auburn 5451; 08 8849 2380)* and **Clare Valley Cycle Hire** *(32 Victoria Rd, Clare, 5453; 0418 802 077)*.

Wine and Heritage Scenic Drive to Mintaro and Martindale Hall.

⑧ Mintaro
SA; 5414
Pretty Mintaro is home to the grand 19th-century Georgian-style mansion **Martindale Hall** *(open Mon–Fri; Sat & Sun pm; fees apply)*, built in 1879. Picnic in the large Conservation Park, or admire the architecture in the marble-floored grand foyer and the hall's original furniture and fittings.
🚗 *From Mintaro, follow signs back to the B82 and turn right to Clare.*

⑨ Clare
SA; 5453
Vine-covered hills welcome visitors to Clare and with 35 cellar doors in the Clare Valley, wine-lovers are spoilt for choice. One not to miss is **Sevenhill Cellars**, 8 km (4 miles) south of Clare off the B82 *(open daily; 08 8843 4222; www.sevenhill.com.au)*, a stone winery founded in 1851 by Jesuit priests fleeing religious persecution in Austria.
🚗 *Head north on the B82 and fork left – keeping on the B82 – to Gladstone. Turn right over the railway line into town.*

Below Agricultural machinery on display at Kapunda Museum, Kapunda

Left Dusty road in the Flinders Ranges, *see pp164–5*
Above Wallaby at Yourambulla Caves, *see p165*

KEY

— Drive route

0 kilometres   20

0 miles   20

⑩ Gladstone
SA; 5473
Established in the 1870s, this quiet
town at the start of the Flinders Ranges
has its roots in farming, the railway and
security. **Gladstone Gaol** *(08 8662 2200;
open daily)* was built in 1881 and stayed
in use until 1975. During World War II it
was used as an internment camp for
Italian and German nationals. Visitors
can learn about the gaol's past, enjoy
the views from the watch-house and
feed the inmates – kangaroos. Back-
packers can stay in a cell overnight.

🚗 *Take B82 north, stopping at Stone
Hut to pick up old-style camel, kangaroo
or crocodile pies at the Old Bakery, then
continuing on to Melrose.*

⑪ Melrose
SA; 5483
Established in 1853, Melrose
offers some fine 19th-
century architecture. Admire
the stonework in the derelict
Jacka's Brewery, which was
built as a flour mill in 1878,
and operated as a brewery
until 1934. The town nestles
at the base of **Mount
Remarkable**, which affords
some great hikes including parts of the
Heysen Trail (Australia's longest). Walk,
hire a bike or drive up to the **War
Memorial Lookout** for the views –
keep an eye out for wallabies. Access
Mount Remarkable National Park from
Stuart Street, following the signs.

🚗 *Head north on the B82.*

⑫ Wilmington
SA; 5485
Five km (8 miles) before Wilmington is
a turn off to **Alligator Gorge**. It is a
beautiful, winding drive to the canyon,

**Poster for the Pichi
Richi Railway, Quorn**

with its jagged burnt-red walls and rich
wildlife. Wilmington itself oozes old-
world charm – drink with the locals in
the 1876 **Wilmington Hotel**, which still
has the old coach stables out the back.
Kids will love the model
cars, trains and antique
Meccano sets at the **Toy
Museum** *(open daily)*.

🚗 *Take B82 right to Quorn.*

⑬ Quorn
SA; 5433
At the edge of the Flinders
Ranges, Quorn is renowned
for its heritage buildings
and the **Pichi Richi Railway**
*(Sat & Sun, Feb–Dec; 1800 440
101)*, which runs on the oldest
surviving length of the narrow-gauge
Old Ghan Railway, built in the 1870s to
link Adelaide and Alice Springs. The
main street is lined with buildings
dating back to 1878, a highlight being
the **Transcontinental Hotel** *(open daily)*.
To explore the **Dutchmans Stern
Conservation Park**, head north on
Arden Vale Road and follow the signs
along unsealed roads west to the
Dutchmans Trailhead car park. It is a
steep 8-km (5-mile) return hike up to
the bluff. For more natural splendour
and wildlife, return to Arden Vale

Road and head 15 km (10 miles) north to the magnificent red rock formations of **Warren Gorge** – the site is known for sightings of the rare yellow-footed rock wallaby among the gum trees.

🚗 *Return to Quorn on Arden Vale Rd and take the B83 towards Hawker.*

⑭ Kanyaka
Flinders Ranges, SA

Just past the Cradock turnoff on the B83, a parking sign alerts drivers to the **Kanyaka Death Rock**. Kanyaka, which means "piece of rock" in the native Adnyamathanhan language, refers to the striking rock formation overlooking the ancient Aboriginal watering hole. The **Old Kanyaka Homestead** (a short way north along the main road) is an 1851 sheep station.

🚗 *Return to B83 north to Hawker, past the turnoff to the Yourambulla Caves.*

⑮ Hawker
SA; 5434

South of Hawker, the **Yourambulla Caves** *(follow the sign just off the main road)* are home to Aboriginal rock art thought to be more than 6,000 years old. The steep one-and-a-half-hour self-guided walk leads up to three sites with ancient etched, abstract motifs. Back in Hawker, do not miss the **Jeff Morgan Gallery** *(open daily)*, featuring the Wilpena Panorama, a 30-m (100-ft) painting of Wilpena Pound *(see below)*, before enjoying a beer at the charming 19th-century **Hawker Hotel**.

🚗 *Follow signs from the main street to Wilpena Rd, leading to Wilpena Pound.*

⑯ Wilpena Pound
Flinders Ranges, SA

Watch the dry countryside turn green on the way into the **Flinders Ranges National Park** to explore the

extraordinary crater-like Wilpena Pound, which is 17 km (10 miles) long and 8 km (5 miles) wide. Aerial and 4WD tours can be booked at the **Wilpena Pound Visitor Information Centre** *(Wilpena Pound, 5434; 08 8648 0048)*. Take the one-hour **Sacred Canyon Walk** past Aboriginal rock carvings, from Sacred Canyon car park, 19 km (12 miles) southeast of Wilpena on Blinman Road. The **Brachina Gorge Geological Trail** is a good option for the less mobile –follow the well-signed 20-km (12-mile) road trail past sedimentary rock formations. For a challenging walk, try the three-hour **Bunyeroo Gorge Hike** from the car park 18 km (11 miles) north of Wilpena on Bunyeroo Gorge Road.

🚗 *If in a 4WD head north on unsealed road through Blinman, otherwise return to Hawker and turn right onto the B83.*

⑰ Parachilna
SA; 5730

Parachilna is a tiny tourist town famous for its "Feral Feast", a platter of bush tucker including emu, crocodile, native limes and bush tomatoes served at the **Prairie Hotel** *(open daily)*. From here, take the unsealed roads (suitable for 2WD vehicles) to the craggy red cliffs and waterholes of **Parachilna Gorge**.

Above left Wide expanse of the Flinders Ranges
Above right Jacka's Brewery in Melrose, which closed during the Depression in the 1930s

EAT AND DRINK

AROUND GLADSTONE

Old Bakery Stone Hut *inexpensive*
This family-run bakehouse is famous for its pies with a native twist. Try camel, emu, kangaroo or crocodile pie.
Main North Rd, Stone Hut, 5480 (between Laura & Wirrabara); 08 8663 2165

HAWKER

The Old Ghan Restaurant *moderate*
Dine on the old platform and enjoy a Ghan burger or dishes made with local produce such as kangaroo meat and quandong (wild peach).
Leigh Creek Rd, 5434; 08 8648 4176; open Wed–Sat

WILPENA POUND

Woolshed Restaurant *moderate*
The fully licensed Woolshed overlooks Rawnsley Bluff and offers good, country-style cuisine – try the delicious seared kangaroo with peppercorn plum sauce.
Rawnsley Park Station, Wilpena Rd, 5434; 08 8648 0126

PARACHILNA

Prairie Hotel
Famous for its "Feral Feast" *(see left)*.
Cnr High St & West Terrace, 5730; 08 8648 4844; www.prairiehotel.com.au

Below Ruins of the Old Kanyaka Homestead, a deserted sheep station

The Top End

Darwin to Territory Wildlife Park

Highlights

- **Tropical Darwin**
  Relax in the Northern Territory's sultry, green, tropical capital, a vibrant, multicultural frontier town

- **Untamed nature**
  Be awestruck by animals in the wild, from crocodiles to abundant birdlife, in lush wetlands and national parks

- **Aboriginal art**
  Explore the astonishing ancient rock art of indigenous peoples at natural galleries in Kakadu National Park

- **Serene waterholes and falls**
  Cool down in tranquil swimming holes beneath thundering waterfalls in Kakadu and Litchfield national parks

Dramatic Florence Falls in full flow, Litchfield National Park

The Top End

Steamy monsoon forests, mangroves teeming with wildlife and spectacular stone escarpments – the tropical "Top End", as the Northern Territory's (NT) northernmost region is known, is a remote, rugged place where there is ample natural beauty to be enjoyed. Home to indigenous peoples who have lived here for 40,000 years, it is spiritually rich, with stories of the Dreamtime and Aboriginal customs depicted in ancient paintings that decorate rock walls. This tour starts in the Territory's capital, Darwin, before taking in the lush wetlands, abundant birdlife and Aboriginal culture of Kakadu National Park. It continues to Litchfield National Park, famous for its termite mounds, waterfalls and tranquil natural swimming holes, ending at the sprawling Territory Wildlife Park, from where it is a short hop back to Darwin.

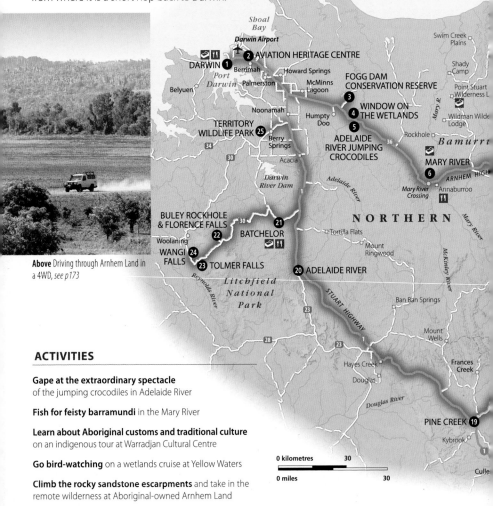

Above Driving through Arnhem Land in a 4WD, *see p173*

Shoal Bay

Van Diema

Darwin Airport

DARWIN **1** **2** AVIATION HERITAGE CENTRE
Berrimah
Port Howard Springs
Darwin Palmerston McMinns Lagoon
Belyuen

Swim Creek Plains

Shady Camp

Point Stuart Wilderness L

Noonamah Humpty Doo FOGG DAM CONSERVATION RESERVE **3**

WINDOW ON **4** THE WETLANDS

Wildman Wilde Lodge

TERRITORY WILDLIFE PARK **25**
Berry Springs **34**
30
Acacia

ADELAIDE RIVER JUMPING CROCODILES **5**

Rockhole *Bamurru*

Darwin River Dam

MARY RIVER **6**

Adelaide River

Mary River Crossing ARNHEM HIGH Annaburroo

BULEY ROCKHOLE & FLORENCE FALLS **30**
Woolaning **22**
WANGI **24**
FALLS **23** TOLMER FALLS
21 BATCHELOR

N O R T H E R N

Tortilla Flats

Mount Ringwood

20 ADELAIDE RIVER

Litchfield National Park

Reynolds River

STUART HIGHWAY
23
28
23

Ban Ban Springs

Mount Wells

McKinlay River

Mary River

Hayes Creek
Douglas

Frances Creek

Douglas River

PINE CREEK **19**
Kybrook

Culle

ACTIVITIES

Gape at the extraordinary spectacle of the jumping crocodiles in Adelaide River

Fish for feisty barramundi in the Mary River

Learn about Aboriginal customs and traditional culture on an indigenous tour at Warradjan Cultural Centre

Go bird-watching on a wetlands cruise at Yellow Waters

Climb the rocky sandstone escarpments and take in the remote wilderness at Aboriginal-owned Arnhem Land

Escape the sticky heat with an invigorating swim in the cool natural rockholes at Litchfield National Park

0 kilometres   30

0 miles   30

KEY

Drive route

Above White-breasted woodswallows,
Territory Wildlife Park, see p177

PLAN YOUR DRIVE

Start/finish: Darwin to Territory
Wildlife Park.

Number of days: 5–7 days, including
one day exploring Darwin, and allowing
for tours, cruises and walks within
Kakadu and Litchfield national parks.

Distance: Approx. 1,255 km (785 miles).

Road conditions: Good signposting
and mostly sealed roads. Roads to Jim
Jim Falls and Maguk (Barramundi
Gorge) and Jarrangbarmi (Koolpin
Gorge) are dirt tracks requiring 4WDs.
Roads are subject to flooding and
closure during the wet season, which
can continue well into May. Check
conditions on 1800 246 199 or
www.ntlis.nt.gov.au/roadreport.

When to go: During the dry season
(May–Sep), skies are clear, temperatures
average 30°C (86°F); Jun–Jul it drops as
low as 10°C (50°F). During Oct–Dec,
humidity rises and there are periodic
showers and spectacular lightning
storms. The wet season (Nov–Apr)
brings daily afternoon downpours,
periodic cyclones, floods, road closures,
and reduced business hours, but the
land is astonishingly lush and green.

Opening times: Normal business hours
during the dry season; shorter hours
and some closures during the Wet.

Shopping: Darwin's main shopping
area, Smith Street Mall, boasts
Aboriginal arts and crafts galleries,
souvenir and gift shops selling
crocodile products, jewellery stores
specializing in pearls, and boutiques.
There are often good Aboriginal arts
and crafts stores at national park
visitor centres too.

Market days: Darwin: Mindil Markets,
Fri nights, Apr–Oct; Parap Markets, Sat
am all year.

Major festivals: Darwin: Deckchair
Cinema, Apr–Nov (www.deckchair
cinema.com.au); Fringe Festival, Jul;
Darwin Beer Can Regatta, Jul (www.
beercanregatta.org.au); Darwin Festival,
Aug; **Kakadu National Park & Arnhem
Land:** Oenpelli (Gunbalanya) Open
Day, Aug; Garma Festival, Aug.

Left Sandy beach in Darwin, see p170

VISITING DARWIN

Parking
There are several car parks around. Park at the foot of Stokes Hill Wharf for the walk.

Visitor Information
Tourism Top End Visitor Centre
Cnr Bennett & Smith St; 1300 138 886; www.tourismtopend.com.au; open daily

SHOPPING IN DARWIN

Mindil Beach Reserve, on the edge of Fannie Bay, is renowned for its Asian-inspired **Mindil Market**, which takes place on Thu and Sun, Apr–Oct, from sunset to 9 or 10 pm. Stalls sell food and handmade arts and crafts. The **Nightcliff Village Markets** are held on Sun am throughout the year.

WHERE TO STAY IN DARWIN

Mirambeena *moderate*
This central, high-rise hotel has huge modern rooms and a shady swimming pool, and serves excellent breakfasts.
64 Cavenagh St, 0800; 08 8946 0111; www.travelodge.com.au

Moonshadow *moderate–expensive*
Luxurious self-contained villas set in tropical gardens with plunge pools and Zen vibe, and stylish apartments.
6 Gardens Hill Crescent, The Gardens, 0820; 08 8981 8850; www.moonshadowvillas.com

Sky City *expensive*
The city's top hotel and casino has comfortable rooms with amenities including a pool, restaurants and bars.
Gilruth Ave, The Gardens, 0801; 08 8943 8888; www.skycitydarwin.com.au

❶ Darwin

Northern Territory (NT); 0800

Darwin is a vibrant city with an eclectic cultural mix enjoying the sultry heat and unhurried pace of life in the tropics. Established as a Singapore-style trading post in 1869, the city has attracted Asians ever since. Its residents are resilient, having survived World War II bombing raids and Cyclone Tracey, which flattened Darwin on Christmas Day 1974. Boasting shady waterfront parks, engaging museums and wonderful seaside dining, Darwin makes a great base for acclimatizing before venturing to Kakadu National Park.

A two-hour walking tour

From the car park walk along **Stokes Hill Wharf** ①, Darwin's southern tip. With plenty of restaurants, the wharf is particularly pleasant in the evening. Backtrack to visit the **Indo-Pacific Marine Exhibition** ② *(open daily)* to learn about Darwin's rich coral environment. Opposite is the **Darwin Waterfront Precinct** ③, with shops, cafés, restaurants and safe swimming lagoons. As Darwin can be very hot, visitors may prefer to return to their car and drive up Kitchener Drive, past the **World War II Oil Storage Tunnels** ④ *(open daily)*, which run beneath the city, and park along the Esplanade near **Survivor's Lookout** ⑤ to continue the rest of the route on foot. At the top of the lookout, take in the wharf views before crossing Smith Street to the park to see the historic buildings that survived Cyclone Tracey, including the ruins of the 1902 **Christ Church**

Cathedral ⑥, incorporated into the modern church; the 1885 **Brown's Mart Theatre** ⑦ next door; and the 1883 **Palmerston Town Hall** ⑧ ruins opposite. Note the huge banyan tree, the **Tree of Knowledge** ⑨, by Brown's Mart – a reminder of Darwin's pre-World War II Chinatown.

Follow Bennett Street towards the Esplanade to the imposing **Parliament House** ⑩ *(open daily)*. Across the Esplanade, note the elegant tropical architecture of the 1883 **Government House** ⑪. From here, walk through **Bicentennial Park** ⑫, and soak up views of Fannie Bay.

To explore Darwin further, return to the car and drive along the Esplanade. Look out for **Lyons Cottage** *(open daily)*, on the corner of Knuckey Street, and **Old Admiralty House**, on the corner of Peel Street, a 1920s tropical-style stilt house. At the end of the Esplanade, turn right, then left

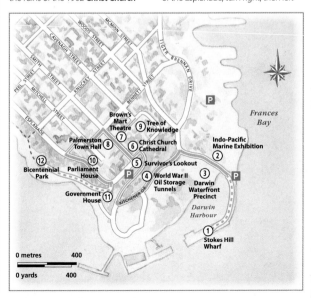

down Doctor's Gully Road to **Aquascene** *(open at high tide; 08 8981 7837)* to feed the fish. Head back up the hill, following Daly Street to Gardens Road and turn left for the luxuriant **George Brown Botanic Gardens** *(open daily)*. Bear right on Gilruth Avenue, left on Conacher Street (2 km/1 mile) to the superb **Museum and Art Gallery of the NT** *(open daily)*.

🚗 *Take Stuart Hwy (1) and turn off at signs to Aviation Heritage Centre.*

② Aviation Heritage Centre

Stuart Hwy, Winnellie, NT; 0821
This **aviation museum** *(open daily)* in a former World War II aircraft hangar houses a number of interesting aircraft, including a huge B-52 bomber, and tells the history of aviation in the NT.

🚗 *Carry on along Stuart Hwy (1). Turn left onto Arnhem Hwy (36) for Kakadu National Park, then left to the Fogg Dam Conservation Reserve.*

③ Fogg Dam Conservation Reserve

off Arnhem Hwy (36), NT
Fogg Dam was created in the 1950s to irrigate an experimental rice project at Humpty Doo. It failed for myriad reasons, including birds eating the crops – the abundant birdlife is one reason to visit this lush wetland reserve. Walk across the barrage to **Pandanus Lookout**, a bird-watching hide with sweeping views of the wetlands and birds, including comb-crested jacanas, geese and egrets. There are other easy, signposted walks through this pristine environment, but saltwater crocodiles inhabit the dam, so heed the signs, do not leave boardwalks and keep away from the lagoon's edge.

🚗 *Return to Arnhem Hwy (36) left to Window on the Wetlands, on the left.*

④ Window on the Wetlands

Arnhem Hwy (36), NT
The striking **Window on the Wetlands Visitor Centre** *(open daily)* sits atop Beatrice Hill, an area of spiritual significance to the indigenous Limilngan-Wulna people. The centre has views across the Adelaide River floodplain and its displays are a great introduction to the environment. Children may like the interactive exhibits on Top End seasons, ecology and problems caused by feral animals.

🚗 *Continue east on Arnhem Hwy to the jetty next to Adelaide River bridge.*

⑤ Adelaide River Jumping Crocodiles

off Arnhem Hwy (36), NT
Several companies offer "jumping crocodile cruises" yet the **Original Jumping Crocodile Cruise** *(several daily; www.jumpingcrocodilecruises.com.au)* on the *Adelaide River Queen* is arguably the best. See saltwater crocs – "salties" – in their natural habitat, rising 2 m (6 ft) out of the river to snap at raw meat – a jaw-dropping, if unnatural, spectacle. Similar cruises also run from Fogg Dam and Window on the Wetlands.

🚗 *Continue along Arnhem Hwy (36) for another 48 km (30 miles) to Mary River (4WD recommended).*

CROCODILE SAFETY

Two types of crocodile are found in northern Australia: the shy freshwater (*Crocodylus johnstonii*), or "freshie", growing up to 3 m (10 ft) long, and the aggressive estuarine (*Crocodylus porosus*), or "saltie", found in both salt and freshwater, and growing up to 6 m (20 ft) long, which takes one or two human lives a year in the north. During the wet season, some swimming holes become host to salties, which have to be trapped and removed, while some swimming spots are never entirely safe. Always check the warning signs at every swimming spot before diving in.

EAT AND DRINK IN DARWIN

Evoo *moderate*
Dine on creative cuisine based on seasonal products at the city's finest restaurant.
Sky City Casino, Gilruth Ave, The Gardens, 0801; 08 8943 8888

Hanuman *moderate*
Enjoy top Thai, Indian and Nyonya (Malaysian) dishes such as poached Hanuman oysters with Asian spices. Reservations essential.
93 Mitchell St, 0801; 08 8941 3500; www.hanuman.com.au; open daily pm; Mon–Fri for lunch

Pee Wee's *moderate*
Experimental fusion cuisine, with a focus on seafood, is served at tables lit by torchlight on an outdoor terrace beside the beach – very romantic.
East Point Rd, 0801; www.peewees.com.au

Other options
Cullen Bay Marina has many waterfront eateries, among them **Buzz Café** *(48 Marina Blvd, Cullen Bay, 0820; 08 8941 1141)*, which serves good food.

VISITING KAKADU NATIONAL PARK

A park entry fee applies, which is paid at **Bowali Visitor Centre** or **Gagudju Lodge** (see p174), **Aurora Kakadu** in South Alligator, or, if in Darwin, **Tourism Top End Visitor Centre** (see p170). Allow 2–3 days to explore the park – it is best to hire a 4WD or join a 4WD tour. To check the accessibility of Kakadu's roads, see *www.kakadu.com.au/access*. Jabiru has a service station, mini-mart, bakery and medical centre.

Camping
Kakadu's 24 camp sites range from well-equipped and inexpensive to basic and free. Most only open during the Dry.

WHERE TO STAY

AROUND MARY RIVER

Point Stuart Wilderness Lodge *moderate*
This lodge offers simple rooms and camping, as well as a restaurant, bar and pool, and an array of activities.
36 km (22 miles) from Arnhem Hwy on Point Stuart Rd, 0836; 08 8978 8914; www.pointstuart.com.au

Bamurru Plains *expensive*
Water buffalo, wallabies and kangaroos graze outside luxurious safari-style bungalows overlooking verdant flood-plains, where flocks of magpie geese, egrets and ibis congregate. Activities include bird-watching, wildlife safaris and airboating. Reservations essential.
Mary River (by pre-arranged pick-up at Swim Creek Station gate or airstrip), 0836; 02 9571 6399; www.bamurruplains.com

AROUND MAMUKALA WETLANDS

Aurora Kakadu *moderate*
Standard and superior motel rooms plus camping and caravan sites set in picturesque tropical gardens with a swimming pool, bistro, and bar.
Arnhem Hwy, South Alligator, 0886; 08 8979 0166; www.auroraresorts.com.au

AROUND BOWALI VISITOR CENTRE

Lake View Park *inexpensive–moderate*
Aboriginal-owned Lake View Park offers options from stylish corrugated-iron self-catering cabins to tent-like "bush bungalows" with exterior bathrooms.
27 Lakeside Drive, Jabiru, 0886; 08 8979 3144; www.lakeviewkakadu.com.au

Gagudju Crocodile Holiday Inn *moderate–expensive*
This extraordinary crocodile-shaped hotel is Kakadu's most luxurious, and has modern rooms, a swimming pool, restaurant and bar.
Flinders Rd, Jabiru, 0886; 08 8979 9000; www.gagudju-dreaming.com

Right A guide interprets ancient Aboriginal art at Ubirr

⑥ Mary River
Arnhem Hwy, NT

Mary River offers a chance for wetlands recreation. Just off Arnhem Highway, **Mary River Crossing** is an accessible fishing spot. Next left is sandy Point Stuart Road *(impassable Oct–Apr)*, and a left turn off it leads to the popular fishing spot at **Rockhole**. Further on, a turn leads to **Point Stuart Wilderness Lodge** *(see left)*, which runs fishing trips. Beyond is a turn for **Shady Camp**, a fishing spot where boats can be hired. A barrage divides fresh and sea water, but beware "salties" on both sides – do not wade in like the complacent local fishermen. For **Bamurru Plains** *(see left)* continue to Swim Creek Station gate.

🚗 *Return to Arnhem Hwy (36) and carry on past Kakadu Park entrance to Mamukala Wetlands, on the right.*

Kakadu National Park
Australia's largest national park, Kakadu boasts an astonishing diversity of wildlife and habitats, from lush tidal wetlands and paperbark swamps to sandstone escarpments and savannah woodlands. Jointly managed by Bininj and Munnguy owners and Parks Australia, Kakadu provides visitors with an insight into Aboriginal culture through rock art, interpretive centres, and indigenous-led tours.

⑦ Mamukala Wetlands
Kakadu National Park, Arnhem Hwy, NT

The first stop in Kakadu National Park, these lush wetlands are home to thousands of magpie geese, especially in the late dry season (Sep–Oct). Observe them from a platform or take a closer look on a 3-km (2-mile) walk.

🚗 *Drive east along Arnhem Hwy (36), then turn right on Kakadu Hwy (21), Bowali Visitor Centre is on the right.*

Indigenous Peoples of the Top End
Aboriginal people believe the spirits shaped Kakadu during Creation Time, bringing with them all the plants, animals and indigenous peoples, the Bininj-Mungguy. The clans are governed by a kinship system. There are two main groups, or "moieties": Duwa or Yirridja. Everyone is born into one or the other – inherited from the paternal side – and cannot marry a person of the same group.

Above Aboriginal "Dreamtime" painting of a turtle at Ubirr

⑧ Bowali Visitor Centre
Kakadu National Park, Jabiru, NT; 0886

Stop at this visitor centre *(08 8938 1120; www.kakadu.com.au)* at the heart of Kakadu National Park to learn about the park through its displays on habitats, wildlife and Aboriginal culture. Pick up walking maps and the Kakadu Visitor Guide, and visit the indigenous-owned **Marrawuddi Gallery** *(08 8979 2777)*, which has an excellent selection of arts and crafts.

🚗 *Return to Arnhem Hwy (36) then left and right along Oenpelli Rd to Ubirr.*

⑨ Ubirr

40 km (25 miles) NE of Arnhem Hwy, NT

Ubirr *(open daily Apr–Nov; open daily pm, Dec–Mar)*, just before the Arnhem Land boundary, is home to impressive Aboriginal "X-ray-style" paintings on rock galleries, accessed via a circular walking track. The ancient paintings provide a fascinating insight into Aboriginal foods and the abundant wetland wildlife, including the Tasmanian tiger or thylacine, which became extinct here over 2000 years ago. Time the visit for morning or sunset, when a scramble up the rocky outcrop provides sweeping vistas of the Nardab floodplain, East Alligator River and Arnhem Land escarpment, bathed in golden sunlight.

🚗 *From Ubirr, take Oenpelli Rd across Cahills Crossing into Arnhem Land, to Oenpelli. Get a permit to visit Arnhem Land, or join a tour (see right).*

⑩ Arnhem Land

NT; 0822

Located between Kakadu National Park and the Gulf of Carpentaria, the 91,000 sq km (3,5135 sq mile) Arnhem Land was designated an Aboriginal reserve in 1931 and never colonized or grazed, retaining its unspoilt wilderness. A permit is required to visit, but the best way to see the area is on a guided tour that takes in an escarpment hike *(see right)*.

At **Injalak Arts and Crafts Centre** *(open Mon–Fri & Sat am, Jun–Oct; 08 8979 0190; www.injalak.com)* in the Aboriginal community of Oenpelli, also called

Gunbalanya, visitors can watch indigenous artists paint and women weave baskets, and buy some locally made crafts. Visitors are not allowed to wander around the community nor visit anything else in the area, so while it is fascinating, to see more, take a tour.

🚗 *Retrace route back to Cahills Crossing, then turn left for 2 km (1 mile) to Guluyambi cruise boat dock on the East Alligator River.*

Wandjina Rock Art

The Aboriginal peoples of the NT believe the Wandjina are the creators of the Dreaming and control the weather using lightning, rain and winds to punish those who do not show respect. Of all the rock art, the Wandjina figures are the most striking, with skeletal white faces surrounded by radiating lines, huge eyes and no mouth. The art is prominent in the nearby Kimberley region.

⑪ Guluyambi Cultural Cruise

East Alligator River, NT

Local indigenous people run the engaging Guluyambi cruises along

Indigenous craft-making, Arnhem Land

East Alligator River *(3–4 times daily; 1800 089113)*, the boundary of Arnhem Land, teaching visitors about their traditions as the cruise zigzags down the river, pointing out the abundant birdlife on the way. During a short stop on the sandy shores of Arnhem Land, the guide demonstrates the use of hunting, gathering and cooking implements.

🚗 *Return to Bowali Visitor Centre. Continue on Kakadu Hwy (21), left for Nourlangie Rock.*

Above left View over Arnhem Land, owned by Aborigines since 1931 *Above right* Pond covered by waterlilies, Arnhem Land

VISITING ARNHEM LAND

Getting a permit

Apply 10 days in advance online or in person to the **Northern Land Council, Darwin** *(08 8920 5178; www.nlc.org.au)* for a permit to visit Arnhem Land, which allows visits to specific places (detours not permitted). Do not take alcohol in. If visiting on a tour *(see below)*, the operator will take care of the paperwork.

Tours

Lord's Safaris is the longest running operator into Arnhem Land and offers small-group 4WD day trips, including a hike up Injalak Hill (Long Tom Dreaming) with an indigenous guide to view rock paintings *(08 8948 2200; www.lords-safaris.com; closed during rainy season)*.

EAT AND DRINK

AROUND MARY RIVER

Bark Hut Inn *inexpensive*

This roadhouse fuel stop serves delicious take-away home-style hamburgers and sandwiches. It is also the last place to buy alcohol before reaching Kakadu National Park. No alcohol is allowed in the park. *Arnhem Hwy, Annaburroo, 0886; 08 8978 8988; www.barkhutinn.com.au*

BOWALI VISITOR CENTRE

Anmak an-me café *inexpensive*

Run by the indigenous-owned Gunjeihmi Association, this excellent little café does great coffee, sandwiches, salad rolls, pies, cakes and drinks. *Bowali Visitor Centre, off Arnhem Hwy, Jabiru 0886; 9am–4.30pm*

Other options

There are no stand-alone restaurants in Kakadu, but there are casual bistros, cafés, bars and barbecue areas at the hotels and motels, which welcome residents and passersby alike.

Eat and Drink: inexpensive under AU$60; moderate AU$60–AU$100; expensive over AU$100

Above left Azure kingfisher, a colourful Kakadu resident, Yellow Waters **Above right** Cruise boats waiting on the lagoon, Yellow Waters

WHERE TO STAY IN YELLOW WATERS

Gagudju Lodge *moderate*
Adjacent to Warradjan Aboriginal Cultural Centre, indigenous-owned Gagudju has a range of accommodation from modern bungalows to camping and caravans, along with pool, bistro, bar and store. *Cooinda, 0886; 08 8979 1500; www.gagudju-dreaming.com*

Camping
Kakadu's 24 camp sites range from well-equipped and inexpensive to basic and free. Most only open during the dry season.

⑫ Nourlangie Rock
Kakadu National Park, NT
This popular place in Kakadu National Park provides access to several important indigenous sites including **Anbangbang Shelter**, which has revealed that Aboriginal people have been here for 20,000 years or so, and **Anbangbang Gallery**, where intriguing paintings on the rock walls portray figures of Aboriginal mythology. An easy 1.5 km (1 mile) walk from the Nourlangie Rock car park takes it all in, including the colossal Nourlangie Rock, while a moderately steep hike up to **Gunwarddehwardde Lookout** provides stunning vistas of Nourlangie Rock and Arnhem Land escarpment. Some walks are only possible May–Sep.
🚗 *Continue on Kakadu Hwy (21), 29 km (18 miles) and turn right on Cooinda Rd to Warradjan Cultural Centre.*

⑬ Warradjan Cultural Centre
Kakadu Hwy, Jim Jim, NT; 0886
Learn about the indigenous people and their culture and traditions at the

Above The sandstone outcrop of Nourlangie Rock, Kakadu National Park

superb turtle-shaped **Warradjan Cultural Centre** *(open daily)*, which boasts one of the most engaging interpretive displays around. The exhibition finishes at the gift shop, which has a good selection of books.
🚗 *Carry on along Cooinda Rd to Yellow Waters.*

⑭ Yellow Waters
Cooinda Rd, off Kakadu Hwy, NT
The wetlands area of Yellow Waters in Kakadu National Park brims with flora and fauna. The area is home to crocodiles, fresh water snakes and turtles, but what makes it special is the thousands of migratory birds it attracts. It is also one of Kakadu's most picturesque spots, with freshwater mangroves and glassy billabongs dotted with crimson and white waterlillies. From the car park, stroll around the billabong on the boardwalk, or take a cruise on the tranquil waterways *(08 8979 0145; www. gagudju-dreaming.com; book in advance)*.
🚗 *With a high-clearance 4WD, drive to the turn off Kakadu Highway to Jim Jim Falls, 58 km (36 miles) away.*

⑮ Jim Jim and Twin Falls
Kakadu National Park, NT
Plunging 150 m (490 ft) off the escarpment, **Jim Jim Falls** are most impressive after the Wet, in June (they stop flowing in August). **Twin Falls** are also magnificent when in flow. Both falls are accessible by 4WD (with snorkel; there is a creek crossing) on a rough track in the dry season. It is a 4-hour return trip. Alternatively join a **Waterfalls Tour** *(08 8979 0145)* from Jabiru or Cooinda. Walks to both falls involve a tough scramble over rocks.
🚗 *Return to Kakadu Hwy (21) and turn left. Turn left after 49 km (30 miles) for Maguk, 11 km (7 miles) down a track.*

Where to Stay: inexpensive under AU$150; moderate AU$150–AU$250; expensive over AU$250

⓰ Maguk (Barramundi Gorge)
Kakadu National Park, NT

At Maguk in the south of Kakadu National Park, a shady path from the car park leads through lush forest to a natural swimming hole. The deep, crystal-clear waters are cool and the rock walls keep the temperature down. Read and heed the warning signs as crocodiles have been found here.

🚗 *Continue 42 km (26 miles) south and turn left to Jarrangbarnmi for 26 km (16 miles) and turn right at the junction; Gimbat is a further 7 km (4 miles).*

⓱ Jarrangbarnmi (Koolpin Gorge)
Kakadu National Park, NT

Jarrangbarnmi's serene pink stone boasts several natural swimming holes, shady spots and sandy shores, but it takes some effort to reach – a 4WD and permit from **Bowali Visitor Centre** *(08 8938 1176; kakadu.permits@ environment.gov.au)* is required as daily visitor numbers to this lovely spot are strictly controlled. Permits are allocated on a first-in-first serve basis, so put your application in advance of your visit. **Gimbat Picnic Area**, 7 km (4 miles) further on, is another peaceful spot with grassy picnic grounds and shade.

🚗 *Return to the junction and drive straight on to Gunlom, 10 km (6 miles).*

⓲ Gunlom (Waterfall Creek)
Kakadu National Park, NT

This wonderful spot in Kakadu National Park was made famous by the movie *Crocodile Dundee*. There is a natural swimming hole below waterfalls (no flow in the Dry), but climb to the top of the falls (20 mins) to a quieter spot for a swim and stunning views. It is possible to camp here and it is great for a picnic.

🚗 *Return to Kakadu Hwy (21) and continue southwest to the park's southern exit at Mary River roadhouse. Drive 68 km (42 miles) to the junction with Stuart Hwy (1) at Pine Creek.*

⓳ Pine Creek
Stuart Hwy, NT; 0847

The location of the NT's first Gold Rush after gold was found in 1871, Pine Creek is one of its oldest towns and the first reached after Kakadu National Park. There are a handful of heritage buildings around town, including the timber-framed and galvanized-iron,1889 **Old Playford Club Hotel** and **Old Bakery**. Miners Park has century-old mining equipment scattered across its dry grass and there is a tiny **museum** *(Mon–Fri pm)* on Railway Terrace with an old locomotive.

🚗 *Drive 118 km (73 miles) northwest to Adelaide River on the Stuart Hwy (1).*

Above left Swimming at Maguk (Barramundi Gorge) **Top right** Picturesque Gunlom in Kakadu National Park **Above right** The swimming hole at Gunlom, as seen in the film *Crocodile Dundee*

ACTIVITIES IN KAKADU NATIONAL PARK

Animal Tracks offer a hands-on full-day interactive tour led by an award-winning Aboriginal guide who teaches visitors to track animals, gather bush tucker, cook, and eat traditional foods *(08 8979 0145, www.animaltracks. com.au)*.

Ayal Aboriginal Tours Kakadu are indigenous-owned and offer natural and cultural tours of the Kakadu National Park. Explore the East and South Alligator regions of Kakadu with a local Aboriginal guide *(0429 470 384; www.ayalkakadu.com.au)*.

Kakadu Culture Camp offers nocturnal wildlife viewing on a torch-lit cruise on Djarradjin Billabong and a night's sleep in safari tents *(08 8979 2048 or 0428 792 048; www.kakaduculturecamp.com)*.

EAT AND DRINK

There are no stand-alone restaurants in **Kakadu National Park**, rather there are casual alfresco bistros, cafés, bars, and barbecue areas at the hotels and motels, which welcome residents and passersby alike.

Above The lush plant foliage around Maguk (Barramundi Gorge)

Eat and Drink: inexpensive under AU$60; moderate AU$60–AU$100; expensive over AU$100

WHERE TO STAY AROUND BATCHELOR

Batchelor Resort *moderate*
A good option if Rum Jungle Bungalows is full, this basic motel has decent rooms, a camp site and a bar serving meals.
37-49 Rum Jungle Rd, 0845; 08 8976 0123; www.batchelor-resort.com

Rum Jungle Bungalows *moderate*
This stylish B&B is set in tropical gardens with a pool. The breakfast is impressive and there is a BBQ to cook dinner.
10 Meneling Rd, off Rum Jungle Rd, 0845; 08 8976 0555; www.rumjunglebungalows.com.au

Camping options
Try **Latitude 1308** *(08 8978 2077; www.latitude1308.com.au)*, with permanent safari-style tents and a café, or **Litchfield Safari Camp** *(08 8978 2185; www.litchfieldsafaricamp. com.au)*, with safari and budget tents.

Below Impressive termite mounds at Litchfield National Park **Below right** The impressive twin cascade of Florence Falls, Litchfield National Park **Below left** Buley Creek through the scrub to Buley Rockhole

20 Adelaide River
Stuart Hwy, NT; 0846
Adelaide River was settled while the Overland Telegraph Line was being installed, but the town did not boom until it became Darwin's supply centre during World War II, and was bombed by the Japanese as a result. The war cemetery is where victims of the air raids are buried. It is a sobering yet picturesque place with shady picnic tables and peacocks, and is a pleasant spot to take a walk or enjoy lunch.

🚗 *Continue north along Stuart Hwy (1), then turn left to Batchelor.*

21 Batchelor
NT; 0845
Established to support post-war efforts to extract uranium from nearby Rum Jungle Mine, Batchelor is more than a company town thanks to Litchfield National Park and the Institute of Indigenous Tertiary Education. For most visitors, Batchelor is little more than a stopover to guarantee an early start for the park, yet its leafy streets and gardens make it a pleasant stay. Visit the Institute's excellent **Coomalie Cultural Centre** *(closed Sun)* for stunning Aboriginal arts and crafts.

🚗 *Follow Rum Jungle Rd, then left on Litchfield Pk Rd into Litchfield National Park and onto Buley Rockhole turn-off.*

Litchfield National Park
Close to Darwin, and with accessible swimming holes, stunning waterfalls and shady picnic grounds, Litchfield National Park is far easier to explore than the vast and isolated Kakadu National Park. Each sight lies within easy distance of the park's one sealed road and the walks are usually quite gentle. The downside, however, is that it really fills up at weekends with day-trippers from Darwin. The park is best visited during the early dry season (May–Jun) when the falls are still flowing.

22 Buley Rockhole and Florence Falls
Litchfield National Park, NT
Consisting of an accessible series of natural swimming holes linked by tiny waterfalls, **Buley Rockhole** is the first stop in Litchfield National Park and a great spot for a swim. From here, it is an easy 3-km (2-mile) trail along Buley Creek to **Florence Falls** (also accessible by car). The twin 20-m (65-ft) cascades are the park's most spectacular and can be viewed from a lookout. Climb 135 steps down to a natural swimming hole at the base of the falls or take the easier 30-minute track down, through monsoon forest and open woodland.

🚗 *Return to Litchfield Park Rd, turn right to Tolmer Falls on the left.*

VISITING LITCHFIELD NATIONAL PARK

Visitor Information Centre
Get a map from the information office in Batchelor on the corner of Tarkarri Road & Nurdina Sreet; *08 8976 0282; www. nt.gov.au/nreta/parks/find/litchfield.html*

Stay safe
Pay attention to crocodile warnings and do not picnic on the platforms as scrub typhus can be transmitted by tiny mites.

Camping
There are national park camp sites with basic facilities at Buley Rockhole and Florence Falls, and at Wangi Falls.

Magnetic Termite Mounds
Look out for the 2-m (6-ft) high magnetic termite mounds in Litchfield National Park, looking like tombstones in a cemetery. Oriented north-south to keep cool – this way the surface is never exposed to the sun – the mounds appear golden red in the morning and late afternoon, and grey in the middle of the day.

㉕ Territory Wildlife Park
Cox Peninsula Rd, NT
This sprawling **wildlife park** *(open daily)* is one of Australia's best, with many walking tracks running through a wide range of different habitats rich in fauna and flora. There are walk-in aviaries, aquariums, a nocturnal exhibit, and birds-of-prey display, and when it all gets too hot to walk, hop on the free train that continually circles the park. From here, it is a 47-km (30-mile) drive back to Darwin.

㉓ Tolmer Falls
Litchfield National Park, NT
Plunging down from two lofty, rocky escarpments to pools far below, the magnificent Tolmer Falls must be Litchfield National Park's most photographed. View them from the clifftop lookout opposite, so as not to disturb the rare orange horseshoe bats and ghost bats that inhabit the area. With a park ranger, visitors can walk along the clifftop to take in ancient cycads, but swimming is not possible.
🚗 *Carry on along Litchfield Park Rd, turn right to Wangi Falls.*

Bird-watching
The Top End national parks provide great bird-watching opportunities. Try to locate red-collared lorikeets, sulphur-crested cockatoos and blue-winged kookaburras by their calls. Around waterholes, look for magpie geese, jacanas or "Jesus birds" – so-called because they walk across the water on lily pads – and, far above, black kites, occasional wedge-tailed eagles and perhaps a sea eagle.

㉔ Wangi Falls
Litchfield National Park, NT
Beautiful Wangi Falls in Litchfield National Park has stairs and ladders into its waterhole for easy swimming. There is a café and BBQ sites, so it does get crowded at weekends. The pool is closed during the Wet due to the undertow and the crocodile threat. A 1.6-km (1-mile) walk winds along a board-walk around the base before climbing up the escarpment above the falls (no swimming here).
🚗 *Return to Stuart Hwy (1) and turn left. Turn left again down Cox Peninsula Rd through Berry Springs into the Territory Wildlife Park.*

EAT AND DRINK AROUND BATCHELOR

Rum Jungle Tavern *inexpensive*
This popular pub-bistro with beer garden serves up generous-sized portions of pub food – anything from salt-and-pepper squid and pastas to enormous steaks and burgers. There is live entertainment some nights, a juke box and pool tables.
5 Nurdina St, 0845; 08 8976 0811

Other options
There are no stand-alone restaurants in the area, rather there are casual alfresco bistros, cafés, bars, and barbecue areas at the hotels and motels, which welcome residents and passersby alike. From Territory Wildlife Park it is a short drive back to Darwin for a good feed.

Above Wildlife viewing platform in Territory Wildlife Park **Below** A jacana on lily pads in Territory Wildlife Park

Eat and Drink: inexpensive under AU$60; moderate AU$60–AU$100; expensive over AU$100

Into the Red Centre

Katherine to Aileron

Highlights

- **Spectacular gorges**
  Explore Nitmiluk National Park's ravishing Katherine Gorge by cruise boat, canoe, helicopter, light plane or simply on foot

- **Relaxing hot springs**
  Soak in the soothing waters of Mataranka's natural hot springs, tranquilly set within palm forests

- **Eccentric pubs**
  Break up the long drives between roadhouses with a cool drink and browse the memorabilia in the wacky Outback pubs at Larrimah and Daly Waters

- **Extraordinary boulders**
  Clamber around the Devils Marbles – monumental red granite stones scattered about the barren landscape

The open road leading into Australia's Red Centre

Into the Red Centre

Golden gorges dramatically carved through spectacular sandstone escarpments, steaming spa pools set amidst a sultry sub-tropical palm forest and a remote highway that leads through the rugged heart of the Northern Territory: these are some of the attractions of this five-day driving tour from Katherine in the Top End to Aileron, just north of Alice Springs in the Red Centre. Highlights include tranquil river cruises and bush walks to see indigenous rock art at Nitmiluk National Park, insights into the harsh Outback life, pioneering heritage and history at Katherine and Mataranka, swimming in the natural hot pools at Elsey National Park, a road-trip-cum-bar-hop to meet eccentric characters at Outback pubs along the Stuart Highway, and the chance to explore striking rock formations such as the Devils Marbles.

Above Canoes for hire at Katherine Gorge, in Nitmiluk National Park, *see p182*

KEY

⚋⚋ Drive route

Below Outback windmills used to pump water, a frequent sight along the Stuart Highway, *see pp188–9*

ACTIVITIES

Fly over the 13 gorges of Katherine Gorge and see the breathtaking natural landscapes of Nitmiluk National Park from above

Canoe, kayak or walk in Nitmiluk National Park to fully appreciate the constantly changing colours of its gorges' sheer sandstone cliffs

Soak in a natural steaming spa at Mataranka's Hot Springs

Learn about the hardship and isolation endured by the pioneers of the "Never Never" at Mataranka

Live like a jackaroo, or stockman, at a working cattle station such as Coodardie Station

Meet the kind of fascinating characters usually only seen in the movies in the Territory's eccentric Outback pubs

Scramble among the colossal red granite boulders known as the Devils Marbles

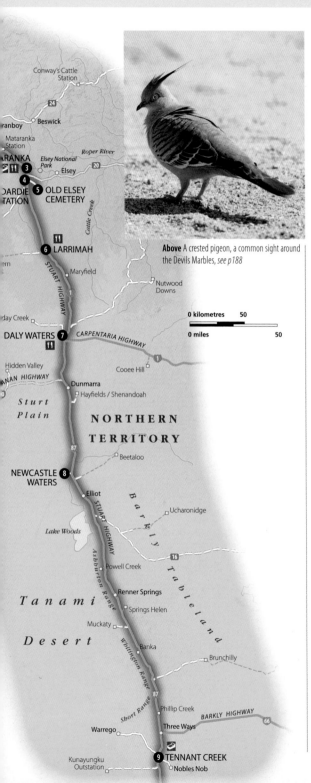

Above A crested pigeon, a common sight around the Devils Marbles, *see p188*

PLAN YOUR DRIVE

Start/finish: Katherine to Aileron.

Number of days: 5 days, including 2 days at Nitmiluk National Park, and a leisurely drive down the Stuart Highway with stops at Mataranka, Elsey National Park and Tennant Creek.

Distance: Approx. 1,049 km (652 miles).

Road conditions: Good signposting and mostly smooth, straight, sealed roads. Check road conditions on *1800 246 199* or *www.ntlis.nt.gov.au/ roadreport* if travelling Oct–May. Katherine is subject to flooding during the Wet when roads can close.

When to go: During the dry season (May–Sep), skies are clear and temperatures average 30°C (86°F); in Jun–Jul they drop as low as 12°C (54°F) at night. Roads are open, but land can appear parched by Sep. The wet season (Oct–Mar) brings regular downpours, floods, road closures and suspension of some tours, but the land is astonishingly lush and green.

Opening times: Normal business hours during the dry season (May–Sep); shorter hours and some business closures during the Wet (Oct–Mar).

Shopping: Pick up Aboriginal art, crafts and artifacts in the gallery at Ti-Tree, a taster of what is to come in Alice Springs (*see pp194–5*).

Major festivals: Katherine: Country Music Muster, May; Katherine Rodeo, Jul; **Mataranka:** Bushman's Carnival, Jun; **Tennant Creek:** Tennant Creek Show, Jul; Tennant Creek Cup (horseracing), May.

Visitor Information Centre
*Cnr Lindsay St & Katherine Terrace,
0851; open daily; 1800 653 142;
www.visitkatherine.com.au*

WHERE TO STAY

KATHERINE

Ibis Styles Katherine *moderate*
This modern and comfortable motel
boasts a good swimming pool, lawns,
barbecues, tennis courts, and a popular
restaurant and bar. There are also family
rooms with kitchens.
*Cnr Cypress Rd & Stuart Hwy, 0850; 08
8972 1744; www.accor.com*

Best Western Pine Tree Motel
moderate
Handily located in the centre of
Katherine, this motel has big rooms, a
laundry for guests and a shady pool.
*3 Third St, 0850; 08 8972 2533;
www.pinetree.bestwestern.com.au*

Paraway Motel *inexpensive–moderate*
Another central motel, the Paraway has
huge rooms (with a queen bed and a
single) and good facilities. There is also a
bar and the Carriage restaurant (Wed–
Mon) is popular for its stonegrill meals.
*Cnr O'Shea & First St, 0850; 08 8972
2644; www.parawaymotel.com.au*

NITMILUK NATIONAL PARK

Camping *inexpensive*
Book camp sites or safari-style tents at
Nitmiluk Gorge and Edith Falls via
Nitmiluk Visitor Centre. It is also
possible to camp at the Dreaming
Place with the indigenous Manyallaluk
community.

Cicada Lodge *expensive*
Staffed by Jawoyn people and
decorated in ochre and earthy tones,
with work by local artists on the walls,
this intimate new eco-lodge has
panoramic views and private plunge
pools. Activities include buffalo
hunting and heli-fishing.
*Gorge Rd, Katherine 0851; 0428 867
348; www.cicadalodge.com*

① Katherine
Northern Territory (NT); 0850
In an area inhabited by the Jawoyn
and Dagoman people, Katherine was
founded in 1862, attracting gold-
miners and drovers thanks to its water
supply. Today, the town is a popular
base for visiting Nitmiluk and an
overnight stop for those travelling
between Darwin and Alice Springs.
The main street, Katherine Terrace, is
home to Aboriginal art galleries, shops,
banks and pubs. The **Northern
Territory Parks and Wildlife Commission** *(32 Giles
St, 0850; 08 8973 8888; www.nt.gov.au/
nreta/parks)* provides information on
Nitmiluk National Park.

From the main street, head north on
Gorge Road to the **Katherine Outback
Heritage Museum** *(open daily)* near
Knotts Crossing. It has a small but
engaging exhibition charting the area's
pioneering history from the 1870s
onwards. Try a Stockman's Dinner *(see
right)*. On the road back to town, the
Katherine School of the Air *(Mon–Fri
am, Mar–Nov; 08 8972 1833)* is a pioneer
of distance education whose tours
reveal how technology has been used
in the field, from radio to the internet.

To relax, head southwest of town on
Victoria Highway (1) and follow signs
to **Katherine Hot Springs** *(Riverbank Dr,
0850; open daily)* on the right. Take a dip
in the warm, palm-shaded pools and
then enjoy a picnic on the lawns.

🚗 *From the centre of Katherine, head
north for 30 km (20 miles) on Gorge Rd,
following signs for Nitmiluk National
Park. Park at the park entrance.*

Above Exploring Katherine Gorge in the Nitmiluk
National Park by canoe

② Nitmiluk National Park
NT; 0852
Ruggedly beautiful, the dramatic
12-km (7-mile) gorge and sandstone
escarpment of Nitmiluk National Park
is a visual feast. There are myriad ways
to explore the 13 deep, red-ochre-
walled gorges that snake through the
park – which is in fact the 12-km
(7-mile) long crevice of Katherine
Gorge, interrupted by boulders, rocks
and sand bars, formed over time by
the torrential rains that fall each year
and the floods that climb towards the
top of the sheer ochre walls. The park
merits at least one full day (leaving
Katherine at the crack of dawn), if not
two (camping out overnight in the
park), to explore it properly.

Right One of the 13 gorges of Katherine
Gorge, Nitmiluk National Park

Spend some time at the engaging **Interpretive Centre** *(open daily Mar–Nov; 1300 146 743)* at the Nitmiluk Centre at the entrance to the park, to learn about the region's geology, flora and fauna, and the indigenous Jawoyn people.

The visitor centre can also provide walking trail maps and guides, and information about ways to see the gorge, or help to arrange activities with Jawoyn-owned **Nitmiluk Tours** *(see right)*. Take a walk led by Jawoyn indigenous guides to view Aboriginal rock art on the gorge walls, or visit the **Dreaming Place** to try basket-weaving, spear-throwing and didgeridoo-playing, and to learn about native medicines and bush tucker. Longer guided walks are also an option – anything from 2 hours to 5 days, with overnight camping.

Another rewarding way to witness the gorge's natural splendour is from the water, on a dawn or sunset cruise,

Cicada Dreaming

The Aboriginal people of the Katherine Gorge area are known as Jawoyn and they call the region Nitmiluk – "Place of the Cicada Dreaming". This comes from an Aboriginal Dreaming legend that tells how Nabilil, a dragon-like figure who camped at Katherine Gorge, named the place Nitmiluk after hearing the "nit, nit" sound of the cicada. Nabilil was later speared by Walarrk, the cave bat, splitting his water bag and filling the Katherine River.

or by canoe. Experienced canoeists can hire canoes to paddle the gorges from Nitmiluk Tours, by the hour, half-day, full-day or overnight – it is a 4-hour return trip to the first gorge. Canoeing is best in the dry season,

Self-guided Walks

Pick up details from the **Nitmiluk Visitor Centre** at the park entrance. The **Southern Walks Information Sheet** has marked trails starting from a 2-km (1-mile) walk, while the **Jatbula Trail Information Sheet** outlines the 4–5-day walk to Edith Falls. Register with the Visitor Centre for overnight walks and book a river crossing and return bus for Jatbula.

water levels permitting, and is not possible from December to April, when the waters are too dangerous. It is also possible to camp (with own gear; a permit and deposit are required for overnight trips). The first camp site is 9 km (6 miles), or a day's paddle, from the Nitmiluk Centre, in the fifth gorge – be prepared to carry canoes over rocks between gorges. Alternatively, **Gecko Canoeing and Trekking** *(08 8972 2224; 1800 634 319; www.geckocanoeing.com.au)* offer organized canoe trips, as well as walking and bird-watching tours. For a different perspective, see the gorge from above with Nitmiluk Tours or **Katherine Aviation** *(08 8971 1277)*.

After all this activity, a swim may be tempting, but is not advised due to the presence of crocodiles. If seeing crocs from a boat appeals, try some after-dark wildlife-spotting with **Travelnorth** *(08 8971 9999; 1800 089 103; www.travelnorth.com.au)*.

Return to Katherine and take the Stuart Highway (1) southeast for 27 km (17 miles) to the signed right turn for **Cutta Cutta Caves** *(open daily; entry by guided tour only)*, a spectacular complex of limestone caves, home to the rare orange horsehoe bat.

🚗 *Continue on Stuart Hwy (1) for 78 km (49 miles) to Mataranka.*

Above The termite mound-dotted landscape east of the Stuart Highway, seen from the air

VISITING NITMILUK NATIONAL PARK

The park is owned by the Jawoyn people and jointly managed by the NT Parks and Wildlife Commission. All guided tours, walks, cruises, canoe hire and helicopter flights can be arranged at the **Nitmiluk Centre** *(at the park entrance; 08 8972 1886; www.parks andwildlife.nt.gov.au)* or booked with Jawoyn-owned **Nitmiluk Tours** *(1300 146 743; www.nitmiluktours.com.au)*. The access road may be closed and activities in the gorge restricted in the wet season (Dec–Apr) due to flooding. Ask about road conditions at the parks office in **Katherine** *(32 Giles Street, 0850; 08 8973 8888)* before setting out.

EAT AND DRINK

KATHERINE

The Terrace Café *inexpensive*
This popular lunch spot is the only alternative to the fast food in town. *Woolworths Shopping Centre, Katherine Terrace, 0850*

Outback Heritage Museum *moderate*
Try a Stockman's Dinner – a chance to listen to yarns around a camp fire, while eating typical bush tucker such as kangaroo, damper, scones and billy tea. *Katherine Outback Heritage Museum; 08 8972 3945; Tue, Thu & Sun, Apr–Oct*

NITMILUK NATIONAL PARK

Nitmiluk Centre *moderate*
There is a general store and café for light meals and snacks on the terrace. *Park entrance; 08 8972 1886*

Far left Aboriginal art in Katherine Gorge
Left Blue-faced honeyeater or banana bird, Nitmiluk National Park

Eat and Drink: inexpensive under AU$60; moderate AU$60–$100; expensive over AU$100

WHERE TO STAY IN MATARANKA

Mataranka Cabins and Camping
moderate
Close to the river and Bitter Springs, this offers good cabins with en suite bathrooms and powered and unpowered caravan and camping sites. *Bitter Springs, 0852; 08 8975 4838; www.matarankacabins.com.au*

Mataranka Homestead Tourist Resort *moderate*
The closest accommodation to Mataranka's hot springs, Mataranka Homestead offers simple motel rooms, self-contained cabins with kitchenettes, a camping ground, bistro and bar. Jeannie's Kitchen serves food year-round and there is live music May–Sep. *Mataranka Hot Springs, 0852; 08 8975 4544 or 1800 754544; www.matarankahomestead.com.au*

Territory Manor *moderate*
It may be famous for its barramundi feeding demonstrations, but the B&B-like Territory Manor also has comfortable rooms as well as powered and unpowered camping sites in shady gardens and a swimming pool. *Mataranka, 0852; 08 8975 4516; www.matarankamotel.com*

Below left Memorabilia-crammed bar at the Daly Waters Pub **Below** Rainbow Springs thermal pools, Mataranka **Below right** Bar at the Larrimah Hotel – the highest in the Northern Territory

➌ Mataranka
NT; 0852

Diminutive Mataranka is regarded as the capital of "Never Never Country", a reference to Jeannie Gunn's 1908 book about pioneer women, *We of the Never Never*, based on her own experiences. Born in Melbourne in 1870, Jeannie moved to Elsey Cattle Station on the Roper River in 1902 with her husband, Aeneas Gunn. After he died of malarial dysentery a year later, she wrote an account of life in the Outback that captured the disappearing pioneering spirit. In 1982, it was made into a popular feature film of the same name, which came from Australian poet Henry Lawson's *The Never Never Country*, about an arid land of rainless skies.

Most visitors make a beeline for the Roper River wetlands for the barramundi fishing or **Elsey National Park** for the thermal springs. The park is a favourite for its lush glades of fern and swimming holes formed from the springs that feed the Roper River.

There are two main entry points to the park. From the northern end of town, take Martin Road east off Stuart Highway to the tranquil, tepid blue waters of **Bitter Springs**, stunningly located within the tropical forest – though the sulphurous smell of algae breaking down may put visitors off.

Then head south of town on Stuart Highway and take Homestead Road east to **Mataranka Homestead Resort** (*08 8975 4544; www.matarankahomestead.com.au*), a fine example of Northern Territory tropical architecture, with louvred windows and stilts. Visitors can go fishing, walk to waterfalls or take a dip in picturesque **Mataranka Hot Springs** – though here bathers must contend with the Flying Fox bats (*see box*) while relaxing in the 34°C (93°F) waters. Also in the grounds of the resort, **Elsey Homestead** is a replica of Jeannie Gunn's original home, built for the movie. The film itself is screened daily at Jeannie's Kitchen (*see right*).

🚗 *From Mataranka, drive south for 10 km (6 miles) along Stuart Hwy (1) and turn right at signed turn on gravel road to Coodardie Station (1 km/half a mile).*

➍ Coodardie Station
NT

A visit to an authentic homestead is a rewarding Outback experience. **Coodardie Station** (*08 8975 4460; www.coodardie.com.au*) offers visitors an opportunity to learn about station life in action. Join the jackaroos (stockmen) on horseback and get up close with the red and grey, humped Brahman cattle, or take a 4WD tour to go bird-watching and wildlife

Left Entrance of the Daly Waters Pub
Below A display of empty beer cars at Larrimah Hotel

spotting, ending the day with a home-cooked meal with the family.

🚗 *Continue south on Stuart Hwy (1) to left turn for Old Elsey Cemetery.*

⑤ Old Elsey Cemetery
NT

The gravestones at this simple bush cemetery identify the final resting places of many of the characters in Jeannie Gunn's book, *We of the Never Never*, which has an important place in Australian folklore.

🚗 *Drive 62 km (40 miles) south along the Stuart Hwy (1) to Larrimah.*

Little Red Flying Foxes

A strong odour greets visitors to Mataranka Hot Springs – the palm forest around the thermal pools reeks of the excrement of the nomadic Little Red Flying Fox colony that nests here from October to July. A boardwalk and canopies have been built to protect visitors, but the bats still wreak havoc on the trees. Park rangers have a conservation dilemma – while some consider the mess to be pollution, the bats are important pollinators, carrying the seeds of native plants over immense distances. Despite the odour, they are fascinating to watch from the pool.

---

⑥ Larrimah
off Stuart Hwy, NT; 0852

Meaning "meeting place" in the local Yangaman language, Larrimah was little more than a fuel stop – until its petrol station burnt down in 2009. Nevertheless, it has an interesting past, revealed at the tiny **Larrimah Museum** *(erratic hours)*. It was a staging camp for soldiers during World War II, when the airfield was established, and remained a busy rail terminus until the railway

closed in 1976. Today, the highlight is **Larrimah Hotel** *(see right)*, crammed with wacky memorabilia and the first of many quirky pubs along this route.

🚗 *Drive along Stuart Hwy (1) and turn off west to Daly Waters.*

⑦ Daly Waters
NT; 0852

Tiny Daly Waters is home to **Australia's oldest international airfield**, in use from the 1930s to the 1950s as a base for distributing mail and as a refuelling stop for Qantas flights to Darwin and Singapore. Tour the airstrip and then visit the hangar, filled with memorabilia and photos. **Daly Waters Pub** is one of the area's oldest hotels; the first pub here received a "gallon licence" in 1893, although the current pub was set up in 1934 to serve passengers and crew from Qantas flights. Its motley collection of memorabilia includes money, ID cards and underwear!

🚗 *Return to Stuart Hwy (1) and drive south to the turn off to Newcastle Waters, 7 km (4 miles) off the highway.*

EAT AND DRINK

MATARANKA

Jeannie's Kitchen *inexpensive*
Live music during the dry season and food year-round are on offer at Jeannie's Kitchen in the Mataranka Homestead Resort, where *We of the Never Never* is screened daily, and cold beers are served in Maluka's Bar next door.
Mataranka Hot Springs, 0852; 08 8975 4544; www.matarankahomestead.com.au

LARRIMAH

Larrimah Hotel *inexpensive*
Boasting a 3-m (10-ft) Pink Panther outside and the highest bar in Australia inside, this bizarre pub will keep visitors entertained. The hotel serves unremarkable pub fare but definitely makes a memorable stop. Basic rooms available.
Larrimah, 0852; 08 8975 9931

DALY WATERS

Daly Waters Pub *inexpensive*
This eccentric pub is a popular lunch stop on the drive between Mataranka and Tennant Creek. It is famous for its generously sized "barra burgers" and plates of barramundi – wonderful washed down with an icy beer.
Daly Waters, 0852; 08 8975 9927; www.dalywaterspub.com

Eat and Drink: inexpensive under AU$60; moderate AU$60–$100; expensive over AU$100

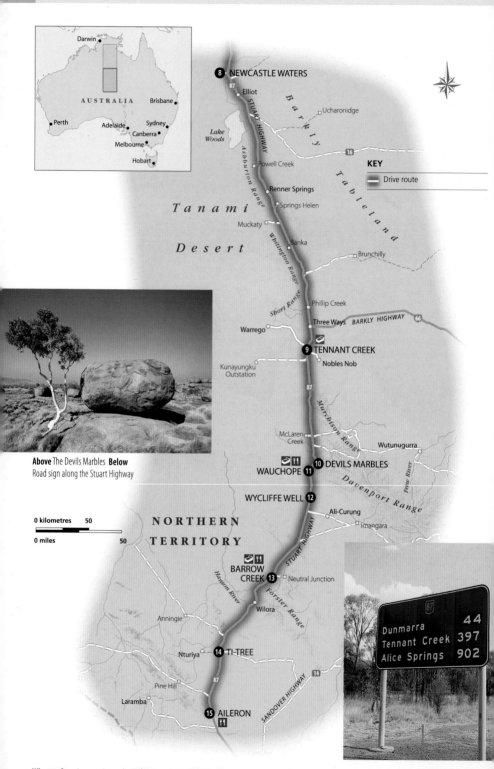

AUSTRALIA

Darwin

Perth

Adelaide

Canberra

Melbourne

Brisbane

Sydney

Hobart

8 NEWCASTLE WATERS

Elliot

Ucharonidge

STUART HIGHWAY

Lake Woods

Powell Creek

Ashburton Range

Renner Springs

Springs Helen

Muckaty

Banka

Brunchilly

Whittington Range

B a r k l y   T a b l e l a n d

16

KEY

Drive route

T a n a m i

D e s e r t

Short Range

Phillip Creek

Three Ways   BARKLY HIGHWAY   66

Warrego

9 TENNANT CREEK

Nobles Nob

Kunayungku
Outstation

87

Murchison Range

McLaren
Creek

Wutunugurra

Perw River

Above The Devils Marbles **Below**
Road sign along the Stuart Highway

WAUCHOPE   10 DEVILS MARBLES

11

Davenport Range

WYCLIFFE WELL 12

Ali-Curung

Imangara

0 kilometres   50

0 miles   50

N O R T H E R N

T E R R I T O R Y

STUART HIGHWAY

Hanson River

BARROW
CREEK   13   Neutral Junction

Forster Range

Anningie

Wilora

Nturiya

14 TI-TREE

Pine Hill

Laramba

87

15 AILERON

SANDOVER HIGHWAY

14

87

Dunmarra   44
Tennant Creek   397
Alice Springs   902

Where to Stay: inexpensive under AU$150; moderate AU$150–$250; expensive over AU$250

8 Newcastle Waters
Stuart Hwy, NT; 0862

The historic droving town of **Newcastle Waters** was largely abandoned in the 1960s, after stock transport by road became the norm and long-distance droving ceased. With their peeling pastel-coloured paint, the ramshackle corrugated iron buildings look rather atmospheric at sunset. The statue of a drover provides a good photo opportunity. There are roadhouses 23 km (15 miles) south at **Elliott**, and the one 90 km (56 miles) further south at **Renner Springs**, is a characterful pub crammed with memorabilia. However, this stretch of road feels very isolated. The roadhouse at **Three Ways**, 135 km (87 miles) further south, is a popular spot to take a photo of the sign at the junction heading east to Queensland.

🚗 *From Three Ways it is another 24 km (15 miles) to Tennant Creek.*

9 Tennant Creek
NT; 0860

Tennant Creek is the best option for a stopover on the long drive between Katherine and Alice Springs. A hub for the Northern Territory's cattle and mining industries, it serves as a supply town to some of the region's oldest and largest cattle stations, the biggest of which runs almost 70,000 head of cattle. Explorer John McDouall Stuart passed through here in the 1860s and the Overland Telegraph Line was established a decade later, paving the way for pastoralists and prospectors, and Australia's last major gold rush, in 1933. Mining and beef remain the area's most important industries today.

From the centre of town, take Peko Road east to **Battery Hill Mining Centre** *(open daily; 1800 500879; call to book tour)*. Located in a disused underground mine, what was once Australia's richest gold mine offers entertaining guided tours and a museum tracing the region's social history.

Return to the Stuart Highway (87) and turn left on what is called Paterson Street, to the **Nyinkka Nyunyu Cultural Centre** *(open daily; 08 8962 2699; www.nyinkkanyunyu.com.au)*, which explains the history and customs of the local Warumungu people. Compelling exhibits show the relationships between Aboriginal groups and the Warumungu's part in the mining and cattle industries. Book ahead for the informative tours.

🚗 *Continue south 105 km (65 miles) along the Stuart Hwy (87) to the Devils Marbles, on the left.*

Tennant Creek Gold Rush

Before large gold deposits were discovered at Tennant Creek in 1932, all that stood here was a telegraph repeater station built in 1872. When news broke about the gold strike, Australia's last gold rush began. Prospectors flocked to this far-flung town, swelling the population to 600 by 1935. In its heyday, the mines made millions of dollars every week. The mines were shut in 1999 until the mid-2000s, when more deposits were found.

Above left Statue of a traditional drover at Newcastle Waters **Above right** Derelict farm vehicle at Battery Hill Mining Centre

VISITING TENNANT CREEK

Visitor Information Centre
Battery Hill Mining Centre, Peko Rd, 0860 (open daily; www.barklytourism. com.au).

WHERE TO STAY IN TENNANT CREEK

Eldorado Motor Inn *moderate*
Tennant Creek's most comfortable motel is on the approach into the northern end of town. It has a good restaurant and an inviting swimming pool.
95 Paterson St, 0860; 08 8962 2402; www.eldoradomotorinn.com.au

Safari Lodge Motel *moderate*
This has simple rooms and is right in the centre, only a short stroll to the pubs where travellers can sit down to a hearty counter meal.
12 Davidson St, 0860; 08 8962 2207; safari.budgetmotelchain.com.au

Other options
For visitors who have missed out on a room, caravan parks have cabins and on-site vans to rent. Try **Tennant Creek Caravan Park** *(208 Paterson St, 0860; 08 8962 2325)* or **Tennant Creek Tourist's Rest** *(Leichhardt St, 0860; 08 8962 2719)*.

Below left The sleek Nyinkka Nyunyu Cultural Centre, Tennant Creek **Below right** Antique equipment at the Battery Hill Mining Centre

Eat and Drink: inexpensive under AU$60; moderate AU$60–$100; expensive over AU$100

Above left and right The spectacular landscape and granite boulders of the Devils Marbles, or Karlu Karlu

Below left A kangaroo seen from the Stuart Highway **Below right** Sulphur-crested cockatoo, found throughout Australia

⑩ Devils Marbles
Stuart Highway, NT

Just off the Stuart Highway, these colossal red granite boulders are the highlight of the 500-km (310-mile) journey from Tennant Creek to Alice Springs, although there is striking arid scenery and bird life to be enjoyed from the car. The local Warumungu people have many myths about these monumental rocks they call Karlu Karlu, which appear to have been rolled like marbles into the spinifex-dotted landscape – one of the most prevalent stories is that they are the eggs of the Rainbow Serpent. Try to arrive shortly after dawn to witness the spectacular effect the golden morning light has on the colour of the boulders. The wildlife is also most active at this time, so visitors should see fairy martins – look for their clay nests in crevices – flocks of zebra and painted finches and reptiles, such as goannas, sheltering in cracks close to the boulders.

🚗 *Continue south along the Stuart Hwy (87), stopping at roadhouses along the way to refuel, on the 507-km (315-mile) journey to Alice Springs.*

⑪ Wauchope
NT; 0872

Wauchope Roadhouse, the first stop after Devils Marbles, has a 1930s pub with a big veranda and pool tables, a restaurant, rooms and camping.

🚗 *Continue south to Wycliffe Well.*

⑫ Wycliffe Well
NT; 0862

Human-size, green alien figures greet visitors at the next fuel stop, **Wycliffe Well**, 18 km (11 miles) down the road, in an area famous for UFO sightings; there is also a shop, a restaurant and opportunities for spotting wildlife.

🚗 *Continue south to Barrow Creek.*

13 Barrow Creek

NT; 0872

Barrow Creek roadhouse, 90 km (57 miles) on, has a 1926 pub plastered with bank notes, and also provides accommodation and has a camp site. The location of a grisly massacre of 90 Aboriginal Kaytetye people in 1874, Barrow Creek is now more commonly associated with the "British backpacker murder" in 2001 of Peter Falconio by drug runner Bradley John Murdoch; Peter's girlfriend, Joanne Lees, survived and wrote a book about the crime.

🚗 *Continue to Ti-Tree (90 km/56 miles).*

14 Ti-Tree

NT; 0872

At the very centre of Australia, Ti-Tree's desert farming community grows surprising quantities of mangoes, grapes and other produce thanks to an abundant underground water supply. The **Red Centre Farm** *(open daily; www.redcentrefarm.com)* has mango orchards and a vineyard and a shop that sells mango jam, chutney, ice cream and mango wine, as well as regular wine. The nearby Aboriginal community sells its vibrant art, crafts and artifacts in the excellent gallery.

🚗 *Continue along the Stuart Hwy (87) for 58 km (36 miles) to Aileron.*

15 Aileron

NT; 0872

Towering above Aileron, the 17-m (56-ft) iron sculpture of an Aboriginal is the **Anmatjere Man**, a memorial to local rainmaker Charlie Quartpot. There is also an art gallery that sells quality locally produced art and crafts, and sometimes features artists at work. The roadhouse here is the

Beautiful Barramundi

A member of the perch family, the Territory's prized fish, barramundi (*Lates calcarifer*), is revered for its delicious taste and for being a feisty sport fish for keen anglers. Found in estuaries in northern Australia, it is increasingly farmed and is regularly seen on roadhouse, restaurant and barbecue menus. Its reputation as a fine, firm-fleshed eating fish is almost folkloric in Australia and while it lives up to its status when it is authentic, fresh and in the hands of a skilled cook, sometimes cheaper fish are sold as barramundi and can result in a disappointing culinary experience.

last chance to fill the fuel tank before Alice Springs, while **Glen Maggie Bar** is the last opportunity to personally refuel – the pub food (especially the Sunday roast) is very popular with the locals. It is another 130 km (82 miles) south along the Stuart Highway (87) to Alice Springs (*see pp194–5*).

Above Sign warning drivers to watch out for people along the deserted roads of the Red Centre **Left** Sealed road curving to the left, an uncommon sight in the Outback

EAT AND DRINK

WAUCHOPE

Wauchope Hotel *inexpensive*
The shady veranda is the perfect place to stop for a cool drink and a meal. *Stuart Hwy, 0862; 08 8964 1963; www.wauchopehotel.com.au*

BARROW CREEK

Barrow Creek Hotel *inexpensive*
Welcome refreshments for travellers. *Stuart Hwy, 0872; 08 8956 9753*

AILERON

Aileron Roadhouse *inexpensive*
The Glen Maggie Bar here serves excellent pub food. *Stuart Hwy, 0872; 08 8956 9703; www.aileronroadhouse.com.au*

Below Billabong on the way to Alice Springs, an oasis of green in the dry Outback

Eat and Drink: inexpensive under AU$60; moderate AU$60–$100; expensive over AU$100

Through the MacDonnell Ranges

Alice Springs to Kata Tjuta

Highlights

- **Vibrant Aboriginal art**
  Browse Alice Springs' excellent galleries and buy some of the vivid indigenous art for sale

- **Dramatic golden gorges**
  Explore the stunning ravines of the East and West MacDonnell Ranges, and splash in refreshing waterholes

- **Colossal canyon**
  Walk the dramatic rim of Kings Canyon, in Watarrka National Park, an important natural reserve

- **Iconic rock formations**
  Stroll the base of Uluru, Australia's big red rock, then explore the enormous rock formations of Kata Tjuta

The unmistakable red mass of Uluru, rising from the plain

Through the MacDonnell Ranges

A place of breathtakingly rugged beauty, the remote Red Centre is Australia's spiritual and geographical heart. Characterized by striking gorges that slice through the dramatic East and West MacDonnell mountain ranges, colossal craters created by meteorites, lush palm-filled valleys and tranquil waterholes, it is one of the country's most rewarding regions to explore. Culturally and artistically rich, for 40,000 years it has been home to many of Australia's traditional indigenous peoples: the Western Desert peoples, the Arrernte, Pitjantjatjara, Yankuntjatjara, Antakarinja, and Luritja. Start at idiosyncratic Alice Springs, then travel through striking Outback landscapes to the "Macs", the East and West MacDonnell Ranges, before driving southwest via Kings Canyon to finish at monumental Uluru and Kata Tjuta.

Papunya

Narwietooma

Mbunghara

Ambu

Milton Park

TANAMI ROAD

Mt Edward
1423m △

Mt Zeil
1531m △

Mt Sonder
1380m △

Haasts Bluff

MacDonnell Ranges

Kulpitarra

ORMISTON GORGE 13 **SERPENTINE GORGE**

GLEN HELEN GORGE 14 12 11

OCHRE PITS 10

GOSSE BLUFF 15 *Missionary Plain* **ELLERY C BIG HO**

Ipolera **HERMANNSBURG MISSION** 16 LARAPINTA D

Areyonga

James Ranges

17 **PALM VALLEY** 18 **WALLA ROCKHO**

Kings Canyon Resort **19 KINGS CANYON**

Tampa Downs

Kings Creek 3 Finke

LURITJA ROAD

Wallara Ranch Palmer River Hen

Lake Neale

Lake Amadeus

NORTHERN 3 **TERRITORY**

Angas Downs

TJUKARURU ROAD 4

Ayers Rock Airport

Ayers Rock Resort Yulara

Mount Ebenezer

Curtin Springs LASSETER HIGHWAY 4 Erldun

KATA TJUTA 21 20 **ULURU**

KEY

— Drive route

0 kilometres 40

0 miles 40

Above right Warning sign on an Alice Springs road, see pp194–5 **Centre right** Aboriginal artwork at Alice Springs, see p194 **Right** Todd River – unusually full of water – at the Old Telegraph Station, Alice Springs, see p195

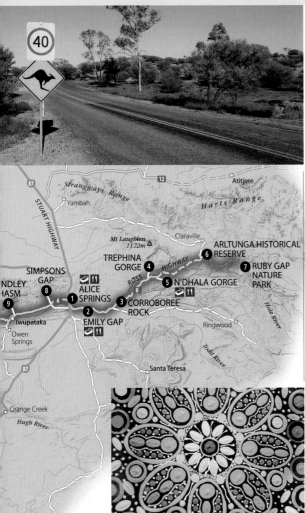

PLAN YOUR DRIVE

Start/finish: Alice Springs to Kata Tjuta.

Number of days: 6–7 days, including at least 1 day in Alice Springs, a night each in the East MacDonnells and West MacDonnells, a night at Kings Canyon and at least 2 days exploring Uluru and Kata Tjuta.

Distance: Approx. 967 km (600 miles).

Road conditions: Good signposting. A combination of smooth sealed roads and dirt tracks. A 4WD is required if attempting the Mereenie Loop (see p199). All roads are subject to flooding and closure during the wet season (Oct–Apr). Check conditions on 1800 246 199 or www.ntlis.nt.gov.au/roadreport.

When to go: In winter, from Apr–Oct, when temperatures average 20–27°C (68–81°F); the weather is dry, and the festival calendar full. In summer, from Oct–Apr, it is hot and sticky, averaging 31–35°C (88–95°F), and 4WD tracks can close for weeks and months at a time after the rain that often falls during this period, although the desert is dotted with green grass and wild flowers grow.

Opening times: Normal business hours from late autumn to early spring (Apr–Sep); shorter hours and some business closures from late spring to early autumn (Oct–Mar).

Main market days: Alice Springs: Todd Mall Markets, every second Sun morning (www.toddmallmarket.com.au).

Shopping: Buying some Aboriginal art is a must, and Alice Springs is the best place to do so.

Major festivals: Alice Springs: Cup Carnival (horse-racing), 1st Mon in May; Bangtail Muster, May; Beanie Festival, Jun (www.beaniefest.org); Camel Cup, Jul; Alice Springs Rodeo, Aug; Henley-on-Todd Regatta, Aug; Desert Mob Exhibition, Sep–Oct; Alice Desert Festival, Sep (www.alicedesertfestival.com.au).

ACTIVITIES

Float over the Red Centre in a hot air balloon from Alice Springs

Watch Aboriginal artists create vibrant paintings at Alice Springs' superb art galleries, and buy their works

Relax on the banks of the Todd River – a dry riverbed for most of the year – by Alice Springs' Old Telegraph Station

Walk through the striking ravine of Trephina Gorge

Swim in icy natural waterholes in the East and West MacDonnell Ranges

Be inspired by the pastel-hued landscapes painted by Albert Namatjira around Hermannsburg Mission

Walk around the base of Uluru to appreciate how huge the rock really is

Above Hot air ballooning over the Outback from Alice Springs

VISITING ALICE SPRINGS

Parking
Park on the street in town, or use the car parks along the Todd River (do not leave cars here overnight).

Visitor Information
60 Gregory Terrace, near Todd St Mall, 0870; 08 8952 5800 or 1800 645 199; www.centralaustraliantourism.com

SHOPPING IN ALICE SPRINGS

Watch Arrernte artists at work and buy their paintings at **Ngurratjuta Iltja Ntjarra** or **Many Hands Art Centre** (29 Wilkinson St, 0870; 08 8951 1953; www.ngurart.com.au; open Mon–Fri) or purchase hand-woven products at nearby **Tjanpi Desert Weavers** (3 Wilkinson St, 0870; 08 8958 2377; open Mon–Fri; www.tjanpi.com.au).

WHERE TO STAY IN ALICE SPRINGS

Aurora Alice Springs moderate
Centrally located, this popular hotel has an excellent bistro and smart contemporary-styled rooms.
11 Leichhardt Terrace, 0870; 08 8950 6666; www.auroraresorts.com.au

Vatu Sanctuary moderate–expensive
These stylish, self-contained apartments are a good place to regroup after a drive, with a pool, BBQ, spa and chill-out areas.
Cnr Knuckey & Babbage St, 0870; 0417 274 431; www.vatusanctuary.com.au

Alice Springs Resort
moderate–expensive
This four-star resort is popular with groups, but is centrally located with a good restaurant, bar and pool. Book a room with views of the Todd River.
34 Stott Terrace, 0870; 08 8951 4545; www.alicespringsresort.com.au

① Alice Springs
Northern Territory (NT); 0870

The once-nomadic Arrernte people have inhabited this area for 40,000 years, but it was not until the establishment of the Overland Telegraph Line by Charles Todd in the 1870s that the town sprung up. The Todd River (usually dry) was named in his honour and the billabong (spring), where the telegraph station was built was named after Alice, his wife. With a population of 28,000, the town has an easy-going charm and larrikin spirit. With its array of indigenous art galleries and engaging sights, Alice Springs is a great place to spend a couple of days.

① Todd Street Mall

The Central and Western Desert art movement's famous dot paintings are on display in a number of galleries on Todd Street Mall and Stott Terrace, including **Gallery Gondwana** (www.gallerygondwana.com), **Papunya Tula Artists** (www.papunyatula.com.au) and **Mbantua Gallery**

Aboriginal weaved crafts, Alice Springs

(www.mbantua.com.au) (opening hours vary; check websites). Acclaimed indigenous artists make Alice Springs Australia's best place to buy Aboriginal art – it may also be possible to see artists at work.

On Todd Street Mall, visit the 1926 **Adelaide House** (open Mon–Fri, Mar–Nov), once the Bush Nursing Hostel, noted for its convection-cooling system designed by Rev John Flynn, founder of the Royal Flying Doctor Service (the John Flynn Memorial Church is next door). Continue south on Todd Street for two blocks and turn right on Stuart Terrace.

At the Old Alice Springs Gaol, the **National Pioneer Women's Hall of Fame** (open daily, Mar–Nov; www.pioneerwomen.com.au) has an exhibition about pioneering women such as Aboriginal rights activist Olive Pink.

Over the Todd River off Tuncks Road, the **Olive Pink Botanical Garden** (open daily; www.opbg.com.au), displays Pink's collection of Central Australian flora.

🚗 *Re-cross the river, turn right into Gap Rd, left into Stott Tce, then Larapinta Dr for Araluen Cultural Precinct.*

② Araluen Cultural Precinct

The precinct (open daily) is home to a collection of cultural venues including the **Araluen Arts Centre** and the **Art Museum**, which hosts the Albert Namatjira collection (see box), along with examples of early Papunya and Hermannsburg School paintings. Outside is a striking 3-m (10-ft) sculpture of the Yeperenye caterpillar, the creative ancestor of Alice Springs' indigenous people. The

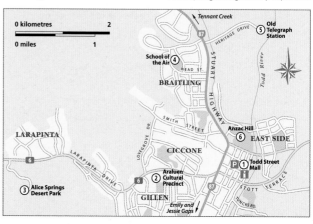

Albert Namatjira

An artist visiting Central Australia's deserts in 1936 showed his Aboriginal guide, Albert Namatjira, how to use watercolours. Albert learnt quickly and showed natural talent – his first exhibition in Melbourne in 1938 sold out. Born in 1902 on the Hermannsburg Lutheran mission, Albert's style of painting started the Hermannsburg School. Now considered one of Australia's greatest artists, his Outback landscapes often feature white gum trees backed by craggy mountain ranges.

Museum of Central Australia has interesting natural history displays, and the **Central Australian Aviation Museum** houses the planes that pioneered Outback travel. **Alice Springs Memorial Cemetery** is the final resting place of Namatjira.

🚗 *Turn left and continue on Larapinta Dr to Alice Springs Desert Park.*

③ Alice Springs Desert Park

Allow two to three hours for the town's most popular attraction, **Alice Springs Desert Park** (*open daily; www. alicespringsdesertpark.com.au*). Walk through various natural habitats typically found in the region, animal enclosures that allow visitors to get close to wildlife and a nocturnal house. Try to see the Birds of Prey show.

🚗 *Return to the centre, turn left at Stuart Hwy (87) and after 2 km (1 mile) turn left up Head St to School of the Air.*

④ School of the Air

Dubbed "the largest classroom in the world" the **School of the Air** (*80 Head St; www.assoa.nt.edu.au; open daily*), a pioneer in distance education, runs guided tours revealing how evolving

technologies, from radio to the telephone and the internet, have been used to teach students in the Outback.

🚗 *Return to Stuart Hwy (87) and turn left. After 1 km (half a mile), double back on Stuart Hwy (87) towards the centre and turn right into Herbert Heritage Drive for the Old Telegraph Station.*

⑤ Old Telegraph Station

Nestled in hills on the banks of the Todd River, the **Old Telegraph Station** (*open daily; 08 8952 3993*) offers original buildings and fascinating historical displays. It is possible to swim in the waterhole after the rains or relax on the grassy riverbanks, popular with kangaroos in the late afternoon.

🚗 *Return to Stuart Hwy (87), turn left and take signposted left turn to Anzac Hill, or walk along the Todd River.*

⑥ Anzac Hill

The war memorial at Anzac Hill is a superb spot to enjoy the sunset and offers panoramic views. Directly south, the break in the MacDonnell Ranges is Heavitree Gap.

🚗 *Take Stuart Hwy south through Heavitree Gap, turning left over the Todd River to Ross Hwy, and follow to the Emily Gap, on the left.*

Writing About a Town Like Alice

The isolation of Alice Springs has fuelled many writers' imaginations. Nevil Shute's 1950 book, *A Town Like Alice*, is about a female prisoner of the Japanese in Malaya who visits Alice Springs in her search to find an Australian soldier she met while captive. Robyn Davidson's *Tracks* (1980) is a personal account of a trip across the desert from Alice Springs to the coast of Western Australia with a dog and four camels.

Above left Aboriginal performance involving didgeridoo playing at the Araluen Cultural Precinct **Above right** Crimson chat in Alice Springs Desert Park

ACTIVITIES AT ALICE SPRINGS

Get an Arrernte perspective on local history with **Trek Larapinta** (*1300 724 795; www.treklarapinta.com.au*) or learn weaving and bush skills on **Beanies, Baskets and Bushtucker Tours** (*0408 436 928*). Cycle to cultural sites with indigenous-led **Dot Painted Mountain Bike Tours** (*0415 815 033*). Float over the Red Centre with **Outback Ballooning** (*www.outbackballooning.com.au*), or fly over the McDonnell Ranges in a plane with **Northern Territory Air Services** (*08 8953 1444*).

EAT AND DRINK IN ALICE SPRINGS

Red Ochre Grill *moderate*
This popular bistro has a welcoming interior and a pleasant patio for plates of bush tucker-inspired cuisine, such as kangaroo tacos, washed down with cold beers and crisp Australian wines. *Todd Mall, 0870; 08 8952 9614*

Barra on Todd *moderate*
Busy and buzzing, this hotel cafe serves up excellent modern Australian fare, with tasty Asian-inspired seafood – barramundi is a speciality. *Alice Springs Resort, 34 Stott Terrace, 0870; 08 8951 4545*

Other options
Overlander Steakhouse (*72 Hartley St, 0870; 08 8952 2159*) dishes up large portions of steaks and native meats; **The Lane** (*58 Todd St Mall, 0870; 08 8952 5522*) does delicious modern Australian cuisine and wood-fired pizzas; and **Thai Room Fan Arcade** (*Todd St Mall, 0870; 08 8952 0191*) is a relaxed BYO and takeaway with authentic Thai curries.

Eat and Drink: inexpensive under AU$60; moderate AU$60–AU$100; expensive over AU$100

VISITING THE EAST MACDONNELL RANGES

The 260-km (165-mile) round trip of the East MacDonnell Ranges, famous for their gaps and gorges and Aboriginal rock engravings, can be done in a day, although an overnight stay at Ross River or camping at Trephina Gorge will give more time for walks at Trephina Gorge, N'Dhala Gorge and Arltunga. Take a picnic lunch, snacks, plenty of water and spare fuel.

Best time to visit
It is most pleasant in the cool, dry winter. During the hot, sticky summer, rain can make many dirt roads impassable. The waterholes can be very cold at any time of year; beware of hypothermia.

WHERE TO STAY

AROUND EMILY GAP
Heavitree Gap Outback Lodge *moderate*
With a decent-sized swimming pool, BBQs, wallaby feeding at dusk and indigenous Red Centre Dreaming performances, this lodge makes a compelling place to stay.
Palm Circuit, 0870; 08 8950 4444; www.auroraresorts.com.au

N'DHALA GORGE
Ross River Resort *inexpensive*
The historic 1890s Loves Creek Homestead of the Ross River Resort provides simple family accommodation with cabins, bunkhouses and camp sites. There is a bar, restaurant (dinner only) and BBQ sites, and fuel available.
Ross Highway, Ross River, 0871; 1800 241 711; www.rossriverresort.com.au

Below right John Hayes Rockhole at pretty Trephina Gorge **Below left** Caterpillar Dreaming petroglyphs at N'Dhala Gorge

---

The MacDonnell Ranges
The rugged MacDonnell Ranges are the longest of many mountain ranges that cross the central Australian desert region, rising up like waves to form ridges before plunging downwards. While their formations are best appreciated from a plane, on the ground the grandeur of their gorges and gaps is best enjoyed by walking along their dry sandy riverbeds and swimming in their icy natural waterholes.

② Emily Gap
Ross Highway, NT
Heavitree Gap, the break in the ranges that forms the southern entrance to Alice Springs, separates the East from the West MacDonnell Ranges and leads to Ross Highway, the route through the East MacDonnells. About 10 km (6 miles) from Alice is lovely **Emily Gap**, the most important Arrernte sacred site, which marks the start of "Caterpillar Dreaming"; note the caterpillars depicted on the rock walls on the far side of the waterhole. **Jessie Gap** is further east, with similar images.
🚗 *Continue 26 km (16 miles) on Ross Hwy to Corroboree Rock, on the left.*

③ Corroboree Rock
Ross Highway, NT
Another significant Arrernte sacred site is **Corroboree Rock**, an ochre dolomite outcrop with crevices that were once repositories for sacred objects. It was believed to be a place of corroborees, or Aboriginal initiation ceremonies, but research has questioned this because there is no water source nearby. There is a marked walk around the rock.
🚗 *Drive 31 km (19 miles) on Ross Hwy and left to Trephina Gorge car park.*

---

④ Trephina Gorge
Ross Highway, NT
The most picturesque ravine of the East MacDonnells, Trephina Gorge is a tranquil spot. It is a short walk along a riverbed lined by shady red gums to a glassy waterhole (dry in dry season) reflecting the gorge's vertical red cliffs. With "ghost gums" (white-trunked eucalyptus trees) sprouting from the walls, it has a dramatic atmosphere. There are two marked moderately hard 30-minute walking trails, including a ridge-top walk and a hike up a hill with panoramic views. At sunrise and sunset, it is possible to see black-footed rock wallabies, which is why so many visitors camp here. A high-clearance 4WD is required to negotiate the rocky 4-km (2-mile) track to nearby **John Hayes Rockhole**, a series of natural waterholes linked by small waterfalls. From the car park, it is an easy walk to the lower pools (10 mins), while the Chain of Pools walk takes 90 minutes.
🚗 *Return to Ross Hwy and continue 5 km (3 miles) to Ross River Resort to register for N'Dhala Gorge. Backtrack 500 m (550 yards) to the high-clearance 4WD track, on left; impassable in rain.*

Seasons of the Centre
The indigenous tribes in the Red Centre observe five seasons: **Piriyakutu/piriya piriya** (Aug–Sep) comes at the end of winter and lasts through to spring – the "piriya" is a wind. **Mai wiyaringkupai/kuli** (around Dec) is the hottest time of the year with lightning but not much rain. **Itjanu/inuntji** (Jan–Mar) brings the rains as well as dramatic lightning. **Wanitjunkupai** (Apr–May) sees plenty of clouds but the rains ease. **Wari** (May–Jul) brings cooler weather.

⑤ N'Dhala Gorge

off Ross Highway, NT

The challenging 11-km (7-mile) track to the N'Dhala Gorge crosses wide sandy riverbeds, by spectacular sheer cliffs where once-horizontal layers of rock have rotated by 90 degrees over time. The scenery is splendid, especially after rain when the emerald-green grass contrasts with the rust-red earth. At the gorge, a moderately hard walking trail (1.5-hour return) passes Aboriginal shelters, art sites and petroglyphs (rock engravings) representing stories of Caterpillar Dreaming. The long feather-like symbol on the rocks depicts a freshly hatched moth taking flight. It is estimated there are over 6,000 prehistoric carvings here.

🚗 *Head back along Ross Hwy and turn right, 6 km (4 miles) before Trephina Gorge, into Atnarpa Rd for 33 km (20 miles) to Arltunga Historical Reserve.*

⑥ Arltunga Historical Reserve

Atnarpa Rd, Ross Hwy, NT

Arltunga was the location of Central Australia's first Gold Rush in 1887 and the atmospheric ruins of the gold-mining settlement are great to explore. There are a number of easy walking routes – pick up itineraries and maps at the **Visitor Centre** *(open daily)*, where there is also an interesting local history display. Note the wooden barrows that the hopeful miners pushed for 600 km (373 miles) from Oodnadatta.

🚗 *Ruby Gap Nature Park is 47 km (29 miles) along Atnarpa Rd, only accessible by high-clearance 4WD (visitors must register on 1300 650 730).*

⑦ Ruby Gap Nature Park

off Ross Highway, NT

When explorer David Lindsay discovered what he thought were rubies (they were garnets) in 1885, **Ruby Gap** became the centre of a mining frenzy. There are no ruins to explore, yet the landscapes are priceless at sunrise and sunset. It is possible to camp, but there are no facilities. There is an easy 2-km (1-mile) walk to peaceful Glen Annie Gorge.

🚗 *Return to Alice Springs on Ross Hwy and head west on Larapinta Drive.*

⑧ Simpsons Gap

West Macdonnell National Park, NT

Simpsons Gap is the most popular of the West MacDonnell gaps. Beside the sandy riverbed, partly shaded by river red and slender ghost gums, a track leads to a waterhole. At sunrise and sunset, black-footed rock wallabies appear on the cliff ledges. There is a visitor centre and barbecue sites.

🚗 *Continue on Larapinta Drive for 23 km (14 miles) and turn right to Standley Chasm. Look out for the twin ghost gums of Albert Namatjira's paintings.*

Above left Emily Gap, a major spiritual site for the Arrernte people **Above right** The impressive outcrop of Corroboree Rock **Below** Old mining buildings at Arltunga Historical Reserve

ACTIVITIES AT SIMPSONS GAP

The very intrepid may wish to walk the 223 km (140-mile) Larapinta Trail from Simpsons Gap to Mount Sonder, or one of its 12 sections. Very careful planning and walker registration essential *(www.nt.gov.au; Apr–Oct)*.

EAT AND DRINK

AROUND EMILY GAP

Tinh & Lan Alice Vietnamese
inexpensive
Run by a husband and wife team, this restaurant serves authentic Vietnamese fare garnished with fresh herbs from their market garden. Bookings essential.
Lot 1900, Heffernan Rd, nr Alice Springs airport, 0870; 08 8952 8396; closed Mon

N'DHALA GORGE

Ross River Resort *inexpensive*
Fuel up on generous-sized steaks in the restaurant at this historic homestead (dinner only), or bring your own sausages to throw on the BBQ.
Ross Hwy, Ross River, 0871; 08 8956 9711; www.rossriverresort.com.au

VISITING THE WEST MACDONNELL RANGES

With golden-hued gorges and plenty of chances to walk and swim, the West MacDonnell Ranges are best enjoyed in one long day with an overnight stay at Glen Helen Resort. The 130-km (80-mile) trip as far as Glen Helen can be done by 2WD. There are unmanned national park **visitor centres** at Simpsons Gap and Ormiston Gorge *(www.nt.gov.au)*.

Best time to visit
It is most pleasant in the cool, dry winter. During the hot, sticky summer, rain can make many dirt roads impassable.

WHERE TO STAY AT GLEN HELEN GORGE

Glen Helen Resort *moderate*
Glen Helen Resort offers the only accommodation in this region. The main building, an old homestead, has a restaurant, café, bar and a tiny shop selling Aboriginal art and essential supplies. Book one of the simple white-washed motel rooms that look onto the rocky red walls of Pacoota Range, or a camp site. The resort also sells fuel and arranges tours. *Namatjira Drive, 0870; 08 8956 7489; www.glenhelen.com.au*

Below Tranquil waterhole at Ormiston Gorge **Below right** The spectacular rocky ravine of Standley Chasm **Below left** Fragment of ochre in Ochre Pits, West MacDonnell Ranges

9 Standley Chasm
West MacDonell National Park, NT
Plan to get to **Standley Chasm** *(open daily)* around 11am for the marked 1.5-km (1-mile) walk through the lush cycad palm- and fern-filled riverbed to the ravine, a narrow passageway formed by sheer, 80-m (260-ft) rock walls. The sun is overhead between 11am and 1pm, illuminating the rock walls in a magical array of red shades. The chasm is located in Aboriginal land and managed by the Iwupataka people, with a café and souvenir shop.
🚗 *Continue along Larapinta Drive and turn right on to Namatjira Drive for 41 km (25 miles), turning off right to Ellery Creek Big Hole.*

10 Ellery Creek Big Hole
West MacDonnell National Park, NT
The still and icy water of Ellery Creek Big Hole is one of the most popular spots for swimming along this route. It is the largest natural waterhole in the area, filling the sand river in a large gap in the West MacDonnell ranges. It is occasionally closed to bathers and there are warning signs advising swimmers to use a flotation device as the cold can be a shock. There are also barbecues and facilities here.
🚗 *Continue along Namatjira Drive for 11 km (7 miles), turning off on the right to Serpentine Gorge.*

11 Serpentine Gorge
West MacDonnell National Park, NT
Winding Serpentine Gorge offers some rewarding walks, including an easy 30-minute trek into the gully and a stiff hike to the top of the gorge for stunning views. The Arrernte believe that a serpent lives in the swimming hole and will not enter the water – this story may have been created to ensure the drinking supply was not polluted.
🚗 *Carry on along Namatjira Drive for 12 km (8 miles) to the Ochre Pits.*

12 Ochre Pits
West MacDonnell National Park, NT
Ochre has always been valuable to the indigenous peoples, used for body decoration, medicine and painting. These pits have long been a key source of this treasured commodity. Park in the designated area and follow the path to view the ochre pits with their spectacular multiple layers of colour. Pay attention to warning signs and do not remove any pieces of ochre.
🚗 *Carry along Namatjira Drive for 17 km (11 miles) to Ormiston Gorge.*

13 Ormiston Gorge
West MacDonnell National Park, NT
With glassy waterholes beneath 250-m (820-ft) red walls, Ormiston Gorge is extremely picturesque. It is also one of the most enjoyable West MacDonnell

⑮ Gosse Bluff
Tnorala Conservation Reserve, NT

Apart from the rugged landscapes and plentiful wildlife, there is little to stop for on the route between Glen Helen and Gosse Bluff, a massive meteorite crater in **Tnorala Conservation Reserve**. It is believed that the crater was caused by a comet hitting Earth 142 million years ago. The 20-km (12-mile) crater has been eroded over time so only the inner 5-km (3-mile) crater remains. There is a picnic area, facilities and ceremonial site (out-of-bounds).

🚗 *Return to Namatjira Drive and head south for 31 km (19 miles) to junction with Larapinta Drive and Mereenie Loop. Turn left for Hermannsburg Mission.*

⑯ Hermannsburg Mission
off Larapinta Drive, NT

Established by the Lutherans in 1877, Hermannsburg was the first Aboriginal mission in the Northern Territory. It is now a Western Arrernte community, so visitors can only stop for fuel and supplies or to tour the restored **Historic Precinct** *(open daily)*.

The artist Albert Namatjira *(see p195)* was born here. In 1944 he built the white-washed **Albert Namatjira's House** *(Larapinta Drive towards Alice Springs)* outside Hermannsburg in the style of the mission buildings. He lived there with his family for just five years, when the death of one of his children led him to move for cultural reasons.

🚗 *Visitors with a high-clearance 4WD can take Palm Valley Rd, just west of town, 16 km (10 miles) along the dry river bed (not after rain) to Palm Valley. Otherwise, head east on Larapinta Drive and turn off right to Wallace Rockhole.*

Left Sign on the way into Ormiston Gorge, West MacDonnell National Park

DRIVING THE MEREENIE LOOP

With a high-clearance 4WD, the 195-km (121-mile) **Mereenie Loop**, west of Hermannsburg, is the fastest route from the West MacDonnells to Kings Canyon and Uluru. Its other attraction is the stunning semi-arid landscape, with only wild horses, donkeys and dingoes as company. However, the dirt road can be challenging: check weather conditions before leaving Hermannsburg and if rain is forecast do not attempt the loop, which is prone to flash flooding and is inaccessible after rain. Do not set out without spare water, fuel and food. A permit is required from Alice Springs tourist office or Glen Helen Resort for the loop. The **alternative** is to backtrack to Alice Springs and take the Stuart Hwy (87) as far as Henbury, turning right for Watarrka National Park, or to carry on along the Stuart Hwy as far as the Lasseter Hwy (4) to Uluru and Kata Tjuta. This route takes 5 hours to drive.

EAT AND DRINK IN GLEN HELEN GORGE

Glen Helen Resort *moderate*
The only proper restaurant between here and Alice Springs, Glen Helen Gorge's dining surpasses expectations with a combination of hearty country meals and international bistro-style dishes. The charming atmosphere – there are tablecloths, antiques, and original art on the walls – makes visitors feel like dressing up, especially if they have been on the road for a while. *Namatjira Drive, 0870 (132 km/82 miles west of Alice Springs); 08 8956 7489; www.glenhelen.com.au*

chasms, with several walks including an easy hike up to **Gum Tree Lookout** for stunning views of the gorge and waterholes below; the strenuous 3-hour **Pound Walk**, which involves scrambling over rocks, and overnight walks. There is camping here, too.

🚗 *Stay on Namatjira Drive for 4 km (3 miles), then left to Glen Helen Gorge.*

⑭ Glen Helen Gorge
West MacDonnell National Park, NT

Not far from the old homestead of Glen Helen Resort *(see left)*, Glen Helen Gorge is a broad gully with towering walls carved through the Pacoota Range. There is a permanent waterhole here, surrounded by reeds in the sandy bed of the Finke River, which is possibly more than 100 million years old. Walk along the road and up the hill to the lookout on the right for stunning views. Sunset or sunrise looks fabulous from here with Mount Sonder, recognizable from Albert Namatjira's paintings.

For a close-up view of **Mount Sonder**, drive on 25 km (16 miles) to Redbank Gorge, then 8 km (5 miles) to the car park. It is an arduous 8-hour return climb to the summit, only recommended for fit, experienced bushwalkers. If hoping to cool down in the waterholes, think again. The ravine sees little sunlight and the water is icy.

🚗 *Buy a permit for the drive to Kings Canyon via Mereenie Loop at Glen Helen Resort and fill up with enough fuel and water to reach Hermannsburg. Continue on Namatjira Drive for 37 km (23 miles), then the dirt road turns sharply to the left and heads south. Turn off to the right for Gosse Bluff.*

Below View of impressive Mount Sonder

Above left and right Two views of the impressive Kata Tjuta rock domes

WHERE TO STAY

KINGS CANYON

Kings Creek Station *moderate*
Kings Creek Station is 35 km (22 miles) from the canyon with safari-style tents and camp site. It also offers camel rides.
Kings Canyon, 0872; 08 8956 7474; www.kingscreekstation.com.au

Kings Canyon Resort *moderate–expensive*
The closest accommodation to the canyon (10 km/6 miles), the luxurious Kings Canyon Resort boasts a range of rooms, including deluxe with spa baths, two restaurants, bars and pools.
Luritja Rd, 0872; 03 9413 6288; www.kingscanyonresort.com.au

ULURU

All Uluru accommodation is on Yulara Drive at **Ayers Rock Resort** *(02 8296 8010, 1300 134 044; www.ayersrockresort.com.au).*

Campground *inexpensive*
Uluru's official camp site, this is well-equipped with BBQs, a shop and pool. There are also permanent tents and air-con cabins with kitchen and TV.
08 8957 7001

Sails in the Desert Hotel *moderate*
The choice for affluent visitors who do not need extreme pampering *(see below)*, the rooms here have huge balconies. It has a notable restaurant.
08 8957 7417

Longitude 131° *expensive*
Among the dunes, this safari-style resort is the premier place to stay at Uluru. Rooms are glamorous, individual canvas-roofed cabins with excellent dining.
08 8957 7131

⑰ Palm Valley
off Larapinta Drive, NT
In **Finke Gorge National Park** *(www.nt.gov.au)*, Palm Valley is a green oasis of cycads and rare red cabbage palms, which have flourished here for more than 10,000 years. There are several marked walks, including a hike to **Kalarranga Lookout** with great views.

🚗 *Return to Larapinta Drive and head east, turning right to Wallace Rockhole.*

⑱ Wallace Rockhole
off Larapinta Drive, NT
This tiny Arrernte community is home to an **Art Centre** *(08 8956 7415)*, which sells Aboriginal art and often holds dot-painting classes. Buy a map and walk to the waterhole to see the petroglyphs or call ahead to the art centre to book a tour. There are fuel and supplies at the general store.

🚗 *Return to Larapinta Drive and turn left on 4WD Mereenie Loop to Kings Canyon in Watarrka National Park.*

⑲ Kings Canyon
Luritja Rd, Watarrka National Pk, NT
More than a vast 270-m (886-ft) chasm, Kings Canyon in **Watarrka National Park** *(www.nt.gov.au)* is an important conservation area for more than 600 species of plants and native animals. Visitor information, maps and details of ranger-guided activities can be picked up at the Kings Canyon car park. All trails are marked. There is a fairly easy

1-hour walk through lush cycads to a spring-fed waterhole for stunning views of the sheer red rock canyon. Or take the challenging 4-hour rim walk (only for the fit), early or late in the day. It starts with a steep ascent, leads through the Lost City's sandstone domes, a palm-filled ravine known as the Garden of Eden and the edge of the south wall, before its descent.

🚗 *Head back down Luritja Rd, carrying on south to the Lassetter Hwy and turn right to Uluru 307 km (191 miles). Refuel first and take advantage of rest stops to stretch the legs and spot some wildlife.*

> **Uluru–Kata Tjuta National Park**
> Uluru–Kata Tjuta National Park is home to the vast red monolith Uluru (formerly known as Ayers Rock) and the striking rock domes of Kata Tjuta (formerly the Olgas). A UNESCO-designated site since 1987, it is jointly managed by National Parks and the traditional Aboriginal owners, the Anangu. The area has great spiritual importance to its indigenous peoples.

⑳ Uluru
Uluru-Kata Tjuta NP, NT
Uluru is located on the lands of the Anangu, the Western Desert peoples, who arrived in the semi-arid area some 20,000 years ago. Learning about their culture is a highlight of a visit to Uluru, as is the immensity and geology of the rock itself. Both can be experienced at the visitor centres

and on guided walks. After the ticket booth, the superb **Uluru–Kata Tjuta Cultural Centre** (open daily; 08 8956 1128; www.environment.gov.au/parks/ uluru) has an exhibition on the customs of the Aboriginal peoples, including displays of Dreamtime stories related to Uluru. It is also home to the **National Parks Information Office**, which explains the parks' diverse habitats, from desert oak woodlands to spinifex-dotted sand dunes. Book ranger-guided walks here. Next door, **Walkatjara Arts** and **Maruku Arts** sell Anangu art and crafts. Most visitors respect the beliefs of the Anangu and do not climb the rock. Instead, take a self-guided walk: follow the Liru Walk from opposite the centre, drive to Mala car park for the Mala Walk, or do the Uluru Base Walk (3–4 hours), passing sacred sites (no photos). Shorter walks lead to rock art sites, caves and waterholes. The best time is at dawn, both for the light on the rock and for the relative cool.

🚗 *Follow signs to Kata Tjuta, 51 km (32 miles) from Ayers Rock Resort.*

㉑ Kata Tjuta
Uluru-Kata Tjuta NP, NT

The cluster of striking domes known as Kata Tjuta (Many Heads) forms a maze of sheer gorges and valleys. It is thought the collection of rocks once formed a monolith ten times larger

than Uluru. Due to the sacred nature of the site, especially to Anangu men, visitor access is restricted to **Walpa Gorge** and the marked **Valley of the Winds** walks. Do not climb the rocks.

Walks can be self-guided or done as part of a tour. The 2.6-km (2-mile) Walpa Gorge Walk leads through a valley to the wall of Mount Olga, the highest rock in the massif at 1,070 m (3,510 ft), or try the 3-hour Valley of the Winds Walk. In hot weather, visitors can only walk to Karu Lookout.

Uluru & Kata Tjuta Tours

Learn about the traditional culture, Dreamtime stories and bush tucker on an **Anangu Tour** (08 8950 3030; www.ananguwaai.com.au) with Aboriginal guides and translators who lead strolls along the Liru, Kuniya and Mala walks. Expert guides from **Discovery Ecotours** (08 8956 2563; www.ecotours.com.au) cover the natural history, geography and culture of Uluru on an informative walk around the base; tours include breakfast. Fly over Uluru and Kata Tjuta in a helicopter with **Professional Helicopter Services** (08 8956 2003) or in a light plane with **Ayers Rock Flights** (08 8956 2345; www.ayersrockflights.com. au). Hop on the back of a camel for a sunrise or sunset ride with **Uluru Camel Tours** (08 8950 3030; www. ananguwaai.com.au) or on the back of a Harley Davidson with **Uluru Motorcycle Tours** (08 8956 2019).

EAT AND DRINK

KINGS CANYON

Kings Canyon Resort *moderate*
Carmichaels Restaurant offers an expansive buffet, while the stylish **Outback BBQ & Grill** dishes up delicious modern Australian bistro food and steaks.
Luritja Rd, 0872; 03 9413 6288 or 1300 233 432; www.kingscanyonresort.com.au

ULURU

There are restaurants at **Ayers Rock Resort** to suit all budgets. There is also a café, takeaway, and supermarket. *1300 134 044 or 02 8296 8010; www.ayersrockresort.com.au (for all Ayers Rock eateries)*

Gecko's Café *inexpensive*
A bistro and bar with a Mediterranean slant – fine steaks and burgers, but try the pastas and wood-fired oven pizzas. *Resort Shopping Centre*

Kuniya Restaurant *expensive*
Kuniya serves modern Australian/ Mediterranean cuisine in refined surroundings. *Sails in the Desert Hotel*

Arnguli Grill *expensive*
This grill serves Australian classics such as a tasting plate of barramundi, smoked kangaroo and slow-cooked crocodile. *Desert Gardens Hotel*

Below Storm clouds over the Mereenie Loop from Hermannsburg Mission to Kings Canyon **Below right** Flourishing palms in Palm Valley, Finke Gorge National Park **Below left** The spectacular red monolith of Uluru

West Coast Wonderland

Perth to Cape Range National Park

Highlights

- **West coast capital**
  Enjoy laidback Perth's Gothic-style architecture and outstanding galleries

- **Striking landscapes**
  Wander among the eerie Pinnacles in Nambung National Park

- **Amazing dolphins**
  Feed wild dolphins by hand in crystal-clear, waist-deep water at Monkey Mia

- **Secluded white-sand beaches**
  Splash in the surf on the superb white-sand beaches of North West Cape

- **Underwater wildlife**
  Swim with sharks and rays over vibrant coral reefs at Ningaloo Marine Park

Ningaloo Reef and Coral Bay

West Coast Wonderland

The Western Australia (WA) coastline is dotted with sleepy fishing villages, holiday towns and stunning white-sand beaches. Along the way, extraordinary sights such as the Pinnacles and Shell Beach, as well as once-in-a-lifetime experiences such as swimming with whale sharks and dolphins, mean it has everything the adventurous traveller could want. Unlike the urbanized east coast, the west coast is sparsely inhabited, allowing visitors to enjoy pristine landscapes and a sense of remoteness. However, it also means that driving distances are long and the terrain can be challenging off-the-beaten-track. This driving tour starts in Perth, WA's lovely capital city, before heading north to the scenic national parks of Kalbarri, Shark Bay and Ningaloo.

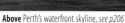
Above Perth's waterfront skyline, *see p206*

ACTIVITIES

Picnic among the plants at Perth's Kings Park and Botanic Garden

Eat sweet crayfish at Cervantes near Nambung National Park

Buy souvenirs from "royalty" in Hutt River Province

Watch for raptors on spectacular Eagle Bluff

Soak in a natural hot tub in Francois Peron National Park

Hand-feed wild dolphins in the shallow waters at Monkey Mia

Snorkel over vivid coral reefs at Ningaloo Marine Park

Join a boat cruise for some marine life spotting, from whale sharks to dolphins, at Coral Bay, Shark Bay and Ningaloo

Explore Yardie Creek's beautiful gorge on a cruise boat and keep an eye out for rare black-footed wallabies

Below A carpet of pink pulla mulla wild flowers in bloom after the winter rains

Above Emu at Vlamingh Head Lighthouse, North West Cape, see p213

KEY

━━━ Drive route

0 kilometres   60
0 miles   60

PLAN YOUR DRIVE

Start/finish: Perth to Cape Range National Park; *see p210 for Hamelin Pool Marine Nature Reserve to Cape Range National Park map.*

Number of days: At least 7 days, with a night in Perth, Geraldton, Kalbarri, Monkey Mia, Carnarvon, Coral Bay and Exmouth, and allowing time to explore Kalbarri National Park, Ningaloo Marine Park and Cape Range National Park.

Distance: Approx. 1,850 km (1,156 miles).

Road conditions: Good signposting and mostly sealed roads. Almost everywhere on this drive is accessible by 2WD, except Francois Peron National Park and parts of Cape Range National Park. Watch out for wildlife on the road, especially from dusk and dawn.

When to go: Any time of year: Perth is known as Australia's sunniest city and rarely gets cold in winter. Avoid school holidays, when accommodation gets booked out a year in advance.

Opening times: Shops and businesses open Mon–Sat 9am–5pm. In the Perth metro area, major retailers and supermarkets open weeknights until 9pm, Sun 11am–5pm.

Main market days: Fremantle: Fri–Sun; **Geraldton:** Farmers' Market, Sat am; **Carnarvon:** Gascoyne Growers' Markets, Sat am (May–Oct).

Shopping: Fremantle Markets offer a quintessential market experience.

Major festivals: Perth: Royal Show, Sep/Oct; Festival of Perth, Feb–Mar; **Fremantle:** Fremantle Festival, Nov; **Geraldton:** Sunshine Festival, Oct; **Dongara-Dension:** Larry Lobster Festival, Nov.

❶ Perth

Western Australia (WA); 6000

Beloved for its fine weather and laidback lifestyle, Perth, Australia's westernmost state capital, sprawls along the Swan River with its Central Business District (CBD) sitting by a glorious expanse of water. Boasting big parks and neat gardens, grand historic buildings and Gothic churches, alfresco cafés and art museums, and a compact shopping centre, it is also one of Australia's most attractive yet underrated cities.

A three-hour walking tour

From the car park, turn left along Murray Street through **Murray Street Mall** ①, Perth's main shopping street. Turn left into William Street to the splendid **Wesley Church** ② (1867) on the right. Carry on and turn left into St Georges Terrace and appreciate the majestic **former Palace Hotel** ③ (1895), on the corner.

A little further on, admire **Trinity Church** ④ (1846), built by architect Henry Trigg (1791–1882). Cross the road right into tiny Howard Street, a hub for the legal profession and home to Victorian architectural gems. Note Edwardian **20 Howard Street** ⑤ on the left, dating from 1905, a wonderful example of the Gothic Revivalist style.

Turn left onto the Esplanade to Barrack Street and the impressive **Weld Club** ⑥ (1892), named after Frederick

Aloysius Weld, a former premier and governor who planted the first pole for the Telegraph Link to South Australia.

Turn right onto Barrack Street and stroll down the hill to Barrack Square, noted for its postmodern 80-m (262-ft) **Bell Tower** ⑦. From the tower, savour the Swan River views. Ferries leave every 15 minutes from **Barrack Street Jetty** ⑧ across the Swan River to Mends Street Wharf at South Perth's Sir James Mitchell Park, which has sublime vistas of Perth's skyline.

Cross the Esplanade again and go up Barrack Street to the Supreme Court Gardens on the right for the Neo-Classical façade of the **Supreme Court** ⑨ (1903) and the tiny Old Court House (1836), Perth's oldest building.

Continue through **Stirling Gardens** ⑩, the state's first botanical gardens and the site of the city's founding in

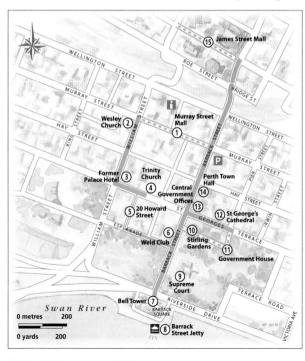

Opposite Perth from Kings Park **Above** The eerie limestone Pinnacles of Nambung National Park

1829. Look for the Gothic **Government House** ⑪, built in 1859. Join the other tourists admiring the life-sized bronze kangaroos. Across the road is the delightful **St George's Cathedral** ⑫ (1888), which is worth a look inside.

Walk back down St Georges Terrace to Barrack Street and the colossal **Central Government Offices** ⑬ (1874) and, by Stirling Gardens, a bronze statue of explorer and former mayor of Perth, Alexander Forrest (1849–1901). Turn right along Barrack Street, past **Perth Town Hall** ⑭ clocktower (1867) and three 1890s façades.

To extend the walk, continue over the railway line into Beaufort Street for the lively cultural area of **Northbridge**. Turn left into **James Street Mall** ⑮, which is home to the **Art Gallery of Western Australia**, housing the world's best Aboriginal art collection and early WA art such as Frederick Garling's 1827 views of the Swan River, along with the **Perth Institute of Contemporary Arts**, **Western Australian Museum**, and **State Library of Western Australia**. At the end of the mall, William Street, on the right, leads to Perth's "Chinatown", whose street corners boast old pubs with wrought-iron lacework balconies.

Either return over the railway tracks to Barrack Street, then left to Murray Street and the car park, or continue to Beaufort Street for the CAT bus to **Kings Park and Botanic Garden** (Kings Pk Rd, 08 9480 3659; www.bgpa.wa.gov. au), a large area of fragrant bushland, and return by CAT bus to the car park.

🚗 Turn right into Murray St, right into Barrack St, left into Wellington St, follow signs onto Mitchell Fwy (south) (2), then Kwinana Fwy (2). Turn right on Leach Hwy (7), then High St to Fremantle. Turn left on Parry St for Queensgate car park.

② Fremantle
WA; 6160
One of Perth's loveliest areas, Fremantle is also one of Western Australia's oldest towns. Ancient home of the Noongar people, its European history started after the *Challenger* landed in 1829. Convicts built most of the fine old buildings, including the **Round House**, **Fremantle Prison** and Fremantle Arts Centre. Home to painters, musicians and writers, 'Freo', as the locals call it, has a relaxed, tolerant and creative vibe. While it is home to a handful of good museums, the best thing to do is simply wander around, taking in the architecture, browse around the busy weekend markets and sip coffee.

🚗 Return along Leach Hwy to Kwinana Fwy (north), then Mitchell Fwy. At the end, turn right onto Burns Beach Rd (87), left onto Joondalup Drive (85), then Neaves Rd (86). Turn left onto Muchea South Rd, left onto Brand Hwy (1). Turn off left to Cervantes. Nambung National Park is 17 km (10 miles) south of town.

③ Nambung National Park
Cervantes, off Brand Hwy, WA; 6511
The Pinnacles at **Nambung National Park** are thousands of limestone pillars up to 5 m (16 ft) tall, standing to attention in an eerie desert landscape. The stylish **Pinnacles Desert Discovery Centre** (www.dec.wa.gov.au) explains the geology. The stones look spectacular in the golden late-afternoon and early-morning light, so consider staying overnight at the crayfishing hamlet of Cervantes. During crayfishing season (mid-Nov–Jun), be sure to try some of the sweet-tasting crustaceans there.

🚗 Take Indian Ocean Drive north and then Brand Hwy 149 km (93 miles) to the twin towns of Dongara-Port Denison.

Eat and Drink: inexpensive under AU$60; moderate AU$60–AU$100; expensive over AU$100

VISITING KALBARRI

Visitor Centre
Grey St, 6536; 08 9937 1104 or 1800 639 468; www.kalbarri.org.au

WHERE TO STAY

DONGARA-PORT DENISON

The Priory Lodge *inexpensive*
This lovely place (once a nunnery) has leafy grounds, a pool, bar and restaurant.
11 St Dominics Rd, 6525; 08 9927 1090

GERALDTON

Ocean Centre Hotel *moderate*
This hotel has large rooms with harbour or beach views and plenty of amenities.
Cnr Foreshore Dr and Cathedral Ave, 6525; 08 9921 7777; www.oceancentrehotel.com.au

KALBARRI

Pelican Shore Villas *moderate*
The units here are some of the best in town – well equipped, with sea views.
Cnr Grey and Kaiber Sts, 6536; 08 9937 1708; www.pelicanshorevillas.com.au

Other options
Kalbarri Seafront Villas *(08 9937 1025; 108 Grey St, 6536; www. kalbarriseafrontvillas.com.au)* offers quality ocean-front units; **Murchison View Apartments** *(cnr Grey and Ruston Sts, 6536; 08 9937 1096)* opposite the waterfront have balconies and are fully self-contained.

Below Heritage stone building at Greenough
Below right Pretty ice plant flowers in Kalbarri National Park **Below left** Surfer riding the waves at Kalbarri Beach

④ Dongara-Port Denison
WA; 6525
These adjoining sleepy fishing hamlets have streets shaded by fig trees and beautiful beaches ideal for fishing, swimming and surfing. Enjoy the sea vistas from **Fisherman's Lookout Obelisk** at Port Denison. Historic buildings include the ruins and old steam engines at the **Royal Steam Flour Mill** (1894) *(Brand Hwy)*; **Russ Cottage** (late 1860s) *(Pt Leander Dr; open Sun am)*, with a kitchen floor of compacted anthills; and the old police station, part of the **Irwin District Museum** *(open Mon–Fri; 08 9927 1323)*. The **visitor centre** *(9 Waldeck St, Dongara; 08 9927 1404; www.irwin.wa. gov.au/tourism)* has information on local attractions, such as visiting the **Dingoes of Dongara**, and self-guided nature walks, including the **Irwin River Nature Trail** to see pelicans, black swans and cormorants.
🚗 *Drive 42 km (26 miles) north along the coastal road to Greenough.*

⑤ Greenough
WA; 6532
This historic settlement, a busy centre in the 1860s, is little more than a ghost town today. However, its striking "leaning trees" and old stone buildings are worth exploring. Take in the display at the **visitor centre** *(open daily; Brand Hwy; 08 9926 1084)*, then buy the **Walkaway Heritage Trail Booklet** to

find out more about the buildings on the route. Discover how early settlers lived, at the nearby **Greenough Pioneer Museum & Garden** *(open daily; Phillips Rd; 08 9926 1890)*.
🚗 *Take Brand Hwy (1) to Geraldton.*

⑥ Geraldton
WA; 6530
The region's main commercial centre, Geraldton has a superb mix of cultural and historic attractions, with wind-swept beaches south and north of town, good for kite- and wind-surfing.

The **Western Australian Museum Geraldton** *(open daily; 08 9921 5080; www. museum.wa.gov.au)* by the marina, has exhibits covering the indigenous, natural and social histories of the region, along with a shipwreck display, which tells the tale of the *Batavia* – the dramatic story of a Dutch East India ship involving shipwreck, mutiny and murder; of 341 people on board when it struck a reef in 1629, only 68 survived.

A few blocks back from the seafront, the striking **HMAS *Sydney* Memorial** is visible from most parts of town and commands sweeping vistas. It commemorates the loss of the HMAS *Sydney* with 645 sailors, lured into battle and sunk by a German cruiser in 1941.

The **Geraldton Regional Art Gallery** *(closed Mon; 24 Chapman Rd, 6530; 08 9964 7170)* is home to an impressive collection of paintings that includes contemporary art alongside work by

EAT AND DRINK

noted Australian artists Norman Lindsay and Elizabeth Durack. Further south, **St Francis Xavier Cathedral** (1938), with its huge dome, towers and Romanesque-style columns, is a superb example of architect-priest Monsignor Hawes' impressive talent.

🚗 *Drive north on North West Coastal Hwy (1) for 52 km (32 miles) to Northampton. After 8 km (5 miles), turn left at sign for Hutt River Province.*

⑦ Hutt River Province
WA; 6535

The **Principality of Hutt River** *(08 9936 6035; www.principality-hutt-river.com)* was formed in 1970 when farmer Leonard Casley, angry over the government's wheat quotas, seceded from Australia (although the province is not officially recognized). Some 40 years later, HRH Prince Leonard and wife Princess Shirley are the "monarchs" of a province with 13,000 citizens. If Prince Leonard is not busy on his sheep station, he will stamp passports with a visa at the post office, give a tour of the property and sell souvenirs.

🚗 *Drive 31 km (19 miles) northwest on Ogilvie Rd, turn left into Hose Rd and right into George Grey Dr for 33 km (20 miles) to Kalbarri, stopping to view cliffs.*

⑧ Kalbarri
WA; 6536

Beloved by locals for its beaches, this is a popular seaside town. Begin the day on the waterfront at Grey Street watching pelican feeding *(8:45am)*; admire birdlife in the lush gardens of **Rainbow Jungle** *(open daily; cnr Grey & Bridgeman Rds; 08 9937 1248)*, 4 km (2 miles) south; and enjoy the native plants at **Kalbarri Wildflower Centre** *(open daily; Clotworthy St; 08 9937 1229)*.

Outside the town are the striking rock formations and gums of **Kalbarri National Park**, a large area of bush. To the south of Kalbarri are the coastal cliffs of Red Bluff, Rainbow Valley, Pot Alley, Eagle Gorge and Natural Bridge – good places for viewing humpback whales *(Aug–Nov)* and dolphins *(all year)*. The southeast of the park along Ajana Kalbarri Road boasts lookouts offering fantastic gorge views.

If not content to just enjoy the park's wild flowers, from vibrant banksias to kangaroo paws in bloom *(Jul–Nov)*, the **visitor centre** *(see left)*, can organize canoeing, cruises, bushwalks or rock-climbing. Rent powerboats, canoes, kayaks, surf cats and boats to explore the Murchison River from **Kalbarri Boat Hire** *(Kalbarri Foreshire; 08 9937 1245; www. kalbarriboathire.com)* or join a guided canoe trip through the park with **Kalbarri Adventure Tours** *(08 9937 1677; www.kalbarritours.com.au)*.

🚗 *Return to North West Coastal Hwy (1). After 179 km (111 miles), turn left to Shark Bay at Overlander Roadhouse and then right on Hamelin Pool Rd.*

DONGARA–PORT DENISON

Southerleys *inexpensive*
The waterfront sun terrace is not the only enticement at this bistro – it is also popular for its well-cooked seafood. *Point Leander Dr, Port Denison 6525; 08 9927 2207*

GREENOUGH

Hampton Arms Inn *inexpensive*
The old-fashioned bar and lovely dining room at this charming inn are wonderful, cozy places to while away an evening. *Company Rd, 6532; 08 9926 1057*

GERALDTON

Freemasons Hotel *inexpensive*
This typical town pub prides itself on its modern brasserie menu full of the usual Australian staples and Asian dishes. Good wines and interesting beers on tap. *Cnr Marine Tce and Durlacher St, 6530; 08 9964 3457*

KALBARRI

Finlay's Fresh Fish BBQ *inexpensive*
No bland bistro, this BYO serves up slabs of laconic Australian humour with fresh seafood and steaks cooked on a BBQ. *Magee Crescent, 6536; 08 9937 1260*

Echo Beach *expensive*
Surprisingly stylish, this restaurant's modern Australian cuisine is excellent, as is the jazzy soundtrack and wine list. Try the local seafood. *Porter St, 6536; 08 9937 1033*

Other options
The Grass Tree *(94–96 Grey St, 6536; 08 9937 2288)* fine all-day dining but shines for dinner; **Black Rock Café** *(80 Grey St, 6536; 08 9937 1062)* gourmet breakfasts to inventive dinners; **Gorges Café** *(Marina Complex, Grey St, 6536; 08 9937 1200)* is a funky daytime café with light meals.

Above The Neo-Romanesque St Francis Xavier Cathedral, Geraldton **Below** The HMAS *Sydney* Memorial, Geraldton

Eat and Drink: inexpensive under AU$60; moderate AU$60–AU$100; expensive over AU$100

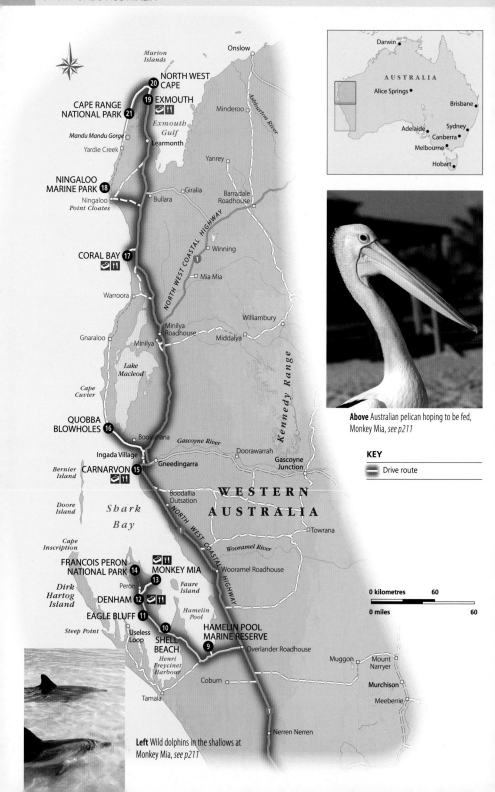

Onslow

Murion Islands

NORTH WEST CAPE **20**

19 EXMOUTH

CAPE RANGE NATIONAL PARK **21**

Minderoo

Exmouth Gulf

Mandu Mandu Gorge

Yardie Creek

Learmonth

Yanrey

NINGALOO MARINE PARK **18**

Ningaloo Point Cloates

Bullara

Giralia

Barradale Roadhouse

Winning **1**

CORAL BAY **17**

Mia Mia

Warroora

Williambury

Gnaraloo

Minilya Roadhouse

Minilya

Middalya

Lake Macleod

Cape Cuvier

Kennedy Range

QUOBBA BLOWHOLES **16**

Boolathana

Gascoyne River

Doorawarrah

Ingada Village

Gneedingarra

Gascoyne Junction

Bernier Island

CARNARVON **15**

Doore Island

Shark Bay

Boodallia Outsation

W E S T E R N

A U S T R A L I A

Towrana

Cape Inscription

FRANCOIS PERON NATIONAL PARK **14**

MONKEY MIA

Wooramel River

Dirk Hartog Island

Peron

Faure Island

Wooramel Roadhouse

DENHAM **12** **13**

EAGLE BLUFF **11**

Hamelin Pool

Steep Point

Useless Loop

10

SHELL BEACH

Henri Freycinet Harbour

HAMELIN POOL MARINE RESERVE

9

Overlander Roadhouse

Muggon

Mount Narryer

Tamala

Coburn

Murchison

Meeberrie

North West Coastal Highway

Nerren Nerren

Left Wild dolphins in the shallows at Monkey Mia, *see p211*

AUSTRALIA

Darwin

Alice Springs

Brisbane

Adelaide

Sydney

Canberra

Melbourne

Hobart

Above Australian pelican hoping to be fed, Monkey Mia, *see p211*

KEY

Drive route

0 kilometres 60

0 miles 60

⑨ Hamelin Pool Marine Nature Reserve

Hamelin Pool Rd, WA; 6532

Wrapped around two narrow peninsulas, **Shark Bay Marine Park** was declared a World Heritage site in 1991 for its unique hypersaline marine waters, its vast seagrass beds, the endangered dugong (sea cow) population that feeds on them, and its "living fossil" stromatolites.

The **Hamelin Pool Marine Nature Reserve** is home to the world's best-known colony of these stromatolites – fragile rock-like formations created out of sediment by microbes almost identical to organisms that existed on earth 3,500 million years ago. The Shark Bay stromatolites are probably 2,000 years old. View them from the board-walk – the best viewing is at low tide.

🚗 *Continue along Shark Bay Rd for 68 km (42 miles) to Shell Beach.*

⑩ Shell Beach

Shark Bay Rd, WA; 6537

The low tidal flow off the blazingly white Shell Beach has made the water hypersalinated – twice as salty as the ocean. One of the only creatures able to prosper in these conditions is the heart cockle, and with no natural predators, it is thriving. The result is a beach with cockle shells piled up to 10 m (33 ft) in depth along a stretch of 60 km (37 miles). After rain, the shells fuse together, a process that inspired some to use them to make the white bricks seen in houses in Denham.

🚗 *Continue on Shark Bay Rd and turn left on gravel road to Eagle Bluff.*

⑪ Eagle Bluff

Eagle Bluff Rd, WA; 6537

The rocky clifftop at Eagle Bluff offers sweeping vistas of the eagles and other birdlife that nest on the cliffs

and tiny islands offshore, as well as views of the sharks swimming in the shallow, clear sea far below.

🚗 *Return to Shark Bay Rd and continue 51 km (32 miles) to Denham.*

⑫ Denham

WA; 6537

A former pearling town, where shells once paved the streets, Denham is a good place to stay and explore the Shark Bay area. Visit **Shark Bay World Heritage Discovery Centre** *(08 9948 1590; www.sharkbay.wa.gov.au; open daily)*, a small but impressive museum with exhibits on Shark Bay and its indigenous peoples.

🚗 *Take Monkey Mia Rd to Monkey Mia.*

⑬ Monkey Mia

WA; 6537

A sublime white-sand beach on a lovely bay, Monkey Mia has become famous for the wild dolphins who turn up every day to be fed in the shallow water. The first session at 7:45am can get crowded, so stay for the second to see the dolphins better. Afterwards, learn local Dreamtime stories, how to track animals and identify bush tucker on walks with a local guide from **Wula Guda Nyinda Aboriginal Cultural Tours** *(0429 708 847; www.wulaguda.com.au)*.

🚗 *Return to Denham and turn right on Monkey Mia Road for the sandy track to Francois Peron National Park (4WD only) or join a tour from the visitor centre.*

⑭ Francois Peron National Park

WA; 6537

The park is famous for its golden cliffs, white-sand beaches and rare marsupials – stop for information at Peron Homestead after 6 km (4 miles). *Return to North West Coastal Hwy, turn left for 194 km (120 miles) to Carnarvon.*

Above left Stromatolite colony at Hamelin Pool Marine Reserve **Above right** Heart cockle shells piled up at Shell Beach **Below** Dolphin-watchers at Monkey Mia

VISITING SHARK BAY MARINE PARK

Visitor Centre
Knight Terrace, Denham, 6537; 08 9948 1590

WHERE TO STAY

DENHAM

Oceanside Village *moderate*
These white-and-blue villas are well equipped; some have sea views.
117 Knight Terrace, 6537; 08 9948 3003; www.oceanside.com.au

MONKEY MIA

Monkey Mia Dolphin Resort *moderate–expensive*
This offers everything from tent piches to well-equipped villas with sea views.
1800 653 611, 08 9948 1320; www.monkeymia.com.au

EAT AND DRINK

DENHAM

Old Pearler Restaurant *inexpensive*
In an old stone house, this place serves favourites such as crayfish mornay.
Knight Terrace, 6537; 08 9948 1373

MONKEY MIA

Bough Shed *moderate*
This waterfront restaurant offers seafood and massive steaks.
Monkey Mia Dolphin Resort, 6537; 08 9948 1171

Where to Stay: inexpensive under AU$150; moderate AU$150–AU$250; expensive over AU$250

Above Spectacular spray at Quobba Blowholes

VISITING NINGALOO AND CAPE RANGE NATIONAL PARK

Exmouth Visitor Centre
Maps, brochures and tour bookings. Information on dive operators in Exmouth and Coral Bay.
Murat Rd, 6707; 08 9949 1176; www.exmouthwa.com.au

Exmouth DEC Office
National Park maps and brochures.
22 Nimitz St, 6707; 08 9947 8000

Milyering Visitor Centre
Maps and information on wildlife, snorkelling and walks in the park.
Yardie Creek Rd, 6707; 08 9949 2808

WHERE TO STAY

CARNARVON

Carnarvon Central Apartments
moderate
These homely, clean, self-contained units are handily located for both the town and the beach.
120 Robinson St, 6701; 08 9941 1317; www.carnarvonholidays.com

CORAL BAY

Ningaloo Reef Resort *moderate*
This resort features a range of options, from motel-style rooms to self-contained apartments with cooking facilities. There is a pub and bottle shop as well as a restaurant with take-away.
1 Robinson St, Coral Bay, 6701; 08 9942 5934; www.ningalooreefresort.com.au

EXMOUTH

Potshot Hotel Resort
inexpensive-moderate
This buzzing resort has dorms, motel-style accommodation and stylish apartments, as well as bars, restaurants and a swimming pool.
Murat Rd, 6707; 08 9949 1200; www.potshotresort.com

Right Turquoise Bay, Cape Range National Park, an excellent spot for snorkelling

---

⑮ Carnarvon
WA; 6701
Laidback Carnarvon is a lush oasis in the dry Gascoyne region, known for its fishing, seafood and fruit and veg plantations. Book a plantation tour at the **visitor centre** (*21 Robinson St; 08 9941 1146; www.carnarvon.org.au*). There is a steam train from the footbridge to the **Historic Precinct**, with heritage buildings. At **One Mile Jetty**, anglers cast for mulloway fish. Explore **Carnarvon Pioneer Cemetery** (*Crowther St*), with graves of local pioneers, some of whom were Chinese and Afghan.

🚗 *Carry on along North West Coastal Hwy (1) for 19 km (12 miles) then turn left on Blowhole Rd to Point Quobba.*

⑯ Quobba Blowholes
Blowhole Rd, WA; 6701
The sign: "KING WAVES KILL" tells visitors they have arrived at Quobba Blowholes. Big waves can catch people by surprise here and sweep them to their deaths, so take care while viewing the thrilling blowhole sprays. Head south a little way for windswept beaches, great for swims or whale watching in season.

🚗 *Go north on North West Coastal Hwy (1) for 199 km (124 miles). Take Minilya–Exmouth Rd left, then left for Coral Bay.*

⑰ Coral Bay
Off North West Coastal Hwy, WA; 6701
At the southern tip of **Ningaloo Marine Park**, Coral Bay's main attraction is its stunning white-sand beach on a beautiful bay. Swimming, snorkelling and fishing are the most popular activities, although most visitors take a tour to the reef. Look out for marine life including whales, manta rays, turtles

---

and the rare dugongs. Snorkelling gear and kayaks can be hired at the beach.

🚗 *Return to Minilya–Exmouth Rd north. If in a 4WD, Ningaloo Marine Park can be reached via unsealed Ningaloo Rd, on left after 38 km (24 miles), but most drivers will choose to continue via Exmouth and North West Cape.*

⑱ Ningaloo Marine Park
WA
Boasting a wealth of sea life, Ningaloo Marine Park is Western Australia's answer to the Great Barrier Reef, only more accessible – just 100 m (328 ft) offshore in parts. Covering 250 km (155 miles) of coast and sea, the park aims to preserve the reef and the marine life that thrives around it. However, it is a particular event after the full moon in March/April that is the big attraction – the mass spawning as the coral release eggs and sperm into the water. This also attracts the largest fish on earth, the huge whale shark (up to 18 m/60 ft), which arrives every year to feast as the water turns into a rich soup.

🚗 *Return to Learmouth–Mirilya Rd, turn left and drive north to Exmouth.*

⑲ Exmouth
WA; 6707
Exmouth is a good base for exploring Ningaloo Marine Park and Cape Range National Park. Stop first at the **visitor centre** to book tours, then enjoy the fresh seafood, go swimming and fishing, and look out for kangaroos, emus and beautiful pink cockatoos around the town. For swimming, try the white-sand **Town Beach** or head on up to the North West Cape.

🚗 *Take Murat Rd to Bundegi Beach.*

Where to Stay: inexpensive under AU$150; moderate AU$150–AU$250; expensive over AU$250

Above Vlamingh Head Lighthouse, offering great views over the North West Cape

⓴ North West Cape
WA; 6707

The area's strategic role is visible in the old US naval communications base, now a motel, on the way to **Bundegi Beach** – an attractive beach with clear waters and sand dunes, washed-up corals and shells. Return to the turn-off to Yardie Creek Road, on the right, and take this to Mildura Wreck Road, turning right onto it.

Along the road, sandy tracks on the right lead to the beach, or continue to the car park at **Surfers Beach** (17 km/ 10 miles), with a viewing platform to watch the surfing – it attracts skilled boarders from all over. At the end of the road it is possible to spot the **Mildura Wreck**, the remnants of a cattle ship that sank offshore in 1907.

Return to Yardie Creek Road, turn right and left to **Vlamingh Head Lighthouse**. Built in 1912, it offers great views of the North West Cape. Return to Yardie Creek Road, turn left and right to the **Jurabi Turtle Centre**; interpretative panels in a striking shelter tell the story of the turtles that breed on the beach – three of the world's seven species nest here in summer *(Nov–Mar)*. It is also the meeting point for tours to see the turtles *(08 9947 8032)* – do not go alone, as visitors disrupt breeding.

🚗 *Turn right on Yardie Creek Rd and continue past beach tracks 32 km (20 miles) to Milyering Visitor Centre.*

㉑ Cape Range National Park
WA

Dominating the North West Cape peninsula, **Cape Range National Park** is fringed by the white-sand beaches of Ningaloo Marine Park *(see left)*. Inland, the park is home to wildlife including lizards, echidnas, emus and kangaroos. It also has magnificent limestone gorges and canyons that can be enjoyed on foot or by 4WD. From the west coast, the park is best seen on a cruise to Yardie Creek Gorge *(tickets from Milyering Visitor Centre; open daily)*, or by driving to the start of a 3-km (2-mile) walk into Mandu Mandu gorge, 20 km (12 miles) south of the visitor centre, for stunning gorge views.

Along the coast south of **Milyering Visitor Centre** *(see left)* are some of the state's most sublime snorkelling spots, where vivid coral can be viewed in calm waters. The best spot is beautiful **Turquoise Bay**. Walk along the beach for 300 m (985 ft), swim out for about 40 m (130 ft), then float back in the current, admiring the breathtaking sea life. A little further south, at **Oyster Stacks**, there is an abundance of fish species just off shore. Continue south and park at the end of Yardie Creek Road. There is an easy 1.5-km (1-mile) return walk to **Yardie Creek**, or take the **Yardie Creek Cruise** *(daily in season; 08 9949 1176)* up the gorge's cobalt waters to see its sheer red walls and spot black-footed rock wallabies.

ACTIVITIES AT NINGALOO MARINE PARK

For whale-watching cruises or scuba diving, contact eco-certified **Ningaloo Dreaming** *(Exmouth Shopping Centre, Maidstone St, 6707; 08 9949 4777; www.ningaloodreaming.com)*. See the coral reef from a glass-bottom boat with **Ningaloo Ecology Cruises** *(08 9949 2255; www.ningalootreasures. com.au)*. Enjoy a range of kayak tours, from half-day paddling to 5-day kayaking, snorkelling and camping safaris, with **Capricorn Kayak Tours** *(0427 485 123; www.capricornsea kayaking.com.au; mid-Mar–Oct)*.

EAT AND DRINK

CARNARVON

Old Post Office Cafe *inexpensive*
This stylish café serves authentic pizzas and pastas, best eaten on the veranda. *10 Robinson St, 6701; 08 9941 1800*

Harbourside Café *moderate*
Enjoy treats such as tandoori scallops or Moroccan snapper on the terrace. *131 Small Boat Harbour Rd, 6701; 08 9941 4111*

CORAL BAY

Coral Bay options
Reef Café *(08 9942 5882)* serves up excellent pizzas; **Fins Café** (08 9942 5900) offers café classics including a decent breakfast menu.

EXMOUTH

Graces Tavern *moderate*
This pub has an eclectic menu and a few eating spaces. Try their delicious pizzas. *Murat Rd, 6707; 08 9949 1000*

Whalers Restaurant *moderate*
With its long veranda, this is more chic than other dining options in Exmouth. Seafood is the order of the day, washed down with a crisp WA white wine. *5 Kennedy St, 6707; 08 9949 2416*

Below The gorge at Yardie Creek – a good place for spotting wallabies

Eat and Drink: inexpensive under AU$60; moderate AU$60–AU$100; expensive over AU$100

Pioneers and Prospectors

Guildford to Boulder

Highlights

- **Bush monastery**
  Stroll around the surprising Spanish-style monastery set in the bush at New Norcia

- **Historic charm**
  Soak up the charming atmosphere in the rural town of York and admire its splendid 19th-century buildings

- **Wheatbelt wild flowers**
  Enjoy the spectacularly colourful flowers that carpet the plains in season

- **Unique geology**
  "Surf" the smooth rock surface of the unique, naturally curved Wave Rock

- **Awesome mines**
  Take in the colossal mine that made the "Wild West" town of Kalgoorlie-Boulder one of Australia's wealthiest

Field of wild flowers near New Norcia

Pioneers and Prospectors

Lush vineyards and wineries, aromatic eucalyptus bushland, endless plains, pastoral settlements with broad streets, wheat silos and windmills, and bustling gold-mining towns with grand old pubs – this four-day driving tour from Guildford through the Avon Valley to the Goldfields towns of Coolgardie and Kalgoorlie takes travellers through some quintessentially Western Australian rural scenes. Along the way, expect to see fields carpeted with vibrant wild flowers and big homesteads with wide verandas and rickety old wooden wagons in the paddock. Stop to explore characterful country towns such as Toodyay and York, where old-fashioned stores are cluttered with arts, crafts and antiques, and coffee shops serve Devonshire cream teas.

Above Field of colourful wild flowers near New Norcia, *see p219* **Below** Spanish-style Abbey Church at New Norcia, *see p219*

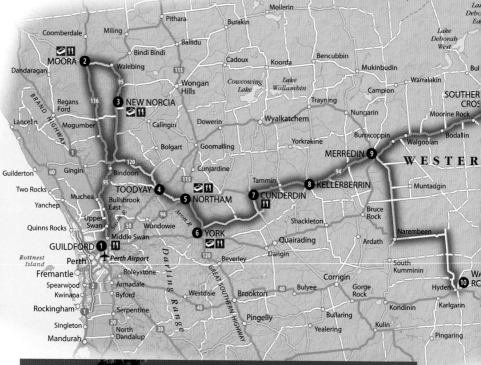

Above Old truck near Wave Rock, *see p222*

KALGOORLIE ⑬
⑭ BOULDER

Broad Arrow
Kanowa

Koolyannobbing
*Lake
Seabrook*

*Boorabbin
National Park*

GREAT EASTERN HIGHWAY

Boorabbin

Quardanoolagin

Yellowdine

⑫ COOLGARDIE

Bullabulling

*Goldfields-
Woodlands
National Park*

Kambalda

*Lake
Lefroy*

Marvel Loch

A U S T R A L I A

*Lake
Carmody*

0 kilometres 50

0 miles 50

KEY

Drive route

ACTIVITIES

Taste local wine and beer and try regional produce on the Swan Valley Food and Wine Trail

Meet a monk on a walking tour at the Spanish monastery settlement of New Norcia

Hunt for treasures at antique stores and crafts galleries in the Avon Valley's charming historic towns

Delight in the breathtaking array of native wild flowers that carpet the roadsides and hills of the Avon Valley in spring

Go white water rafting or hot-air ballooning at Northam

Strike a surfer's pose as you "ride" the red granite Wave Rock

Pan for gold in a creek bed at Kalgoorlie

Take a look into one of the largest man-made holes on the planet at Boulder

PLAN YOUR DRIVE

Start/finish: Guildford to Boulder.

Number of days: 4 days, including time to explore New Norcia, the Avon Valley towns, Wave Rock and the gold-mining towns.

Distance: Approx. 1,160 km (725 miles).

Road conditions: Good signposting and smooth sealed roads, with some dirt roads to Wave Rock (but still ok for 2WD).

When to go: Late autumn, winter and spring (May–Nov) are best, when temperatures are comfortable, the wild flowers are in bloom and the towns are bustling. Summer (Dec–Apr) can be scorching and should be avoided – Toodyay, York and Northam become ghost towns when people retreat to the beaches at weekends.

Opening times: Shops and cafés open 9am–5pm (bakeries open earlier) from Mon–Fri, and until noon on Sat, except in Toodyay and York where places stay open all weekend for day-trippers.

Main market days: Boulder: Burt St, 3rd Sun of month.

Shopping: Follow the Swan Valley Food and Wine Trail to buy wine, arts and crafts.

Major festivals: Swan Valley: Valley and Vines Festival, Mar; Swan Valley Winemakers, Mar; **Avon Valley:** Avon Descent, Aug; **York:** York Easter Fair, Easter weekend; **Northam:** Avon Valley Vintage Festival, Easter weekend; Avon Valley Gourmet Food and Wine Festival, Jun; **Coolgardie:** Coolgardie Day, Sep; **Kalgoorlie:** Kalgoorlie Community Fair, Mar; Spring Festival, Oct; **Boulder:** Back to Boulder Fest, Oct.

VISITING GUILDFORD

Parking
Park near Guildford Train Station or on James Street or one of the side streets such as Stephen Street or Ethel Street.

Visitor Information
Collect a Swan Valley brochure with maps and details of driving trails, wineries and restaurants at **Swan Valley Visitor Centre** *(Guildford Courthouse, Cnr Meadow & Swan St; 08 9379 9400; www.swanvalley.com.au; open daily).*

WHERE TO STAY

MOORA

Moora Motel *inexpensive*
The spacious, spotlessly clean rooms at this friendly country motel have toasters and kettles, so guests can make their own breakfast.
44 Roberts St, 6510; 08 9651 1247; office closes at 6pm

NEW NORCIA

New Norcia Hotel *moderate*
This is certainly a unique property, being a slice of old Spain in the heart of the Australian bush. While the hotel has adequate accommodation, the Monastery guesthouse is a more interesting stay.
Benedictine Community of New Norcia, 6509; 08 9654 8034; www.newnorcia.wa.edu.au

❶ Guildford
Western Australia (WA); 6936

Guildford, along with Perth and Fremantle, was one of the founding settlements of the Swan River Colony – the British settlement established on the west coast of Australia in 1829. The town is home to many handsome colonial and Federation-era buildings, as well as big old pubs, charming art galleries, cluttered antique shops and lively cafés. As well as being the Swan Valley's main town, it is the start of the award-winning Swan Valley Food and Wine Trail.

A one-hour walking tour

From the car park on Ethel Street, walk along James Street, stopping to look in the antique and bric-a-brac shops. Along the way, take a look at **Seaton Ross House** ①, near the corner of James and Johnston Street, which served as a maternity hospital from 1930–46.

At the corner of Meadow Street, pause to look at the fine white Art Deco **Guildford Town Hall** ② (1938), the Uniting Church nearby, and Guildford Council Chambers Library (1900). Visit the **Guildford Art Market** ③ behind the town hall on Meadow Street, then admire the nearby grand buildings, including the **Garrick Theatre** ④ (1878), Du Cane's House (1852) and, opposite, **Kings Cottage** ⑤.

Cross James Street and the railway line to explore Guildford's main historic precinct: admire the magnificent 1897 **Post Office** ⑥, on the corner of Stirling and James Street, beside it the Mechanics Institute, established in 1862, and the **Old Courthouse and**

General store sign, Guildford

Gaol ⑦ (1866), which is now the visitor centre. Turn right on Terrace Road to see the splendid old **Rose and Crown Hotel** ⑧, dating to 1841, then cross the road past a few charming shops and cafés, and the historic **Barker and Gull's Store** ⑨, just up from the corner of Terrace Road and Meadow Street. Continue along Meadow Street towards the Swan River to see **St Charles Seminary** ⑩ and across the road, **Moulton's Landing** ⑪, a scenic spot where the original town wharf once stood. Next, backtrack along the opposite side of the road for **Moulton's Cottage** ⑫, built in 1841. Turn right onto Swan Terrace to see the enormous **Crosslands House** ⑬, also known as Riverleigh. Dating to 1897, the mansion is a fine example of Gold Rush architecture with a lovely Art Nouveau turret. Cross the road and wander through pretty Stirling Square to view **St Matthews Church** ⑭, before crossing the railway line back to James Street and the car.

🚗 *Head east down James St, turn left onto Meadow St, which becomes West Swan Rd, and follow the signed Swan Valley Food and Wine Trail through an array of little towns, stopping at wineries (see right) and galleries along the way. At the end of West Swan Rd, turn left (leaving the Food and Wine Trail) onto Great Northern Hwy (1) to Moora, 142 km (88 miles) away. Stay on the Great Northern Hwy (95) for 55km (34 miles), then turn left on the Bindoon-Moora Rd (116) for 86 km (54 miles) to Moora.*

Moulton's Landing ⑪

Swan River

Moulton's Cottage ⑫

St Charles Seminary ⑩

Barker and Gull's Store ⑨

Crosslands House ⑬

Rose and Crown Hotel ⑧

St Matthews Church ⑭

STIRLING SQUARE

VICTORIA STREET

Old Courthouse and Gaol ⑦

Post Office ⑥

Guildford Town Hall ②

JAMES STREET

STIRLING STREET

Kings Cottage ⑤

Seaton Ross House ①

Guildford Art Market ③

Garrick Theatre ④

0 metres 150
0 yards 150

Far left The Spanish-style Benedictine monastery at New Norcia **Left** Connors Mill and Museum, dating from 1870, Toodyay

VISITING TOODYAY

Visitor Information
7 Piesse St, 6566; 08 9574 2435;
www.toodyay.com

Shopping
Toodyay is packed with arts and crafts, antiques and boutique shops. Try the
Toodyay Emporium *(16 Stirling Terrace, 08 9574 2062)* for Australian "antiques".

EAT AND DRINK

AROUND GUILDFORD

Houghton's *moderate*
One of the original wineries in Western Australia, this is an easy one to visit from Guildford – about 8 km (5 miles) up the Great Northern Highway – for fine food, made for sharing, accompanied by good wine from the adjacent vineyards.
Middle Swan, 6936; 08 9274 9540; www. houghton-wines.com.au; closed pm

MOORA

Drovers Inn *inexpensive*
The charmingly old-fashioned Drovers Inn restaurant is a classic old Australian corner pub with big verandas outside and stylish Art Deco touches inside; expect huge country portions.
Cnr Dandaragan and Padbury St, 6510; 08 9651 1108; open Wed–Sun pm

NEW NORCIA

New Norcia Hotel *moderate*
Simple, large portions of standard Australian fare served in a grand old dining room or on the veranda. Sunday night is pizza night.
New Norcia, 6509; 08 9654 8034; www.newnorcia.wa.edu.au

Swan Valley Food and Wine Trail

With wineries, breweries, galleries, buzzy cafés and roadside produce stalls, the Swan Valley, stretching up the Swan River from Guildford, just outside Perth, to Upper Swan, is an easily accessible wine region. The best way to see the area is on the **Swan Valley Food and Wine Trail**, a signed 32-km (20-mile) loop taking in the main attractions. Pick up a map from the visitor centre in Guildford.

② Moora
WA; 6510

Part of the Central Wheatbelt *(see p221)*, Moora, established in 1895, is set among fields of wheat, barley and canola. However, the town's main attractions are its grand architecture, vivid murals and, in season, its colourful wild flowers. In winter and spring, there are yellow wattle and lilac hibiscus, and in summer, orange eremaeas, yellow kangaroo paws and the cream bottlebrushes of the saltmarsh honey myrtle. **Moora Visitor Centre** *(65 Padbury St; 08 9653 1053)* has information on wild flower drives and walking trails.
🚗 *Drive southeast along Midlands Rd (116), turning right onto Gt Northern Hwy (95) to New Norcia. Park behind the main building on the right on the way in.*

③ New Norcia
WA; 6509

Founded in 1847 by Benedictine monks intent on converting the local Aboriginal people to Christianity, New Norcia is Australia's only monastic town. Among the striking Spanish-style buildings – the first two monks were Spanish – is the **Museum and Art Gallery** *(08 9654 8056; www.newnorcia. wa.edu.au; open daily)*. Book a guided tour at its visitor centre to visit the two grand schools (St Ildephonsus' for boys and St Gertrude's for girls), Abbey

Church (1860) and flour mills – New Norcia is renowned for its bread, baked in wood-fired ovens – and take a look inside the grand old **New Norcia Hotel**.
🚗 *Continue south on Gt Northern Hwy (95) for 42 km (26 miles), then turn left (southeast) onto Bindoon Dewars Pool Rd (120) for 34 km (21 miles), right onto Bindi Bindi-Toodyay Rd (120) to Toodyay.*

④ Toodyay
WA; 6566

Delightful little Toodyay, founded in 1836, was one of the earliest inland settlements of the Swan River Colony and a handful of buildings from that period remain, including **Connors Mill and Museum** *(Cnr Stirling Terrace & Piesse St; open daily)* and **Old Newcastle Gaol** *(Clinton St; open daily)*. Visit **St Stephen's Church**, opposite the mill on the riverbank, and the old **Mechanics' Institute** *(Stirling Terrace)*, now a library. The town bustles at the weekends, when visitors flock here to browse among the arts and crafts and antique shops, and lunch in the old pubs.
🚗 *Drive south on Bindi Bindi–Toodyay Rd, turn left onto Northam–Toodyay Rd for 22 km (14 miles) into Northam. Carry straight on over the river then left into Fitzgerald St to the centre of town.*

Below Traditional corner pub in Moora, with a wide, shady veranda

Eat and Drink: inexpensive under AU$60; moderate AU$60–AU$100; expensive over AU$100

VISITING THE AVON VALLEY

Visitor Information
All visitor centres can book tours and accommodation and have maps detailing walks and drives.

Northam Visitor Centre: *2 Grey St, 6401; 08 9622 2100; www.avon valleywa.com.au; open daily.*

York Visitor Centre: *81 Avon Terrace, York, 6302; 08 9641 1301; www.avon valleywa.org; open daily.*

VISITING THE CENTRAL WHEATBELT

Central Wheatbelt Visitor Centre
(85 Barrack St, 6415, Merredin; 08 9041 1666; www.wheatbelttourism.com; open daily) has information and maps.

WHERE TO STAY

NORTHAM
Avon Bridge Hotel *inexpensive*
The most stylish accommodation in town, this imposing old corner pub has comfy rooms and hotel- and motel-style accommodation.
322 Fitzgerald St, 6401; 08 9622 1023; www.avonbridgehotel.com.au

YORK
Faversham House *inexpensive*
This delightful, grand mansion, dating from around 1840, has several rooms in the main house with ensuite rooms, some with access to the veranda. There is a courtyard with several rooms with shared bathrooms.
24–26 Grey St, 6302; 08 9641 1366; www.favershamhouse.com.au

Imperial Hotel *inexpensive*
This beautifully renovated old Australian pub has luxurious garden suites that are popular for weekend getaways from Perth. Rooms do not have TVs or fridges and there are no facilities for children.
83 Avon Terrace, 6302; 08 9641 1255; www.imperialhotelyork.com.au

Nosh and Nod *moderate*
This modern accomodation has four furnished rooms. Two of the rooms have spas, while one is self-contained, complete with utilities such as a washing machine and kitchen.
75 Avon Terrace, 6302; 08 9641 1629; www.noshnod.com.au

Above and right Stunning wild flowers found in the Avon Valley

⑤ Northam
WA; 6401
Established in 1833 by Governor Stirling, founder of the Swan River Colony, Northam was an important departure point for explorers and miners venturing east to make their names and fortunes. It is now a major commercial centre for Central Wheatbelt farmers. Although it is set on the Avon River, famous for its white swans and suspension bridge, Northam is the least attractive of the Avon Valley towns, with a handful of historic buildings, including the 1836 **Morby Cottage** *(Katrine Rd; open Sun)* and the 1886 **Old Railway Station Museum** *(Fitzgerald St; open Sun).*

🚗 *From Fitzgerald St, drive east, then turn right into Peel Terrace, which becomes the Northam–York Rd. Drive for 33 km (21 miles) to York, turn right into Pool St and left onto Avon Terrace.*

⑥ York
WA; 6302
Known for its sandalwood production, York was WA's first inland settlement and the best preserved. Founded as a convict outpost in 1826, it's the most atmospheric of the Avon Valley towns,

oozing history and charm. Boasting restored 19th-century buildings, with historic shop-fronts, retro signage and corrugated-iron awnings, wandering along York's main street, Avon Terrace, is like stepping back in time. The most notable buildings are the Town Hall, Settlers House, Residency Museum and the old pubs. While it is a delight to stroll along the main drag past the old book and antiques shops and old-fashioned stores, there are attractions worth visiting, including **York Motor Museum** *(open daily)* with an impressive vintage car collection, **Old Courthouse** *(open daily)* and **Sandalwood Yards**. Close to Avon Terrace is the Avon River spanned by **York Suspension Bridge**.

🚗 *Return to Northam–York Rd (120) for 4.5 km (3 miles), turn right into Goldfields Rd for 47 km (29 miles), then turn left onto Mills Rd and left onto Cunderdin–Quairading Rd to Cunderdin.*

⑦ Cunderdin
WA; 6407
First settled in 1894 when the railway arrived, Cunderdin's key sights include a restored water pumping station converted into the town **Museum** *(100 Forrest St; open daily)*, which has displays on the gold mining and pastoral

history, and a replica of the cartoon **Ettamogah Pub** *(75 Main St)*, which featured in the long-running comic of the same name by Ken Maynard in the now-defunct *Australasian Post* magazine. The original cartoon replica was at Albury-Wodonga in NSW.

🚗 *Continue east for 47 km (29 miles) along Gt Eastern Hwy to Kellerberrin.*

⑧ Kellerberrin

WA; 6410

The first town building to be built in 1897, Kellerberrin's Agricultural Hall served as the town school, courthouse and roads department office. It is now a **Pioneer Museum** *(get key from Visitor Centre, Shire Offices, 110 Massingham St; 08 9045 4006)* within Pioneer Park, with displays on pastoral life, farm machinery and local memorabilia. **Kellerberrin Hill Lookout** offers good vistas of the surrounding countryside.

🚗 *Continue east for 57 km (35 miles) along Gt Eastern Hwy (94) to Merredin.*

Central Wheatbelt

Stretching from the fertile Avon Valley to the dusty Goldfield cities of Coolgardie and Kalgoorlie-Boulder, the Central Wheatbelt has pastoral towns with old-fashioned pubs, amid pastures and plains dotted with windmills, wheat silos and salt lakes. The Great Eastern Highway (94), also known as the Golden Way, joins the towns along the route beside the "Golden Pipeline", which carries water from Mundaring Reservoir to Kalgoorlie-Boulder. Wild flowers such as acacia, wreath flowers and everlastings bring colour to the region, Jul–Oct.

⑨ Merredin

WA; 6415

Once a sandalwood centre, Merredin is now a grain-producing town and boasts a handful of sights related to its early development and its role in World War II. These include engineering equipment dating to 1898 that was used to harvest water from rock, the 1928 heritage-listed **Cummins Theatre** and the **Military Museum** *(key from Central Wheatbelt Visitor Centre; 08 9041 1668)* featuring equipment and memorabilia from the World War II sites around Merredin, when the town once hosted an important army hospital. During wild flower season, from Jul–Oct, the area becomes especially attractive when almost a thousand species of wild flowers come into bloom.

🚗 *Take Great Eastern Hwy east, turn right on Merredin–Narembeen Rd for 68 km (42 miles). Turn left on Mt Walker Rd for 40 km (25 miles), then right for 45 km (28 miles) on Hyden–Mt Walker Rd becoming McPherson St; turn left on Hyden Lake King Rd to Wave Rock.*

Above left The Visitor Information Centre in the Town Hall, York **Above right** The York Suspension Bridge **Below** The tranquil Avon River, York

EAT AND DRINK

NORTHAM

Avon Bridge Hotel *inexpensive*
The restaurant at this popular pub is Northam's best, dishing up generous portions of modern bistro cuisine. There is also a more casual café.
322 Fitzgerald St, 6401; 08 9622 1023; www.avonbridgehotel.com.au

YORK

Café Bugatti *inexpensive*
This friendly, Bugatti-themed café has become a York institution, serving a range of Italian-influenced dishes. A selection of gelati, cake and other desserts is also available.
104 Avon Terrace, York, 6210; 08 9641 1583; www.bugatti.yorkwa.com.au

CUNDERDIN

Ettamogah Pub *inexpensive*
This rather odd re-creation of the famous cartoon Ettamogah does excellent counter meals – big steak sandwiches and even bigger steaks.
75 Main St, 6407; 08 9635 1777

Below Federation-era façade of the Marvel Bar Hotel (1898), Coolgardie **Below right** The monumental mine known as the Super Pit, Boulder **Below left** Bank in The Australian Prospectors and Miners Hall of Fame, Kalgoorlie

⑩ Wave Rock
Hyden, WA; 6359

Hyden is famous for its striking 15-m (49-ft) wave-shaped rock formation, Wave Rock. As well as providing a popular photo opportunity (a surfer pose seems to be the favourite), the 60-million-year-old granite rock offers walking opportunities and the drive here is scenic in wild flower season.

🚗 *Return to Merredin then head northeast for 109 km (68 miles) on Gt Eastern Hwy (94) to Southern Cross.*

⑪ Southern Cross
WA; 6426

Settled in 1888 after the discovery of gold, Southern Cross was WA's first Gold Rush town. Its streets are wide enough to turn a camel train around – and it has a few historic buildings, such as the mud-brick **Yilgarn History Museum** *(open daily)*, which features a prospectors' camp. The **Old Cemetery** is a solemn reminder of the challenges faced by the pioneers and prospectors.

🚗 *Carry on northeast along Gt Eastern Hwy 186 km (116 miles) to Coolgardie.*

⑫ Coolgardie
WA; 6429

The original Gold Rush settlement, Coolgardie was flooded by 10,000 prospectors in 1892 after Arthur Bayley discovered 16 kg (35 lbs) of gold. Now much smaller, the town is focused around a main street lined with Federation-era buildings. Stop at the visitor centre in the **Mining Warden's Court Building** *(62 Bayley St; 08 9026 6090; open Mon–Fri)* to see the comprehensive **Goldfields Exhibition Museum** *(open Mon–Fri)*, and the adjoining **Pharmacy Museum** *(open daily)*, with its curious collection of 18th- and 19th-century medicines and posters. Nearby, view the beautifully restored **Warden Finnerty's House**.

🚗 *Drive northeast along Gt Eastern Hwy for 38 km (24 miles) to Kalgoorlie. Park in the main road, Hannan St.*

The Goldfields

WA's Goldfields region is still one of the world's richest gold-producing areas. While its remoteness, disease and a lack of water made life difficult for the first prospectors, the wealth of the Goldfields and its population growth led to WA's statehood in 1901. Mining remains the area's main industry: Australia's largest open cut gold mine, the **Kalgoorlie-Boulder Super Pit**, produces 24,000 kg (850,000 ounces) of gold annually. It is an important source of employment and also draws many tourists, who come to gape at the colossal hole.

VISITING KALGOORLIE

Kalgoorlie-Boulder Visitor Centre,
316 Hannan St, 6430; 08 9021 1966;
www.kalgoorlietourism.com; open daily.

Kalgoorlie Brothel Tours
After visiting the mines, the most
popular activity in Kalgoorlie is to
visit the city's diminutive red light
district on Hay Sreet to do a brothel
tour. **Questa Casa** *(133 Hay St, 6429;*
08 9021 4897; daily 3pm) offers tours
during the quiet hours, covering the
history of prostitution in the Goldfields.

⑬ Kalgoorlie
WA; 6429

The discovery of gold in the area led
to a spate of tunnelling, which
required lots of wood to hold up the
mine shafts. As a result, the local
landscape became desertified and
pit-scarred, while the twin towns of
Kalgoorlie–Boulder became two of
Australia's richest and wildest
outposts. Start with a stroll along
Kalgoorlie's Hannan Street to admire
the flamboyant façades of the
restored Federation-era buildings
and grand old pubs with wide
verandas and elegant wrought-iron
work. The towering red 33-m (108-ft)
head-frame at the top of the road
belongs to the excellent **Western
Australian Museum** *(open daily; 08
9021 8533; www.museum.wa.gov.au).*
The museum has an exhibition on
the history of the Goldfields, as well
as the sandalwood industry and
Aboriginal culture. It also has great
views of the city and mines.

Head along the Goldfields
Highway to the **Hannan's North
Tourist Mine** *(open Mon–Fri; www.
mininghall.com),* located on the site of
a former mine, where visitors can
wander around a re-created mining
town, take an underground tour
guided by former miners, and even
try their hand at panning for gold.
The Hall of Fame features exhibitions
on the history of the area, with
displays of rocks and minerals and
contemporary art that has been
supported by the mines.

🚗 *Return on the Goldfields Hwy, past
Hannan St, and turn left at the signed
turn-off to the Super Pit and the top of
Boulder's main road, Burt St, on the
right (there is parking here).*

⑭ Boulder
WA; 6432

Initially a separate settlement, built to
serve the mines, Boulder was later
absorbed into Kalgoorlie, and is now
virtually a suburb of the city. A tinier
and quaint version of its twin, Boulder's
small main streets boasts a similar array
of splendid old edifices and a few
grand old pubs; however, Kalgoorlie is
a more engaging place to stay.

Do not leave town without visiting
the gigantic hole in the ground – the
Super Pit mine. While it is fascinating
simply to look from the **viewing point**,
watching a blast is a more memorable
experience. Visit or phone the **Super
Pit Shop** *(open Mon–Fri & the 3rd Sun
of the month; 2 Burt St; 08 9021 2211;
www.superpit.com.au)* to find out
when a blast is scheduled and time
your visit accordingly. Alternatively,
fling on safety glasses and a high-
visibility vest, and join a **Super Pit
Tour.** For tour times and bookings,
contact **Kalgoorlie Tours and
Charters** *(250 Hannan St; 08 9021
2211; www.kalgoorlietours.com).*

EAT AND DRINK IN KALGOORLIE

Balcony Bar & Restaurant *moderate*
It is best to book a veranda table
here in the warmer months, to
watch the sunset and dine on some
modern-Australian cuisine with a
Mediterranean lilt. Excellent wood-
fired pizzas and friendly service.
137 Hannan St, 6430; 08 9021 2788;
www.palacehotel.com.au

Blue Monkey *moderate*
Great all-day dining (including a big
hearty breakfast) with excellent
modern-Australian classics is what you
can expect at this easy-going eatery.
Extensive dinner menu including
home-made pizzas.
418 Hannan St, 6430; 08 9091 3833

Above The extraordinary curved rock
formation, Wave Rock **Below** Period theatre,
Boulder, built in the 1930s

Eat and Drink: inexpensive under AU$60; moderate AU$60–AU$100; expensive over AU$100

Waves, Whales and Wine

Bunbury to Cape Leeuwin

Highlights

- **Beautiful beaches and bays**
  Bask in the sun or play beachcomber on the sandy beaches at Busselton or Dunsborough, some of Western Australia's most scenic towns

- **Sublime surf**
  Carve some spectacular waves – or watch some surfing legends do so – at the renowned surf spots of Yallingup and Prevelly

- **Wonderful wineries**
  Taste superb, award-winning wines and enjoy lunch overlooking the glorious vineyards at Margaret River's renowned wineries

- **Craggy coastline**
  Watch whales migrate, learn about shipwreck history and admire the wild and windswept Cape Leeuwin

Road sheltered by eucalypts in the Margaret River region

Waves, Whales and Wine

A fine combination of coastal and inland delights makes Western Australia's southwest region one of the state's most rewarding areas to visit. Expect laidback holiday towns with white-sand coves and crystal-clear seas interspersed with sections of wild, windswept coastline and some of Australia's best surfing beaches. Inland, the gently undulating bushland is dotted with picturesque wineries and farms producing some of the country's finest wine and food. This leisurely 4–5-day drive from Bunbury to beautiful Cape Leeuwin follows the coastline for much of the way, taking in the sleepy seaside towns of Busselton and Dunsborough, the natural beauty of Geographe Bay and Cape Naturaliste, the surf beaches of Yallingup and Prevelly, the Margaret River wine region, and the lovely town of Augusta, a popular whale-watching area, before reaching desolate Cape Leeuwin.

Above Viewpoint at Yallingup, *see p230*

ACTIVITIES

Swim with wild dolphins at Koombana Bay, Bunbury

Inspect the reef from the underwater observatory on Busselton Jetty

Dive the wreck of the HMAS *Swan*, off Dunsborough

Keep an eye out for migrating whales off the coast of Leeuwin-Naturaliste National Park

Complete a section of the windswept Cape to Cape walk

Ride the classic waves at Prevelly, one of Australia's top surfing spots

Hop from vineyard to vineyard tasting superb wines in the Margaret River wine region

Do a guided tour of the spectacular underground Margaret River Caves

Learn how to survive in the wild on a bush tucker tour in the Margaret River region

Climb up Australia's tallest lighthouse at Cape Leeuwin

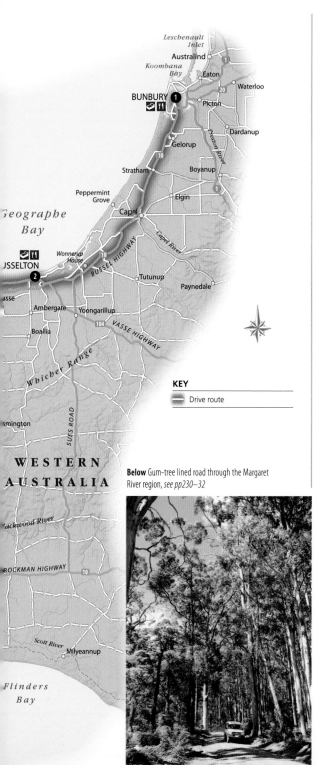

KEY

― Drive route

Below Gum-tree lined road through the Margaret River region, *see pp230–32*

PLAN YOUR DRIVE

Start/finish: Bunbury to Cape Leeuwin.

Number of days: 4–5 days, including a leisurely day driving to the Margaret River region, 2–3 days spent exploring the region, and an easy day's drive to Augusta and Cape Leeuwin.

Distance: Approx. 371 km (232 miles).

Road conditions: Good signposting and good smooth sealed roads with the occasional 2WD dirt road through a national park or to a beach.

When to go: Any time in spring, summer or autumn (*Sep–May*) is suitable, when the weather is loveliest and temperatures rarely rise above 32°C (90°F). Beach resorts are booked out well in advance from Christmas until the end of January for school holidays. Winters (*Jun–Aug*) are pleasant for touring the vineyards, with temperatures averaging 18°C (64°F) by day, 10°C (50°F) at night.

Opening times: Shops and cafés open 9:30am–5pm (bakeries open earlier) from Mon–Fri and until noon on Saturday, except in Margaret River where many shops open all weekend. Most wineries shut by 5pm, and their restaurants only open for lunch. Restaurants in towns open for dinner from 6pm, last orders by 9pm.

Main market days: Bunbury: Sun; Busselton: Sun; Dunsborough: 2nd & 5th Sat of month; Margaret River: Sun; Farmers' Market, summer weekends; Augusta: Sat in summer.

Shopping: Buy cases of Margaret River wines at cellar doors, regional produce such as venison, truffles, cheese, olive oil, honey and preserves from gourmet shops in Margaret River, and contemporary art, Aboriginal arts and crafts, jewellery and ceramics.

Major festivals: Busselton: Beach Festival, Jan; Busselton Jetty Swim, Feb; **Dunsborough:** Jazz Festival, Jun; Whale season, Aug–Dec. **Prevelly:** Margaret River Classic (surf competition), Nov; **Margaret River:** Big Wave Challenge, Apr–Jun; Wine Festival, May; Wild flower season, Sep–Dec; **Augusta:** Augusta Festival, Mar; Whale season, Jun–Sep.

Above left View out to sea over Bunbury and its harbour **Above right** Busselton's 19th-century wooden jetty stretching out to sea **Below right** Dolphin leaping through the waves at Koombana Bay

WHERE TO STAY

BUNBURY

Quality Hotel Lord Forrest *moderate*
An ideal base for Bunbury's dolphins, beaches and forests, with good rooms and facilities, including a pool.
20 Symmons St, 6230; 08 9726 5777; www.lordforresthotel.com.au

The Rose Hotel *moderate*
A historic pub dating back to 1865, with refined heritage rooms, a well-regarded restaurant and two bars.
Victoria St, 6230; 08 9721 4533; www.rosehotel.com.au

BUSSELTON

Busselton Jetty Chalets *inexpensive*
These self-contained chalets opposite a park and the beach, and an easy walk from the jetty, offer good value.
94 Marine Tce, 6280; 08 9752 3893; www.busseltonjettychalets.com

Busselton Holiday Village
inexpensive
This well-shaded holiday park in the heart of Busselton offers a range of accommodation, from luxury guest houses to chalets and camp sites, with a large enclosed garden and BBQ areas.
118 Peel Tce, 6280; 08 9752 4499; www.busseltonholidayvillage.com.au

DUNSBOROUGH

Newberry Manor *moderate*
This quaint B&B has three comfortable suites, one with kitchenette and fridge. There is a lovely lounge and breakfast room overlooking the gardens.
16 Newberry Rd, 6281; 08 9756 7542; www.newberrymanor.com.au

Pullman Resort *expensive*
A sleek, stylish resort with stunning vistas of Bunker Bay. There is a fabulous swimming pool, all within splashing distance of the sea.
Bunker Bay Road, 6281; 08 9756 9100; www.mirvachotels.com

① Bunbury
Western Australia (WA); 6230
Laidback Bunbury may not be the most beautiful beach town on the coast, but its relaxed vibe, historic buildings, mangroves and bottlenose dolphins make it worth a visit.
Make a beeline for the **Dolphin Discovery Centre** *(Koombana Drive; open daily; 08 9791 3088; www.dolphindiscovery.com.au)*, which offers boat tours with marine biologist guides and the opportunity to swim with wild dolphins at Koombana Bay. Bunbury's **visitor centre** in the old train station *(Carmody Place; open daily; 1800 286 287; www.visitbunbury.com.au)* has information on walking trails around the mangroves and a heritage walk taking in 50 historic attractions, including splendid buildings from the 1800s, such as St Mark's Church (1842), Rose Hotel (1865), King Cottage Museum (1880), and the Old Post Office and Courthouse (1880s).
🚗 *From Bunbury, head south on Blair St and follow Bussell Hwy (10) for 49 km (30 miles) to Busselton centre. Park on and around Peel or Stanley St.*

② Busselton
WA; 6280
Named after a local pioneering family, pretty Busselton is a family holiday town beloved for its 30 km (19 miles) of sandy beaches and the charming 1865 wooden **Busselton Jetty** *(open daily; 08 9754 0900; www.busseltonjetty.com.au)*. The restored pier is home to an observatory 8 m (26 ft) beneath the sea, where visitors can admire the corals and marine life on the reef below. The seaside park has a good restaurant and picnic tables. Busselton also boasts some lovely old buildings, including the old courthouse in town, dating to 1854, and the 1838

Australian National Trust-listed **Wonnerup House** *(opening times vary, contact Busselton Visitor Centre: 08 9752 1288; www.geographebay.com)*, which gives an insight into early settlers' lives.
🚗 *Follow Bussell Hwy for 8 km (5 miles), then carry on along Caves Rd for 15 km (9 miles), turning right onto Seymour Blvd, then at the next roundabout, take the first exit, Dunsborough Lakes Dr, for Dunsborough.*

Caves Road
Caves Road, running from Busselton and Dunsborough in the north to the outskirts of Augusta in the south, is the main artery through the Margaret River region. It is possible to spend a couple of days exploring Caves Road alone, stopping off at wineries, breweries and arts and crafts galleries, such as **Gunyulgup Galleries** *(open daily; www.gunyulgupgalleries.com.au)*, which features contemporary art, ceramics, pottery and jewellery by local artists, and next door the brilliant restaurant **Lamonts** *(see Eat and Drink, p231)*. The best studios, galleries, eateries and wineries are on maps available at visitor centres.

③ Dunsborough
WA; 6281
The delightful town of Dunsborough, overlooking gorgeous Geographe Bay is popular with divers exploring wrecks off the coast, ramblers hiking nearby nature trails, and those who love swimming and sunbathing on some of Western Australia's most beautiful beaches and sheltered bays. The centre of town includes galleries, boutiques, bakeries, cafés and pubs. Look in on the **visitor centre** *(Dunsborough Park Shopping Centre; open daily; 08 9752 5800; www.geographebay.com)*, which has

walking maps and can book tours. However, the real attractions are the calm coves out of town on the way to Cape Naturaliste, where turquoise water laps the squeaky white sands at **Meelup**, **Eagle** and **Bunker Bay**.

🚗 *Follow Naturaliste Terrace to Cape Naturaliste Rd, then continue for 12 km (7 miles) to the cape and car park.*

Dunsborough Diving

Dunsborough's coast is home to the former HMAS *Swan*, now the largest accessible dive wreck site in the southern hemisphere. This 113-m (372-ft) destroyer was scuttled in Geographe Bay, off Meelup Beach, in December 1997. Diving tours are available most of the year, subject to weather conditions and can be booked at the Dunsborough and Busselton visitor centres.

🚗 *Backtrack along Cape Naturaliste Rd into Naturaliste Terrace for 15 km (9 miles) then take the first right turn onto Caves Rd for 7.5 km (5 miles), then turn right onto Yallingup Beach Rd.*

Above Rocky shore and clear waters of Leeuwin–Naturaliste National Park

④ Cape Naturaliste

WA; 6290

At Cape Naturaliste, the most western point of Geographe Bay, visit the truncated white **lighthouse** *(open daily)*. It dates from 1903 and was built using limestone taken from Bunker Bay. The cape is a good place to spot humpback and southern right whales during the annual migration season *(Sep–Dec)*. Cape Naturaliste also marks the beginning (or end) of the 140-km (87-mile) **Cape to Cape Walk** *(see box on p232)*, which can be done in small sections. Alternatively, try the easy **Cape Naturaliste Track**, leading through limestone pinnacles to a lookout boasting spectacular views of the cape.

Leeuwin–Naturaliste National Park

Stretching 120 km (75 miles) from Cape Naturaliste and Bunker Bay in the north to Cape Leeuwin and Augusta in the south, the Leeuwin-Naturaliste National Park is marked by a wild, windswept coastline, ruggedly beautiful cliffs, striking granite rock formations, heath-covered headlands and stunning sandy beaches. The national park is home to abundant birdlife, rare species of wild flowers, including the Naturaliste Nancy and Dunsborough spider orchid, towering karri trees and some 350 limestone caves and tunnels. Sealed and unsealed roads give access to lookouts and walking trails.

EAT AND DRINK

BUNBURY

Vat2 *moderate*
Vat2 has an eclectic menu ranging from Moroccan- and Turkish-influenced dishes to steaks and pasta. Enjoy the seafood platters and extensive breakfast menu.
2 Jetty Rd, 6230; 08 9791 8833; www.vat2.com.au

BUSSELTON

The Goose *moderate*
The Goose has a pretty location adjacent to the famous jetty, with brilliant views from its alfresco area. The menu has the usual modern-Australian eclecticism with standout seafood, particularly the seafood chowder.
Geographe Bay Rd, Jetty foreshore, 6280; 08 9754 7700; www.thegoose. com.au; closed Sun–Mon

DUNSBOROUGH

Dunsborough Bakery *inexpensive*
This bakery is famous for the delicious pies it has been making since the 1940s – try the Surfer's Pie.
243 Naturaliste Tce, 6281; 08 9755 3137; www.dunsboroughbakery.com

AROUND DUNSBOROUGH

Bunkers Beach Café *moderate*
A simply stunning beach location at Bunker Bay between Dunsborough and Cape Naturaliste is matched by the excellent modern-Australian cuisine coming out of the kitchen. Perfect for breakfast or lunch after a dip or a walk along the beach.
Farm Break Lane, Bunker Bay, Naturaliste, 6281; 08 9756 8284; www.bunkersbeachcafe.com.au

Above The unspoiled sandy beach at Bunker Bay, Dunsborough

Eat and Drink: inexpensive under AU$60; moderate AU$60–AU$100; expensive over AU$100

VISITING THE MARGARET RIVER REGION

Visitor Information
The visitor centre (*open daily; 100 Bussell Hwy, 6285; 08 9780 5911; www.margaretriver.com*) can book accommodation and tours, and stocks the excellent Margaret River Map and Guide, which identifies all wineries, as well as the Map to Studios and Galleries of the South West Cape Region (*www.margaretriverartisans.com.au*).

Indigenous Tours
The **Wardan Aboriginal Cultural Centre** (*Injidup Springs Rd, Yallingup, 6282; 08 9756 6566; www.wardan.com.au*) offers bush tucker walks where visitors are shown how to use traditional tools and identify bush medicines. Visitors can also learn about bush tucker from the back of a canoe with **Bushtucker Tours** (*08 9757 9084; www.bushtuckertours.com*).

WHERE TO STAY

AROUND YALLINGUP
Windmills Break *expensive*
A five-star boutique hotel, just north-east of Yallingup, offering well-designed rooms and suites, a large garden and generous swimming pool.
Cnr Caves & Hemsley Rd, 6281; 08 9755 2341; www.windmillsbreak.com.au

Cape Lodge *expensive*
This boutique hotel has excellent rooms and suites, lovely gardens and a fine restaurant. It is 10 km (6 miles) down Caves Road towards Prevelly, opposite Driftwood Estate Winery.
3341 Caves Rd, 6280; 08 9755 6311; www.capelodge.com.au

MARGARET RIVER
Bridgefield *inexpensive*
This charming, historic guesthouse has rooms full of antiques and also offers excellent self-contained chalet accommodation. Close to centre.
73 Bussell Hwy, 6285; 08 9757 3007; www.bridgefield.com.au

Margaret River Hotel *moderate*
This large hotel dating from 1936 has stylish hotel rooms and suites with basic cooking facilities. It also has a popular bistro and bar.
125 Bussell Hwy, 6285; 08 9757 2655; www.margaretriverhotel.com.au

Central Avenue Apartments *moderate*
These contemporary, open-plan apartments all have private balconies, and modish amenities.
1 Charles West Ave, 6285; 08 9758 7025; www.centralavenue.com.au

Right Stunning dune-backed, surfing beach at Yallingup

⑤ Yallingup
WA; 6282
The small seaside settlement of Yallingup – Aboriginal for "place of love" – is stunningly set on a hillside overlooking the superb **Yallingup Beach**, which, along with nearby **Smiths Beach** and **Injidup Beach**, offers some of the best surf breaks in the world. The beach car parks see an endless stream of surfers watching the waves and waiting for the big one. In recent years, the beach shacks down this coast have been replaced by sleek architect-designed holiday houses and real estate prices have rocketed, but the coastal hamlets still retain the laidback feel that made them so appealing in the first place. The coastline is also one of the most dramatic around – the granite outcrop at **Canal Rocks**, to the south (*turn right off Caves Road along Canal Rocks Road*), is a good spot to look out for whales.

🚗 *Return to Caves Rd, turn right and head south for 38 km (24 miles), then right on Wallcliffe Rd to Prevelly.*

⑥ Prevelly
WA; 6285
Prevelly is not only one of the most picturesque places on the coast, it is also one of Australia's best surfing beaches, playing host to November's annual **Margaret River Classic** surfing championship. Learn to surf or simply brush up on your wave skills at the **Margaret River Surf School** (*1 Resort Place, Gnarabup; 08 9757 1111*). Prevelly is also home to the **Greek Chapel of St John**, a memorial

Above Surfers at Yallingup Beach, on a rare bad surf day

dedicated to Crete's Preveli Monastery, which gave protection to Australian and other Allied soldiers during World War II. Architecture buffs will enjoy the stylish holiday houses in the area.

🚗 *Backtrack along Wallcliffe Rd and cross over Caves Rd heading inland to Margaret River township, turning left on Bussell Hwy (10), to the town centre.*

⑦ Margaret River
WA; 6285
Located on the banks of a pretty river and set amid fragrant bushland close to the coast and national park, the laidback township of Margaret River is a great base for exploring one of Australia's premier wine regions. Start with the main street, crammed with gourmet food shops, arts and crafts galleries and chic boutiques. In the evenings, when the out-of-town

Above Experienced surfers enjoying the excellent waves at Prevelly

winery restaurants are closed, its fine eateries, lively cafés and wine bars come into their own.

Pick up a winery map from the **visitor centre** *(see left)* to explore some of the wineries along the Bussell Highway between Carbunup River and Cowaramup, along Caves Road back towards Yallingup, and in the area south of Margaret River, between Wallcliffe Road and Redgate Road and in the area east of Witchcliffe. Allow time to visit some of the other gourmet producers along the way – look out for local beer, cheese, preserves, olive oil, truffles, venison, berries, fudge and chocolate. The **Good Olive** *(97 Bussell Hwy; open daily; 08 9758 7877, www. thegoodolive.com.au)* stocks a wide range of edible delicacies.

Alternatively, choose a day's **wine tour** *(see box)* so that the driver can relax and enjoy tasting the wines at the cellar doors, and include a long lunch at one of the fine winery restaurants or cafés, such as those at **Leeuwin Estate**, **Xanadu**, **Palandri** and **Hamelin Bay**. Be aware that most winery restaurants are not open for dinner, so expect to eat back at Margaret River in the evening. If continuing by car beyond Western Australia, consider asking wineries to ship wine purchases home so they do not spoil in the boot of the car.

🚗 *Drive along Wallcliffe Rd to Caves Rd and turn left. The caves are all located off Caves Rd – Lake Cave is near Conto Rd, Jewel Cave and Mammoth Cave are near the intersection with Bussell Hwy (10).*

Margaret River Wines

This wine region owes its heritage to a 1965 report by Dr John Gladstone, who pinpointed the area's great potential, comparing its soils and cool climate to those in Bordeaux, France. Within two years a winery had been established, and now, over 40 years later, Margaret River has become one of the premier wine-growing regions of the world. Renowned wineries include **Leeuwin** and **Voyager estates** as well as **Chapman Grove Wines**. The region is especially noted for its Sauvignon Blanc, Semillon, Cabernet Sauvignon, and Shiraz wines. Many companies offer winery tours, such as **Margaret River Discovery Tours** *(04 3991 0064; www.margaretriverdiscovery.com.au)* and **Wine For Dudes** *(04 2777 4994; www.winefordudes.com)*. The **Margaret River Wine Festival** in the autumn *(www.margaretriverfestival. com; mid-Apr)* is a showcase for all things wine related.

EAT AND DRINK

AROUND YALLINGUP

Lamonts *moderate*
This well-regarded restaurant and winebar, located on the beachfront, is worth checking out for lunch or dinner. The short menu is packed full of local ingredients – try the marron (like freshwater crayfish). It has a deli serving breakfast and food to-go, as well as an excellent wine store.
Smiths Beach Rd, 6282; 08 9750 1299; www.lamonts.com.au; open daily

Cape Lodge *expensive*
This elegant lake-view restaurant is a stunner and the cuisine and service here is an equal match. Chef Tony Howell is obsessed with fresh produce – from the garden and the sea – and it shows in every expertly cooked dish. It is about 10 km (6 miles) down Caves Road towards Prevelly, on the left-hand side, opposite Driftwood Estate Winery.
3341 Caves Rd, 6280; 08 9755 6311; www.capelodge.com.au

MARGARET RIVER

Wino's *moderate*
As many winery restaurants do not serve dinner, Wino's is a great, unpretentious place to take some sustenance in the evening after a day of wine tasting. Enjoy fine tapas and modern-Australian cuisine.
85 Bussell Hwy, 6285; 08 9758 7155

Must Margaret River *moderate*
The Must team, well known for their buzzing Perth bistro, are a great fit here after taking this space over in early 2009. Their bistro classics go well with the big local wines and the service is extremely convivial.
107 Bussell Hwy, 6285; 08 9758 8877; www.must.com.au; noon–late

Below Orderly rows of vines at one of the Margaret River wineries

Eat and Drink: inexpensive under AU$60; moderate AU$60–AU$100; expensive over AU$100

WHERE TO STAY IN AUGUSTA

Augusta Hotel Motel *inexpensive*
This hotel-motel has simple self-contained cottages and rooms, most with excellent views of the ocean at Flinders Bay or the Blackwood River.
Blackwood Ave, 6290; 08 9758 1944; www.augustahotel.com.au

Clovelly Holiday Units *inexpensive*
These basic, self-contained holiday units provide a decent base for the attractions of the area.
78 Blackwood Avenue, 6290; 08 9758 1577; www.augustaclovellyunits.com.au

Surfing Mecca

The 130 km (81 miles) between capes Naturaliste and Leeuwin make up the Margaret River surfing region, home to some of the best surfing in Australia. Swells hit the coast here virtually year-round, although it is best in winter and spring. Margaret River's **Surfers Point** is the most well known and most accessible spot on the coast. It is also home to a pro surfing contest held annually in Mar–Apr. Keen surfers should pick up a surfing map of the region from the tourist office. Learning to surf is the most popular activity after wine tasting. **Margaret River Surf School** *(08 9757 1111; www.margaretriversurf school.com)* offers two-hour lessons and three-day courses while **Escape Safaris** *(08 9755 2488; www.escape safaris.com.au)* runs women-only surfing lessons.

⑧ Margaret River Caves
WA; 6285

The Margaret River region is home to nearly 350 limestone caves hidden beneath the Leeuwin-Naturaliste Ridge, created from water that has seeped through and eroded the porous limestone rock, forming stalactites and other fascinating formations. The most interesting is **Jewel Cave**, which has an impressive

6-m (20-ft) stalactite, while **Lake Cave** is the prettiest with illuminated stalactites and stalagmites reflected in its underground waters. Lake Cave is also the deepest with more than 300 steps down to the entrance. Only a handful of caves are open to the public and all except for **Mammoth Cave** must be visited on guided tours.

The peaceful hamlet of **Hamelin Bay**, a former timber port with a caravan park and bush cabins, is located on Caves Road on the way to Jewel and Mammoth Cave and is worth stopping off for. It has a lovely sheltered beach that is ideal for swimming, beachcombing and fishing. The shipwrecks offshore keep snorkellers and scuba divers happy.

🚗 *From Hamelin Bay, return to Caves Rd and turn right (past Jewel and Mammoth Cave turn-off) and on to the Bussell Hwy. Turn right to Augusta.*

Cape to Cape Walk

Walk a section of the 140-km (87-mile) Cape to Cape Walk, from Cape Naturaliste in the north down the coast to Cape Leeuwin in the south. Enjoy brilliant views of the coast and beaches, with panoramic whale look-outs on the way. All visitor centres in the region have maps detailing the full walk as well as shorter trails.

Below Idyllic Hamelin Bay, a safe and pleasant place to swim **Below right** The 39-m (128-ft) high Cape Leeuwin Lighthouse **Below left** Lookout at spectacular Cape Leeuwin on the Cape to Cape Walk

EAT AND DRINK IN AUGUSTA

The Colourpatch Café *inexpensive*
This sweet café on the riverbank proudly calls itself "the last eating house before the Antarctic", and the view from its balcony stretches out over the Blackwood River as it flows into the Southern Ocean, and on towards the South Pole. For the last meal, it offers a selection of locally sourced seafood such as battered Blackwood River whiting, flake (shark) with chips and salad, and a platter of fresh seafood.
98 Albany Terrace, 6290; 08 9758 1295; daily for lunch

⑨ Augusta
WA; 6290
The charming seaside holiday town of Augusta, at the mouth of the scenic Blackwood River, is popular for fishing, windsurfing and whale-watching. It is also one of the state's oldest settlements, after Albany and Perth, with several historic sights, including a limestone-encrusted Water Wheel constructed in 1895. The engaging **Augusta Historical Museum** *(Blackwood Ave; open am daily May–Aug & daily Sep–Apr)* has fascinating exhibitions on the history of the area, its pioneers and the many shipwrecks that occurred on the treacherous reef offshore. The **visitor centre** *(Ellis Street; 08 9758 0166; www.margaretriver.com; open daily)* can book accommodation, provide maps and arrange tours.
🚗 *From the Bussel Hwy, continue south through Augusta's town centre and follow Leeuwin Rd to Cape Leeuwin.*

Matthew Flinders
The name of Flinders is liberally scattered across the map of Australia, marking the spots charted by navigator Matthew Flinders. Flinders first sighted Cape Leeuwin on 6 December 1801 before going on to circumnavigate Australia. He encountered the French corvette *Le Géographe* and assisted its captain, Nicholas Baudin, at what came to be called Encounter Bay. Flinders' help to the French ship did not, however, prevent him being detained by the Governor of French Mauritius for more than six years (1803–1810) on his journey home (France and Britain were at war). His classic tale of Australian exploration, *A Voyage to Terra Australis*, was published a day before his death in 1814.

⑩ Cape Leeuwin
WA; 6290
Desolate, windswept Cape Leeuwin marks the end of the long-distance Cape to Cape Walk that starts at Cape Naturaliste *(see p229)*. Named after a ship by its Dutch captain in 1622, Cape Leeuwin (the name means Lioness) is home to the striking **Cape Leeuwin Lighthouse** *(open daily; regular tours)*, mainland Australia's tallest lighthouse, and one of its oldest. Built in 1895, it is still operational and is of great historical significance; it was here, on this spot, in 1801 that Matthew Flinders began the ambitious job of mapping Australia. From June to September, the cape is a good place to watch southern right and humpback whales migrate, while at other times of year visitors can hope to catch a glimpse of dolphins and fur seals. There is a popular café, gallery and shop at the entrance to the site, which marks the southwesterly tip of Australia.

Above The pleasant holiday resort of Augusta
Below Fishing boats and jetty at Augusta

Eat and Drink: inexpensive under AU$60; moderate AU$60–AU$100; expensive over AU$100

The Great Southern

Blackwood River Valley to Cape Arid National Park

Highlights

- **Cheese and wine**
  Enjoy Denmark's handmade cheeses, washed down by its excellent wines

- **Whale encounters**
  Learn about whales at Whale World in Torndirrup National Park and see them on tours from Albany

- **Easygoing Esperance**
  Stroll along the esplanade at Esperance, a popular seaside town

- **Wild, remote beaches**
  Delight in the sight of kangaroos on white-sand beaches at beautiful Cape Le Grand National Park

The Salmon Holes beach in Torndirrup National Park

The Great Southern

Western Australia's southwest region, known as the Great Southern, boasts some of the state's most beautiful scenery, from gently undulating hills and soaring forests of ancient karri and tingle trees, to bushland blanketed in wild flowers and snow-white sandy beaches lapped by aquamarine waters. This driving tour begins in the Blackwood River Valley, and then winds its way through the southwest's wooded national parks, and the Valley of the Giants, where visitors can walk through the tree tops, 40 m (131 ft) above ground, before taking in quaint Denmark. Next is the historic town of Albany, with its heritage architecture and whale-watching opportunities. From here, the drive carries on east to the laidback holiday town of Esperance and then to remote Cape Arid, stopping off to explore spectacular coastal national parks and pretty bays and inlets along the way. The highlight is nature at its most pristine and breathtaking.

Above Coastal scenery at Nanarup Beach, Two Peoples Bay Nature Reserve, see p243

Below Driving along Nanarup Beach, Two Peoples Bay Nature Reserve, see p243

Above Pretty wild flowers on West Beach, Esperance, *see p244*

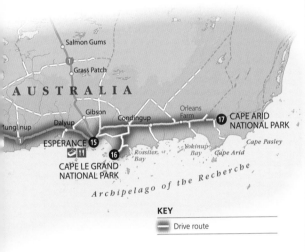

KEY

— Drive route

ACTIVITIES

Paddle a canoe through the delightful Blackwood River Valley

Climb the tallest fire lookout in the world in Pemberton

Explore the treetops on a walkway in the Valley of the Giants

Learn how to surf the great waves on the spectacular beaches at Denmark

Taste delicious gourmet regional produce and excellent wines on the Shadforth Scenic Drive and in the Mount Barker region

Hike the challenging trails through the wild flowers in Porongurup National Park or the Stirling Range

Watch dolphins and humpback and southern right whales on their annual migration along the coast at Bremer Bay

Observe the sea lions at Hopetoun, Ravensthorpe

Walk the trails on the peaks and headlands of the Cape Le Grand and Cape Arid national parks

PLAN YOUR DRIVE

Start/finish: Blackwood River Valley to Cape Arid National Park.

Number of days: 5 days, including a day travelling from Pemberton to Denmark, allowing time to explore the forests, a day in Albany, a day to explore Torndirrup National Park and Two Peoples Bay Nature Reserve, a day in Esperance and a day exploring Cape Le Grand National Park.

Distance: Approx. 1,476 km (930 miles).

Road conditions: Good sealed roads with some 2WD-accessible dirt roads in the national parks and wine region. Shadforth Scenic Drive is partly unsealed and Red Gum Pass in the Stirling Range National Park is entirely unsealed. Excellent signposting.

When to go: Spring, summer and autumn (Sep–May) are the best times to go, when the weather is pleasant. Summer (Dec–Feb) is when the region is at its very best, but accommodation at holiday towns such as Esperance and Albany is booked out well in advance from Christmas through to the end of Jan for the school holidays. Winters can be chilly.

Opening times: Shops and cafés open 9:30am–5pm (bakeries open earlier) Mon–Fri and until noon Sat. Most wineries shut by 5pm; their restaurants only open for lunch. Restaurants in towns open for dinner from 6pm, last orders often by 8:30pm.

Main market days: Bridgetown: River Park markets, alternate Sun; Albany: Farmers' Market, Sat.

Shopping: Buy splendid Mount Barker wines, gourmet produce such as fine cheeses, honeys, preserves and fudge, along with fine hand-carved wood products in Pemberton.

Major festivals: Pemberton area: marron fishing & cherry season, Dec–Feb; salmon fishing, Mar–Apr; Mount Barker: Grapes & Gallops Festival, Jan; wild flower season, Aug–Nov; Wild flower Celebration, Sep-Oct; Albany: Taste Great Southern Festival, Feb–Mar; Festival of the Sea, Apr; Southern Art and Craft Trail, Sep-Oct.

Above Towering eucalyptus trunk in the forests around Walpole

GETTING TO THE BLACKWOOD RIVER VALLEY

From Perth take Southwestern Hwy to Bunbury and on to Bridgetown. From Augusta, take Bussell Hwy north and Brockman Hwy east to Nannup.

VISITING PEMBERTON

Visitor Information
Information about the Southern Forests with maps, tours and activities such as walking trails, horseriding, fly-fishing and canoe/bike rental.
Brockman St, 6260; 08 9776 1133; www.pembertonvisitor.com.au

WHERE TO STAY

PEMBERTON

Old Picture Theatre *moderate*
Built in 1929, this building has been converted into a set of comfortable apartments, each with extensive living areas, kitchen and original features.
Cnr Ellis & Guppy St, 6260; 08 9776 1513; www.oldpicturetheatre.com.au

AROUND PEMBERTON

Stonebarn *expensive*
A true retreat, this luxurious forested barn offers personal service and great cuisine.
Off Telephone Rd, near where South-west Hwy (1) crosses Warren River; 08 9773 1002; www.stonebarn.com.au

Other options
Pump Hill *(Pump Hill Road; 08 9776 1379; www.pumphill.com.au)* has cozy cottages on a working farm in Pemberton. **Treenbrook Cottages** *(2 km/1 mile beyond Pemberton–Northcliffe Rd turn-off on Vasse Hwy (10) towards Nannup; 08 9776 1638; www. treenbrook.com.au)* have open fireplaces and are nestled among a towering karri forest.

① Blackwood River Valley
Western Australia (WA)

The riverside logging towns of Nannup and Bridgetown in the Blackwood River Valley are easily reached either from Augusta *(see p233)* or direct from Perth *(see pp206–207)* and are linked by scenic roads. **Nannup**, 60 km (37 miles) southeast of Busselton, is idyllically set among gentle wooded hills. Stop at the **visitor centre** *(4 Brockman St, 6275; 08 9756 1211; www.nannupwa.com.au)* for information on the Blackwood River.
Blackwood Canoeing *(08 9756 1209; www.blackwoodrivercanoeing.com)* offers self-guided canoe trips. From Nannup, follow Kearney Street into pretty Brockman Highway 44 km (28 miles) east to **Bridgetown**. It is renowned for its superb produce, especially marron (crayfish) and olive oil, and Bridgetown **visitor centre** *(Hampton St, 6255; 08 9761 1740; www.bridgetown.com.au)* has plenty of good information on local producers. The main street is worth exploring to browse its craft shops and enjoy a Devonshire cream tea.

🚗 *From Bridgetown, head south on Southwestern Hwy (1), turning right on Vasse Hwy (10) to Pemberton.*

② Pemberton
WA; 6260

Set amid lush green farmland and lofty 400-year-old forests, Pemberton has a tiny main road lined with quaint cafés, craft shops and art galleries, and the surrounding countryside is home to boutique wineries, trout farms and walking trails. Take a stroll through the town centre and time your walk to

Below Road through the lofty forest surrounds of Walpole

Tall Timber Country

The area between the Margaret River region and Albany, known as Tall Timber Country, is home to majestic karri forests and arboreal attractions such as the towering **Gloucester Tree** and the treetops walk in the **Valley of the Giants**. Logging towns, such as Pemberton and Manjimup, have rebuilt their economies around tree plantations and nature tourism since tree clearing was reduced in 2001. Now they offer the chance to experience some of the planet's last temperate old-growth forest while providing opportunities for scenic drives, walks and canoeing.

allow a ride on the **old diesel tram** *(www.pemtram.com.au; departs 10:45am & 2pm)* through the forest from Pemberton to Warren Bridge, which rattles over the rickety timber bridges that span trickling brooks along the old logging railway.

At the **Pemberton Visitor Centre** *(08 9776 1133; www.pembertonvisitor. com.au)*, explore the **Karri Forest Discovery Centre** *(open daily)*, which boasts an excellent interactive exhibition on the local environment and its fauna and flora and is an essential stop before heading into the forests. In the same building, the compelling **Pioneer Museum** *(open daily)* has a life-size settlers' hut and artifacts from the pioneering period, along with engaging photographs and other memorabilia.

Don't forget to stop at the **Gold 'n' Grape Gallery** *(Cnr Vasse Hwy & Fox Rd; 08 9776 0304; www.goldngrape.com.au)*,

Where to Stay: inexpensive under AU$150; moderate AU$150–AU$250; expensive over AU$250

Above left Café advertising marron, Pemberton **Above right** Weather-boarded church at Pemberton

which offers a stunning range of locally crafted items: carvings, furniture made from reclaimed wood, glassware and jewellery.

🚗 *Gloucester Tree is in Gloucester National Park, 3 km (2 miles) from Pemberton; follow the signs left off Vasse Hwy (10) on the way into town.*

③ Gloucester Tree
WA; 6260

The 61-m (200-ft) tall Gloucester Tree, just southeast of Pemberton, is the area's top attractions. A spiral of horizontal stakes form stairs up to a platform on what is the world's tallest fire lookout tree. While most people visit with the intention of scaling the tree, only a few courageous people actually do it. If you are scared of heights, do not attempt the climb; instead, enjoy the surrounding karri woodlands by driving beneath the shaded canopies or strolling the many walking trails.

🚗 *Return to Vasse Hwy (10) and retrace route 13 km (8 miles) to Southwestern Hwy (1). Turn right and drive 104 km (65 miles) to Walpole.*

④ Walpole
WA; 6398

While there is little to see at Walpole itself, it is set in a pretty location and makes a good base for exploring the lofty forests, sheltered bays, tranquil inlets and ocean lookouts around town. On the South Coast Highway (1), on the approach into town, the **Walpole-Nornalup Visitor Centre** *(open daily; South Coast Hwy; 08 9840 1111; www.walpole.com.au)* is a good place to pick up information about scenic drives and walks.

   If there is only time to visit one beach, then make it the splendid,

windswept white sand of **Conspicuous Beach**. This is relatively accessible via a track 6 km (4 miles) west of town.

🚗 *Continue driving east along what is now the South Coast Hwy (1) to the left turn for the Valley of the Giants.*

⑤ Valley of the Giants
South Coast Highway, WA

The ancient forest of colossal karri and tingle trees that comprises the Valley of the Giants is one of the region's most popular attractions and the **Tree Top Walk** *(open daily; 08 9840 8263)* is a must-do activity. This impressive feat of engineering consists of a 600-m (1,968-ft) long wheelchair-accessible walkway, which rises to a height of 40 m (131 ft) above the forest floor. While the walkway is very safe, those with a fear of heights may be made anxious by the swaying (it is closed in high winds) and might prefer to follow the **Ancient Empire Walkway** along the forest floor.

🚗 *Return to the South Coast Hwy (1), and continue driving 58 km (35 miles) east to Denmark.*

Elevated Eucalypts

The massive trees seen on the **Tree Top Walk** and in the **Ancient Empire** are mostly different types of eucalyptus trees, growing as high as 30–80 m (100–260 ft). Red tingle *(Eucalyptus jacksonii)* and karri *(Eucalyptus diversicolor)* are the most common here as well as yellow tingle *(Eucalyptus guilfoylei)* and marri *(Corymbia calophylla)*. The walk on the forest floor through the Ancient Empire heads through a grove of veteran tingle trees, which are unique to this area. Some of these can grow to 70 m (230 ft), with a diameter of 4.5 m (15 ft).

EAT AND DRINK

BLACKWOOD RIVER VALLEY

The Barking Cow *inexpensive*
The café at this deli serves gourmet sandwiches, home-made breads, salads and smoothies – it is a good place to stock up for a picnic too.
88a Hampton St, Bridgetown, 6255; 08 9761 4619

Blackwood Bistro *moderate*
Dine al fresco amid beautiful gardens, or by the cozy fire inside, at this winery restaurant overlooking a lake in Nannup. Hearty breakfasts, home-style lunches and sumptuous afternoon teas are on offer through the day – followed by a leisurely game of boules or a wine tasting at the cellar door.
Kearney St, Nannup, 6275; 08 9756 0077; closed Mon–Wed

PEMBERTON

King Trout Restaurant & Marron Farm *moderate*
It is pretty clear what is on the menu here and while everyone is familiar with trout, marron is a delicious farmed crustacean that is just like freshwater crayfish. If so inclined visitors can even catch their own!
Cnr Northcliffe & Old Vasse Rd, 6260; 08 9776 1352; phone ahead to book for dinner

Jarrah Jacks *moderate*
Beer connoisseurs will love Jarrah Jacks, where they can enjoy exquisite home-brewed beers with a light meal prepared with fresh local produce. For oenophiles, there are also award-winning regional wines on offer.
Kemp Rd, 6260; 0427 760 200; www.jarrahjacks.com.au

Eat and Drink: inexpensive under AU$60; moderate AU$60–AU$100; expensive over AU$100

VISITING DENMARK AND MOUNT BARKER

For winery maps and national park permits, stop off at **Denmark Visitor Centre** (73 South Coast Hwy, Cnr Ocean Beach Rd, 6333; 08 9848 2055; www.denmark.com.au; open daily) or **Mount Barker Visitor Centre** (Albany Hwy, 6324; 08 9851 1163; www.mountbarkertourismwa.com.au).

MOUNT BARKER WINERIES

Ferngrove: 278 Ferngrove Road, Frankland River, 6396; 08 9855 2378; www.ferngrove.com.au
Galafrey Wines: 432 Quangellup Road, Mount Barker, 6324; 08 9851 2022; www.galafreywines.com.au
Plantagenet Wines: Lot 45, Albany Hwy, Mount Barker, 6324; 08 9851 3111; www.plantagenetwines.com
Poacher's Ridge: 1630 Spencer Road, Mount Barker, 6324; 08 9857 6066; www.prv.com.au

WHERE TO STAY IN DENMARK

Denmark Waterfront moderate
This offers a range of accommodation from cottages to studio apartments, some with water views. All have tea/coffee facilities and ensuite bathrooms.
63 Inlet Drive, 6333; 08 9848 1147; www.denmarkwaterfront.com.au

Denmark Observatory Resort moderate
Stylish resort in a splendid location with great views. The plush, Australian-style bungalows and studios have mod-cons and spa baths. There are cheaper caravan and RV bays, too.
427 Mt Shadforth Rd, 6333; 08 9848 2233

Below left The pretty Catholic St Mary's Church in Denmark **Below right** The Denmark Heritage Rail Bridge

6 Denmark
WA; 6333

Located on the tranquil Denmark River, this little town is a lovely place to browse among the arts and craft shops and galleries and enjoy lunch at a relaxing café. For a good picnic spot on the riverbank, follow the river south (along Hollings Drive) to the **Denmark Heritage Rail Bridge**. From the town centre, Ocean Beach Road leads to the river mouth, where fishermen cast their lines into the calm lagoon of Wilson Inlet. At the end of the road, **Ocean Beach** boasts magnificent views across Ratcliffe Bay and is a popular spot for learning to surf. **South Coast Surfing** (08 9848 2814) is one of the best of Denmark's surfing schools, offering one-to-one and group lessons, and renting surfboards and wetsuits.

When the attractions of the coast begin to pall, it is time to head up into the hills above Denmark. The 39-km (24-mile) partly unsealed **Shadforth Scenic Drive** snakes through some of the region's most attractive scenery, passing wineries and small food producers. Get a map from the visitor centre and follow the signs (west along Mount Shadforth Road, north on Macleod Road and east down Scotsdale Road back into Denmark), stopping to taste and buy wine, cheese and honey. There are myriad animal farms along the way where the animals can be petted for a fee or wildlife such as koalas and emus photographed.

🚗 Head east, following signs down South Coast Hwy (1) towards Mt Barker. Turn left onto Mt Barker Rd.

The Great Southern

Stretching from Denmark all the way to Esperance, the area known as "The Great Southern" has a windswept coastline that is dotted with sheltered white-sand coves, separated by rugged granite headlands. In stark contrast, the inland area consists of idyllic countryside – rolling vineyards, thick forests and natural bushland blanketed with wild flowers. It is also famed for its pretty hamlets filled with craft shops and galleries, the wine-making region around Mount Barker and the beautiful Porongurup and Stirling Range national parks.

7 Mount Barker
WA; 6324

The quiet country town of Mount Barker boasts a few historic buildings, including the convict-built **Old Police Station** (1868), now a museum (08 9848 1781), **St Werburgh's Chapel**, built in 1872 and the Plantagenet Hotel and Motel. Try an award-winning home-made pie at **Mount Barker Country Bakery** (Lowood Rd), but the reason most people visit is to taste the wines at the cellar doors of some of Western Australia's finest wineries, including **Plantagenet**, **Galafrey Wines**, **Ferngrove**, and **Poacher's Ridge** (see left). The area is best known for its Riesling, planted in the late 1970s, and its more recent Chardonnay, as well as its red Cabernet Sauvignon and Pinot Noir.

🚗 From Lowood Rd, cross the railway track and turn right onto Albany Hwy (30) and left on Mt Barker–Porongurup Rd for 17 km (11 miles) to Porongurup National Park.

Where to Stay: inexpensive under AU$150; moderate AU$150–AU$250; expensive over AU$250

Porongurup National Park
Mt Barker–Porongurup Rd, WA

One of the world's oldest volcanic formations, at 1,100 million years old, the granite Porongurup mountain range lies in **Porongurup National Park**. The summits of a dozen or so striking domes and peaks – the highest reaching 670 m (2,200 ft) – protrude from a 12-km (7-mile) long ridge that offers up countless walking and picnicking opportunities with spectacular views. Walks range from a short stroll to **Tree in a Rock**, close to the northern entrance of the park, to more challenging half-day hikes, including a walk to **Devils Slide** (671 m/2,200 ft) via **Nancy** and **Hayward Peaks**. The park is also rightly famous for its huge numbers of wild flowers (there are over 750 species) and is popular with bird-watchers.

🚗 Continue southeast along Mt Barker–Porongurup Rd to Chester Pass Rd, and turn left (north) into Stirling Range National Park.

Stirling Range National Park
WA; 6338

On the drive north on Chester Pass Road, the jagged high peaks of the 65-km (40-mile), Stirling Range National Park will loom into view, often wreathed in clouds. Like Porongurup, Stirling Range is famed for its stunning wild flowers (in bloom Aug–Dec). Here, too, there are great walking opportunities. Try the gruelling 3-hour hike to **Bluff Knoll** (1,095 m/3,520 ft), or the similarly tough 3-hour climb to **Toolbrunup Peak** (1,052 m/3,592 ft). For a shorter walk, try the hike to **Talyuberlup** (783 m/2,569 ft) from the park's camp site, with some stunning views. Or try the scenic drive along the unsealed 45-km (28-mile) track that winds through the peaks to **Red Gum Pass**.

🚗 From Red Gum Pass, follow signs back to Albany Hwy (30) and turn left to Mount Barker. Continue to Albany.

Above left The historic Plantagenet Hotel and Motel, Mount Barker **Above right** Vineyards near Mount Barker **Below** Weathered roadside store in Mount Barker

VISITING STIRLING RANGE NATIONAL PARK

Check road conditions and pick up maps and a national park permit from the tourist office in Mount Barker or Denmark (see left).

EAT AND DRINK IN DENMARK

McSweeneys Gourmet Café
inexpensive
There are few options for eating out in Denmark, so a delicious breakfast or lunch at McSweeneys is a must.
5b Strickland St, 6333; 08 9848 2362

Southern End *moderate*
The best restaurant in the area is found in the Denmark Observatory Resort. Staff are friendly and the modern versions of classic bistro-style dishes are delicious.
427 Mt Shadforth Rd, 6333; 08 9848 2600

Flower Power

The Stirling Range is extremely important for wild flowers – the area alone is home to more plant species than the entire British Isles, and 87 of them occur nowhere else on Earth. With 123 orchid species, the Stirling Range also contains over one third of all known WA orchids. While there is always interesting plant life to see here, the wild flowers are in bloom Aug–Dec, with Sep and Nov generally the best months, as the southwest warms up before summer.

Above left Yellow wild flowers at Two Peoples Bay Nature Reserve **Above right** Sheltered swimming area, Two Peoples Bay

VISITING ALBANY AND TORNDIRRUP NATIONAL PARK

Albany Tourist Information Centre
Old Railway Station, Proudlove Parade, Albany, 6330; 08 98419290; www.albanytourist.com.au

Whale Watching
Albany Whale Tours *(0408 451 068; www.albanywhaletours.com.au; Jun–Oct)* offer 3-hour whale watching cruises to King George Sound. **Silver Star Cruises** *(0428 429 876; www.whales. com.au; Jun–Oct)* offer whale watching and cruises to historic whaling sights.

Torndirrup National Park
www.dec.wa.gov.au

WHERE TO STAY IN ALBANY

Albany Foreshore Guest House
inexpensive
This historic guesthouse with harbour views has been renovated as a five-room B&B. An easy stroll to points of interest, with a cozy guest lounge.
86 Stirling Terrace, 6330; 08 9842 8324; www.albanyforeshoreguest house.com.au

Dog Rock Motel *moderate*
A quality motel with modern rooms, it is only a few minutes walk from the town centre and has a very good restaurant.
303 Middleton Rd, 6330; 08 9845 7200; www.dogrockmotel.com.au

My Place Colonial Accommodation
moderate
With charming early 1900s rooms, this place also offers mod cons.
47–61 Grey Street East, 6330; 08 9842 3242; www.myplace.com.au

Right The vast expanse of sandy beach at Two Peoples Bay

🔟 Albany
WA; 6330
Western Australia's first settlement, in 1826, Albany is a popular holiday town. Its natural harbour, where the **Princess Royal Fortress** *(Forts Rd; open daily)* was built in 1893, became a strategic port on the route between England and Botany Bay. Take the road around the headland to Albany's main bay, **Middleton Beach,** with views of the harbour and the restored fortress.

Many of Albany's main sights are located on the foreshore, the site of the first settlement. The **Amity** *(open daily; 08 9841 5403)* is a replica of the ship that brought 60 settlers here in 1826 after six months at sea. The **Western Australian Museum - Albany** *(open daily; 08 9841 4844)* has fascinating displays of the town's early history, as well as exhibits on Aboriginal bush tucker and medicine. Dating to 1852, the **Old Gaol & Convict Museum** *(open daily; 08 9841 6174)* is one of Australia's oldest colonial buildings.

🚗 *Follow Princess Royal Drive west around the lagoon, turning left over the railway track into Frenchman Bay Rd; follow signs to Torndirrup National Pk.*

⓫ Torndirrup National Park
Frenchman Bay Rd, WA
Torndirrup National Park is home to a string of gorgeous bays and coves, such as calm **Shoal Bay** and sheltered **Frenchman Bay**, popular swimming spots on the northern side of the peninsula *(left off Frenchman Bay Road)*. Some of the coast's most dramatic cliffs and wild beaches can be found on the southern side of the peninsula, at **Cable Beach** *(right off Frenchman Bay Road)* and the **Salmon Holes** *(right off Frenchman Bay Road, near the end)*. There are spectacular coastal views from **Stony Hill** *(also right off Frenchman Bay Road)* and **Isthmus Hill** *(at the end of Frenchman Bay Road)*. From the latter, there is an invigorating 4-km (2-mile) walk to **Bald Head** at the end of the Flinders Peninsula. Many people come to see the **Blowholes** *(right off Frenchman Bay Road)* and natural attractions of the **Gap** and **Natural Bridge** *(right off Frenchman Bay Road)*. Take extreme care here as people have slipped to their deaths or been swept out to sea by freak waves.

Located in Australia's last whaling station, which ceased operations in 1978, **Whale World** *(at end of Frenchman Bay Road; open daily; 08 9844 4021; www. whaleworld.org)* is dedicated to the whales that were once hunted here.

🚗 *Return back to Princess Royal Drive, head right then left up York St, straight over into Lockyer Ave, which becomes Ulster Rd and then Lower King Rd. This leads to Two Peoples Bay Rd and Two Peoples Bay Nature Reserve.*

Left The spectacular coastline and white sandy beaches at Torndirrup National Park

⑫ Two Peoples Bay Nature Reserve

Two Peoples Bay Rd, WA

The coastal wilderness of Two Peoples Bay boasts beautiful wind-swept beaches punctuated by wild rocky points. From Two Peoples Bay Road, Nanarup Road leads to **Nanarup Beach**, a popular spot for beach fishing. Backtrack to Two Peoples Bay Road leading to Two Peoples Bay, one of Western Australia's most gorgeous beaches, backed by a lovely shady camping area, from where there is a pleasant nature trail around the headland to **Little Beach**, known for its splendid white sands and clear waters. A protected area, it is home to a few threatened animal species including the rare noisy scrub bird, along with small marsupials, such as quokkas and quendas.

🚗 *Backtrack along Two Peoples Bay Rd, turn off right along Hunton Rd, turn right on Hassel Hwy then the South Coast Hwy (1). At Boxwood Hill, turn right on Borden–Bremer Rd to Bremer Bay.*

⑬ Bremer Bay

WA; 6338

Located at the mouth of the Bremer River, beautiful Bremer Bay is a tiny seaside hamlet surrounded by heath-covered headlands and fringed by white sand. Its serene setting and fine beach make it a popular holiday spot. Its limited accommodation, however, ensures it can never get too crowded. Situated on the Wellstead Estuary, named after John Wellstead, the area's first settler, it offers the usual water-based activities, such as swimming, surfing, snorkelling and fishing. The sheltered **main beach** is an easy walk from the centre. Dolphins can be spotted all year, but from Jul–Nov, whales like to rest here on their long journey across the southern coast.

🚗 *From Bremer Bay, backtrack to the South Coast Hwy (1) and turn right for 146 km (91 miles) to Ravensthorpe.*

⑭ Ravensthorpe

WA; 6346

Shaded by stately salmon gums *(Eucalyptus salmonophloia)*, so-called for their salmon-pink bark, the small town of Ravensthorpe has a rich mining heritage, evident in its old buildings, particularly the **Palace Hotel** (1907) and **Dance Cottage**. Set among varied landscapes, from rocky hills and valleys to stark plains and fertile farmland, the area boasts scenic drives and walks with opportunities to stroll among the wild flowers. Pick up information and maps from the **visitor centre** *(Morgans St; 08 9838 1277; www.ravensthorpe.wa.gov.au)* along with maps for the **Railway Heritage Walk Trails** *(www.railtrails.org.au)*. Head to **Hopetoun**, on the coast, to visit the **Ocean Discovery Centre & The Deck** *(open daily Sep–May; Veal St, 6348; 08 9838 3303; www.gotothedeck.com.au)* and see the sea lions offshore at Seal Island.

🚗 *Follow South Coast Hwy for 184 km (114 miles), turn right at Harbour Rd, left on Pink Lake Rd to centre of Esperance.*

Below The Natural Bridge rock formation at Torndirrup National Park

Eat and Drink: inexpensive under AU$60; moderate AU$60–AU$100; expensive over AU$100

Above left The wonderful open beach at Esperance **Above right** A building in the Historic Museum Village, Esperance

VISITING ESPERANCE AND THE NATIONAL PARKS

Esperance Visitor Centre
Information and maps for drives and walks, to book accommodation and tours and to rent bicycles.
Historic Museum Village, Dempster St, 6430; closed Wed & Sun pm; 08 9083 1555; www.visitesperance.com

National Parks Office
The DEC office in Esperance has information on Cape Le Grand and Cape Arid national parks and sells park permits.
92 Dempster St, Esperance, 6430; 08 9083 2100; www.dec.wa.gov.au

WHERE TO STAY IN ESPERANCE

Esperance Clearwater Motel Apartments *moderate*
These family-owned apartments have excellent facilities, including massive flat-screen TVs and broadband internet, and are in a good location, walking distance from the centre of town.
1A William St, 6430; 08 9071 3587; www.clearwatermotel.com.au

Island View Apartments
moderate–expensive
These stylish one-, two- and three-bedroom self-contained apartments are great for a stay of a few days, with good kitchens, laundries, balcony barbecues, and views of the Esplanade and sea. Bikes are available to hire.
14–15 The Esplanade, 6430; 08 9072 0044; www.esperanceapartments. com.au

⑮ Esperance
WA; 6450

There are few more rewarding places to rest for a few days than the tranquil seaside town of Esperance, a favourite summer holiday spot for many Western Australians. A Dutch vessel first passed through the archipelago in 1627, but it was two French ships, *L'Esperance* and *Recherche*, which sought shelter here in 1792, that are credited with the European discovery of the area.

Esperance flourished as a supply port during the region's Gold Rush around 1895, and it prospered once again after World War II, when a way of making its salty soil fertile was discovered.

Start exploring on Esperance's main road, Dempster Street, at the visitor

> **WARNING**
> Lives have been lost in this area even on calm days.
>
> **DANGER**

Sign about the dangers of the sea, Esperance

centre, and pick up a Heritage Walk booklet explaining the history of the buildings at **Museum Village** *(open daily)*. This is a handful of heritage cottages converted into craft shops, galleries and cafés. One block away, on James Street, **Esperance Museum** *(open daily pm)* is located in a former railway goods shed and displays memorabilia charting the town's history. A must-do activity is a stroll along the Norfolk pine-lined esplanade to visit **Sammy the Seal**, under the jetty.

Pay attention to signs warning against swimming. Freak waves, currents and rips can be dangerous, even if the beach looks harmless enough.

🚗 *Follow The Esplanade, turning right into Norseman Rd then right onto Fisheries Rd. Continue for 40 km (25 miles) before turning right onto Ovens Rd, then Merivale Rd, then Cape Le Grand Rd to Le Grand Beach.*

Exploring Esperance
Esperance has a number of excellent walks and drives. The **Kepwari Wetland Walk Trail** (3.6 km/2 miles) is a 5-minute drive from town and is lined with interpretative displays on the wetlands environment. Rent a bike or drive the scenic **Great Ocean Drive** (40 km/25 mile) loop west of Esperance, which leads to the **Rotary Lookout** for coastal vistas; pictures-que **Twilight Cove**, a sheltered spot that is considered one of the most beautiful beaches on the southern coast; **Observation Point Lookout**, from where there are sweeping views of the windswept coast, and a naturist beach; and, inland from here, the **Pink Lake**, which gets its extraordinary colour from the algae *Dunaliella salina*, which can withstand high levels of salt.

Above One of Esperance's stars, Sammy the Seal, often found under the jetty

16 Cape Le Grand National Park
Off South Coast Highway, WA

For many visitors to Western Australia, a visit to Cape Le Grand National Park, with its spectacular wild coastline and dazzling white sandy beaches, is the highlight of their trip. First stop at the end of Cape Le Grand Road is scenic **Le Grand Beach**. Backtrack a little, turn right and right again down Hellfire Road to tranquil **Hellfire Bay**. Back inland, **Frenchman's Peak** (262 m/860 ft) offers a pleasant hike to the summit with great views. There is a more challenging walk (3 hours) from here back to Le Grand Beach and an easier walk (2 hours) east to **Thistle Cove**. Alternatively, visitors can drive on along Lucky Bay Road to Thistle Cove, site of the state's most beguiling beach, **Lucky Bay**, which is famous for its beach-loving kangaroos. The beach is also a great spot for swimming, snorkelling and canoeing, and there is a small camping ground here with good facilities. Another 6 km (4 miles) east is the wide expanse of **Rossiter Bay**.

🚗 *Backtrack along Cape Le Grand Rd and turn right at Merivale Rd then left at Orleans Bay Rd and right at Fisheries Rd for 68 km (42 miles).*

17 Cape Arid National Park
WA

Situated on the western edge of the Great Australian Bight coastline (see p251), remote Cape Arid National Park boasts yet more breathtakingly beautiful white sandy beaches. A 4WD vehicle is required to explore the park, but the rewards are the chance to spot southern right whales, which can be seen from here late winter to spring,

when an abundance of wild flowers blanket the heath-covered headlands. The park also boasts some excellent walking trails, including the **Len Otte Nature Trail** (1 hour) with spectacular views over the park; **Tagon Coastal Walk** (4 hours) with more stunning coastal views and the opportunity to see whales in season; **Boolenup Walk** (2 hours), which leads to the brackish Lake Boolenup; and **Mount Ragged Walk** (3 hours), a harder hike up to the top of Tower Peak, from where fit walkers will be rewarded with panoramic coastal vistas. Make sure to take extra care when walking along this stretch of coastline, as there are occasional unpredictable king waves that have been known to sweep people away from the exposed shores.

Above left Pretty wild flowers near the coast in Cape Le Grand National Park **Top right** Purple coastal wild flowers **Above right** Kangaroo, a frequent visitor to the beaches at Cape Le Grand National Park

EAT AND DRINK IN ESPERANCE

Loose Goose *moderate*
This popular restaurant is a friendly, family-run concern, serving up hefty portions of brilliant local seafood and French-inspired cuisine.
9A Andrew St, 6450; 08 9071 2320; dinner only

Taylor Street Jetty Café-Restaurant *moderate*
Adjacent to the Taylor Street Jetty, this café and restaurant serves up food from morning to night, from big breakfasts to pasta and seafood dinners.
Taylor St Jetty, 6450; 08 9071 4317

The Coastal Trail

The 15-km (9-mile) Coastal Trail along the beaches and headlands of the Cape Le Grand National Park takes 6–8 hours in total. However, it can be broken up into shorter walks, including **Le Grand Beach to Hellfire Bay** (2–3 hrs, hard); **Hellfire Bay to Thistle Cove** (2 hrs, hard); **Thistle Cove to Lucky Bay** (40 mins, easy); and **Lucky Bay to Rossiter Bay** (2–3 hrs, moderate). The **Le Grand Heritage Trail** is an easy 40-minute walk. Pick up a brochure detailing the trails from the Esperance visitor centre.

Above A sweeping bay at Cape Le Grand National Park

Eat and Drink: inexpensive under AU$60; moderate AU$60–AU$100; expensive over AU$100

The Nullarbor Crossing

Norseman to Port Augusta

Highlights

- **Extreme isolation**
  Experience the silence of the Nullarbor Plain on Australia's famous road trip

- **Dramatic scenery**
  Take in the spectacular cliffs and rugged, rocky coastline of the Great Australian Bight

- **Sublime seafood**
  Savour the sea's bounty on the Eyre Peninsula, from oysters at Coffin Bay to scallops at Port Lincoln

- **Outback history**
  Learn about pioneers and Aboriginal culture at Wadlata Outback Centre

- **Arid gardens**
  Appreciate unique desert flora on a walk among the sand dunes at the Australian Arid Lands Botanic Garden

Murphys Haystacks: surreal granite rocks on the way to Point Labatt

The Nullarbor Crossing

Driving the incredibly straight roads across the vast arid expanses of the Nullarbor Plain – from Western to South Australia – is the ultimate Australian road trip. Few Australian road movies are made without setting a sequence here. It is a rite of passage and something every Australian dreams of doing once in their lifetime. Whether driving across the plain in two long, exhausting days or a more leisurely three, be sure to collect an "I've crossed the Nullarbor" certificate from the visitor centres at Norseman or Ceduna. While the drive is short on sights, there is stunning scenery along the way, including spectacular cliffs rearing from the sea and the poignant ruins of a telegraph station buried by shifting sands. However, the most pleasure is gained from the car, admiring the changing forms and colours of the landscapes, spotting the wildlife, from kangaroos to eagles, and the daily magic of sunrises and sunsets. Visitors should reward themselves at the end of the journey with a feast of fresh seafood overlooking a stunning sandy beach somewhere on the Eyre Peninsula.

Above Old-fashioned petrol pumps on the Nullarbor Plain, *see p251*

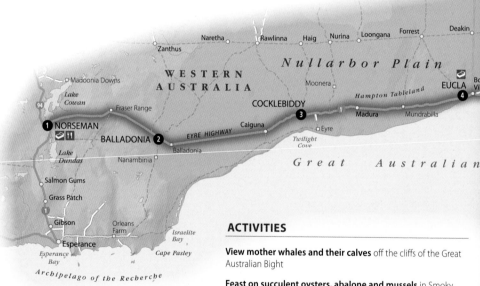

ACTIVITIES

View mother whales and their calves off the cliffs of the Great Australian Bight

Feast on succulent oysters, abalone and mussels in Smoky Bay, Streaky Bay and the Eyre Peninsula

Watch the sea lions frolicking on the beach at Point Labatt or do some dolphin-spotting at Tumby Bay

Take a hike and see the brush-tailed bettongs and grey kangaroos in the wildlife-rich Venus Conservation Park, Venus Bay

Dive with deadly great white sharks on a cage-diving trip from Port Lincoln

Spot desert flora and abundant birdlife on dune walking trails at the Australian Arid Lands Botanic Park, Port Augusta

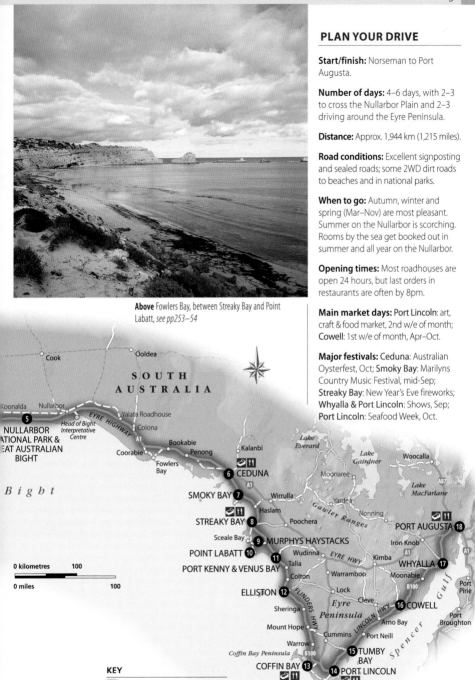

Above Fowlers Bay, between Streaky Bay and Point Labatt, *see pp253–54*

PLAN YOUR DRIVE

Start/finish: Norseman to Port Augusta.

Number of days: 4–6 days, with 2–3 to cross the Nullarbor Plain and 2–3 driving around the Eyre Peninsula.

Distance: Approx. 1,944 km (1,215 miles).

Road conditions: Excellent signposting and sealed roads; some 2WD dirt roads to beaches and in national parks.

When to go: Autumn, winter and spring (Mar–Nov) are most pleasant. Summer on the Nullarbor is scorching. Rooms by the sea get booked out in summer and all year on the Nullarbor.

Opening times: Most roadhouses are open 24 hours, but last orders in restaurants are often by 8pm.

Main market days: Port Lincoln: art, craft & food market, 2nd w/e of month; **Cowell:** 1st w/e of month, Apr–Oct.

Major festivals: Ceduna: Australian Oysterfest, Oct; **Smoky Bay:** Marilyns Country Music Festival, mid-Sep; **Streaky Bay:** New Year's Eve fireworks; **Whyalla & Port Lincoln:** Shows, Sep; **Port Lincoln:** Seafood Week, Oct.

Above left Corrugated iron camel sculptures at Norseman **Above right** The ruins of the Old Telegraph Station at Eucla

VISITING NORSEMAN

Visitor Information
Welcome Park, 68 Roberts St, 6443; 08 9039 1071; www.norseman.info

WHERE TO STAY

There are few settlements on the Nullarbor Plain, so accommodation is limited to motels, caravan parks and camp sites attached to roadhouses.

NORSEMAN
Art Deco Railway Hotel-Motel *inexpensive*
Built in 1937, during the boom years, this offers budget accommodation as well as more upmarket en suite rooms. It also has a restaurant serving good pub fare for guests on request.
106 Roberts St, 6443; 08 9039 0003

Other options on the road
At Balladonia, the **Balladonia Hotel Motel** *inexpensive* (08 9039 3453) has basic rooms, a caravan park and camping grounds. **Cocklebiddy Roadhouse** *moderate* (08 9039 3462) offers simple accommodation. Madura, 92 km (57 miles) east of Cocklebiddy, offers rooms and caravan sites at **Madura Pass Oasis Motel** *moderate* (08 9039 3464). Mundrabilla, 116 km (72 miles) further on, on the Nullarbor Plain proper, also has a motel and caravan/camp site, and the **Mundrabilla Roadhouse** (08 9039 3465).

EUCLA
Eucla Motor Hotel *moderate*
A popular stop, this hotel caters for all types – book in advance. (The studio-style motel rooms are best.) It has all the usual facilities and a fair restaurant.
Eyre Hwy, 6443; 08 9039 3468

The Nullarbor Plain
Crossing the vast Nullarbor Plain on the Eyre Highway (1) is a quintessential Australian Outback experience. Aboriginals call this area "Oondiri", meaning "the waterless". Ironically, the limestone plateau was once covered by ocean and is now home to abundant wildlife, including emus, kangaroos, camels and wombats. It gets its English name from Alfred Delisser who, in 1867, surveyed the treeless plain, naming it "Nullarbor" after "nulla arbor", Latin for "no trees".

① Norseman
Western Australia (WA); 6443
Norseman is the last proper town at the Western Australian end of the Eyre Highway. This historic goldfields town, the second richest in the state, was established in 1894 after a prospector's horse called Norseman kicked up a large nugget. There is a statue of the horse on the corner of Roberts and Ramsay streets. The corrugated iron camel sculptures on the Prinsep and Roberts Street roundabout recall the early camel trains that transported mail and other freight. Follow the signs to the **Beacon Hill Lookout** and **Walk Trail**, 2 km (1 mile) from town, for a stroll through fragrant bushland with expansive vistas of the country.

🚗 *Drive north on Roberts St or the parallel Coolgardie–Esperance Hwy (1) to the signposted start of the Eyre Hwy (1), which heads east 188 km (117 miles) to Balladonia Roadhouse.*

② Balladonia
Eyre Highway, WA; 6443
Named after an Aboriginal word meaning "big red rock", Balladonia is famous for being the spot where debris from Skylab fell down from

space in 1979. Inside the **Balladonia Roadhouse**, there is an exhibition on the incident and a small museum on the history of the area. The café has good coffee as well as the usual meat pies and sausage rolls to snack on.

🚗 *Continue driving east along the Eyre Hwy on the "90-mile straight", Australia's longest straight stretch of highway. After 151 km (94 miles) lies Caiguna, with its famous blowhole, 5 km (3 miles) to the west; carry on east for 64 km (40 miles) to Cocklebiddy.*

③ Cocklebiddy
Eyre Highway, WA; 6443
Stretch the legs and grab a coffee at this former Aboriginal mission, now a roadhouse-cum-hotel-motel. There is a pleasant picnic spot at **Chapel Rock**, 4 km (2.5 miles) east of town. Visitors with a 4WD who are planning to stay the night might consider heading south 32 km (20 miles) along a track to **Twilight Cove** for fishing and whale watching, or phone ahead and arrange to visit the bird observatory at the historic **Eyre Telegraph Station** *(by arrangement only; 08 9039 3450).*

🚗 *Continue east along the Eyre Hwy for 275 km (170 miles) to Eucla. Stop for fuel/snacks at 206 km (128 miles) at Mundrabilla Roadhouse.*

Fruit Fly Quarantine
At the border between the states of Western Australia and South Australia, be prepared to jettison absolutely all fresh fruit and vegetables in the car. This is to prevent the spread of fruit fly and thereby protect South Australia's AU$480 million horti-cultural industry. Those violating the quarantine risk a fine of AU$2,500. For more information, contact 1300 666 010; www.pir.sa.gov.au.

Where to Stay: inexpensive under AU$150; moderate AU$150–AU$250; expensive over AU$250

❹ Eucla

Eyre Highway, WA; 6443

It is hard to believe that this roadhouse-motel was once Australia's busiest telegraph station and, in the early 1900s, a bustling little town (population 100). If there are no rooms at Eucla, try the roadhouse at **Border Village**, 12 km (8 miles) east, where a plaque commemorates John Eyre, the first European to traverse the coastline of the Great Australian Bight and the Nullarbor Plain by land, in 1840–41.

Try to arrive at Eucla before sunset and follow the signposted road from the roadhouse 4 km (2 miles) down the hill to the **Old Telegraph Station** ruins. Atmospherically set amid sand dunes, the station was established in 1877, linking Western Australia with the rest of the country and the world. Spend time exploring the ruins and photographing the eerie sight from the dunes – it is also pretty at sunrise.

🚗 *Drive east along Eyre Hwy to the South Australia border and quarantine checkpoint (see box). Continue east for 196 km (122 miles) to the turn-off for the Head of Bight, stopping along the way at the Bunda cliff lookouts. From the turn-off, it is 12 km (8 miles) to the Head of Bight Interpretative Centre.*

❺ Nullarbor National Park and Great Australian Bight

Eyre Highway, South Australia (SA)

The Nullarbor National Park extends from the state border to the Yalata Aboriginal Community. Running parallel along the coast is the Great Australian Bight marine national park, famous for its spectacular Bunda cliffs,

blowholes and migrating whales. There are numerous signposted turn-offs to cliff lookouts – take care as many are not fenced and drop away to the sea below.

The highlight here is without doubt the **Head of Bight Interpretative Centre** *(08 8625 6201)*, managed by the local Yalata Aboriginal Community. There are a few informative panels, and then it is a short walk to the cliffs where boardwalks and viewing platforms provide the best vantage points from which to spot whales. During the migration and breeding seasons (May–Oct), some 20 types of whale might cruise past this stretch of coast, but most visitors come to look for the endangered southern right whales *(see box)* that calve in these waters. Take some binoculars and look also for dolphins, sea lions and fur seals.

🚗 *Return to Eyre Hwy (A1), and turn right, continuing east 285 km (177 miles) to Ceduna.*

Southern Right Whales

As winter starts to set in, southern right whales – so called because they were once the "right" whales to hunt – begin their migration from Antarctica to the warmer waters of Africa, South America, New Zealand and Australia to breed. They arrive in South Australia between May and October. The Head of Bight is a popular calving area, so there is a good chance of seeing whales with calves in tow making their way back south near the end of the season.

Above The Bunda cliffs along the southern edge of the Nullarbor Plain **Below** Sign on the Eyre Highway near Yalata

CROSSING THE NULLARBOR

To avoid danger on the Nullarbor Crossing, a certain amount of planning is required. Besides the usual precautions of making sure the vehicle is in good working order and there is plenty of food and water in case of breakdown, make sure to plan fuel stops as some of the service stations close at dusk. For vehicles with a small fuel tank, a spare fuel container is vital; some car rental companies can supply these.

Planning overnight stops is also key as rooms are often booked up in advance. Fatigue is a common cause of accidents on this route, so plan breaks ahead of time and note that dusk, dawn and night are times when animals such as emus and kangaroos are most active and can be road hazards.

EAT AND DRINK

Between Norseman and Ceduna, the only places to get something to eat and drink are the simple motel restaurants or cafeterias, takeaways and mini-marts that are attached to roadhouses. Take advantage of these when stopping for fuel and take plenty of snacks for the car.

NORSEMAN

Travelers Restaurant *moderate*
This restaurant at the Norseman Great Western Motel is the only proper restaurant in town, providing country-style food at a very country-style pace. *Norseman Gt Western Motel, Prinsep St, 6443; 08 9039 1633; www. norsemangreatwesternmotel.com.au; open early evenings only*

Next 92 km

Above The waters of Streaky Bay, coloured by oils released from seaweed

⑥ Ceduna
SA; 5690

Arriving in Ceduna, the first real town on the South Australian side of the border, comes as either a relief to those finding the drive monotonous or a disappointment to those enjoying the isolation and adventure. Most travellers make a beeline for the tourist office to get their Nullarbor Certificate to prove they made the crossing. Ceduna's name is derived from the Aboriginal word "Chedoona", meaning "resting place", and the town is a fine spot to spend the night and enjoy a seafood dinner – it is famed for its fish and oysters. The largest commercial centre in the area, it is also a good place to refuel and stock up on supplies before driving around the Eyre Peninsula.

The superb **Ceduna Aboriginal Arts and Culture Centre** (cnr Eyre Hwy and Kuhlmann St, 5690; open Mon–Fri; 08 8625 2487) is worth visiting for an insight into the customs and traditions of the local indigenous peoples. It is also a wonderful place to pick up some original arts and crafts.

🚗 *Head southeast along the Flinders Hwy (B100) for 38 km (24 miles), following signs for Smoky Bay.*

Above Fishing boat at Ceduna, famed for its King George whiting

The Eyre Peninsula

A popular holiday destination and reward after the long drive across the Nullarbor, the Eyre Peninsula, stretching from Ceduna to Port Augusta, offers up over 2,000 km (1,240 miles) of coastline boasting sheltered sandy coves, sweeping surf beaches and sheer limestone cliffs. In the warmer weather, visitors can break up the drive with stops for swimming and fishing, while in winter, brisk seaside walks and fish and chips at the end of a pier are the order of the day. Whatever the time of year, there is always flora and fauna to enjoy somewhere.

VISITING CEDUNA

Visitor Information
Ceduna Travel Centre, 58 Poynton St, 5690; 08 8625 2780; www.cedunatourism.com.au; open 9am–5pm

WHERE TO STAY

CEDUNA

Ceduna Foreshore Hotel-Motel *moderate*
This hotel has excellent views over the bay from its renovated rooms as well as its bars and bistro. Different levels of rooms, with the executive ones affording the best views.
32 O'Loughlin Terrace, 5690; 08 8625 2008, 1800 655 300; www.ceduna. bestwestern.com.au

STREAKY BAY

Streaky Bay Hotel-Motel *inexpensive*
Centrally located with colonial-style architecture and alfresco dining, this simple hotel offers good-value accommodation. The best rooms have bay views and wide verandas.
Cnr Alfred Terrace & Bay Rd, 5680; 08 8628 1008; www.streakybayhotel. com.au

Right Murals of mechanical farming on the exterior of the Powerhouse Restored Engine Museum in Streaky Bay

Where to Stay: inexpensive under AU$150; moderate AU$150–AU$250; expensive over AU$250

Left The wind-eroded pink granite stones, Murphys Haystacks

SHOPPING IN CEDUNA

Ceduna is known for its indigenous arts and crafts, which can be acquired at the Ceduna Aboriginal Arts and Culture Centre *(see left)*.

EAT AND DRINK

CEDUNA
Ceduna Oyster Bar *moderate*
Stop in at the Ceduna Oyster Bar on the highway on the northern edge of town and buy a dozen oysters and drive to one of the scenic picnic spots on the foreshore at Ceduna to savour them. *Eyre Highway, 5960; 08 8626 9086*

STREAKY BAY
Mocean Café *moderate*
Do not let all that seafood escape to the big cities – take a seat on the deck overlooking the jetty and feast on fresh and well-prepared produce and South Australian wines. Beware, it can get busy. *34b Alfred Terrace, 5680; 08 8626 1775; closed Mon*

⑦ Smoky Bay
SA; 5690
Located on a beautiful bay, this small, laidback fishing town, 40 km (25 miles) south of Ceduna, is a popular summer retreat with beach houses lining the coast and a 100-year-old wooden jetty. The town is also known for its oysters – plump, juicy and grown in the cool, clean and nutrient-rich waters. Watch them being landed at the boat ramp. Landscapes are ruggedly handsome from here on with white sandy beaches backed by dunes and heath. Refuel and buy supplies, tackle and bait at the **general store** *(08 8625 7066)*.
🚗 *Drive southeast for 70 km (43 miles) along Flinders Hwy (B100) to Streaky Bay. Stop off at Haslam 30 km (19 miles) south of Smoky Bay to admire the beach.*

⑧ Streaky Bay
SA; 5680
Named in 1802 by Captain Matthew Flinders after the bands of colour in the water caused by oils released from seaweed, Streaky Bay is a larger fishing town than Smoky Bay but it still oozes a gentle charm. Made famous in the 1970s, when the movie *Blue Fin* was filmed here, the town is now pretty low-key.

An agricultural and mining centre – granite from here has been used in some of Australia's most striking buildings, including Canberra's Parliament House – Streaky Bay is best known for its seafood, especially its oysters, scallops and abalone, which wing their way to some of the country's finest restaurants. Anglers can try their hand at fishing from the jetty, beach or boat – excellent whiting, salmon, snapper and blue swimmer crabs are all found here. For

the mechanically minded, the **Powerhouse Restored Engine Museum** *(Alfred Terrace; 2–5pm Tue & Fri or by appt; 08 8626 1628)* has an interesting display of vintage restored machinery.
🚗 *Drive 40 km (25 miles) southeast along the Flinders Hwy (B100) to the turn-off right (west) to Murphy's Haystacks, on the Calca-Point Labatt Rd.*

⑨ Murphys Haystacks
Eyre Peninsula, SA
Thought to be over 1,500 million years old, these ancient sculptural granite rock formations, or inselbergs, are actually found all over the Eyre Peninsula, although these are the most accessible. Carved by the wind into exotic aerodynamic shapes, the enormous pink-red outcrops look especially striking in the early morning or late afternoon light. Entry fee is by donation paid at the entrance gate. On-site facilities include toilets and picnic tables.
🚗 *Head west towards Calca and Sceale Bay, then follow the signs south to Point Labatt Conservation Park car park.*

Below Stone church near Murphys Haystacks

Eat and Drink: inexpensive under AU$60; moderate AU$60–AU$100; expensive over AU$100

VISITING PORT LINCOLN

Visitor Information
This office books accommodation, fishing charters, shark-cage diving, marine-life-spotting tours and winery visits from Port Lincoln as well as providing information on the rest of the Eyre Peninsula. *Adelaide Place, 5606, Port Lincoln; 08 8683 3544; www.visitportlincoln.net; open daily*

WHERE TO STAY

COFFIN BAY

Coffin Bay Hotel Motel *inexpensive*
A relaxed old-style hotel with bar, beer garden and dining room, this has basic but comfortable en suite rooms. *Shepherd Ave, 5607; 08 8685 4111*

Coffin Bay Beach Units *moderate*
Across from the foreshore, between the boat ramp and Coffin Bay National Park, these self-contained units, which sleep six, are perfect for families. *347–51 Esplanade, 5607; 08 8685 4173*

PORT LINCOLN

Port Lincoln Hotel *moderate*
This stylish modern hotel is right across the road from the waterfront and has large, well-appointed rooms overlooking the sea, as well as a good bar and restaurant. *1 Lincoln Hwy, 5606; 1300 766 100; www.portlincolnhotel.com.au*

Limani Motel *moderate*
This older-style motel has a variety of rooms, all with the benefit of sea views and well-equipped kitchens. *50 Lincoln Hwy, 5606; 08 8682 2200; www.limanimotel.com.au*

Below left and right Rocks and cliffs at Point Labatt

🔟 Point Labatt
Eyre Peninsula, SA
It is a short walk from the car park to the viewing platform perched atop 50-m (150-ft) high cliffs from where visitors can watch the country's only mainland breeding colony of Australian sea lions frolicking on the rocks and swimming in the surf below. Male sea lions can weigh up to 400 kg (882 lb) and measure up to 2 m (6 ft) long. Females are a little shorter and much lighter. Look up to see the occasional white-bellied sea eagle and osprey soaring in the sky.

🚗 *Backtrack to Calca and Murphy's Haystacks to Flinders Hwy, turning right for 21 km (13 miles) to Port Kenny.*

🔟 Port Kenny and Venus Bay
SA; 5671/5607
Tiny **Port Kenny** may not be the area's prettiest town, but it overlooks lovely lagoon-like Venus Bay and is a great spot for fishing for garfish, flounder, whiting and trevally. From Port Kenny, go northwest on the Flinders Highway for 12 km (8 miles) to Witera Silos and turn left on the Calca Road for **Venus Conservation Park** (*www.environment.gov.sa*). It protects the Weyland Peninsula and seven islands within the bay and is home to 100 bird species, as well as mammals including the tiny marsupial brush-tailed bettong.

The little town of **Venus Bay**, 18 km (11 miles) southeast around the bay from Port Kenny, is a summer holiday spot that is popular for its fishing, boating and surfing. From the well-signposted **South Head Walking Trail** – pick up a map from Venus Bay Caravan Park on the seafront *(32 Matson Terrace, 5607; www.venusbaycaravanparksa.com)* – and **Needle Eye Lookout**, visitors can spot sea lions, dolphins and southern right whales *(May–Oct)*. Also well signposted off Flinders Highway, **Talia Cave Tourist Drive** starts south of Venus Bay near Elliston and leads to two spectacular caves, **The Tub** and **The Woolshed**.

🚗 *Take Flinders Hwy south to Elliston, 57 km (35 miles) from Venus Bay.*

Great White Sharks
Made notorious by the film *Jaws* and reaching up to 6 m (20 ft) in length, the great white shark is one of the most fearsome predators in the sea. An endangered species, it is often sighted off the South Australian coast. Some Port Lincoln companies offer cage-diving trips allowing visitors the chance to see these magnificent beasts close up. Contact **Goin' Off Safaris** (*www.goinoffsafaris.com.au*) or **Calypso Star Charter** (*www.calypsocharter.com.au*).

Where to Stay: inexpensive under AU$150; moderate AU$150–AU$250; expensive over AU$250

⑫ Elliston

SA; 5670

Colourful and historic murals adorn Elliston's old town buildings, but the main attraction here is the sea. Famed for its superb fishing, dramatic coastal cliffs and surfing beaches, Elliston is another laidback town splendidly set on a sheltered bay. Follow the 12-km (7-mile) long **Great Ocean Drive** beside spectacular coastal cliffs to tranquil **Waterloo Bay**, where locals like to fish for garfish, King George whiting and squid, or **Locks Well**, a famous salmon fishing beach. Alternatively, simply enjoy some whale, dolphin or sea lion spotting *(Mar–Oct)*.

🚗 *Drive south on Flinders Hwy to Coffin Bay. Park on the Esplanade.*

⑬ Coffin Bay

SA; 5607

Renowned throughout the country for being the home of Australia's finest oysters, Coffin Bay is also one of the most picturesque hamlets on the Eyre Peninsula with a tranquil estuary, windswept surfing beaches and stunning **Coffin Bay National Park**. Park near the caravan park on the Esplanade and stroll along a stretch of the signposted, 8-km (5-mile) **Oyster Walk**, which meanders around the foreshore by former fishermen's shacks, then feast on sublime oysters. If planning to stay, book ahead during summer when the village's population swells from 500 to several thousand.

🚗 *Continue east along Flinders Hwy for 46 km (29 miles) to Port Lincoln on the eastern coast of the Peninsula.*

⑭ Port Lincoln

SA; 5606

Discovered by Matthew Flinders in 1802, this affluent city has built its wealth from exporting its excellent seafood to the restaurants of Sydney and Melbourne – much of it is loaded straight from the trawlers onto trucks bound for the east coast. A picturesque place with a smattering of historic buildings dotted around town, towering pine trees lining the beach and port, bustling cafés and a few decent restaurants, Port Lincoln makes a good overnight stop. There is plenty to do here, including fishing, wine tasting and even diving in specially built cages to see the largest predatory fish in the sea, the great white shark.

Plaque of Flinders' ship, Port Lincoln

🚗 *From Port Lincoln, drive north along the Lincoln Hwy (B100) for 46 km (29 miles) to the turn-off right (east) 3 km (2 miles) to Tumby Bay.*

Eyre Peninsula's Seafood

The star of South Australia's pristine waters and fresh seafood is the Eyre Peninsula. From wild and farmed fish to the region's spectacular oysters, abalone and mussels, the peninsula provides 65 per cent of the state's seafood. Dec–Mar is the best season for oysters, Apr–Sep sees the capture of tuna that can fetch up to AU$5,000 at the fish market, while in Nov–Dec prawns are at their best. Cowell, Port Lincoln, Coffin Bay, Streaky Bay and Ceduna are the best places to either buy fresh seafood to cook yourself or buy a seafood takeaway to indulge in on a picnic by the sea.

Far left Elliston's much-photographed mural-covered community hall

ACTIVITIES ON THE EYRE PENINSULA

To make the most of the seafood, pick up a leaflet at the Port Lincoln visitor centre and follow the **Eyre Peninsula Seafood & Aquaculture Trail** between Ceduna and Whyalla for seafood-themed tours and cruises, and guided tours of oyster sheds and beds. *1300 788 378; www.seafoodtrail.com*

EAT AND DRINK

COFFIN BAY

The Oysterbeds *moderate*
This charming, casual restaurant has a great supply of oysters – some of the best to be found in the state. While the temptation is to just have them natural, the different styles they serve are worth trying, too.
61 Esplanade, 5607; 08 8685 4000; closed Tue

PORT LINCOLN

Sarins Restaurant and Bar *inexpensive*
Given that so much seafood comes in at Port Lincoln, a feast of the sea is the order of the day at this restaurant where the platters are perfect.
1 Lincoln Highway, 5606; 1300 766 100; www.portlincolnhotel.com.au

The Boardwalk Bar and Bistro *moderate*
Right at the entrance to the main commercial fishing port, expect great seafood and bistro classics served on a deck overlooking the sea. Try the wasabi and lime oysters for a real kick.
Marina Hotel, 13 Jubilee Drive, 5606; 08 8682 6141; www.marinahotel.com.au

Below left Quiet sandy beach in Coffin Bay National Park **Below right** A pelican swimming in lagoon-like Coffin Bay

Eat and Drink: inexpensive under AU$60; moderate AU$60–AU$100; expensive over AU$100

Above Huge, glowing cuttlefish in the waters around Whyalla

VISITING PORT AUGUSTA

Visitor Information
Book tours, including whale and dolphin watching cruises, fishing charters, and scenic flights.
41 Flinders Terrace, 5700; 08 8641 9194; www.wadlata.sa.gov.au

WHERE TO STAY IN PORT AUGUSTA

Augusta Westside Motel *inexpensive*
In a quiet beachside location on the western side of Port Augusta, this comfortable motel is a good place to unwind after the long drive and prepare for trips into the Flinders Ranges. It is also well located for the Wadlata Outback Centre.
3 Loudon Road, 5700; 08 8641 0722; www.augustawestside.com.au

Majestic Oasis Apartments *moderate*
These chic four-star serviced apartments – some with water views – are within walking distance to the local pubs and shops. There is secure parking and a "home delivery" deal with local restaurants for tired drivers.
Marryatt Street, 5700; 08 8648 9000; www.majestichotels.com.au

Standpipe Golf Motor Inn *moderate*
A little way from the centre, the clean rooms in this motor inn, clustered around an 1883 homestead, have views of Port Augusta's golf course and the Flinders Ranges. It has its own Tandoor restaurant.
1 Daw Street (cnr Eyre and Stuart hwys), 5700; 08 8642 4033; www.standpipe.com.au

Right Small fishing boats moored in Port Augusta's harbour

⑮ Tumby Bay
SA; 5605
Surrounded by gently undulating farmland and with a fine collection of heritage buildings – from grand old pubs with big verandas to historic log huts with thatched roofs – Tumby Bay must be the Eyre Peninsula's most charming town. The 10-km (6-mile) long sandy beach, crystal-clear sea, jetty and marina, resident sea lions and visiting dolphins make the place a popular holiday destination.
🚗 **Return to the Lincoln Hwy (B100), then turn right and drive northeast for 114 km (71 miles) to Cowell.**

⑯ Cowell
SA; 5602
Settled in 1853, Cowell, like Tumby Bay, is dotted with delightful old heritage buildings, including the

former post office and residence, dating to 1888, which now house the **Franklin Harbour Historical Museum** *(hours vary; 08 8629 2262)*. While Cowell is a popular fishing destination and renowned for the seafood and farmed oysters from its natural harbour, it is also well known for its jade, one of the world's largest and oldest deposits, discovered in 1965 at nearby Minbrie Range.
🚗 **Drive northeast along Lincoln Hwy (B100) for 111 km (70 miles) to Whyalla.**

⑰ Whyalla
SA; 5600
Cloaked in a layer of red dust, the industrial city of Whyalla, with its smattering of Art Deco buildings, is an interesting place to spend an afternoon. Established in 1901 as an iron ore port, the town flourished as a result of its steelworks. After steel, Whyalla is best known for its huge, glowing cuttlefish, which arrive for a colourful courtship and spawning in May–Aug each year. At the same time, the city is inundated with divers and snorkellers who come to see the display provided by these luminous "chameleons of the sea". For diving tuition, contact **Whyalla Diving Adventures** *(08 8645 5693)* or **Whyalla Diving Services** *(08 8645 8050)*.

Follow signs off Lincoln Highway to **Hummock Hill Lookout**, on the eastern side of the city centre near the foreshore. Once a gun battery, built to protect the shipyards during World War II, the lookout boasts views of the marina, Spencer Gulf and steelworks,

which are lit up at night. With binoculars, visitors can see the Southern Flinders Ranges across the gulf and, behind the city, the iron-ore rich Middleback Ranges. War buffs will appreciate the restored guns, and there is a pleasant picnic area.

Head down the hill and back to the Lincoln Highway, towards Port Augusta, to the **Whyalla Maritime Museum** *(open daily; 08 8645 8900)*. The long naval history of the city is charted in this exhibition, located in the former HMAS *Whyalla*, the first modern warship built in South Australia in 1941. If the exhibits on the shipbuilding industry are of interest, book a tour of **OneSteel Whyalla Steelworks** *(1800 088 589; times vary; book at the Whyalla visitor centre next to HMAS Whyalla)* for an insight into the steel and iron ore process.

🚗 *Drive northeast along Lincoln Hwy for 74 km (46 miles) to Port Augusta.*

Native bird in the Botanic Garden

Clever Cuttlefish

Reputed to be one of the most intelligent invertebrates, cuttlefish are extraordinary creatures. Preying on crabs and small fish, these molluscs have well-developed eyes, and shoot out two of their 10 tentacles to catch prey and pull it towards a central beaked mouth. They are not only able to change their colour to blend in with the ocean floor but also their skin texture. Cuttlefish also contain an ink sac, which can be emptied to create a dark, nasty-tasting cloud to confuse would-be predators – this was also once the source of sepia ink, a dark brown pigment used by artists.

18 Port Augusta
SA; 5700

The first major centre after the long drive across the Nullarbor or down from Alice Springs, Port Augusta is an obvious place to stay. With its lovely waterfront, historic buildings and attractions, it is a good place to relax in comfort before heading on into the Flinders Ranges. Restaurants are grouped along the Stuart Highway, while cafés and shopping are in the centre.

On the eastern approach to town, the Lincoln Highway meets the Stuart Highway and becomes the main road. Once over the bridge, take the first right and then right into Flinders Terrace for the **visitor centre** and **Wadlata Outback Centre** *(open daily; 08 8641 9193; www.wadlata.sa.gov.au)*. Spend a couple of hours here learning about the Outback, its indigenous peoples and pioneers, through exhibits on flora and fauna, Aboriginal customs, communications and train travel.

Drive north out of town along the Stuart Highway (A87) to the **Australian Arid Lands Botanic Garden** *(open daily; 08 8641 9116; www.aalbg.sa.gov.au)*. Hike the 12 km (8 miles) of trails and bird-watching walks at this sprawling desert garden, which showcases native desert flora and birdlife. Stop by the visitor centre first to pick up a detailed map and guide. The garden is best visited in the first hour after opening or an hour or two before closing, to avoid the worst of the heat and enjoy a gentler light; remember to carry some water.

Hannahville Hotel *inexpensive*
The casual bistro at the old Hannahville Hotel serves endless plates of modern Australian bistro classics to guests both in the restaurant and at the pavement seating. It is a local favourite for its consistent standards.
Cnr Gibson and Flinders St, 5700; 08 8642 2921

Other options
There are several cafés dotted around town, of which the best is **Ozzies Coffee Lounge** *inexpensive* at the top end of the shopping mall *(22 Commercial Road, 5700; 08 8642 4028; www.ozzies.com.au)*. The Arid Lands Botanic Garden Café *inexpensive* is a good pitstop if visiting the gardens *(Stuart Hwy, 5700; 08 8641 9117)*. South Australian fast food chain **Barnacle Bill** *inexpensive* serves an astonishingly good value fresh seafood platter *(60 Victoria Parade; 08 8641 0000; www. barnaclebill.com.au)*, while most of the pubs serve counter meals – try the **Commonwealth Hotel** *(73 Commercial Road, 5700; 08 8642 2844)* and **Hotel Augusta** *(1 Loudon Road, 5700; 08 8642 2701)* on the western foreshore, which serves oyster tempura.

Eat and Drink: inexpensive under AU$60; moderate AU$60–AU$100; expensive over AU$100

General Index

Acknowledgments

Dorling Kindersley would like to thank the many people whose help and assistance contributed to the preparation of this book.

Main Contributors
Jarrod Bates has a degree in history, a postgraduate qualification in communications and is a contributing editor of DK's *The Sports Book*.

Lara Dunston, born in Sydney, has lived in Perth, Adelaide and Alice Springs on a five-year caravanning adventure around Australia – her favourite of the 60 countries she has visited as a travel writer.

Andrew Harris is a Melbourne-based writer and photographer who covers everything from adventure travel to destination spas, from Iceland to Borneo and back to his home turf in Victoria.

Jessica Syme lives on the Gold Coast in Queensland and has written several books, including *We'll Meet Again*, an account of the infamous Surfers Paradise pyjama parties of the late 1950s.

Elizabeth Re is an experienced writer and television producer, who has recently tracked the endangered Tasmanian devil in the island state, and declining koala numbers in Queensland, for TV.

Steve Womersley has contributed to numerous travel guides as a writer and editor. He lives near the Central Victorian Goldfields town of Chewton.

Editorial Consultants
Margo Daly, Fay Franklin and David Leffman

Fact checkers
Deborah Soden, Naomi Stallard and Kim Wildman

Proofreader
Debra Wolter

Indexer
Hilary Bird

Revisions Team
Erin Bell, Richard Brennan, Sean Brennan, Tim Dub, Tony Eichmann, Tim Hardy, Sumita Khatwani, Hayley Maher, Deb McLennan, Sally McPherson, Claire Naylor, Ryan Paine, James Paxton, Sachin Pradhan, Ellen Root, Sharon Scurr, Connor Slattery, Beverly Smart, Paul Smedley, Deborah Soden, Naomi Stallard, Avantika Sukhia, Rebecca Taylor, Scott Trenorden, Stuti Tiwari, Ajay Verma

Maps
John Plumer, JP Map Graphics Ltd, www.jpmapgraphics.co.uk
This book incorporates Data which is © Commonwealth of Australia 2000-2009. The Data has been used in Back Roads Australia with the permission of the Commonwealth. The Commonwealth has not evaluated the Data as altered and incorporated within Back Roads Australia, and therefore gives no warranty regarding its accuracy, completeness, currency or suitability for any particular purpose.

Photography
Terry Carter, Andrew Harris, Kathrine Seppings, Jessica Syme

Additional Photography
Max Alexander, Ian Keohane, Rob Reichenfeld, Chris Stowers, Matthew Ward

Picture Credits
The Publishers would like to thank the following individuals, companies and picture libraries for their kind permission to reproduce their photographs:

t-top; tc = top centre; tl = top left; tr = top right; c= centre; cl = centre left; clb = centre left below; cr = centre right; crb = centre right below; bc = bottom centre; bl = bottom left; br = bottom right.

Alamy Images: Cephas Picture Library/Jeffery Drewitz 87bl; redbrickstock.com/Stefan Jannides 46-7; Mark Sunderland 87tr. **Busselton Jetty** www.busseltonjetty.com.au: 228tc. **Corbis**: JAI/Doug Pearson 229tr. **Dolphin Discovery Centre**, Bunbury, Western Australia: 228crb. **Dreamstime.com**: Ben185 113tc. **Getty Images**: 162tl; Digital Vision/Natphotos 30-1; Gallo Images/Travel Ink 68br, 228tl; The Image Bank/Aaron Black 5tc; The Image Bank/Philippe Bourseiller 256tl; The Image Bank/Scott E Barbour 4br, 80-1; Photographer's Choice/Andrew Holt 62br; Photolibrary 202-3; Riser/John W Banagan 10br; Robert Harding World Imagery// Jochen Schlenker 70-1, 79tl; Robert Harding World Imagery/Ken Gillham 13tr; Taxi/James Braund 170tl. **Lonely Planet Images**: Andrew Bain 79tr; Christopher Groenhout 68clb; Richard I'Anson 40-1. **Mount Tomah Botanic Garden**: 88bl. **National Library of Australia**: 28-9. **Saltwater Cafe & Restaurant**: 65tr. **Yarraman Estate**: 91tl.

Sheet Map
Corbis: Tony Waltham/Robert Harding World Imagery.

Jacket
Front - **Corbis**: Tony Waltham/Robert Harding World Imagery. Back – **Getty Images**: The Image Bank/Walter Bibikow tc; Stock Image/Jean-Pierre Pieuchot tl; **Lonely Planet Images**: Christopher Groenhout tr. Spine – **Auscape**: John Carnemolla t.

All other images © Dorling Kindersley
For further information see: www.dkimages.com

Road Signs

SPEED LIMITS AND GENERAL DRIVING INDICATIONS

Give way

STOP

Compulsory stop

No entry

No left turn

No right turn

Speed limit

End of speed limit

School zone – special speed limit

Shared zone – special speed limit

School zone – special speed limit

ALL TRAFFIC

Right turn only

ALL TRAFFIC

Left turn only

One way

NO U TURN

No U-turn

U TURN PERMITTED

U-turn permitted

Two-way traffic

Tram lane

Truck lane

Buses only

Roundabout

PARKING AND ACCESS

Exit from motorway in 2 km

Exit from motorway now

Wrong way – go back

Reduce speed now

End of motorway

WARNING SIGNS

No parking area

Parking permitted for length of road

Meter parking permitted for length of road

Restricted parking area – permits only

No stopping